Duncan Petersen's

Charming Small Hotel Guides

Britain
& Ireland

DUNCAN PETERSEN'S

CHARMING SMALL HOTEL GUIDES

Britain & Ireland

EDITOR Tamara Grosvenor

CONTRIBUTING EDITORS George Pownall, Christopher
and Sara Steele, Jacqui Sayers

SERIES EDITOR Fiona Duncan

DUNCAN PETERSEN

16th (expanded) edition

Conceived, designed and produced by
Duncan Petersen Publishing Ltd,
C7 Old Imperial Laundry, Warriner Gardens, London SW11 4XW

Editorial director Andrew Duncan
Contributing editors George Pownall, Christopher and Sara Steele,
Jacqui Sayers
Production editor Jacqui Sayers
Cover design Lizzie Ballantyne
Maps Map Creation Ltd

A CIP catalogue record for this book is available
from the British Library

ISBN 978-1-903301-49-4

DTP by Duncan Petersen Publishing Ltd
Printed by E.G. Zure SA in Spain

Additional photography: 4 Corners Images; Fotolia

Contents

Introduction

Welcome to this 2008 edition of Charming Small Hotel Guides *Britain and Ireland* — a major new upgraded edition:

• *All hotels now have two colour photographs rather than one — often giving an inside as well as an outside view of the hotel.*

• *The layout has been changed in order to take you more quickly to essential booking information.*

We hope that you will think these real improvements, rather than change for its own sake. In all other respects, the guide remains true to the values and qualities that make it unique (see opposite), and which have won it so many devoted readers. This new edition has 368 pages, giving full coverage of Ireland, rather than the highly selective coverage in earlier editions. This is the guide's sixteenth consecutive update since it was first published in 1986. It has sold hundreds of thousands of copies in the U.K., U.S.A. and in five European languages.

Why are we unique?

This is the only independently-inspected (no hotel pays for an entry) UK-originated accommodation guide that:

• has colour photographs for every entry;

• concentrates on places that have real charm and character;

• is highly selective;

• is particularly fussy about size. Most hotels have fewer than 20 bedrooms; if there are more, the hotel must have the feel of a much smaller place. We have found that a genuinely warm welcome is much more likely to be found in a small hotel;

• gives proper emphasis to the description, and doesn't use irritating symbols;

• is produced by a small, non- bureaucratic company with a dedicated team of like-minded inspectors.

See also 'So what exactly do we look for?', page 8.

So what exactly do we look for?
Our selection criteria

• A peaceful, attractive setting. Obviously, if the entry is in an urban area, we make allowances.

• A building that is handsome, interesting or historic; or at least with real character.

• Adequate space, but on a human scale. We don't go for places that rely too much on grandeur, or with pretensions that could be intimidating.

• Good taste and imagination in the interior decoration. We reject standardized, chain hotel fixtures, fittings and decorations.

• Bedrooms that look like real bedrooms, not hotel rooms, individually decorated.

• Furnishings and other facilities that are comfortable and well maintained. We like to see interesting antique furniture that is there to be used, not simply revered.

• Proprietors and staff who are dedicated and thoughtful, offering a personal welcome, but who aren't intrusive or overly effusive. The guest needs to feel like an individual.

• Interesting food. There are few entries in this guide where the food is not of a high standard.

• A sympathetic atmosphere; an absence of loud people showing off their money; or the 'corporate feel'.

Introduction

A fatter guide, but just as selective

In order to accommodate all entries with a whole-page description and colour photograph, we've had to print more pages. But we have maintained our integrity by keeping the selection to around 330 entries. Over the years, the number of charming small hotels in Britain and Ireland has increased steadily – not dramatically. We don't believe that there are presently many more than about 330 truly charming small hotels in Britain and Ireland, and that, if we included more, we would undermine what we're trying to do: produce a guide which is all about places that are more than just a bed for the night. Every time we consider a new hotel, we ask ourselves whether it has that extra special something, regardless of category and facilities, that makes it worth seeking out.

Types of accommodation in this guide

Despite its title, the guide does not confine itself to places called hotels or places that behave like hotels. On the contrary, we actively look for places that offer a home from home (see page 10). We include small and medium-sized hotels; pubs; inns; restaurants-with-rooms; guest-houses and bed-and-breakfasts. Some places, usually private homes which take guests, operate on house-party lines, where you are introduced to the other guests, and take meals at a communal table. If you don't like making small talk to strangers, or are part of a romantic twosome that wants to keep itself to itself, this type of establishment may not be for you. On the other hand, if you are interested in meeting people, perhaps as a foreign visitor wanting to get to know the locals, then you'll find it rewarding.

No fear or favour

To us, taking a payment for appearing in a guide seems to defeat the object of producing a guide. If money has changed hands, you can't write the whole truth about a hotel, and the selection cannot be nearly so interesting. This self-evident truth seems to us to be proved at least in part by the fact that pay guides are so keen to present the illusion of independence: few admit on the cover that they take payments for an entry, only doing so in small print on the inside.

Not many people realize that on the shelves of British bookshops there are many more hotel guides that accept payments for entries than there are independent guides. This guide is one of the few that do not accept any money for an entry.

Home from home

Perhaps the most beguiling characteristic of the best places to stay in this guide is the feeling they give of being in a private home – but without the everyday cares and chores of running one. To get this formula right requires a special sort of professionalism: the proprietor has to strike the balance between being relaxed and giving attentive service. Those who experience this 'feel' often turn their backs on all other forms of accommodation – however luxurious.

Our pet dislikes

Small hotels are not automatically wonderful hotels; and the very individuality of small, owner-run hotels, makes them prone to peculiarities that the mass-produced hotel experience avoids. For the benefit of those who run the small hotels of Britain - and those contemplating the plunge - we repeat once more our list of pet hates:

Price too high Prices are much higher, like for like, than in France and Italy. This is not always the fault of hotels, but it is disappointing.

Not entirely child-friendly Again, compared with mainland European hotels, children are much more often seen as a nuisance by hoteliers.

Poor English at reception The surge in recent years of foreign workers, prepared to work for low wages, means guests sometimes have to adapt to a non-fluent English speaker. Especially irritating if you arrive tired after a long journey.

'Contemporary-formulaic' decoration Too many hotels think they can appeal simply by putting 'modern' grey and brown paint on the walls. The more we see of this, the more of a cliche it becomes.

The hushed dining room Owners have a duty to create an atmosphere in which conversation can flow.

The ordinary breakfast Even hotels that go to great lengths to prepare special dinners are capable of serving prefabricated orange juice, sliced bread and tea made with tea bags at breakfast.

The schoolteacher mentality If you run a hotel, you should be flexible and accommodating enough to deal with the whims of travellers.

The excess of informality At one not-cheap London address (which did not find its way into the guide) we were shown around by a young man in jeans (which might be acceptable) but without socks (which is not).

The inexperienced waiter Or waitress. Running a small operation does not excuse the imposition on the paying public of completely untrained (and sometimes ill-suited) staff who can spoil the most beautifully cooked food.

The lumpy old bed Beds have improved much in recent years. There's no excuse for a creaking frame or an old mattress.

The erratic boiler It doesn't often happen, but tepid baths are unforgiveable. Even the cheapest places should regard this as a basic.

Check the price first

In this guide we have adopted the system of price bands, rather than giving actual prices as we did in previous editions. This is because prices were often subject to change after we went to press. The price bands refer to the approximate price of a standard double room (high season rates) with breakfast for two people. Prices for Ireland are quoted in Euros. They are as follows:

£	under £70	€	under 100 euros
££	£70 – £120	€€	100 – 170 euros
£££	£120 – £180	€€€	170 – 260 euros
££££	more than £180	€€€€	more than 260 euros

To avoid unpleasant surprises, always check what is included in the price (for example, VAT and service, breakfast, afternoon tea) when making the booking.

How to find an entry

In this guide, the entries are arranged in geographical groups. First, the whole of Britain and Ireland are divided into five major groups, starting with Southern England and working northwards to Scotland; Ireland comes last.

Within these major groups, the entries are grouped into smaller regional sub-sections such as the South-West, Wales, the Midlands and the Highlands and Islands – for a full list, see page 5. Within each sub-section, entries are listed alphabaetically by nearest town or village; if several occur in or near one town, entries are arranged in alpha order by name of hotel.

To find a hotel in a particular area, use the maps following this introduction to locate the appropriate pages.

To locate a specific hotel, whose name you know, or a hotel in a place you know, use the indexes at the back, which list entries both by names and by nearest place name. The name of the county follows the town name in the heading for each entry.

The three main sections of the book (England and Wales, Scotland and Ireland) are introduced by area introductions.

Introduction

HOW TO READ AN ENTRY

Postal address and other key information.

Places of interest within reach of the hotel.

This sets the hotel in its geographical context and should not be taken as precise instructions as to how to get there; always ask the hotel for directions.

Rooms described as having a bath usually also have a shower; rooms described as having a shower only have a shower.

This information is only an indication for wheelchair users and the infirm. Always check on suitability with the hotel.

Essential booking information.

THE SOUTH-WEST   SOUTHERN ENGLAND

Gittisham, Devon

Gittisham, Honiton, Devon
EX14 3AD

Tel (01404) 540 400
e-mail stay@thishotel.com
website www.thishotel.com

Nearby Gittisham village, Honiton antique trail, Dartmoor National Park, Jurassic Coast, Ottery St Mary
Location set in 3,500 acres of grounds, 2 miles from A30 and Honiton with ample car parking
Food breakfast, lunch, dinner
Price ££££
Rooms 16 including cottage; all en suite with plasma TV, phone, hairdryers; most rooms have wi-fi internet
Facilities two bar/lounge rooms, two dining rooms, Georgian kitchen, extensive parkland, helipad; fishing, shooting and riding all nearby
Credit Cards MC, V
Children welcome
Disabled access to restaurant only
Pets well-behaved dogs, £7 per night
Closed last two weeks of January
Proprietors Ken and Ruth Hunt

Combe House
Country hotel

Through delightful unspoiled Gittisham village, up a long drive, past wild flower meadows you find this large manor house dating from Elizabethan times. Perhaps it's not as mellow as some photos make it look, but you're definitely in the isolated world of an old country estate. Inside, old and new rub shoulders amusingly, perhaps eccentrically. In the main public space downstairs, the hall, gay splashes of colour contrast effectively with magnificent dark, heavy old panelling. Antique wallpaper has been preserved in a little reception room off the hall and the dining room walls are charmingly hand painted by former owners. It's full of quirky corners and surprises (including an outdoor bath house) to keep you amused. You'll see the odd imperfection downstairs, which could not matter less, because this is far from being a haphazard operation. Ruth and Ken Hunter are natural but astute hoteliers who have built up Combe House's reputation from nothing over a decade of hands-on hard work. Now, all the basics are right: award-winning food; upstairs, fresh, imaginative rooms, some traditional, some more contemporary, some pretty, at a useful range of prices. For a treat, book the Linen Suite with its copper bath tub. People of most ages can feel comfortable here.

50

City, town or village, and region, in which the hotel is located.

Name of hotel.

Type of establishment.

Description – never vetted by the hotel.

Breakfast, is normally included in the price of the room. We have not quoted prices for lunch and dinner. Other meals, such as afternoon tea, may also be available. 'Room service' refers to food and drink, either snacks or full meals, which can be served in the room.

Always let the hotel know in advance if you want to bring a pet. Even where pets are accepted, certain restrictions may apply, and a small charge may be levied.

Children

Where children are welcome, there are often special facilities, such as cots, high chairs, baby listening and high teas. Always check whether children are accepted in the dining room.

We list the following credit cards:

AE   American Express
DC   Diners Club
MC   Mastercard
V   Visa

Reporting to the guide

Please write and tell us about your experiences of small hotels, guest houses and inns, whether good or bad, whether listed in this edition or not. As well as hotels in Britain, we are interested in hotels in France, Spain and the Balearics, Austria, Germany, Switzerland, the U.S.A and Greece. We assume that reporters have no objections to our publishing their views unpaid. Readers whose reports prove particularly helpful may be invited to join our Travellers' Panel. Members give us notice of their own travel plans; we suggest hotels that they might inspect, and help with the cost of accommodation.

The address to write to us is:
Editor, *Charming Small Hotel Guides*
C7 Old Imperial Laundry, Warriner Gardens, London, SW11 4XW

Checklist
Please use a separate sheet of paper for each report; include your name, address and telephone number on each report.
Your reports will be received with particular pleasure if they are typed, and are organized under the following headings:

Name of establishment
Town or village it is in, or nearest
Full address, including postcode
Telephone number
Time and duration of visit
The building and setting
The public rooms
The bedrooms and bathrooms
Physical comfort (chairs, beds, heat, light, hot water)
Standards of maintenance and housekeeping
Atmosphere, welcome and service
Food
Value for money

We assume that in writing you have no objections to your views being published unpaid, either verbatim or in an edited version. Names of major outside contributors are acknowledged, at the editor's discretion, in the guide.

Hotel location maps

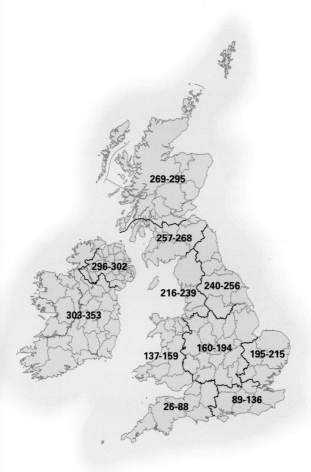

269-295

257-268

296-302

216-239

240-256

303-353

137-159

160-194

195-215

89-136

26-88

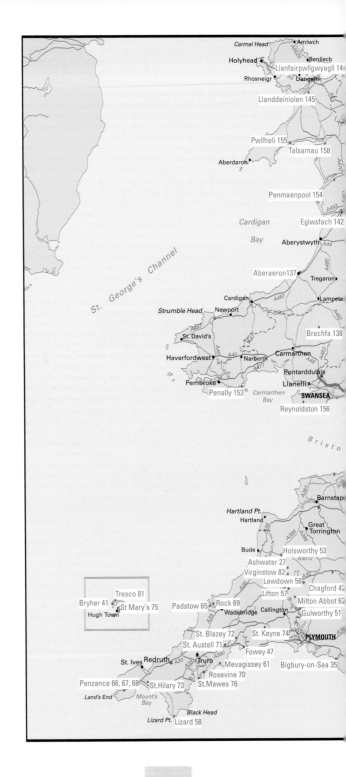

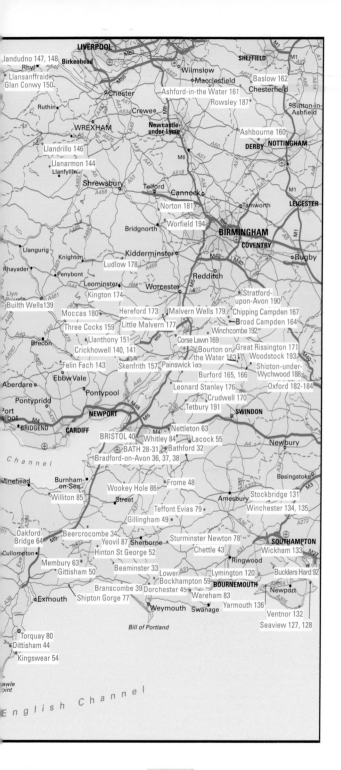

Llandudno 147, 148
Rhyl
Llansanffraid
Glan Conwy 150
Birkenhead
LIVERPOOL
Wilmslow
Macclesfield
Ashford-in-the-water 161
Rowsley 187
SHEFFIELD
Baslow 162
Chesterfield
Sutton-in-Ashfield
Ruthin
Chester
Crewe
Ashbourne 160
DERBY NOTTINGHAM
WREXHAM
Newcastle-under-Lyme
Llandrillo 146
Llanarmon 144
Llanfyllin
Shrewsbury
Telford
Cannock
Norton 181
Tamworth
LEICESTER
Worfield 194
BIRMINGHAM
Bridgnorth
COVENTRY
Llangurig
Knighton
Kidderminster
Ludlow 178
Rugby
Rhayader
Penybont
Leominster
Redditch
Worcester
Stratford-upon-Avon 190
Builth Wells 139
Kington 174
Moccas 180
Hereford 173
Malvern Wells 179
Chipping Campden 167
Broad Campden 164
Three Cocks 159
Little Malvern 177
Winchcombe 192
Brecon
Llanthony 151
Corse Lawn 169
Great Rissington 171
Crickhowell 140, 141
Bourton on the Water 163
Woodstock 193
Felin Fach 143
Skenfrith 157
Painswick 155
Shipton-under-Wychwood 188
Ebbw Vale
Burford 165, 166
Aberdare
Leonard Stanley 176
Oxford 182-184
Pontypridd
Pontypool
Crudwell 170
Port Talbot
NEWPORT
Tetbury 191
SWINDON
BRIDGEND
CARDIFF
Nettleton 63
Newbury
BRISTOL 40
Whitley 84
Lacock 55
BATH 28-31
Bathford 32
Bradford-on-Avon 36, 37, 38
Channel
Basingstoke
Minehead
Burnham-on-Sea
Frome 48
Williton 85
Wookey Hole 86
Stockbridge 131
Street
Teffont Evias 79
Amesbury
Winchester 134, 135
Gillingham 49
Oakford Bridge 64
Beercrocombe 34
Yeovil 87
Sherborne
Sturminster Newton 78
SOUTHAMPTON
Cullompton
Hinton St George 52
Chettle 43
Wickham 133
Membury 63
Beaminster 33
Ringwood
Gittisham 50
Lower Bockhampton 59
Lymington 120
Bucklers Hard 92
Branscombe 39
Dorchester 45
BOURNEMOUTH
Newport
Exmouth
Shipton Gorge 77
Wareham 83
Weymouth
Swanage
Yarmouth 136
Ventnor 132
Seaview 127, 128
Bill of Portland
Seaton 132
Torquay 80
Dittisham 44
Kingswear 54
awle oint
English Channel

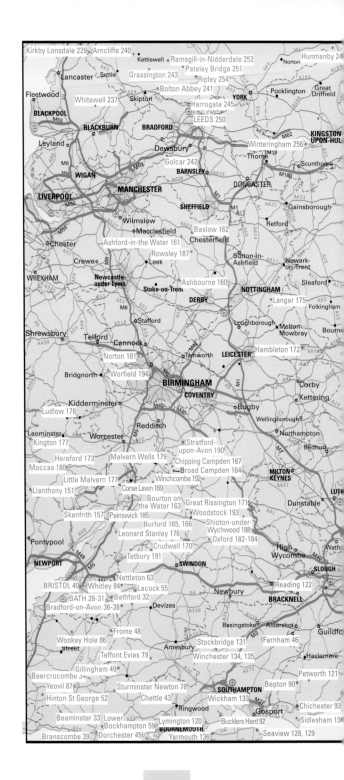

Kirkby Lonsdale 229 · Arncliffe 240
Kettlewell · Ramsgill-in-Nidderdale 252
Pateley Bridge 251 · Norton · Hunmanby 24
Lancaster · Settle · Grassington 243 · Ripley 254
Bolton Abbey 241 · Pocklington · Great Driffield
Fleetwood · Whitewell 237 · Skipton · Harrogate 245 · York
BLACKPOOL · Harrogate 245
BLACKBURN · BRADFORD · LEEDS 250
KINGSTON UPON-HUL
Leyland · Dewsbury · Winteringham 256
Golcar 242 · Thorne
WIGAN · BARNSLEY · Scunthorpe
MANCHESTER · DONCASTER
LIVERPOOL · SHEFFIELD · Gainsborough
Wilmslow · Retford
Chester · Macclesfield · Baslow 162 · Chesterfield
Ashford-in-the-Water 161 · Sutton-in-Ashfield · Newark-on-Trent
Crewe · Rowsley 187 · Leek
WREXHAM · Newcastle-under-Lyme · Ashbourne 160 · NOTTINGHAM · Sleaford
Stoke-on-Trent · Langar 175 · Folkingham
DERBY
M6 · Stafford · Loughborough · Melton Mowbray · Bourn
Shrewsbury · Telford · Cannock · Tamworth · LEICESTER · Hambleton 172
Norton 181
Bridgnorth · Worfield 194 · BIRMINGHAM · Corby
COVENTRY · Kettering
Kidderminster · Rugby · Wellingborough
Ludlow 178 · Redditch · Northampton
Leominster · Worcester · Stratford-upon-Avon 190 · Bedford
Kington 177
Hereford 173 · Malvern Wells 179 · Chipping Campden 167 · MILTON KEYNES
Moccas 180 · Broad Campden 164
Little Malvern 177 · Winchcombe 192 · LUT
Llanthony 151 · Corse Lawn 169 · Great Rissington 171 · Dunstable
Bourton on the Water 163 · Woodstock 193
Skenfrith 157 · Painswick 185 · Shipton-under-Wychwood 188
Burford 165, 166 · Oxford 182-184
Leonard Stanley 176
Pontypool · Crudwell 170 · High Wycombe · Watfo
Tetbury 191
NEWPORT · SWINDON · SLOUGH
Nettleton 63
BRISTOL 40 · Whitley 84 · Lacock 55 · Reading 122
BATH 28-31 · Bathford 32 · Newbury · BRACKNELL
Bradford-on-Avon 36-38 · Devizes
Frome 48 · Basingstoke · Aldershot · Guildfo
Wookey Hole 86 · Stockbridge 131 · Farnham 46
Street · Amesbury
Teffont Evias 79 · Winchester 134, 135 · Haslemere
Gillingham 49
Beercrocombe · Petworth 121
Yeovil 87 · Sturminster Newton 78 · Bepton 90
Hinton St George 52 · Chettle 43 · SOUTHAMPTON · Chichester 9
Wickham 133 · Gosport · Sidlesham 9
Beaminster 33 · Lower · Ringwood
Bockhampton 59 · Lymington 120 · Bucklers Hard 92 · Seaview 128, 129
Branscombe 39 · Dorchester 45 · BOURNEMOUTH
Yarmouth 136

18

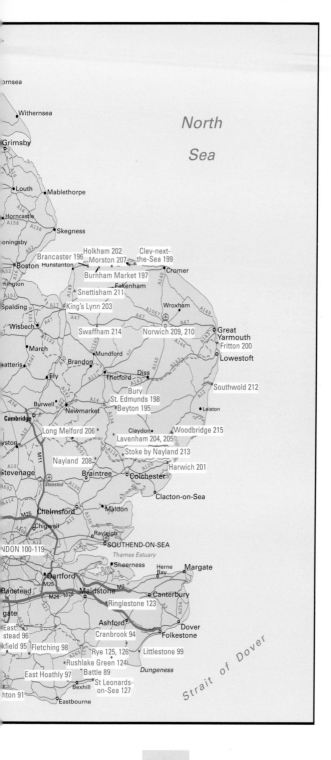

North

Sea

ornsea

Withernsea

Grimsby

Louth · Mablethorpe

Horncastle
A158 · Skegness
oningsby

Boston Hunstanton Brancaster 196 Morston 207 Clev-next-
the-Sea 199
Holkham 202
hington Burnham Market 197 Cromer
Snettisham 211 Fakenham
Spalding King's Lynn 203 Wroxham
A1067
Wisbech Swaffham 214 Norwich 209, 210 Great
Yarmouth
March Mundford Fritton 200
atteris Brandon Lowestoft
Ely Thetford Diss
Burwell Bury Southwold 212
St. Edmunds 198
Newmarket Beyton 195 Leiston
Cambridge
Long Melford 206 Woodbridge 215
yston Claydon
Lavenham 204, 205
Nayland 208 Stoke by Nayland 213
Stevenage Braintree Harwich 201
Stansted Colchester
Chelmsford Maldon Clacton-on-Sea

Chigwell
Rayleigh
NDON 100-119 SOUTHEND-ON-SEA
Thames Estuary
Banstead Sheerness Herne Margate
Dartford Bay
gate Maidstone Canterbury
East Ringlestone 123
stead 96 Ashford Dover
kfield 95 Fletching 98 Cranbrook 94 Folkestone
Rye 125, 126 Littlestone 99
East Hoathly 97 Rushlake Green 124 Dungeness
hton 91 Battle 89
Bexhill St Leonards-
Eastbourne on-Sea 127

Strait of Dover

19

Strontian 294
Tobermory
Kinlochleven
Killiecrankie 282
Pitlochry
Ballinlu
Salen
Lochaline
Port Appin 287
Aberfeldy
Loch Lyon
Craignure
Isle of Eriska 280
Tyndrum
Killin 283
Oban
Dalmally
Fionnphort
Mull
Seil
Balquidder 273
Comrie 275
Luing
Inveraray
Cairndow
Auchterarder
Scarba
Callander
Per
Colonsay
Kilmartin
Strachur 293
Bunblane
Kinros
Ardlussa
Luss
Loch Lomond
Stirling
Dunfermline
M80
M9
Jura
Greenock
Kirkintilloch
Cumbernauld
Bo'nes
Craighouse
M8
GLASGOW 262
M8
Bridgend
Kilberry 265
Largs
Johnstone
Hamilton
Carluke
Islay
Clachan
Lochranza
Strathaven
Ardbeg
Arran
Brodick
Kilmarnock
Galston
Skirling 26
Lamlash
Muirkirk
A74(M)
Abington
Machrihanish
Campbeltown
Ayr
Cumnock
Sanquhar
Rathlin Island
Turnberry
Beattock
Sanda Island
Girvan
SOUTH AYRSHIRE
Moniaive
Thornhill
Bennane Head
St. John's Town of Dalry
Lochmaben
Ballantrae
Barrhill
Dumfrie
Kirkcolm 266
Cairnryan
Loch Ken
Dalbeattie
Stranraer
Wigtown
Creetown
Portpatrick 267
Kirkcudbright
Aspatri
Drummore
Whithorn
Maryport
Mull of Galloway
Burrow Head
Low Lorton 23
Newlands
Wasdale Head 236
Ramsey
Peel
Laxey
Isle of Man
Port Erin
Douglas
Castletown

I r i s h   S e a

Carmel Head
Amlwch
Holyhead
Conwy
Llandudno 147, 148
Llanfairpwllgwyngyll 149
Bangor
Llansanffraid Glan Conwy 150
Llanddeiniolen 145
Ruthin
Betws-y-Coed
Corw

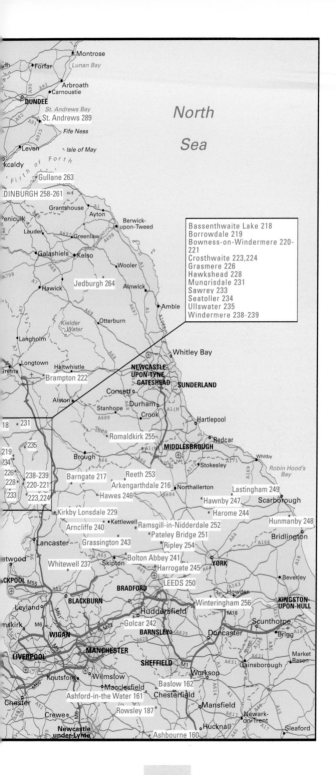

North

Sea

Montrose
Forfar   Lunan Bay
Arbroath
Carnoustie
DUNDEE
St. Andrews Bay
St. Andrews 289
Fife Ness
Leven   Isle of May
kcaldy   of   Forth
Firth of Forth
Gullane 263
DINBURGH 258-261
Grantshouse
eniculk   Ayton
Lauder   Berwick-upon-Tweed
Greenlaw
Galashiels Kelso
Wooler
Hawick   Jedburgh 264   Alnwick
Amble
Kielder   Otterburn
Water
Langholm
Longtown   Haltwhistle
aretna   Brampton 222
Alston
Consett
Stanhope   Durham
Crook
A689
Tees
Romaldkirk 255
Brough
A66
Barngate 217   Reeth 253
Arkengarthdale 216
Hawes 246
Kirkby Lonsdale 229
Arncliffe 240   Kettlewell   Ramsgill-in-Nidderdale 252
Grassington 243   Pateley Bridge 251
Ripley 254
Whitewell 237   Skipton
Bolton Abbey 241
Harrogate 245
etwood
CKPOOL M55
Leyland
nskirk   M6
WIGAN
LIVERPOOL   MANCHESTER
Knutsford   Wilmslow
Macclesfield
Chester   Ashford-in-the-Water 161
Crewe
Newcastle
under-Lyme
Ashbourne 160

Bassenthwaite Lake 218
Borrowdale 219
Bowness-on-Windermere 220-221
Crosthwaite 223,224
Grasmere 226
Hawkshead 228
Mungrisdale 231
Sawrey 233
Seatoller 234
Ullswater 235
Windermere 238-239

Whitley Bay
NEWCASTLE-UPON-TYNE
GATESHEAD   SUNDERLAND

A1(M)   Hartlepool

A1(M)   Redcar
MIDDLESBROUGH   Whitby
A171   Stokesley   Robin Hood's Bay
Northallerton   Lastingham 249
A684   Hawnby 247   Scarborough
Harome 244
Hunmanby 248
Bridlington

18   231
219   235
234
226   238-239
228   220-221
233   223,224

York
Beverley
Howden
Winteringham 256   M18
KINGSTON-UPON-HULL
BRADFORD   LEEDS 250
Scunthorpe
BLACKBURN
Huddersfield   A163
Golcar 242
BARNSLEY   A635   Doncaster   Brigg
SHEFFIELD   M1   Market Rasen
Worksop   Gainsborough
Baslow 162   Chesterfield
Rowsley 187   Mansfield
Newark-on-Trent   Sleaford
Hucknall

Papa Westray North Ronaldsay
Westray
Sanday
Rousay Eday
Brough Head Sanday Sound
ORKNEY Stronsay
ISLANDS Mainland Shapinsay
Finstown
Stromness Kirkwall
Mull Head
Rora Head St. Mary's
Hoy Burray
South Ronaldsay
Burwick
Pentland Firth

Haroldswick
Gutcher Unst
Isbister Mid Yell Fetlar
Yell
Uyea
Hillswick Yell SHETLAND
Toft ISLANDS
Sullom
Whalsay
Mainland
Walls 295 Lerwick
Scalloway Bressay

Sumburgh
Sumburgh Head

Strathy Scrabster
Dounreay John o' Groats
Melvich Thurso
Dounreay Loch Sinclair's
Bay
Loch More
Kinbrace Latheron Lybster
Lybster

Helmsdale

Golspie
Dornoch Dornoch Firth
Tarbat Ness
Tain

Firth
Burghead Lossiemouth
Cromarty Elgin Buckie Cullen Fraserburgh
Auldearn 271 Forres Fochabers
Aberchirder Mintlaw
Rothes Keith Turriff Peterhead
Charlestown Dufftown Huntly
of Aberlour
Grantown- Glenlivet 279 Oldmeldrum Ellon
on-Spey Rhynie Inverurie
Carrbridge Tomintoul Kintore Dyce
Alford ABERDEEN
Aviemore Girdle Ness
Kingussie 284 Ballater Banchory Peterculter
wtonmore Crathie Aboyne 269
Braemar Stonehaven

Laurencekirk Inverbervie
Milton Ness
Killiecrankie 282 Brechin Montrose
Pitlochry 286 Kirriemuir Scurdie Ness
Loch Lunan Bay
Tummel Forfar North
more Blairgowrie Meigle Arbroath Sea
DUNDEE
Perth Newport-
on-Tay St. Andrews Bay
Comrie 275 Newburgh St Andrews 289
uchterarder Cupar
Fife Ness

23

Atlantic

Ocean

Aran Island

Gweebarra Bay

Ardara 30

Rossan Pt.

Killybeg

Dunkineely 33

Donegal Bay

Inishmurray

Benwee Hd.

Erris Hd.

Downpatrick Head

Belmullet

Killala Bay

Sligo Bay

Slig

Inishkea

Bangor Erris

Crossmolina

N59

Dromore West

Ballyseda

Blacksod Bay

Ballycroy

L.Conn

Ballina

SLIGE

Tobercurry

Achill Island

Mulrany 347

MAYO

Riverstown 352

L Gara

Newport

Swinford

Boy

Clare

Clew Bay

Westport

Castlebar

Ballymote 310

Ballaghaderreen

Castlebaldw

Inishturk

L.Carra

Ballyhaunis

Ca 315 ea

Inishbofin

Kylemore 340

L Mask

Claremorris

N60

Inishark

Leenane 341

Clifden 317-320

CONNEMARA

Recess 351

ugh

Tuam

Slyne Head

N59

Cashel Bay 314

GALWAY

Galway 331

Ballinaslo

Inishmore

Galway Bay

Aran Islands

Inishmaan

Loughrea

Inisheer

N67

Gort

Portumna

Lisdoonvarna

Lough Derg

Hags Head

342, 343 non

Liscannor Bay

Milltown Malbay

CLARE

Ennis

Newmarket-on-Fergus 349

Nena

348

Kilkee

Kilrush

Shannon

Loop Head

Shannon

Foynes

Limerick

Mouth of The Shannon

Ballybunion

Glin 332

Kerry Head

Listowel

Rathkeale

Tipperary

Brandon Head

Tralee Bay

Abbeyfeale

Rath Luirc

LIMERICK

Kilmallock

Castlegregory 316

Tralee

Ballingarry 306

Dingle 323

Castleisland

Mitchelstown

Slea Head

Dingle Bay

KERRY

Fermoy

Killorglin

N72

Caragh Lake L. Leane

Killarney

Mallow 344

312

Valencia I.

Cahirciveen

Aghadoe 303

Bray Head

N70

Kenmare 338

CORK

Cloyne 3

Bolus Head

Macroom

Midleton

Cobb

Glengarriff

Innishannon 337

Shanagarry 3

Ballylickey 307, 308

Cork Harbou

Dursey Head

Bandon

Kinsale

Bantry Bay

N71

Clonakilty

Butlerstown 311

Goleen 333, 334

Skibbereen

Mizen Head

Galley Head

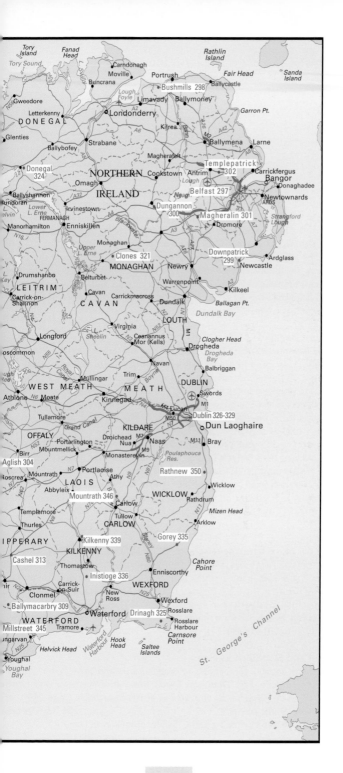

England and Wales area introduction

This section covers the largest geographical area in the guide, from the sheltered coves and sunken lanes of Devon and Cornwall in the south-west to the stark peaks and tranquil lakes of Cumbria in the north, and from the rugged moorland hills, windswept headlands and bays of the west Pembrokeshire coast to the flat east Norfolk fens. In both England and Wales, you can scarcely travel a mile without discovering something worth seeing: whether a historical sight, a picturesque village, a Georgian town or a spectacular view. For this edition of the guide, we have made many new discoveries throughout the country: among them, sophisticated town house B&Bs, comfortable country manors and guest-houses, seaside family hotels, stylish retreats and cosy village inns. All are within a wide range of prices and all have the special qualities of character and charm that we prize.

Southern England
Notable new places to this edition include the impressive **Combe House** in Gittisham (page 50), **Millers at Glencot House** (page 86), and the stylish **Zanzibar**, on the Sussex coast at St Leonards on Sea (page 130). Just before we went to press, yet another Hotel du Vin/Malmaison boutique hotel opened in Cambridge, where there has always been a lack of interesting places to stay. This seems to be one of the better Hotels du Vin and is, of course, sparkling new (tel 01223 227330).

Always on the look-out for different London hotels, we have found nine for this edition, including **B&B Belgravia** (page 100), **The Mayflower** (page 111), **Sydney House** in Chelsea (page 117), and **The Levin** (page 110). Our Scilly Isles coverage has improved, with some new entries such as **The Star Castle** (page 75) and **Hell Bay** (page 41). St Martin's on the Isle has been replaced by **The Island Hotel**, Tresco (page 81), which is more up to date and has a good atmosphere.

Wales
Among our most interesting established Welsh hotels are **Ty'n Rhos**, a secluded, comfortable farm (page 145) and **Pen-y-Gwyrd**, a perennial favourite with climbers (page 152). Some new Welsh hotels for this edition include **The Drawing Room** in Builth Wells (page 139); **The Felin Fach Griffin Inn** (page 143); and **Plas Bodegroes** in Pwllheli (page 155). Also worth a mention is **Rhiwafallen** in Gwynedd, a traditional granite farmhouse we have heard good things about (tel 01286 830172).

Central and Northern England
In Northern England, surrounded by stunning Lakeland scenery, our recommendations include **The Drunken Duck Inn**, full of character and charm (page 217); **The Charles Bathurst Inn** at Arkengarthdale (page 216); and **The Tower Bank Arms** in Sawrey (page 233). On page 208 **The White Hart** in Nayland is a charming 15thC Suffolk coaching inn.

Ashwater, Devon

Ashwater, Beaworthy,
Devon EX21 5DF

Tel (01409) 211224
Fax (01409) 211634
e-mail stay@blagdon.com
website www.blagdon.com

Nearby National Trust Coast; golf
courses.
Location just off A388 Launceston –
Holsworthy road, 4 miles (6.5 km) S
of Holsworthy, in 20 acres; ample car
parking and helicopter pad
Food breakfast, dinner
Price £££
Rooms 7; 5 double, 2 twin, all with
bath; all rooms have phone, TV,
hairdryer
Facilities sitting room, library, dining room, bar; terrace, garden, croquet **Credit cards** MC, V **Children**
welcome over 12 **Disabled** access
difficult **Pets** not accepted
Closed 2 weeks in Nov and 2 weeks
in Jan **Proprietors** Steve and Liz
Morey

Blagdon Manor
Country house hotel

Don't be put off by Blagdon Manor's isolated situation: it lies plum in the middle of the West Country, so no place of interest is really very far away.

This Grade II listed former farmhouse, surrounded by rolling countryside, was derelict when previous owners Tim and Gill Casey discovered it and brought it back to life. Successors Steve and Liz Morey purchased Blagdon Manor because, between them, they had worked in the hotel industry for 40 years and thought "it was time to do it themselves".

They told us that their goal isn't to make money, but to use their experience to provide quality. With that in mind, they completely refurbished all seven rooms, and Steve took charge of the kitchen, which produces home made jams, breads and ice cream. What can't be made on the premises comes from local businesses.

The new conservatory makes an ideal spot for breakfast and lunch and with views toward the north side of Dartmoor, definitely adds to the place. Bedrooms are comfortable, with pretty fabrics.

The Morey's assured us that they will be at Blagdon for many years to come, "We want to be here until we retire." We would welcome comments on how they are doing.

Bath

Newbridge Hill,
Bath BA1 3PT

Tel (01225) 336966
Fax (01225) 425462
e-mail info@apsley-house.co.uk
website www.apsley-house.co.uk

Nearby Bath centre.
Location on A431 to NW of city;
ample car parking
Food breakfast, light supper in qui-
eter times
Price ££
Rooms 12 double, all with shower,
10 with baths; all rooms have phone,
TV, hairdryer
Facilities sitting room, bar, breakfast
room; garden
Credit cards AE, MC, V
Children accepted
Disabled one ground floor room
Pets not accepted
Closed Christmas
Proprietors Claire and Nicholas
Potts

Apsley House
Town hotel

Once upon a time this was a grand house with huge grounds leading down to the River Avon. It was built for the Duke of Wellington in 1830, thus miss-ing the flourishing Georgian period for which Bath is famous. The grounds were sold off long ago to make way for the houses which now surround Apsley House, leaving enough garden to ensure privacy for the occupants.

There are, however, still remnants of its eminent past within, from the grand sweep-ing staircase to the high ceilings of the spa-cious rooms. There is a large, comfortable drawing room, with a grand piano, for guests' use, as well as a licensed bar.

Owners Claire and Nicholas Potts have updated the bedrooms and bathrooms, added some new furniture and generally set about making the place "a lot cleaner". Bedroom No. 9 is fashioned from the old kitchen, complete with bread oven and a splendid marble fireplace. Since the last edi-tion the Potts have opened up three fur-ther bedrooms in the hotel, complete with four-poster beds. They have also turned their attention to the grounds and put some well-needed love into the gardens.

Claire is particularly proud of her cooked breakfasts, although the classical radio piped in over breakfast may not be to everyone's liking.

1 Upper Oldfield Park,
Bath, Avon BA2 3JX

Tel (01225) 426336
Fax (01225) 444699
e-mail info@dorianhouse.co.uk
website www.dorianhouse.co.uk

Nearby Bath centre.
Location from Bath, take A367
signposted Shepton Mallet, after 1
minute's drive, take first road on the
right; with car parking
Food breakfast
Price ££
Rooms 11 doubles; all with bath or
shower, all rooms have TV, phone,
hairdryer, wi-fi **Facilities** sitting
room, dining room, honesty bar;
garden
Credit cards MC, V
Children accepted by arrangement
Disabled access difficult
Pets not accepted
Closed never
Proprietors Tim and Kathryn Hugh

Dorian House
Bed-and-breakfast

Although Bath has a large number of hotels, Dorian House stands out as a place of elegance and charm. Tim and Kathryn Hugh have made the most of this Victorian building built in 1880 of Bath stone, standing on a hill overlooking the city centre – bedrooms have splendid views towards Royal Crescent.

With high ceilings and large windows (including some impressive bay windows), rooms are drenched in light and, with tan, beige and cream tones, have a feeling of airiness. The house retains all of its original features and many rooms have fireplaces and fine antiques. Since our last edition there's been extensive redecoration in bedrooms, bathrooms and elsewhere.

Breakfast is taken in a tastefully decorated breakfast room also with views of the city. The sitting room (with honesty bar) is equally refined. You can't have dinner here, but there are plenty of good restaurants in Bath and Tim and Kathryn provide a book of menus collected from the better restaurants in town. Tim happens to be a cellist for the London Symphony Orchestra and his concert recordings form part of Dorian House's own-label cd. His artistic flair is evident in this smart bed and breakfast.

14 Raby Place, Bath,
Northeast Somerset
BA2 4EH

Tel (01225) 465120

Nearby Bath centre.
Location on S side of city; street parking
Food breakfast
Price £
Rooms 4; 2 double, both with shower; 1 twin with separate shower; 1 family room with shower; all rooms have TV, hairdryer
Facilities dining room; garden
Credit cards not accepted
Children accepted **Disabled** not suitable
Pets by arrangement **Closed** occasionally **Proprietor** Muriel Guy

Fourteen Raby Place
Town guest-house

Bath has many hotels and guest-houses that exact a heavy toll from the visitors who come to view the Roman Baths and splendid Georgian architecture. The few that manage to keep their prices reasonable are usually either far from the centre, or uninspiring, and we don't know of any that can match Muriel Guy's delightful Georgian house on the lower slopes of Bathwick Hill.

The house is in a typical Bath terrace, single-fronted, with a spacious and light open-plan kitchen/dining room, where breakfast is cooked to order and served on a large mahogany table. On a recent visit we were impressed with Mrs Guy's enthusiasm for all things organic – breakfast even included delicious stewed rhubarb, fresh from her own allotment.

Mrs Guy has been collecting paintings and ceramics for over 35 years and her delightfully eclectic collection fills the house. Bedrooms are well proportioned and tastefully done in an interesting mix of colours and styles. Our inspector stayed on the fourth floor and was treated to great views over the city. Rooms to the rear look out over the gardens.

Mrs Guy is a charming, friendly host – quietly enthusiastic about Bath and this Georgian town house, which has been her home for more than 35 years.

Russel Street, Bath,
Northeast Somerset
BA1 2QF

Tel (01225) 447928
Fax (01225) 446065
e-mail reservations@bathqueensberry.com **website** www.bathqueensberry.com

Nearby Assembly Rooms; Museum of Costume; The Circus.
Location in middle of city, close to main shopping area; paved gardens behind; daytime car parking restricted – but valet parking available
Food breakfast, lunch, dinner; room service
Price £££
Rooms 29, 1 with shower, rest with bath; all rooms have phone, TV, hairdryer, CD player
Facilities sitting room, bar, restaurant; courtyard **Credit cards** AE, MC, V **Children** welcome **Disabled** access possible, lift/elevator **Pets** guide dogs only **Closed** never
Proprietors Laurence and Helen Beere

The Queensberry
Town house hotel

This Bath hotel is slightly large for our purposes, but cannot be allowed to escape the net. Laurence and Helen Beere bought this discreet, quiet and beautifully decorated haven right in the centre of Bath in 2003. It has the advantage of a lift to all levels, which cuts down on confusion in the maze of stairwells, corridors and different levels resulting from the linking of three buildings. Despite the small-scale appearance of the hotel, the majority of the bedrooms are surprisingly spacious, and are kitted out to the highest standards of comfort and elegance. Double beds generally mean king-size here, almost guaranteed to give you a good night's sleep, and made up with lovely cotton sheets. Rooms on the first floor are largest, with armchairs and breakfast tables; bathrooms are lavish, with quality toiletries and proper towels.

All of the rooms have been refurbished in the last two years, successfully giving them a more contemporary feel, while still making use of the original features and antiques.

Downstairs, the principal sitting room is beautifully furnished in muted colours. The basement restaurant, the Olive Tree, attracts non-residents.

Bathford, Avon

Church Street, Bathford,
Bath, Somerset
BA1 7RS

Tel (01225) 859946
Fax (01225) 859430
e-mail jonap@eagleho.demon.co.uk
website www.eaglehouse.co.uk

Nearby Bath
Location 2.5 miles (4 km) E of Bath,
off A363, in village; in 2-acre gar-
dens, with ample car parking
Food breakfast
Price ££
Rooms 8; 4 double with bath, 2 sin-
gle with shower, 2 family with bath;
all rooms have phone, TV, hairdryer
Facilities breakfast room, drawing
room; garden, lawn tennis, croquet.
treehouse and swings for children
Credit cards MC, V **Children** wel-
come
Disabled access difficult
Pets accepted
Closed l0 days over Christmas
Proprietors John and Rosamund
Napier

Eagle House
Village guest-house

A stalwart of our guide, Eagle House provides a tranquil alternative to the bustle of staying in nearby Bath. Despite its outwardly grand Georgian exterior – the house was designed by John Wood the Elder – this is above all a family home, where John and Rosamund Napier go out of their way to provide a relaxed welcome to their guests.

Aquila the black Labrador wanders about and toys are readily available for the children, yet John's early training at the Savoy and Claridges underpins informality with an innate professionalism. Personal service is the watchword here, but not in the nannying sense. As there is no licence to serve alcohol, the Napiers are quite happy for people to bring their own to drink in the large, elegant drawing room hung with family heirloom portraits which include Mary Queen of Scots and Charles I and II.

The bedrooms are decorated in pretty wallpapers and comfortably furnished in country style. There is also the option of the Walled Garden Cottage for those who value complete privacy. Equipped with kitchen, sitting room and two bedrooms each with bath and shower, guests can still have breakfast in the main house. As ever at Eagle house, there is no pressure.

Beaminster, Dorset

Beaminster, Dorset
DT8 3AY

Tel (01308) 862200
Fax (01308) 863700
e-mail enquiries@bridge-house.co.uk **website** www.bridge-house.co.uk

Nearby Mapperton Gardens; Forde Abbey.
Location on A3066 in centre of town; ample car parking
Food breakfast; lunch; dinner
Price ££
Rooms 14; 12 double and twin, 1 family all with bath, 1 single with shower; all rooms have phone, TV
Facilities sitting room, bar, restaurant, conservatory; walled garden
Credit cards AE, DC, MC, V
Children accepted
Disabled 4 bedrooms with easy access **Pets** dogs accepted in coach house rooms
Closed never
Proprietors Mark and Joanna Donovan

Bridge House
Country hotel

Dating from the 13th century, Bridge House is reputedly a former monastery or clergy house and the oldest building in Beaminster. Whatever its antecedents, it is certainly a venerable and charming building and has been run as a hotel by Mark and Joanna Donovan for the last three years. Mark, a former television producer, and Joanna, a former retail buyer, took on the hotel as a major change of lifestyle. Their aim has been to build on the previous owner Peter Pinkster's good reputation, by 'updating where necessary, without destroying the hotel's unique charm'.

The sitting room and bar areas are cheefully decorated in cherry and green tartans; local artists' paintings hang on the cream walls. Lunch and dinner are served in the pretty pink-panelled dining room or the conservatory which looks out on to the walled gardens. Chef Linda Pagett has been here for several years. Young and enthusiastic, her cooking has made waves in an area blessed with quality local produce: fish, meat and cheese all come from nearby. Bread, biscuits, ice-cream and chocolates are all made in the Bridge House kitchens; even the marmalade that accompanies the satisfying breakfasts is made on the premises.

Bedrooms are all different, as would be expected in a building so full of nooks and crannies – including a priest's hole.

Beercrocombe, Somerset

Beercrocombe,
Taunton, Somerset
TA3 6AF

Tel (01823) 480430

Nearby Barrington Court; Vale of
Taunton.
Location on SW side of village, 10
miles (16 km) SE of Taunton; in gar-
dens, with ample car parking
Food breakfast, dinner
Price £
Rooms 3 double, 2 with bath, 1 with
shower; all rooms have hairdryer,
radio
Facilities 3 sitting rooms, dining
room; terrace, garden **Credit cards**
not accepted **Children** accepted by
arrangement
Disabled not suitable **Pets** not
accepted **Closed** Nov to Mar
Proprietors Veronica and Henry
Cole

Frog Street Farm
Farm guest-house

Veronica Cole has been running her farmhouse retreat, a flower-bedecked 'longhouse' hidden deep in the Somerset countryside, for some 30 years now. Her husband has
recently leased the farmland and is now able
to give Veronica a helping hand.

The house has considerable character
and warmth, with a handsome oak-beamed
inglenook in the sitting room and some very
antique panelling. Guests walk through the
front door straight in to the highly polished
dining room. Veronica, an accomplished
cook, makes as much as she possibly can for
her carefully-prepared set dinner menus,
from soups to ice-creams. Eggs come from
her own hens, vegetables from Henry's
organic garden, beef from the farm. The couple also own a successful National Hunt stable, and horse-racing features prominently
in their lives. The stables at the back of the
farm invariably hold a variety of brood
mares, hunters and young horses, guarded
by the farm collie.

Bedrooms look out on to farmland, cider
apple orchards and the pretty garden. They
are all spacious and comfortable, with floral
duvets, and a mix of antique furniture. The
atmosphere is friendly, restful and unpretentious. We hear Veronica is planning to scale
things down soon, and that her daughter
may take over. Reports welcome.

Bigbury-on-Sea, South Devon

Folly Hill, Bigbury-on-Sea,
South Devon TQ7 4AR

Tel (01548) 810240
Fax (01548) 810240
e-mail
thehenleyhotel@btconnect.com
website www.thehenleyhotel.co.uk

Nearby Burgh Island, Avon Estuary.
Location 20 minutes from A38
beyond Bigbury-on-Sea towards sea;
ample car parking
Food breakfast, dinner
Price ££
Rooms 6 double and twin, 4 with
bath, 2 with shower; all have phone,
TV, radio
Facilities conservatory/dining room;
garden, private cliff path, beach
Credit cards MC, V **Children** over
12 only **Disabled** not suitable
Pets welcome **Closed** Nov to March
Proprietors Martyn Scarterfield and
Petra Lampe

The Henley
Coastal hotel

Recommended to us by an astute reader, The Henley was described to us as 'the sort of place that I always hope to discover on holiday, and alas, rarely do.' Originally built as a holiday cottage during Edwardian times, the hotel has a beach-house feel and spectacular views that stretch from the Avon Estuary around to Burgh Island. And if simply looking at the sea isn't enough, you can climb down the private cliff path to a stretch of pristine beach.

Although owner Martyn Scarterfield was a PE and Art teacher in a previous life, he comes from a family hotel in Sidmouth and has been in the trade for many years. Co-owner Petra Lampe brings both charm and a sense of warmth and elegance to the hotel. Together, they create a relaxing atmosphere that is, above all, unpretentious.

Bedrooms are simple, yet comfortable and spacious. The dining room has Lloyd Loom furniture and overlooks the sea. Martyn does the cooking and it can be described as "real home cooked food" – excellent quality without any artificial presentation. The menu features a choice of three starters and two mains, one of which will be fresh, locally caught fish.

A winning combination of great food, beautiful views and friendly owners.

Bradford-on-Avon, Wiltshire

4 Masons Lane, Bradford-on-Avon,
Wiltshire BA15 1QN

Tel (01225) 866842
Fax (01225) 866648
e-mail website@bradfordoldwind-
mill.co.uk **website** www.bradfor-
doldwindmill.co.uk

Nearby Bath; Kennet and Avon
Canal.
Location just N of town centre;
with cottage garden and parking for
3 cars
Food breakfast, dinner (Mon, Thur,
Sat only)
Price ££
Rooms 3; 2 double, 1 family suite,
all with bath; all rooms have TV
Facilities sitting room, dining room;
terrace **Credit cards** MC, V
Children welcome over 6 **Disabled**
access difficult
Pets not accepted **Closed** Nov - Feb
Proprietors Peter and Priscilla
Roberts

Bradford Old Windmill
Town guest-house

Peter and Priscilla Robert's extraordinary
home, an old windmill, continues to
provide guests with a unique experience.
Built in 1807, the windmill functioned for
only 20 years but left a memorable building
in its stead. It boasts a 4-story Cotswold
stone tower, conical tiled roof, pointed
Gothic windows and restored sail galley.

The rooms, with curved walls and odd-
angled corners, offer excellent views over
old Bradford and beyond. The suite
includes a minstrel gallery and the smallest
room has a waterbed. Each room contains
curiosities and guidebooks from the
Roberts' extensive travels. Bathrooms
have been updated.

There is a pretty terrace that also overlooks old Bradford, where breakfast and dinner are occasionally served, weather permitting. You get breakfast at a communal table,
but special provision is made for those honeymoon couples booking the 'celebration
special break' who wish to eat late and alone.

Priscilla will cook dinner (always vegetarian) if given notice. Recent menus
include Caribbean, Thai and Nepalese. The
breakfast menu is extensive and includes
free-range bacon. Ingredients are 90 per
cent organic. This is a very different kind of
guest-house, and one with great character.
See also our other windmill, Cley Mill, on
page 199.

Bradford-on-Avon, Wiltshire

Newtown, Bradford-on-Avon,
Wiltshire BA15 1NQ

Tel (01225) 862230
Fax (01225) 866248
e-mail priorysteps@clara.co.uk
website www.priorysteps.co.uk

Nearby Barton Tithe Barn; Bath.
Location off A363 on N side of
town; in 0.5 acre garden, with car
parking
Food breakfast, dinner (to order)
Price ££
Rooms 5 double and twin, all with
bath; all rooms have TV
Facilities sitting room, dining room;
terrace, garden
Credit cards MC, V
Children accepted
Disabled access difficult **Pets** not
accepted
Closed occasionally **Proprietors**
Carey and Diana Chapman

Priory Steps
Town guest-house

High above the lovely little wool town of
Bradford-on-Avon, Carey and Diana
Chapman's converted row of weavers' cottages look out over the predominantly
Georgian houses interspersed with a smat-
tering of Saxon and medieval buildings.
Although only three minutes walk from the
centre, Priory Steps is not easy to find. It is so
discreetly signposted that it looks like a private home – which it is for the Chapmans
and their children. As a result, the pictures
and pieces that decorate the house have family connections and the atmosphere is informal and easy-going, especially in the book-
lined sitting room.

Each of the bedrooms has a theme –
Indian, Chinese and so on. In spite of the cottage architecture, there is nothing cramped
about them: they are light and airy, with wonderful views. Beautifully decorated by Diana's
mother-in-law, each has its own character
and is furnished mainly with antiques. This is
a well-maintained place with a continuing
refurbishment programme.

Diana is a keen cook and dinner is served
either at a communal table in the elegant dining room or, on fine days, out on the terrace
of the garden looking down over the town.
Dinners are three courses, with no choice,
but special requirements are happily met,
given notice. You will be made to feel like a
house guest in a particularly well-run home.

Bradford-on-Avon, Wiltshire

1 Church Street, Bradford-on-Avon,
Wiltshire, BA15 1LN

Tel (01225) 868686
Fax (01225) 868681
e-mail theswan-
hotel@btconnect.com
website www.theswan-hotel.com

Nearby sights of Bradford-on-Avon;
Avoncliffe; Bath.
Location in town centre, entrance
on quiet side street. Off-road car
parking.
Food breakfast, lunch, dinner
Price ££-£££
Rooms 12; 9 with bath, 3 with
shower only; all have phone, TV, wi-
fi **Facilities** sitting room, bar, restau-
rant, private dining room, garden,
function room
Credit cards MC, V
Children accepted
Disabled by arrangement
Pets not accepted **Closed** never
Proprietors Stephen and Penny
Ross **Manager** Tom Bridgeman

The Swan Inn
Town inn

In 2007 this 600-year-old Bradford-on-Avon institution got a new lease of life – a complete makeover. It's now somewhere you might actually want to stay, no small claim considering how ghastly it was before. However, the listed building was a nightmare to renovate, and the result lacks the finesse we like to look for in this guide. This shouldn't stop you staying here, if you want what it offers: a mixture of small town hotel, pub and informal restaurant. Locals and residents enjoy the bar and the (good) food; prices are fair; and – big bonus – you can get to Bath by train in 15 minutes. This makes it a serious alternative to lodging in Bath, where hotel prices are now higher than in London. And Bradford-on-Avon is a fine town, with plenty to interest visitors.

Lack of finesse? The interior design relies too much on predictable 'contemporary' colours, carpets and curtains. The little sitting room near the main entrance is underwhelming; the dining areas need softening; the bed creaked; there was some traffic noise. That said, rooms 8 and 12 are spacious and good value.

We're hoping that the management, independent hotelier Stephen Ross and chef-manager Tom Bridgeman, can improve on what they've got – after all it was early days when we visited.

Branscombe, Devon

Branscombe, Devon
EX12 3DJ

Tel (01297) 680300
Fax (01297) 680500
e-mail reception@masonsarms.co.uk
website www.masonsarms.co.uk

Nearby South Devon coastal path; Sidmouth.
Location in village 8 miles (11 km) S of Honiton, off A3052 between Sidmouth and Seaton; with ample car parking
Food breakfast, lunch, dinner
Price ££-£££
Rooms 22; 20 double, twin and family with bath ensuite, 2 with separate bath; self-catering cottages; all rooms have phone, TV, hairdryer
Facilities sitting room, bar, restaurants; terrace, garden **Credit cards** MC, V **Children** welcome **Disabled** access not possible
Pets accepted **Closed** never
Proprietors Slaney family
Managers Scott Wayne, Richard Slaney

Masons Arms
Seaside village inn

Branscombe is a picturesque little Devon village, at the end of a winding lane, surrounded by steep, wooded hillsides and overlooking the sea. The National Trust owns most of the land around, and the South Devon Coastal Path passes through it. In other words, this village is a hive of activity, inspiring visits from walkers in winter and beachcomers in summer, many of whom pitch up at the Masons Arms. Welcoming, yes; popular, certainly. It's just what a village pub should be, although its success has led to expansion: what was a simple inn, converted from four cottages, now has two restaurants, a large function room, 22 rooms spread out over two buildings and eight Garden Cottages.

Since our last edition The Masons Arms was taken over by the Slaney family, who wanted to make improvements, while preserving the character of the place. They have refurbished the reception, lounge and restaurant, and all cottage rooms, and all rooms now have their own bath.

The bedrooms have a cottagey feel, with pretty fabrics, beamed ceilings and sloping floors. The recently upgraded Cottage Rooms are modern and stylish. The bathrooms are a smart slate grey. Food is good pub grub, with the restaurants offering a more up-market, and therefore more costly, menu. Reports welcome.

The Sugar House,
Narrow Lewins Mead,
Bristol, Avon BS1 2NU

Tel (0117) 925 5577
Fax (0117) 925 1199
e-mail reception.bristol@hoteldu-vin.com
website www.hotelduvin.com

Nearby city centre; docks; Christmas steps.
Location in city centre, residents only car parking
Food breakfast, lunch, dinner
Price £££
Rooms 40 double and twin, all with bath; all rooms have phone, TV, CD player, minibar, hairdryer
Facilities sitting room, billiards room, dining room, bar, humidor, courtyard
Credit cards AE, DC, MC, V
Children accepted
Disabled access possible, lift/elevator **Pets** guide dogs only
Closed never **Manager** Steven Lewis

Hotel du Vin
Town hotel

Since our last edition, the Hotel du Vin chain has been taken over by Malmaison, a large group. Signs of big-business management and of the standardisation that goes with it, are beginning to be seen. However, for our money, this is still probably the most interesting and stylish place in Bristol.

Converted from a collection of derelict 18thC sugar warehouses, the hotel's gracious Queen Anne frontage belies the wizardry behind. Open brickwork, black-painted girders and sweeping stairs with a curving steel bannister combine industrial elements with contemporary style to great effect.

Sponsored by and named after different wine houses, the huge bedrooms contain custom-made, superbly comfortable beds, alongside equally huge bathrooms with showers and free-standing baths. Though it fronts on to Bristol's main thoroughfare, the hotel's double glazing effectively blocks any traffic noise. The aptly-named Sugar Bar is dominated by a large mural of grapes on the vine, while whitewashed walls, big squashy sofas, wood flooring and rugs contribute to the unhurried, plantation house feel. Sadly, the future of the cigar room was uncertain as we went to press, because of the smoking ban. See pages 91, 134, and 245 for the other Hotels du Vin included in the guide – because of the new owners, we have a small selection now.

Bryher, Isles of Scilly

Bryher, Isles of Scilly

Tel (01720) 422947
Fax (01720) 423008
e-mail contactus@hellbay.co.uk
website www.hellbay.co.uk

Nearby Tresco subtropical garden
Location access by ferry from
Tresco – no cars; in own extensive
grounds
Food breakfast, lunch, dinner
Price £££
Rooms 25; all suites, no singles, but
can be double or twin; all rooms
have phone, TV, hairdryer, DVD
and CD players
Facilities swimming pool, children's
play area, games and fitness rooms,
sauna, gym, par 3 golf
Credit Cards MC, V **Children**
accepted **Disabled** no special
arrangements; location makes arrival
difficult **Pets** accepted **Closed** early
Jan-early Feb
Proprietor Robert Dorrien-Smith
Manager Philip Callan

Hell Bay
Seaside hotel

California meets the Atlantic Ocean at
this wonderfully sited island hotel,
which reopened recently after a metamor-
phosis. It takes commitment to get here
(helicopter or ferry from Penzance to
Tresco, then ferry and tractor-bus), but
when you do you'll find grass, golden sand,
a jumble of rocks, and nothing except
ocean to separate you from America.
Bryher is the tiny (otherwise uninhabited
island) separated from neighbouring
Tresco by a narrow strait of almost tropi-
cal blue water.

Hell Bay is the work of Robert and Lucy
Dorrien-Smith, hereditary owners of the
neighbouring island of Tresco. Robert has
filled the place with his own collection of
modern art and sculpture, all with a
regional connection, as well as eye-catching stained glass and mirrors. Bedrooms
are suites, each sleeping up to four, with a
huge double bed and two attractive armchair beds, and they are decorated in fresh
'seaside' colours. Elsewhere cheerful seaside blue and comfortable cane chairs
dominate the contemporary decorative
scheme. There have been mixed reports
about the food. Prices are relatively high –
as you would expect this far off the beat-
en track. Its primary appeal is to a well-
heeled, trendy crowd.

Chagford, Devon

Chagford, Devon
TQl3 8HH

Tel (01647) 432367
Fax (01647) 432574
e-mail gidleighpark@gidleigh.co.uk
website www.gidleigh.com

Nearby Castle Drogo; Dartmoor; Rosemoore, Knighthayes Court gardens.
Location 2 miles (3 km) W of Chagford; in 45 acre grounds with ample car parking
Food breakfast, lunch, afternoon tea, dinner; room service
Price ££££
Rooms 23 double, all with bath; 1 cottage in the grounds; all rooms have phone, TV, hairdryer, wi-fi, safe
Facilities sitting room, bar, loggia, 3 dining rooms; terrace, garden, croquet, fishing, tennis, bowls, 18 hole putting course **Credit cards** AE, DC, MC, V **Children** accepted; under 7 not allowed in dining room for dinner **Disabled** ground floor bedroom **Pets** welcome
Closed never **Proprietors** Andrew and Christina Brownsword

Gidleigh Park
Country house hotel

This quintessential country house hotel was created 30 years ago by Americans Paul and Kay Henderson, and taken over recently (with a major refurbishment) by Andrew Brownsword. It used to be all about ticking clocks, curled-up Siamese cats and enveloping, understated luxury and it still has great character. However, the atmosphere is now more openly plutocratic – its main appeal is very much to the well-off and elderly and to be honest it has become, despite its quality, a marginal entry in the guide.

Take your walking boots and your Labrador and prepare for the very rich, highly-praised cooking of Michael Caines (which merits two Michelin stars).

On the edge of Dartmoor, lost in woods, the house is situated at the end of a long, bumpy, tree-lined lane which opens out to present an idyllic park setting. Behind the house are attractive terraced gardens, giving way to woods; in front, the rocky River Teign.

All the refurbished bedrooms give an immediate feeling of comfort but also friendliness. Prices are sky high and service excellent – but (in the dining room) very ceremonious, with every course described at some length as it arrives on the table.

Chettle, Dorset

Chettle, near Blandford Forum,
Dorset, DT11 8DB

Tel (01258) 830096
Fax (01258) 830051
e-mail
enquiry@castlemanhotel.co.uk
website www.castlemanhotel.co.uk

Nearby Kingston Lacy House;
Cranborne Chase; Salisbury.
Location in village, signposted off
A354, 6 miles (9 km) NE of
Blandford; ample car parking
Food breakfast, Sunday lunch,
dinner
Price ££
Rooms 8 double, all with bath; all
rooms have phone, TV, hairdryer
Facilities dining room, 2 sitting
rooms, bar; garden **Credit cards**
MC, V **Children** welcome **Disabled**
access difficult **Pets** not accepted in
house; 2 stables available for guests'
horses and dogs **Closed** Feb
Proprietors Edward Bourke and
Barbara Garnsworthy

Castleman
Country house hotel

Chettle is one of those rare estate villages that has hardly changed in the 150
years it has been in the benign ownership of
one family – who live in the fine Queen
Anne manor house, open to the public during summer months. Teddy Bourke, one of
the family, took on the decrepid ex-dower
house ('locals all thought it was haunted') in
1996, together with his partner, Barbara
Garnsworthy, transforming it into a charmingly eccentric and very reasonably priced
hotel and restaurant. Part of the building
dates back 400 years, but it was much altered
in Victorian times when it was tricked out
with a galleried hall; a richly carved oak
Jacobean fireplace was also installed in one of
the reception rooms (the other is Regency
style) with bookcases to match. Upstairs, the
elegant proportions of the rooms have been
left intact, and bedrooms are just right: comfortable and in good taste, but without room
service or unnecessary frills so as to keep
prices sensible; several of the bathrooms have
Victorian roll top baths. The 'large' rooms are
enormous, one with a huge bay window
overlooking the fields, whilst the smaller ones
are still spacious. The Castleman's restaurant
– a long, rather plain room at the rear –
serves straightforward traditional and modern British dishes – and the bill is not indi-
gestible. 'Superb value', say regular guests.

Dittisham, Devon

Old Coombe Manor Farm,
Dittisham, near Dartmouth,
Devon Q6 OJA

Tel (01803) 722398
Fax (01803) 722401
e-mail richard@fingals.co.uk
website www.fingals.co.uk

Nearby Dartmouth Castle.
Location 7 miles (6 km) N of
Dartmouth, 1 mile (1.5 km) from village; with garden and ample car
parking
Food breakfast, snack lunch, dinner
Price ££
Rooms 11; 9 double, 2 family
rooms, all with bath; all rooms have
phone; some have TV **Facilities** dining room, bar, library, TV room,
swimming pool, jacuzzi, sauna,
snooker, croquet, tennis, table-tennis, cinema; rowing boat available
Credit cards AE, MC, V **Children**
accepted **Disabled** access difficult
Pets accepted but not in public
rooms **Closed** after New Year to
before Easter **Proprietor** Richard
Johnston

Fingals
Manor house hotel

Fingals is different, and those who love it will really love it – which sums up why we remain enthusiastic about this manor farmhouse in a secluded valley, close to the River Dart. Owner Richard Johnston, calls it a 'hotel and restaurant', but in practice, Fingals comes much closer to the 'country house party' type of guest-house, where it is normal (though not obligatory) for guests to share a table in the wood-pan-elled dining room at mealtimes.

The house – 17thC with Queen Anne front additions – has plenty of charm, with a stylish blend of new and old furniture, pine and oak. An adjacent self-catering barn is ideal for a family or for those want-ing extra space and privacy.

Fingals is an exceptionally relaxed place – you pour your own drinks, eat breakfast whenever you like, be it morning or after-noon – and those who insist on everything being just so are likely to be disappointed. The four-course dinners, chosen from a short menu, are modern in style, compe-tent in execution, and ample in quantity. A laid-back place with a laid-back yet thor-oughly professional proprietor.

Dorchester, Dorset

49 High East Street, Dorchester,
Dorset DT1 1HU

Tel (01305) 264043
Fax (01305) 260884
e-mail reception@casterbridgeho-
tel.co.uk
website www.casterbridgehotel.co.uk

Nearby Hardy country; Dorset
coast.
Location on main road in centre of
town; limited street parking
Food breakfast
Price ££
Rooms 15; 10 double, 5 single, all
with bath or shower; all rooms have
phone, TV, hairdryer **Facilities** sit-
ting room, bar, conservatory/break-
fast room; patio garden
Credit cards AE, MC, V **Children**
welcome
Disabled 2 rooms on ground floor
Pets not accepted
Closed Christmas Day and Boxing
Day **Proprietors** Stuart and Rita
Turner

Casterbridge
Town hotel

You might easily drive straight past the
Casterbridge, assuming it to be just
another one of those dreary country
town hotels which seem to dominate
British high streets. However, when you
learn that it is owned by the same family as
the Priory (see page 83) you might stop
and wisely think again. The hotel has been
in the Turner family since 1930, but in the
1980s family scion Stuart and wife Rita
took it over and started on the monumen-
tal task of updating its moribund interior.

They succeeded in bringing life to an old
Georgian building that remains faithful to
its origins, but incorporates the modern
touches we all crave; above all it is a very
comfortable place in which to stay. A
drawing room has been decorated in soft
blue-greys and pink, with several large,
pleasing oil paintings and an abundance of
reading matter. The Georgian furniture is
all in keeping. A well-stocked bar next
door leads into a delightful conservatory
and to a little courtyard with fountain
beyond. Unlike the Priory, the Casterbridge
only offers bed and breakfast. The bedrooms are prettily decorated, with delightful wallpapers, quality fabrics and pleasant
bathrooms. Bedrooms in the modern
annexe beyond the courtyard are equally
comfortable, but have less charm than
those in the main building.

Farnham, Dorset

Farnham, Blandford Forum,
DT11 8DE

Tel (01725) 516261
Fax (01725) 516988
e-mail themuseuminn@supanet.com
website www.museum.inn.co.uk

Nearby Blandford Forum;
Cranborne Chase; Dorchester,
Salisbury.
Location in village, 7.5 miles NE of
Blandford Forum, off A354 to
Salisbury
Food breakfast, lunch, dinner
Price ££
Rooms 8 double and twin, all with
bath and shower; all rooms have
phone, TV, hairdryer
Facilities bar, conservatory, sitting
room, dining room
Credit cards DC, MC, V
Children accepted over 8
Disabled 4 rooms on ground floor
Pets accepted
Closed never; restaurant open Fri
dinner, Sat dinner, Sun lunch
Owners Mark Stephenson and
Vicky Elliot

The Museum Inn
Village hotel

The Castleman Hotel in Chettle is now joined by another really excellent place in which to eat and stay in the neighbouring, and equally delightful, village of Farnham on Cranbourne Chase. The Museum Inn was built by the father of modern archaeology, General Augustus Henry Lane-Foxx Pitt-Rivers, as accommodation for visitors to his nearby museum. It is exceedingly clean and the food is good. It is popular with locals – reputedly including Madonna and Sting.

Today, the museum has undergone a complete refurbishment after a long spell as a low-key, rather dismall pub, and it now combines a popular inn, with imaginative bar food served in several different areas, a more formal restaurant, and eight guest bedrooms. These are simple and stylish, with attractive prints on cream walls, and toille-de-jouey or checked fabrics for bedspreads, curtains and upholstered chairs. Owners Mark Stephenson and Vicky Elliot ensure a laid-back atmosphere, employing friendly young staff from Australia and New Zealand. There's always a buzz around the bar, and Clive Jory's food in the restaurant is popular.

Fowey, Cornwall

28, Fore Street, Fowey,
Cornwall PL23 1AQ

Tel (01726) 833302
Fax (01726) 833668
e-mail info@theoldquayhouse.com
website www.theoldquayhouse.com

Nearby The Lost Gardens of
Heligan, Lanhydrock, coastal walks
Location on main street; no hotel
car park but in summer low-cost
permits available for car park 800
yards away; in winter, long term pay
and display car park, Caffa Mill, 700
yards
Food breakfast, lunch, dinner
Price ££-££££
Rooms 11; all double, most with
bath and shower, some with shower
only; all have phone, TV, wireless
internet, TV, video player
Facilities bar, riverfront terrace,
restaurant, sitting areas
Credit Cards AE, DC, MC, V
Children not under 12 **Disabled** no
lift/elevator – not suitable **Pets** only
guide dogs **Closed** never
Proprietors Jane and Roy Carson
Manager Joanne Wansbury

Old Quay House
Seaside hotel

Location, location, location. This is a long, thin building jutting out over the wonderful Fowey River in the heart of charming Fowey, loved by yachties, and the rest; and it is rightly geared around the endless amusement you'll get from the comings and goings on the river, not to mention the prettiness of it all.

You can eat or just sit with a drink on the terrace right over the water watching it all go by, or when cold, move just inside to a sitting area. Most of the bedrooms have the view, the best being corner rooms and the (£300) top-floor suite. The interior design is cool, uncluttered, contemporary, to attract a core market of 30s-50s: grey paint, pine floors, perspex tables. The long, thin downstairs combined bar, restaurant and sitting area is a sea of somewhat in-your-face wicker chairs. Food was fairly priced at around £30 for three courses when we visited; the list of wines by the glass was perhaps limited.

They aim for a personal welcome and with 11 bedrooms, and the current competent, friendly management, that's a reasonable claim. However, with so many non-residents coming in to eat, it's not especially strong on the private, unique character we appreciate. It's a 'hotel and restaurant' formula, one that can work well, but in different hands might be merely formulaic.

Frome, Somerset

Babington, near Frome,
Somerset BA11 3RW

Tel (01373) 812266
Fax (01373) 812112
e-mail
enquiries@babingtonhouse.co.uk
website www.babingtonhouse.co.uk

Nearby Bath; Bradford-on-Avon.
Location in countryside, 15 miles
(24 km) S of Bath; ample car parking
Food breakfast, lunch, dinner; room
service
Price ££££
Rooms 28 double and twin, all with
bath; all rooms have phone, TV,
DVD player, CD player, fax/modem
point, minibar, hairdryer **Facilities**
sitting room/bar, snooker room, dining room, bistro, computers, indoor
and outdoor swimming pools, health
club, crèche, cinema, chapel; terrace,
garden, tennis court
Credit cards AE, DC, MC, V
Children welcome
Disabled bedrooms on ground floor
and adapted WC **Pets** accepted
Closed never **Proprietor** Nick
Jones

Babington House
Country house hotel

Babington was the bright idea of Nick Jones, owner of the trendy Soho Club in London, and bought as a country retreat for club members. There is still talk about 'members' and 'non-members' but in prac-tise anyone can stay here, although it might be better if you were young, or at least young at heart, street-wise, and preferably in the media business. Having said that, everyone is made to feel welcome, in an atmosphere which is so laid-back that it's almost horizontal yet at the same time professional. If you are tired of stuffy coun-try house hotels, with too many swags and drapes and no concessions to children, you will find Babington enormously refreshing: a contemporary hotel set in an elegant country house that offers metro-politan chic and unpretentious luxury. Bedrooms are wonderful, with huge bot-tles of complimentary lotions in the bath-rooms (no mean sachets here) and 24-hour room service. You can have any num-ber of beauty treatments in the Cowshed, where there is also an indoor pool and a gym. Small children are kept occupied in the well-equipped crèche. We would par-ticularly welcome feedback on Babington: how does it feel staying here if your face doesn't fit?; how did you cope with life in the bar/sitting room?

Gillingham, Dorset

Gillingham,
Dorset, SP8 5NR

Tel (01747) 823626
Fax (01747) 825628
e-mail
reception@stockhillhouse.co.uk
website www.stockhillhouse.co.uk

Nearby Shaftesbury; Stourhead
House and Gardens.
Location 5 miles (8 km) NW of
Shaftesbury on B3081; in 11-acre
grounds with ample car parking
Food breakfast, lunch, dinner
Price ££££
Rooms 9 double, 8 with bath, 1 with
shower; all rooms have TV, phone,
hairdryer
Facilities sitting room, dining room,
breakfast room, parkland, kitchen
garden, tennis court, croquet, put-
ting green, helipad
Credit cards MC, V
Children welcome over 7
Disabled not suitable **Pets** not
accepted **Closed** restaurant only, Sat
and Mon lunch **Proprietors** Peter
and Nita Hauser

Stock Hill House
Country house hotel

This restored Victorian manor house,
reached up a long drive through wooded grounds, has been immaculately furnished and decorated in indivual, opulent
and somewhat heavy turn-of-the-century
style by its hands-on owners, the Hausers,
who have been at the helm for more than
20 years. Bedrooms are luxurious, and
although the atmosphere is definitely formal, one is relieved to discover that it is also
genuinely warm and friendly. Three of the
bedrooms are in a separate coach house,
and are more contemporary in style.

Peter Hauser and Lorna Connor do all
the cooking and produce superb results.
Peter's Austrian roots are reflected in the
varied, generous menu, which changes
daily. Fruit and vegetables come from his
impressive walled kitchen garden. While he
works away in the kitchen, guests are apt
to pop in for a chat or to see what he is
planning for dinner that evening. Many of
the hotel's staff are recruited from across
Europe and they are attentive and friendly.

The extensive grounds include formal
gardens and a tennis court. More reports
would be appreciated.

Gittisham, Devon

Gittisham, Honiton, Devon
EX14 3AD

Tel (01404) 540 400
e-mail stay@thishotel.com
website www.thishotel.com

Nearby Gittisham village, Honiton antique trail, Dartmoor National Park, Jurassic Coast, Ottery St Mary
Location set in 3,500 acres of grounds, 2 miles from A30 and Honiton with ample car parking
Food breakfast, lunch, dinner
Price ££££
Rooms 16 including cottage; all en suite with plasma TV, phone, hairdryers; most rooms have wi-fi internet
Facilities two bar/lounge rooms, two dining rooms, Georgian kitchen, extensive parkland, helipad; fishing, shooting and riding all nearby
Credit Cards MC, V
Children welcome
Disabled access to restaurant only
Pets well behaved dogs, £7 per night
Closed last two weeks of January
Proprietors Ken and Ruth Hunt

Combe House
Country hotel

Through delightful unspoiled Gittisham village, up a long drive, past wild flower meadows you find this large manor house dating from Elizabethan times. Perhaps it's not as mellow as some photos make it look, but you're definitely in the isolated world of an old country estate. Inside, old and new rub shoulders amusingly, perhaps eccentrically. In the main public space downstairs, the hall, gay splashes of colour contrast effectively with magnificent dark, heavy old panelling. Antique wallpaper has been preserved in a little reception room off the hall and the dining room walls are charmingly hand painted by former owners. It's full of quirky corners and surprises (including an outdoor bath house) to keep you amused. You'll see the odd imperfection downstairs, which could not matter less, because this is far from being a haphazard operation. Ruth and Ken Hunter are natural but astute hoteliers who have built up Combe House's reputation from nothing over a decade of hands-on hard work. Now, all the basics are right: award-winning food; upstairs, fresh, imaginative rooms, some traditional, some more contemporary, some pretty, at a useful range of prices. For a treat, book the Linen Suite with its copper bath tub. People of most ages can feel comfortable here.

Gulworthy, Devon

Gulworthy, Tavistock,
Devon PL19 8JD

Tel (01822) 832528
Fax (01822) 832528
e-mail
enquiries@thehornofplenty.co.uk
website www.thehornofplenty.co.uk

Nearby Cotehele House, Dartmoor,
Plymouth.
Location 3 miles (5 km) W of
Tavistock on A390; with ample car
parking
Food breakfast, lunch, dinner
Price £££
Rooms 10; 8 double and twin, 6
with bath, 2 with shower, 2 suites
with bath; all rooms have phone, TV,
video, minibar, hairdryer
Facilities sitting room, bar, restaurant; terrace, garden
Credit cards MC, V **Children**
accepted; over 7 in restaurant for
dinner **Disabled** 2 suitable bedrooms **Pets** accepted by arrangement **Closed** Christmas
Proprietors Paul and Andie Roston
and Peter Gorton

Horn of Plenty
Country restaurant-with-rooms

The Horn of Plenty has long featured in this guide, despite the several changes of ownership which it has undergone in recent years. On a recent visit we found that a major reinvestment was now complete, with all the rooms a high standard, including one imaginatively done in mauve: this goes for those in the main house and those in the coach house, overlooking the charming walled garden.

Built in 1830 by the Marquess of Tavistock, the secluded, creeper-covered house is approached down a short avenue of tall trees and has a splendid location overlooking the Tamar Valley, a view shared by the bedrooms, some of which have small terraces.

The Horn of Plenty is primarily a restaurant, and dinner is the main event, skilfully prepared by chef, and now co-owner, Peter Gorton (well-known now, thanks to a recent television series) and served in front of picture windows in the two-part dining room.

It's not especially cheap, but we reckon you get what you pay for here – a view backed up by a guest we overheard expressing his satisfaction. Competent, friendly front of house manager.

Hinton St George, Somerset

High Street, Hinton-St-George
Somerset, TA17 8SE

Tel (01460) 73149
e-mail steveandmichelle@lord-poulettarms.com
website www.lordpoulettarms.com

Nearby local cider makers;
Montacute House, Sherborne
Castle, Forde Abbey;
Jurassic coast, Blackdown Hills.
Location in village street, plenty of
free car parking; own small private
car park.
Food breakfast, lunch, dinner
Price ££
Rooms 4; 2 with bath in the room,
two with separate private bathroom
across corridor; all rooms except one
have WC, radio, flat screen TV on
request (except one room where no
signal), leaf tea and coffee making
Facilities bar, garden, boule area
Credit cards MC **Disabled** not
suitable **Children** one room can be
converted to family room **Closed**
Christmas Day and Boxing Day
Proprietors Steve Hill and Michelle
Paynton

The Lord Poulett
Village inn

We reacted with pleasure to this country inn from the moment we were through the door. First, the arresting birdcage pattern wallpaper in the passage. Then the pleasant atmosphere in the bar – actually divided into three areas. A cheery local was installed in his favourite spot. Two mothers with babies were meeting for a tomato juice. Steve and Michelle, the proprietors, who took over in 2002 with no previous experience of the business, say they wanted to create a country get-away for visitors and a meeting place for locals – and they have. Tables and chairs were a mellow jumble of different antique country types. Food was the best we can remember in a pub. Upstairs, the bedroom corridor was decorated with a bold, striped wallpaper reminding us of a French inn, and the four simple, pretty but not over-feminine, homely bedrooms were charming, individual, again relying on unusual wallpapers rather than contemporary sludge-colours. Prices are fair.

At the back are two gardens for eating out in fine weather, one a herb garden, the other grassy, with an old *pelota* or fives wall at the end.

A pub that's got it just right, thanks to the owners' natural taste and emphasis on quality and things that matter.

Holsworthy, Devon

Clawton, Holsworthy,
Devon EX22 6PS

Tel (01409) 271219
Fax (01409) 271309
e-mail courtbarnhotel@talk21.com
website www.hotels-devon.com

Nearby Bude, Boscastle, Tintagel,
Hartland Abbey, Dartmoor.
Location on A388 from Launceston
to Holsworthy, at Clawton; ample
car parking
Food breakfast, lunch, dinner
Price ££
Rooms 8; 7 double and twin, 1 suite,
all with bath; all rooms have phone,
TV, hairdryer **Facilities** dining
room, breakfast, drawing room, TV
room; garden, croquet, badminton,
lawn tennis, 4-hole pitch and putt
Credit cards AE, DC, MC, V
Children accepted
Disabled access difficult
Pets accepted by arrangement
Closed never **Proprietors** Robert
and Susan Wood

Court Barn
Country house hotel

Court Barn lacks any trace of stuffiness or pretentiousness; and it has an abundance of easy-going warmth. It is a four-square house, dating from the 16th century but partly rebuilt in 1853, where antiques, souvenirs, books and games jostle with sometimes unusual furnishings in a carefree medley of patterns. The result is reassuring: this home-like environment spells comfort far beyond the meretricious harmony of hotels colour-matched by designers. And its owners, Susan and Robert Wood, spare no effort to make you feel at home and welcome.

Downstairs, there is a drawing room with open log fire and views over the garden, a breakfast room which looks out on to the croquet lawn, and an elegant dining room which is candle-litlit in the evenings. The food, on our most recent visit, was satisfying, accompanied by an extensive wine list, annotated by Robert ('Norwegian wines are terrible and may account for the country's lowest wine consumption in Europe').

Beautifully kept park-like grounds surround the house; croquet hoops, putting holes, badminton and lawn tennis suggest plenty to do outside. Beyond are gently rolling hills; and Court Barn is perfectly placed for exploring Devon and Cornwall.

Church Hill, Kingswear,
Dartmouth, Devon TQ6 0BX

Tel (01803) 752829
Fax (01803) 752357
e-mail enquiries@nonsuch-house.co.uk
website www.nonsuch-house.co.uk

Nearby Dartmouth; Dartmoor; Torquay.
Location from Dartmouth ferry to Kingswear, take Fore Street, then turn sharp right after 100 yards on to Church Hill; street car parking
Food breakfast, dinner (Sun, Mon, Thu, Fri)
Price ££
Rooms 4 double, 2 with shower, 1 with bath, one with bath/shower; all rooms have TV, CD player, wi-fi
Facilities sitting room, dining room, conservatory; terrace, garden
Credit cards MC, V **Children** accepted over 10
Disabled 1 room suitable **Pets** not accepted **Closed** never
Proprietors Kit and Penny Noble

Nonsuch House
Riverside village guest-house

The Noble family are old friends of this guide, having for many years run Langshott Manor near Horley in Surrey with great warmth and professionalism. They moved to Nonsuch House in Devon ten years ago, and it is now run by their son Kit and his wife Penny.

Nonsuch House is a tall, slim building which stands, rather unprepossessingly, on a hairpin bend in a one-way system high above the Dartmouth ferry at Kingswear. The views, looking across the river towards Dartmouth, are superb, and can be had from all the windows. Bedrooms are named after shipping forecasts and are smart, comfortable and well-equipped – certainly a cut above the normal guest-house. All of the rooms have now been refurbished and have their own baths. The sitting room is decorated in rich, warm colours and furnished with large, comfy sofas and an open fire. Food is served in the modern conservatory that also has stunning views over the river to the sea. This in turn leads down the hill to a lovely little garden for residents to use.

Kit's cooking is simple yet delicious, with fresh seafood every day and an award-winning breakfast. The family will organise any of the varied activities around Dartmouth, such as sailing, river trips, or bracing walks.

Lacock, Wiltshire

6 Church Street, Lacock,
near Chippenham,
Wiltshire SN15 2LB

Tel (01249) 730230
Fax (01249) 730527
e-mail angel@lacock.co.uk
website www.lacock.co.uk

Nearby Lacock Abbey; Bowood
House; Corsham Court; Sheldon
Manor.
Location 3 miles (5 km) S of
Chippenham off A350, in middle of
village; with gardens, and some car
parking
Food breakfast, lunch, dinner
Price ££
Rooms 10; 8 double, 2 twin, all with
bath; all rooms have phone, TV,
rooms in main inn have fax/modem
points **Facilities** 3 dining rooms, sit-
ting room; terrace, garden
Credit cards AE, DC, MC, V
Children accepted **Disabled** 1 room
on ground floor **Pets** accepted
Closed Christmas; restaurant only,
Mon lunch **Proprietors** George
Hardy and Lorna Levis

At the Sign of the Angel
Village inn

Lacock and The Sign of the Angel go
hand-in-hand: the 'perfect' English village (almost entirely in the preserving
hands of the National Trust) and the epit-
ome of the medieval English inn – half-timbered without, great log fires, oak panelling, beamed ceilings, splendid old beds
and polished antique tables within.

There are many such inns sprinkled
around middle England, but most are better enjoyed over a beer or two, or a meal,
than overnight. Even here, the rooms vary
in comfort and none could be called spacious. But they are all cosy and charming
nonetheless, and full of character. The Angel
is emphatically run as a small hotel rather
than a pub – tellingly, there are no bars, and
the residents' oak-panelled sitting room on
the first floor is quiet. It has belonged to
the Levis family for over 40 years, and is
now jointly run by daughter-in-law Lorna
Levis and George Hardy with the help of
village ladies. Lorna and George also share
the traditional cooking (best for Sunday
lunch). Breakfast offers old-timers such as
junket and prunes, as well as a huge cooked
meal if you want it.

If the rooms in the inn itself are booked,
consider the cottage annexe, which is
equally attractive and pleasantly secluded.
The gardens have been described as scruffy
– perhaps due to the ducks – is this fair?

Lewdown, Devon

Lewdown, near Oakhampton,
Devon EX20 4PN

Tel (01566) 783256
Fax (01566) 783332
e-mail info@lewtrenchard.co.uk
website www.lewtrenchard.co.uk

Nearby Dartmoor; Tintagel; Exeter;
Boscastle.
Location from old A30 at Lewdown,
take road signposted Lewtrenchard;
in 11-acre grounds with ample car
parking
Food breakfast, light weekday lunch,
Sun lunch, dinner
Price ££–£££
Rooms 9; 7 double and twin, 2
suites, all with bath; all rooms have
phone, TV, hairdryer **Facilities** sitting room, bar lounge, restaurant,
breakfast room, ballroom; garden,
croquet, fishing lake **Credit cards**
AE, DC, MC, V **Children** under 5
by arrangement **Disabled** access difficult **Pets** accepted **Closed** never
Proprietors Von Essen Hotels **Chef
patron** Jason Hornbuckle

Lewtrenchard Manor
Manor house hotel

Driving east down the narrow road
from Lewdown, on the edge of
Dartmoor, nothing quite prepares you for
the first sight of Lewtrenchard Manor, a
magnificent 16thC stone manor house,
with some Victorian additions, approached
by an avenue of beech trees and set in
stunningly beautiful grounds which lead
down to a lake studded with swans.

The interior is equally impressive. The
massive reception rooms are rich in ornate
ceilings, oak panelling, carvings and large
open fireplaces. Despite its size, however,
the hotel has the warm and hospitable
atmosphere of a much humbler building,
engendered in great part by its hostess, Sue
Murray. The drawing invites you to curl up
with a good book.

On the first floor, a splendid long gallery,
full of family paintings and portraits, leads
to the spacious bedrooms, all of which
have extensive views through leaded windows and over the Devon countryside.

A former owner of Lewtrenchard was
the Reverend Sabine Baring Gould (who
wrote, amongst others, the hymn *Onward,
Christian Soldiers*). Mercifully, he largely
resisted the Victorian habit of embellishing
an already beautiful building.

Von Essen Hotels took over since our
last edition, but we understand, and hope
that this means no changes for the worse.

Lifton, Devon

Lifton, Devon
PL16 0AA

Tel (01566) 784666
Fax (01566) 784494
e-mail
reservations@arundellarms.com
website www.arundellarms.com

Nearby Dartmoor; Tintagel;
Boscastle, Port Isaac, Exeter.
Location 3 miles (5 km) E of
Launceston, just off A30 in Lifton;
with ample car parking
Food breakfast, lunch, dinner
Price £££
Rooms 21; 18 double and twin, 3
single, all with bath; all rooms have
phone, TV, hairdryer, fax/modem
points **Facilities** 2 restaurants, 2
bars, games room, drying room; garden, salmon and trout fishing (20
miles of private rights), fishing lake,
fly fishing lessons, organise shooting
parties **Credit cards** AE, DC, MC,
V **Children** accepted **Disabled**
access possible **Pets** dogs accepted
Closed 3 nights at Christmas
Proprietor Anne Voss-Bark

Arundell Arms
Fishing inn

A 200-year-old coaching inn, on a site that dates back to Saxon times, which is famous – indeed an institution – for fishing and for food. Traditional country pursuits are taken seriously here: the hotel run courses on fly fishing. People also come for riding, golf, bird watching and to enjoy some of the loveliest countryside in England. Anglers have 20 miles of private fishing and a 90-feet-deep lake at their disposal (containing some very large, wily trout). On a recent visit we were impressed by the flexibility of fishing arrangements – don't be shy of coming here if you are a beginner.

Then there is the food, for which resident chef Philip Burgess has established a fine reputation. You might start with a homemade soup followed by pan-fried salmon with a ginger and chilli salsa, and end with basil ice-cream with poached pears and raspberries. Almost all the staff are local people and tend to stay for a long time, following the example of charming, softly-spoken proprietor Anne Voss-Bark who has managed the hotel since 1961 and is a well-know figure in the fishing world.

From the sitting room you can see the garden and the 250-year-old former cockpit, now a tackle room. There are two rather grand interconnecting dining rooms and, of course, a bar. Bedrooms are homely, pretty and fresh. A unique place.

The Lizard, Cornwall

Church Cove, The Lizard,
Cornwall TR12 7PQ

Tel (01326) 290877
Fax (01326) 290192
e-mail luxurybandb@ladewednack-house.com
website
www.landewednackhouse.com

Nearby The Lizard peninsula; St Ives; Isles of Scilly.
Location from Helston take A3083 to Lizard; before entering village turn left to Church Cove, then left towards lifeboat station
Food breakfast, dinner
Price ££
Rooms 3 double and twin, 1 with bath, 2 with shower; all rooms have phone, TV, hairdryer **Facilities** dining room, drawing room, breakfast room; garden, swimming pool, bowls, access to boats **Credit cards** MC, V **Children** not accepted
Disabled access difficult
Pets accepted by arrangement
Closed Christmas **Proprietors** Mr and Mrs Thorbek

Landewednack House
Country bed-and-breakfast

This beautiful 17thC former rectory, taken over and updated by Mrs and Mrs Thorbek in 2004, is a warm and elegant private home where paying guests are made very welcome. The parish of Landewednack, at the end of the Lizard peninsula, is the most southerly in England and is fortunate enough to have a climate mild enough for most of the year to encourage a wide variety of trees, plants and shrubs to flourish. The gardens are a delight.

Inside, the house is equally enchanting. Leading off the flagstoned hall is the dining room with a beamed ceiling and massive granite fireplace where guests can dine by candlelight in front of a crackling log fire. Breakfast is taken in a separate, smaller room. The resident chef, Anthony, is proud of his work here, which has earned him a mention in the Michelin guide (though not a star, since Landewednack caters only for its guests).

House guests can relax in the elegant drawing room at any time of the day, or in the evening for pre-dinner drinks. The three bedrooms are all different, and all charming. The best view is from the Yellow Room, with a mahogany half-tester. Through its large bay window you can see across the garden to the church and the sea beyond – a wonderful sight at sunset.

Lower Bockhampton, Devon

Lower Bockhampton, Dorchester,
Dorset, DT2 8PZ

Tel (01305) 262382
Fax (01305) 266412
e-mail YalburyEmails@aol.com
website www.yalburycottage.com

Nearby Hardy's Cottage,
Dorchester, Dorset coast.
Location in sleepy hamlet, on road,
with ample private car parking.
Food breakfast, dinner
Price ££
Rooms 8; one twin-bedded, rest
double; all with bath and shower; all
rooms have phone, TV, DVD,
hairdryer, tea and coffee making
facilities
Facilities sitting room, dining room,
DVD collection, garden
Credit cards MC, V
Disabled 6 ground floor bedrooms
Children welcome
Pets accepted
Closed 1 week Nov, 2 weeks Jan;
Sun and Mon nights Nov to Easter
Proprietors Mark Collier and Roy
Friddemont

Yalbury Cottage
Village hotel

Is it a small hotel? Or a B & B in someone's
home? It's hard to tell, and it doesn't really
matter, which is why we like it. The long,
thatched cottage you see from the road contains the heart of the place, the sitting room
with inglenook fireplace exposed brick, low
beams and pleasant, mainly homely country
furniture. Here you could almost be in a private house. Next to it, no less important to
this operation, is the long, narrowish dining
room where breakfast and dinner are served,
the latter six choices per course and changing about every ten days – and it has an enviable reputation. Roy and Mark welcome you
personally, serve the drinks and food, but the
sitting room is definitely guest territory –
they don't intrude.

The characterful, charming part of the
property ends quite abruptly when you enter
the modern rear extension where the bedrooms are. They are neat and comfortable,
but lack flair. The bathrooms are OK, but
Mark and Roy know their limitations and
would like to upgrade them. They are refreshingly keen not to over-sell Yalbury, warning
people to expect a relatively simple operation, and perhaps then find themselves surprised when it delivers more than expected.

Yalbury is on the market, and might change
hands sometime after this editions goes to
press, but we're assured that the formula
won't change.

Membury, Devon

Membury, near Axminster,
Devon EX13 7AQ

Tel (01404) 881881
Fax (01404) 881890
e-mail reception@leahill.co.uk
website www.leahill.co.uk

Nearby Lyme Regis; Axminster;
Sidmouth.
Location in 8-acre grounds, 1 mile
(2.5 km) S of Membury; ample car
parking
Food breakfast
Price ££
Rooms 4 double and twin, all with
bath, 3 holiday cottages; all rooms
have TV, hairdryer
Facilities breakfast room; terrace,
garden **Credit cards** none
Children accepted
Disabled access difficult
Pets dogs accepted **Closed**
Christmas **Proprietor** Sue Avis

Lea Hill
Country bed-and-breakfast

Lea Hill has changed a good deal since our last visit. It used to be a country hotel, but owner Sue Avis has cut it back to a four-room bed-and-breakfast, with self-catering units. Because of the charm of both the building and its owner, and its stunning location, we're glad to keep it in the guide.

The setting really is enchanting: on a prominent hilltop with views over woodland and meadows. The building itself is a prime example of a thatched Devon longhouse with parts dating from the 14th century when it was a farmhouse. Two bedrooms are located in a 400-year-old converted barn. Decorated with chintzy fabrics, they have a country farmhouse feel. The two further rooms are located in the main house with exposed beams and charming uneven floors. You eat a generous breakfast in the main farmhouse, overlooking the Membury Valley.

In the summer Lea Hill is now primarily given over to self catering accommodation in its three cottages, with B&B being offered in the quieter months. This picturesque place is above all friendly and cosy: we received a warm welcome from both Sue and Florrie, her collie cross rescue dog.

Mevagissey, South Cornwall

School-Hill, Mevagissey, South
Cornwall PL26 6TH

Tel (01726) 842468
Fax (01726) 844 482
e-mail stay@trevalsa-hotel.co.uk
website www.trevalsa-hotel.co.uk

Nearby Roseland Peninsula, Eden
Project, Lost Gardens of Heligan,
Caerhays Castle
Location Off B3273 with ample car
parking
Food breakfast, lunch and dinner
Price ££
Rooms 12 doubles all with bath and
shower; all rooms have TV, hairdry-
er, wi-fi, some have CD player
Facilities dining room, sitting room,
garden, terrace, summer house
Credit Cards AE, MC, V
Children 12 years and upwards
Disabled access difficult
Pets not accepted
Closed ring to check
Proprietors Klaus Wagner and
Matthias Mainka

Trevalsa Court
Seaside hotel

This is a cliff-top hotel with spectacular
views, courteous staff; a simple but
refreshingly different style – and an interesting history. It was been built in the
1930s as a private, cliff-top home with
breathtaking sea views and a Daphne du
Maurier character: oak-panelled walls,
stone-framed mullion windows.

Klaus Wagner and his friend Matthias
Mainka bought it in 1999, and two years
later it nearly failed. But they carried on, and
here it is thriving, new to the 2007 edition.

The place reflects Matthias's eclectic,
Berlin/deco-inspired taste, with leather
sofas, and black-and-white photographs
and etchings by East German artists. No
two of the 13 bedrooms are the same, in
shape, size or colour. They are refreshing
rather than luxurious, and some of the
bathrooms need updating. There's an intimate dining room where the food is excellent for the price: fennel and orange soup,
melting scallops, herb-crusted lamb. The
garden contains a little summerhouse for
two. The beach at the bottom of the cliff is
reached by a vertiginous metal stairway.

Trevalsa isn't isolated: houses have
grown up around it. We don't rate this as
ideal for a beach holiday, but it's a great
base for the local sights. The coastal path is
literally at the bottom of the garden.

Milton Abbot, Devon

Milton Abbot, Tavistock, Devon
Pl19 0PR

Tel (01822) 870000
Fax (01822) 870578
e-mail mail@hotelendsleigh.com
website www.hotelendsleigh.com

Nearby Tavistock market, Tamar
Valley, Plymouth historic dockyards,
Exeter cathedral
Location 5 minutes from Tavistock
down mile long drive in own exten-
sive grounds; ample car parking
Food breakfast, lunch and dinner
Price ££££
Rooms 16; all have bath and shower;
all have phone, TV, DVD player,
internet access
Facilities dining room, sitting room,
garden, terrace, library, helipad,
swimming pool in the near future
Credit Cards AE, MC, V
Children accepted
Disabled good access, 1 ground
floor suite with private garden
Pets accepted, dog beds provided
Closed 2 weeks in Mid Jan
Proprietors Alex and Olga Polizzi

Endsleigh
Country house hotel

Endsleigh, on the edge of Dartmoor, and
sister hotel of Olga Polizzi's Tresanton in
Cornwall (page 76), is one of the most
talked about new British hotels. Our
reporter found it 'effortlessly elegant and –
crucially – unpretentious, unlike many of its
try-hard, oh-so-hip rivals.'

It's down a mile-long private drive in 'one
of the loveliest locations I've seen in 20
years of writing about hotels.' The sixth
Duke of Bedford built the 16-bedroom fishing and shooting lodge as a retreat, in the
cottage orné style. The gardens are by
Humphrey Repton.

Olga Polizzi has decorated it in her cool,
inimitable style, but the spirit of the old
house remains intact – old pull-down maps
of Devon in the hall, the family crests in the
dining room, the floor made of sheeps'
knuckles on the veranda. Bedrooms are
lovely: stylish and unfussy, with original baths
and basins and a welcome lack of puzzling
technology. You'll get a TV and DVD player,
but you are more likely to spend time pour-
ing over the absorbing collection of books
in the library. Apart from that, there's little
to do, other than to fish, walk or picnic in
the grounds, a fantasy of dells and grottoes.

The Polizzis prefer to employ locals as
staff, and, though willing, we felt that they
needed time to perfect the service. No
problems with the chef, Shay Cooper.

Nettleton, Wiltshire

Nettleton Shrub, Nettleton, near
Chippenham, Wiltshire NS14 7NJ

Tel (01249) 782286
Fax (01249) 783066
e-mail
CaronCooper@compuserve.com
website
www.fossefarmhouse.8m.com

Nearby Castle Combe; Cotswolds.
Location in countryside off B4039,
6 miles (9.5 km) NW of
Chippenham, in 1.5 acres of garden
with car parking
Food breakfast, lunch, dinner
Price ££
Rooms 6; 4 double and twin with
bath or shower, 1 single with shower,
1 family room with bath; all rooms
have TV, hairdryer
Facilities sitting room, dining room,
tea room; terrace, garden
Credit cards MC, V **Children**
accepted **Disabled** access difficult
Pets accepted by arrangement
Closed never **Proprietor** Caron
Cooper

Fosse Farmhouse
Country hotel

Caron Cooper presides over a small
corner of France in the Wiltshire
countryside. She has decorated Fosse
Farmhouse with some style, mainly à la
française. The sitting room is in a provincial
Normandy style, while across the courtyard the converted stables feature a low,
uneven beamed ceiling. Antiques, including
many French pieces, fill the house and
Caron, who owns a shop on Portobello
Road, also sells pieces around the house.

Bedrooms in the main house feel very
much a part of Caron's home. The two doubles are a good size, while the single is small
with a shower that could use an update. In
the stable block, original cobbled flooring in
the downstairs sitting room and light airy
bedrooms, makes a pleasing alternative. Self
catering accommodation in the Garden
House has been added, providing two further double rooms, as well as the Dovecote
– an open-plan studio, which sleeps two.

Caron's food blends French with English
influences. The menu is no-choice, but
guests can let her know beforehand of any
special needs. You might get rack of lamb
with a mint and port wine sauce or chicken
basquaise; dessert might be sticky toffee
pudding or crème brulée.

We have had some readers' reports let-
ters questioning the quality of the food.
More reports welcome.

Oakford Bridge, Devon

Oakford Bridge, Near Bampton,
Devon EX16 9HZ

Tel (01398) 351236
e-mail bark.house.hotel@btinter-net.com
website www.barkhouse.co.uk

Nearby Exmoor; Knightshayes
House; Marwood and Rosemoor
gardens
Location in own grounds, on A396
near Bampton; car parking
Food breakfast, dinner
Price ££
Rooms 5 double and twin with bath
or shower; all rooms have phone,
TV **Facilities** sitting room, dining
room; garden, garden croquet
Credit cards not accepted
Children accepted **Disabled** access
difficult **Pets** accepted
Closed occasionally
Proprietors Mr M French and Miss
M McKnight

Bark House
Country guest-house

Tucked away in the beautiful Exe Valley, this delightful guest-house is about 200 years old and was originally used to store bark for tanning. It's everyone's idea of a Devon cottage, particularly in spring when the facade is smothered by a magnificent old wistaria. By day, you can explore the woodland paths and gardens behind the house and, opposite the building, a sitting area provides a sunny spot for afternoon tea. By night, the tiny hamlet of Oakford Bridge sparkles in the velvet-black valley while the only sounds are the trickling of a small cascade in the garden and the burbling River Exe. Just before we went to press Alistair Kameen handed over Bark House to new owners, who are continuing to run it as a guest-house along much the same lines.

Inside, the cosy and intimate sitting room, with an open fire, is the perfect place to relax and anticipate dinner. The new owners describe the food as more traditional than Alistair's cooking, and dinner might be a starter of potted salmon, roast shoulder of lamb, and a choice of home-made pavlovas and puddings.

The bedrooms reflect the essential simplicity of Bark House. Mr French plans to add a further two rooms by 2008, 'without spoiling the unique exterior'.

Reports welcome.

Padstow, Cornwall

Riverside, Padstow,
Cornwall PL28 8BY

Tel (01841) 532700
Fax (01841) 532942
e-mail reservations@rickstein.com
website www.rickstein.com

Nearby surfing beaches; Trevose
Head **Location** in village centre, 4
miles (6 km) NW off A39 between
Wadebridge and St Columb; car
parking
Food breakfast, lunch, dinner
Price ££
Rooms 35 doubles, (some can be
twins) in 3 different buildings, most
with bath, some with shower; all
rooms have phone, TV, hairdryer;
some have minibar **Facilities** 3
restaurants, bar, sitting room, con-
servatory **Credit cards** MC, V
Children welcome in St Petroc's
Hotel and the Café, over 3 in restau-
rant **Disabled** access possible
Pets dogs accepted in rooms except
St Edmund's House **Closed**
Christmas; restaurants closed on 1st
May **Proprietors** Rick and Jill Stein

Seafood Restaurant & St Petroc's Hotel
Restaurant-with-rooms

Rick Stein's Padstow empire now extends to three different places to stay, at vary-ing prices, and three places to eat: his flagship Seafood Restaurant, the Bistro in St Petroc's Hotel, and the Café in Middle Street.

If you are intent on eating at the quayside Seafood Restaurant (superb seafood, straight from the fishing boats, served by friendly staff in a lively dining room) then the bedrooms above make the best choice for a night's stay. They are spacious, understated and more than comfortable, with superb estuary views from Nos 5 and 6. What the place lacks in public rooms, it makes up for in laid-back atmosphere and its prime posi-tion on the quay. St Edmund's House, behind the restaurant, has six new pricey suites. Less expensive, but no less tasteful, are the rooms in St Petroc's Hotel just up the hill, a little removed from the bustle of the quay-side. This is an attractive white-painted building with views across the older parts of town as well as of the estuary. Some rooms are on the small side. The place exudes a friendly ambience, not least in the Bistro, where a short, very reasonably priced menu features meat and vegetable dishes as well as seafood. There are three attractive, inex-pensive rooms above the Café in Middle Street, and four new rooms are opening behind St Petrocs as we go to press.

Abbey Street, Penzance,
Cornwall TR18 4AR

Tel (01736) 366906
Fax (01736) 351163
e-mail hotel@theabbeyonline.co.uk
website www.theabbeyonline.co.uk

Nearby Tregwainton Garden; St
Michael's Mount; Land's End.
Location in middle of town, over-
looking harbour; parking for 6 cars
in courtyard
Food breakfast, dinner; room service
Price £££-££££
Rooms 7; 4 double and twin, 1 suite,
2 single, 4 with bath, 3 with shower;
all rooms have TV, hairdryer
Facilities sitting room, dining room;
walled garden
Credit cards AE, MC , V **Children**
accepted **Disabled** access difficult
Pets accepted in bedrooms only
Closed never **Proprietors** Jean and
Michael Cox

The Abbey
Town hotel

After several years of management
problems, we believe that things are
changing at The Abbey, and that it is back
on track to being one of the most exceptional places to stay in the West Country.
Jean and Michael Cox took a house with
character in the heart of old Penzance (it
was built in the mid-17thC and given a
Gothic façade in Regency times); decorated and furnished it with unstinting care,
great flair and a considerable budget; and
they call it a hotel. In reality, they run it
much more as a private house, and visitors
who expect to find hosts eager to satisfy
their every whim may be disappointed.

For its fans, the absence of hovering
flunkies is of course a key part of the
appeal of The Abbey. But there are other
attractions – the confident and original
decoration, with abundant antiques and
bric-a-brac, the spacious, individual bedrooms (one with an enormous pine-panelled bathroom); the welcoming, flowery
drawing-room and elegant dining-room
(both with log fires burning 'year-round');
the delightful walled garden behind the house.
Dinner can be had at the restaurant next
door, holder of a Michelin star. Front rooms
overlook the harbour and the dry dock.

Penzance, Cornwall

Chapel Street, Penzance
TR18 4AQ

Tel (01736) 363761
Fax (01736) 363761
e-mail reception@pen-
zanceartsclub.co.uk **website**
www.penzanceartsclub.co.uk

Nearby Tate at St Ives, Newlyn
Gallery, Barbara Hepworth
Museum, St Michael's Mount.
Location in centre of town at the
lower end of Chapel Street, across
from the church
Food breakfast, lunch in summer,
dinner
Price ££
Rooms 7 double, 1 with bath, rest
with shower; all rooms have TV
Facilities bar, sitting room, restau-
rant, exhibit space; writing and art
courses
Credit cards MC, V
Children welcome
Disabled not accessible **Pets** small
dogs by arrangement, £10 per week
Closed never **Proprietor** Belinda
Rushworth-Lund

St Michael's Mount

Penzance Arts Club
Town hotel

As you might expect, the Penzance Arts
Club claims to provide accommodation with artistic flair. Built as the
Portuguese Embassy in 1781, the building
is a Grade II listed Georgian house. The
Club offers a variety of painting and writing courses for members, but non-members can stay too. The focus on local art is
evident, with a fortnightly-changing show
in the entry hall exhibit space and a
plethora of paintings lining the stairwells
and rooms. For those who are interested
in the South Cornwall art scene or who
want a break, this could be the place.

Although not luxurious, the rooms are
light and airy in cheerful blue, peach and
lemon hues and hold an eclectic collection
of furniture and floral fabrics. Four rooms
have free standing showers and wash basins
in the corner. Most rooms have views of the
harbour. We've had some negative comments about the housekeeping from well-
heeled, metropolitan types, but who even
so concede that the place has character.

Dinner and lunch are available in the
member's restaurant. Rooms fill up quickly, so be sure to book in advance. The club
produces an events guide and some of the
activities maybe non-member friendly. It's
not very well signposted. Keep an eye out
for it on the left as you pass by the church.

Penzance, Cornwall

Cornwall Terrace, Penzance,
Cornwall TR18 4HL

Tel (01736) 363744
Fax (01736) 360959
e-mail reception@summerhouse-cornwall.com
website www.summerhouse-cornwall.com

Nearby Trengwainton Garden; St
Michael's Mount; Land's End; St
Ives; Newlyn School art colony.
Location close to the harbour; drive
alongside the harbour and turn right
immediately after the Queen's Hotel;
car parking
Food breakfast, dinner (Thur-Sun)
Price ££
Rooms 5; 4 double, 2 with bath, 2
with shower, 1 twin with shower
Facilities sitting room, dining room;
small walled garden
Credit cards MC , V **Children** not
accepted
Disabled access difficult
Pets not accepted **Closed** Nov-Mar
Proprietors Ciro and Linda Zaino

Summer House
Town restaurant-with-rooms

Linda and Ciro Zaino moved to the tip
of Cornwall from London, where Ciro
had managed some of the capital's top
restaurants, to open this restaurant-with-
rooms in a Grade II listed Georgian house
close to the sea front. They run it with
great panache, reports our inspector, who
considers it a 'great find'. He describes it as
Mediterranean in colour and feel, quirky in
style and breezy in atmosphere. Brighton
meets the Neapolitan Riviera.

The former home of one of Cornwall's
leading naïve artists, the house is still full of
paintings, indiosycratic furniture and lush
pot plants. Downstairs there is a little cosy
sitting room as well as the most important
room in the building, the restaurant. Here
blues and yellows predominate in a room
that spills out in to a small walled garden
burgeoning with terracotta pots and palm
trees. Ciro's sunny cooking, using fresh
local ingredients, has become a great draw.

Upstairs, the five simple bedrooms are
highly individual with a diverse mix of family pieces and collectables. Fresh flowers
are everywhere. Linda is charming and her
front-of-house presence is just right:
enthusiastic, friendly and welcoming. Since
our last edition all of the bathrooms have
been redone in limestone and now have
power showers. More reports please.

Rock, Cornwall

Rock, Wadebridge, Cornwall
PL27 6LA

Tel (01208) 863394
Fax (01208) 863970
e-mail info@enodoc-hotel.co.uk
website www.enodoc-hotel.co.uk

Nearby Polzeath 2 miles; Padstow
(by ferry).
Location overlooking the Camel
Estuary, bordering St Enodoc golf
course in Rock, 2 miles off B3314
from Wadebridge; car park
Food breakfast, lunch, dinner
Price £££
Rooms 16 double, all with
bath/shower, 4 suites; all rooms have
phone, TV, radio, hairdryer, fan
Facilities sitting room, library, dining room, bar, billiard room, gym,
sauna; outdoor heated swimming
pool
Credit cards AE, DC, MC, V
Children welcome **Disabled** ramp
side entrance; adapted WC on
ground floor
Pets not accepted **Closed** Jan to mid
Feb **Manager** Victoria Hutton

St Enodoc
Seaside hotel

Well-heeled British families have
flocked to Rock for their bucket-
and-spade holidays for generations, but
hotels which are both stylish and child-
friendly have been thin on the ground hereabouts – until, that is, the emergence in 1998
of the old-established St Enodoc Hotel from
a change of ownership and total makeover.

The imposing building is typical of the
area: no beauty, but solid and purposeful,
with pebbledash walls and slate roof.

Emily Todhunter's interior decoration
suits its seaside location, with its bright
colours (paint, fabrics, painted furniture,
modern art), clean lines, and easy-going
comfort. The Californian-style Porthilly Bar
and split-level Grill is popular with non-residents, although reports indicate that the
Pacific Rim food could improve. It has
panoramic views, with a wide terrace for
outdoor dining. Bedrooms feel like bedrooms rather than hotel rooms, with marvellous views across the Camel Estuary.

With its child-friendly facilities, the hotel is
particularly popular during holidays and half
terms. Although the hotel has been recently
been sold, the management and staff remain
unchanged. More reports please.

Rosevine, South Cornwall

Rosevine, near Portscatho,
South Cornwall, TR2 5EW

Tel (01872) 580644
Fax (01872) 580801
e-mail info@driftwoodhotel.co.uk
website www.driftwoodhotel.co.uk

Nearby Eden Project, Tate Gallery,
the gardens of Heligan, Glendurgan
and Trebah.
Location in countryside just off
A3078, S of Truro; ample parking
for cars and boats
Food breakfast, dinner
Price ££££
Rooms 14 double and 1 twin, 3 with
bath, 1 with shower; rest with bath
and shower, cabin with double and
twin; all rooms have phone, TV,
hairdryer
Facilities sitting room, drawing
room, dining room, bar; garden,
beach **Credit cards** AE, MC, V
Children welcome **Disabled** access
difficult **Pets** not accepted **Closed**
mid Dec to mid Feb **Proprietors**
Paul and Fiona Robinson

Driftwood Hotel
Coastal hotel

'Situated on seven glorious acres of Cornwall's finest heritage coastline,' says the brochure – and Driftwood does indeed provide all you could want on a sea-side break. It's a clapboarded converted family house that has been refurbished and renovated into a stylish yet comfortable haven by interior designer Fiona and husband Paul. All fourteen bedrooms, including the cabin overlooking the beach, have a clean, fresh style that helps maximise the space, as do the cosy sitting and drawing rooms.

Those who love seafood will be happiest here, but the rest of the food is good too. The menu is concentrated on well prepared dishes with fresh local ingredients. The restaurant has spectacular views of the rugged Cornish coastline and you can eat outside, weather permitting. For children there is a TV room with computer games and video library. If you fancy getting out and about there are numerous small pubs and restaurants nearby St Mawes; or hampers can be made up for lazing on the beach.

All around Driftwood there are varied activities that suit different tastes. Great walks and gardens such as Trelissick, the Eden Project, within a short drive; for art lovers, the Tate Gallery at St Ives; or for the energetic, watersports, riding, tennis and golf.

St Austell, Cornwall

Boscundle, St Austell,
Cornwall PL25 3RL

Tel (01726) 813557
Fax (01726) 814997
e-mail reservations@boscundle-manor.co.uk **website**
www.boscundlemanor.co.uk

Nearby Eden Project, Heligan
Gardens, Lanhydrock House
Location 2.5 miles (4 km) E of St
Austell, close to A390; in 8 acre
woodland gardens; ample car parking
Food breakfast, dinner
Price £££ **Rooms** 14; 7 double and
twin, 2 suites, all with bath; 1 single
with shower, 1 garden room, 1 cottage with 3 doubles; all rooms have
phone, TV, minibar, safe, fridge
Facilities sitting room, bar, dining
room, conservatory/breakfast room;
heated indoor and outdoor pool;
garden, croquet, woodland walks,
helicopter landing pad, civil wedding
licence **Credit cards** AE, MC, V
Children welcome **Disabled** access
possible to cottage **Pets** no **Closed**
Jan 1 to Feb 14 **Proprietors** David
and Sharon Parker

Boscundle Manor
Country house hotel

David and Sharon Parker took over
Boscundle Manor a while ago. It's
been a mainstay of the guide for many
years, and last time we looked was becoming tired and frayed around the edges. The
Parkers stepped in, however, with a full-
scale refurbishment plan, which is now
complete. The previous owners took most
of the antiques with them, so new furniture, mainly oriental mahogany, features
throughout. Carpets and curtains have
been replaced, fresh coats of paint bright-
en the walls and the bathrooms and bedrooms sparkle.

The grounds are now 5 acres of terraced gardens and woodland, with several
pleasant walks through the woods. There
are ponds and old tin mine remains.

The Parkers have also changed the
sunny conservatory into a brasserie for
casual dining. The formal dining room has a
daily-changing menu using Cornish produce whenever available. The butter on
the table comes from hand-milked cows
and is hand-packed at the local dairy. Chef
Jonny Gilbert looks after the cooking and
David eagerly seeks guests' reactions to
new dishes.

St Blazey, Cornwall

Prideaux Road, Luxulyan Valley,
near St Blazey, Cornwall PL24 2SR

Tel (01726) 814488
e-mail keith@nanscawen.com
website www.nanscawen.com

Nearby Fowey; Lanhydrock House;
the Eden Project; Polperro; Looe.
Location in countryside, 0.5 mile (1
km) off A390, NW of St Blazey, 3
miles (5 km) NE of St Austell; in 5-
acre grounds, with car parking
Food breakfast
Price ££
Rooms 3 double and twin, all with
bath; all rooms have phone, TV,
hairdryer
Facilities drawing room, conservatory; terrace, garden, heated outdoor
swimming pool, whirlpool spa
Credit cards MC, V **Children**
accepted over 12
Disabled access difficult **Pets** not
accepted
Closed never **Proprietors** Keith
and Fiona Martin

Nanscawen Manor
Country guest-house

Dating from the 16thC, Nanscawen
Manor has been carefully extended in
recent years and sits amidst five acres of
mature and very pretty gardens and
grounds, with a 'wonderfully located' outdoor swimming pool. Its seclusion is enviable: approached by a fairly steep uphill track
from the road, you can't see the house until
you are almost upon it. As well as the pool,
you can also sink into the whirlpool spa, and
there is a terrace on which to sit in the sunshine amongst palm trees and hydrangeas. A
recent inspection confirmed readers'
reports that the Martin's family home is an
excellent bed-and-breakfast guest-house.

The entrance hall, with polished parquet
floor, leads to a large, attractive sitting room
with an honesty bar. Breakfast is taken in a
sunny, cane-furnished conservatory; it's very
good, and includes dishes such as locally
smoked salmon with scrambled eggs. A semi-
spiral staircase takes you up to the three
bedrooms, described by one reader as
'charming, but perhaps a touch too feminine
for some tastes.' Rashleigh, in the newer part
of the house, is vast, with a huge hand-carved
four poster, while the two in the original
wing have large beds, one a four-poster, and
views of the garden to the south. With ongoing refurbishments, Keith told us they are
"making things better as they go along".

St Hilary, Cornwall

St Hilary, Penzance, Cornwall
TR20 9BZ

Tel (01736) 740262
Fax (01736) 740055
e-mail ennys@ennys.co.uk
website www.ennys.co.uk

Nearby Lands End; Penzance;
Lizard peninsula.
Location in gardens with car park-
ing; from B3280 from Marazion turn
left into Trewhella Lane, just before
Relubbus
Food breakfast
Price ££
Rooms 5; 3 double, 2 with bath, 2
with shower, 2 suites, all with bath;
all rooms have TV, hairdryer, wi-fi
Facilities breakfast room, sitting
room; garden, grass tennis court,
heated outdoor swimming pool
Credit cards MC, V
Children accepted over 3
Disabled access difficult **Pets** not
accepted
Closed Nov 1 to Dec 20; Jan 4 -
Mar 15 **Proprietor** Gill Charlton

Ennys
Country bed-and-breakfast

Travel journalists don't often move over
into the hospitality business themselves, but Gill Charlton is one who has, and
she has brought her considerable knowledge of what makes an intersting place to
stay to this excellent country guest-house.

Ennys is a beautiful, creeper-clad 17thC
Cornish manor house situated at the end
of a long tree-lined drive in little St Hilary,
a few miles from Penzance. The sheltered
gardens are full of shrubs and flowers and
include a swimming pool and grass tennis
court. The fields stretch down to the River
Hayle, along which you can walk and picnic.

Bedrooms in the main house are prettily decorated, furnished in country house
style, and all have window seats with garden or country views. Two family suites are
in an adjacent converted stone barn near
which self-catering accommodation is also
available. Proper cream teas are laid out in
the rustic farmhouse-style kitchen.
Afterwards, you can curl up in the large
comfortable sitting room with open log
fire. Gill is the perfect hostess, and a mine
of information on the surrounding area.

St Keyne, Cornwall

St Keyne, Nr Looe, Cornwall
PL14 4RN

Tel (01579) 342001
Fax (01579) 343891
e-mail enquiries@wellhouse.co.uk
website www.wellhouse.co.uk

Nearby Looe; Plymouth; Bodmin Moor; Eden Project.
Location in countryside just outside village of St Keyne, 2 miles (3 km) S of Liskeard, off B3254; in 3.5-acre gardens with ample car parking
Food breakfast, lunch, dinner; room service
Price £££
Rooms 9; 8 double, 1 family room, all with bath; all rooms have phone, TV, hairdryer **Facilities** sitting room, dining room, bar; garden, tennis, heated swimming pool, croquet; nearby heilpad; classic car hire
Credit cards MC, V
Children welcome, if well behaved
Disabled no special facilities **Pets** not accepted**Closed** New Year's Eve
Proprietor Richard Farrow

Well House
Country hotel

The Well House has been a trademark charming small hotel since the guide started in 1986 – and over the years we had consistently satisfied feedback. In 2006 Nicholas Wainsford sold the hotel to Richard Farrow, who intended to provide more of the same, while gradually upgrading.

We visited in 2007 and found that this was so. Maybe the welcome is a little less personal – you might be met by the manager rather than the owner; the food is still very good for the price, though possibly it may not have the sparkle of before – but it still attracts non residents. The dining room has been refreshed with contemporary leather chairs and new paintings, but the rest of the public spaces continue to endear themselves to an older age group who like unflashy, country house style.

The house was built by a tea planter in 1894, with no expense spared. The beautifully tiled entrance hall, the staircase and woodwork are all original. The dining room, terrace and most of the bedrooms have wonderful views across the Looe Valley. An outdoor heated pool is sensitively located. The large grounds have truly charming corners. Richard is an enthusiastic, sociable type and we wish him well in the balancing act faced by many owners of places such this: preserving traditional charm while not becoming dated.

St Mary's, Isles of Scilly

St Mary's, Isles of Scilly,
TR21 0TA

Tel (01720) 422317/423342
Fax (01720) 422343
e-mail info@star-castle.co.uk
website www.star-castle.co.uk

Nearby other Scilly islands including Tresco; bird watching; swimming with seals
Location in own grounds
Food breakfast, lunch, dinner
Price ££-£££
Rooms 38; 4 singles, 34 double or twin; all rooms have bath and shower, phone, TV
Facilities sitting room, bar, 2 restaurants, tennis, indoor swimming pool
Credit Cards AE, MC, V
Children accepted
Disabled difficult, but some ground level rooms
Pets accepted
Closed 3 days before Christmas, four weeks after New Year
Proprietor Robert Francis

Star Castle
Island hotel

There's only a handful of upmarket hotels in the Scillies, some of which strive to appeal to the mainland's chic set. They tend to lack heart, but this one decidedly does not. The welcome begins at the airport, or ferry, where Robert, his son James or one of the staff meet guests personally.

Castles often make dismal hotels, but this one, inside its walls in the shape of an eight-pointed star, has something of the charm and intimacy of a Cotswold cottage. As well as the cosy bar, first floor sitting room and ground floor, stone-walled dining room, there are eight charming bedrooms in the castle itself, all recently redecorated.

Each morning at breakfast, Robert and James enquire from their guests what they feel like doing, making suggestions, arranging boat trips and providing packed lunches and maps for walkers. Many regulars simply say they are "going with Tim", a hugely popular local boatman who takes guests on trips to the off-islands.

The spacious bedrooms in the annexe have also been overhauled. An exotic garden is growing up between the two wings to detract from their somewhat Butlinesque appearance.

We could not fault the food, and there's an interesting personal wine list. This is not a chic hotel, but a very good one.

St Mawes, Cornwall

St Mawes, Cornwall
TR2 5DR

Tel (01326) 270055
Fax (01326) 270053
e-mail info@tresanton.com
website www.tresanton.com

Nearby Trelissick, Glendurgan,
Heligan and Trebah gardens; Truro;
Eden Project; National Maritime
Museum.
Location in town, just below castle,
14 miles (22 km) S of Truro; car
parking
Food breakfast, lunch, dinner; room
service
Price £££-££££
Rooms 29; 26 double and twin, 3
suites, all with bath; all rooms have
phone, TV, video, fax/modem point,
hairdryer, wi-fi **Facilities** sitting
room, dining room, bar, cinema, terraces; boats, 8-metre yacht **Credit
cards** AE, MC, V
Children welcome **Disabled** not
suitable **Pets** accepted in two rooms
Closed 2 weeks in Jan **Proprietor**
Olga Polizzi

Tresanton
Seaside town hotel

It's easy to drive past the hotel, as it has no obvious entrance, particularly for cars. Look closer and you will see a discreet sign and some steps next to a pair of white-painted garages. Stop, and within seconds someone will appear to welcome you, take your luggage and park your car. This is not any old seaside hotel.

Tresanton was opened in the summer of 1998 by Olga Polizzi, daughter of Lord Forte, and it is now well established as the West Country hotel for chic townies who prefer not to forego sophistication when by the seaside. Yet St Mawes is a happy-go-lucky holiday village, full in summer of chirpy families, bucket and spade in hand, and the two must rub along together. A whitewashed former sailing club and a cluster of cottages on the sea front make up the hotel, which was well known back in the 1960s, but had long lost its glamour before Olga Polizzi came across it. She set about redesigning it in minimalist, elegant style, using restful, muted tones of oatmeal and flax, accentuated by blues, greens, browns or yellows. Bedrooms are a study in understated luxury and have stunning sea views. The warm and comfortable sitting room and bar are more traditional.

Tresanton has become the most sought-after hotel in the South of England, and rightly so. The food, in particular, is gaining many plaudits.

Shipton Gorge, Dorset

Shipton Gorge, Bridport,
Dorset DT6 4LJ

Tel (01308) 456137
e-mail innsacre.farmhouse@btinter-net.com

Nearby coastal path; Lyme Regis;
Chesil Beach; Dorchester, Jurassic
Coast.
Location in quiet countryside, 2
miles (3km) E of Bridport, S of A35;
with ample car parking
Food breakfast, dinner
Price ££
Rooms 4; 3 double, 1 twin, all with
bath; all rooms have TV
Facilities bar, sitting room
Credit cards MC, V **Children**
accepted over 9
Disabled no special facilities **Pets**
accepted (small charge)
Closed Christmas Day to New Year
Proprietors Sydney and Jayne
Davies

Innsacre Farmhouse
Farm guest-house

Set on the side of a steeply rising, hill, this 17thC farmhouse is surrounded by 22 acres of its own land, conveniently placed three miles from the sea and National Trust coastal path. The Davies's own flock of Jacob sheep graze the hillside, contributing to the atmosphere of peace and rural charm. Sydney and Jane have recently planted 3,000 indigenous trees, with the aim of becoming carbon neutral.

The farmhouse itself is quite dark inside, with one main room serving the triple purpose of sitting room, bar and dining room. Warmed by a woodburning stove in winter, the beamed room is divided by screens to separate diners and drinkers. It is decorated in an eclectic mix of objects, including colourful Provençal fabrics and strikingly large arrangements of flowers.

Jayne Davies is responsible for cooking the excellent suppers. There is no choice, although she takes into account the various likes and dislikes of guests and the three courses are all freshly prepared using local ingredients. Jayne will also make up picnic lunches for the many walkers that come to stay. Sydney has painted the bedrooms in strong heritage colours and furnished them with provincial French furniture in keeping with the rustic appeal of the place. Informality is the keyword here.

Sturminster Newton, Dorset

Hazelbury Bryan Road, Sturminster
Newton, Dorset DT10 2AF

Tel (01258) 472507
Fax (01258) 473370
e-mail book@plumbermanor.com
website www.plumbermanor.com

Nearby Thomas Hardy country;
Shaftesbury; Sherborne.
Location 2 miles (3 km) SW of
Sturminster Newton; private car
parking
Food breakfast, Sun lunch, dinner
Price ££-£££
Rooms 16; 14 double, all with bath,
2 small doubles with bath; all rooms
have phone, TV
Facilities dining room, sitting room,
bar; garden, croquet, tennis court
Credit cards AE, DC, MC, V
Children welcome
Disabled easy access to barn bed-
rooms and dining room **Pets** accept-
ed by arrangement **Closed** Feb
Proprietor Richard Prideaux-Brune

Plumber Manor
Manor house hotel

This is a handsome Jacobean manor
house, 'modernized' in the early
20thC, that has been in the Prideaux-
Brune family for well over 300 years. Since
1973, brothers Richard, Tim and Brian have
been running it as an elegant but relaxed
restaurant with comfortable bedrooms.
Richard Prideaux-Brune is much in evidence front-of-house, as is his brother
Tim. Together with Brian, who is responsible for the highly-regarded food, they draw
in restaurant customers from far and wide
– expect plenty of bustle on Friday and
Saturday evenings, and non-residents in
the dining room.

The brothers make charming hosts, and
have created a very relaxed and welcoming atmosphere. Old family portraits hang
in the house; labradors lounge in the bar;
the decoration is homely and comfortable
rather than smart. The large bar area might
detract from the feeling of a family home,
but it helps the Prideaux-Brunes' operation in a practical way (shooting parties
are a feature in winter).

Bedrooms are divided between those in
the main house (which lead off a gallery
hung with portraits) and those in a converted stone barn and courtyard building which
overlook the extensive gardens and stream.
They are all spacious and comfortable.

Teffont Evias, Wiltshire

Teffont Evias, Salisbury,
Wiltshire SP3 5RJ

Tel (01722) 716392
Fax (01722) 716820
e-mail enq@howardshousehotel.com
website www.howardshousehotel.com

Nearby Salisbury Cathedral; Wilton
House; Stonehenge; Old Sarum.
Location in village, off B3089 (signposted from Teffont Magna), 10
miles (16 km) W of Salisbury; car
parking
Food breakfast, Sunday lunch,
dinner
Price £££
Rooms 9; 8 double and twin, 1 family, all with bath; all rooms have
phone, TV, hairdryer **Facilities** dining room, sitting room; terrace, garden **Credit cards** AE, MC, V
Children welcome
Disabled ground-floor dining room
accessible **Pets** accepted **Closed**
Christmas **Proprietor** Noële
Thompson

Howard's House
Village restaurant-with-rooms

Teffont Evias, in the Nadder valley, has
been owned by the same family, father to
son, since 1692. It is picturesque and has
great charm without being twee. In the
grounds stands Howard's House, opposite a
marvellously knotty topiary hedge, and
embellished by a Swiss gabled roof in the
early 19th century – its then owner had fall-
en for all things Swiss on the Grand Tour. It
is surrounded by two acres of pretty garden.

Its *raison d'être* is the food, created by
chef Nick Wentworth. Dishes might
include seared scallops with *sauce vierge*
and crab mayonnaise, rack of lamb with
onion puree and tomato and olive salsa,
followed by summer berry jelly and elder-
flower ice cream. The smallish dining room,
mint green with white tablecloths, is soothing but predictable, as is the decoration in
the cosy sitting room and the bedrooms:
pastel-coloured walls, floral fabrics, pine furnishings. The four-poster room is the prettiest; rooms 1 and 2 look out over the garden.

Breakfast here is above reproach: excellent coffee, warm croissants and toast
wrapped in a white napkin, and the mouth-
watering orange juice. You might choose a
boiled egg, or something more sophisticated such as poached egg tartlet with
Hollandaise sauce. Noële Thompson took
over ownership recently and promises us
more of the same.

Torquay, Devon

Rockhouse Lane, Maidencombe,
Torquay, Devon TQ1 4SX

Tel (01803) 328098
Fax (01803) 328336
e-mail info@orestonemanor.com
website www.orestonemanor.com

Nearby South Devon Coastal Path,
National Trust properties,
Dartmouth, Totnes.
Location from Torquay follow the
A379 signposted Teignmouth up
Watcombe Hill, signposted at the
top of Rockhouse Lane
Food breakfast, lunch, dinner, room
service
Price £££
Rooms 12 double or twin, all with
bath; all have phone, TV, compli-
mentary sherry **Facilities** dining
room, sitting room, bar, conservato-
ry, private dining room, meeting
room; terrace, heated swimming
pool **Credit cards** AE, MC, V
Children welcome **Disabled** 1 room
Pets welcome **Closed** never
Proprietors Jean and Allan May

Orestone Manor
Country house hotel

Not a conventional charming small
hotel – it's a large house, run on conventional hotel lines, with uniformed staff,
but it does have two things we like very
much. The five-star location, overlooking
Tor bay, with ever-changing wide sea views;
and a pleasing, ecclectic decorative style.
The large conservatory, filled with Lloyd
Loom chairs and palm trees lends a
Mediterranean feel; while Mediterranean
fabrics and elephant-themed decorations
contribute a 'colonial' element. The atmosphere is essentially middle aged to elderly
and many will find this an appealing anti-
dote to the formulaic trendiness of places
going for the younger market.

Food, on our visit, was good to very
good, service flawless. The Mays, who took
over in 2006, are professional hoteliers from
Torquay, and know what they are about.

Although all rooms are well-appointed,
our favourite is number six because of its
long bathroom with a clawfoot bath and
balcony overlooking the sea.

Tresco, Isles of Scilly

Tresco, Isles of Scilly, TR24 0PU

Tel (01720) 422883
Fax (01720) 423008
e-mail islandhotel@tresco.co.uk
website www.tresco.co.uk

Nearby Tresco's sub-tropical Abbey Garden; boat trips to other Scilly Isles; ferry to Bryher – see page 41.
Location On Tresco's north side, overlooking Grimsby Sound.
Food breakfast, lunch, dinner
Price dinner included ££££ (no b & b rate, but meals can be cross charged with New Inn on Tresco and Hell Bay on Bryher)
Rooms 48; 43 double or twin, 5 single; all rooms bath except one with shower only; all rooms with phone, TV, DVD, hairdryer
Facilities sitting room (with wi-fi), dining room, terrace bar, tennis, croquet, private beach, water sports
Credit cards MC, V **Children** welcome **Disabled** 3 rooms suitable
Pets not accepted **Closed** Nov-Feb
Manager Euan Rodger

The Island Hotel
Seaside hotel

We include Tresco's well known and long-established luxury hotel in this new edition as a replacement for St Martin's on the Isle (see page 26). It's not an obvious choice, since with 48 rooms it exceeds our usual size limit. What made us change our minds? Most of the rooms have been updated recently, gaining in character and charm. (All but three have sea views.) But above all, the location: not only on charming, traffic-free Tresco, but spread out around its own bay with (on fine days) clear tropical-blue water and beyond an amazing, often violent seascape infested with deadly rocks throwing up mountains of spray when the swell runs.

It's a large colonial-style complex of low buildings that harmonize with their surroundings. The atmosphere is peaceful, service discreet, reminiscent of a gentler age. Activities include kite flying, fishing, shrimping, bike hire, water sports. In the dining room, fresh fish and Tresco beef. Family friendly. Privately run by the Dorrien-Smith family, owners of Tresco. See also Hell Bay Hotel, page 41.

Virginstow, Devon

Virginstow, Devon EX21 5EA

Tel (01409) 211236
Fax (01409) 211460
e-mail info@percys.co.uk
website www.percys.co.uk

Nearby Dartmoor; Tintagel;
Clovelly; Tamar Otter Sanctuay.
Location from the A30, travelling
W, turn off after Okehampton to
Broadwidger, then follow signs to
Virginstow
Food breakfast, lunch, dinner
Price £££
Rooms 8 double and twin, all with
bath or shower; all rooms have TV,
hairdryer, minibar; some have DVD
Facilities restaurant, bar, 2 sitting
rooms; heated deck/patio; garden
Credit cards AE, MC, V **Children**
over 12 **Disabled** 4 ground-floor
rooms, 1 specially adapted **Pets** in
bedrooms only **Closed** never
Proprietors Tony and Tina
Bricknell-Webb

Percy's Country Hotel
Country hotel and restaurant

Percy's Country Hotel (formerly called
Percy's at Combeshead) was originally
bought as a retirement home by the
Bricknell-Webbs, who ran a restaurant in
London called Percy's. They decided to
open the 16thC farmhouse in rural Devon
as a hotel and restaurant, as well as running
the 130 acres of land that went with it,
where they now breed racehorses, and
raise pigs and sheep (some for the hotel's
table). The bedrooms, in an adjacent converted barn, are spacious and (after recent
refurbishment) smart in an understated
way: everything is of a high standard: the
showers are power showers, the beds are
king-size, and the real coffee comes in
cafetieres. Two rooms, with stripped wood
floors, fresh flowers and a wood-burning
stove make up the intimate and calming
restaurant which is for residents only. Tina
cooks in the modern English style, with
almost all ingredients, such as salad, eggs
and venison, coming from the estate. Fish
features strongly, and it is very good, not
surprisingly as Tony has a licence to bid
directly at the Looe fish auction. The scallops are superb, or you might opt for squid
sauteed and served on a bed of mixed
leaves. The wine list is equally good, with
bottles listed in ascending order of price
regardless of country of origin, and almost
all available by the glass.

Wareham, Dorset

Church Green, Wareham,
Dorset BH20 4ND

Tel (01929) 551666
Fax (01929) 554519
e-mail reservations@theprioryhotel.co.uk **website** www.theprioryhotel.co.uk

Nearby Poole Harbour; Swanage; Lulworth Cove.
Location in town near market square; in 4.5 acre gardens with ample car parking
Food breakfast, lunch, dinner
Price ££££
Rooms 18; 14 double, 2 single, 2 suites, all with bath; all rooms have phone, TV, hairdryer, minibar
Facilities sitting room, bar, restaurant; terrace, garden, croquet, pontoon, organise gold and fishing outings **Credit cards** DC, MC, V
Children accepted over 8 **Disabled** access difficult **Pets** guide dogs only
Closed never **Proprietor** Turner family

The Priory
Country town hotel

Hidden behind the church, this 16thC Priory is the perfect retreat for anyone who appreciates a sense of history, as well as peace, comfort and good food. It has been run for the last thirty years by the Turner family, and is currently under the guiding hand of Jeremy, who is ensuring that everything, from the excellent antiques to the pretty fabrics in the bedrooms, has been done with taste and in keeping.

The bedrooms are all that should be expected from a 16thC priory: beams, sloping ceilings and floors, as well as being supremely comfortable and well-equipped with books (no *Reader's Digest* here) and attractive toiletries in the bathrooms. To keep up with the demand for rooms the boathouse has been converted to provide four extra bedrooms, or rather suites, equipped with luxury baths and French windows opening on to the River Frome. Indeed, by boat is the best way to arrive at the Priory: moorings are available and, after a quick walk through the stunning gardens (from which Mrs Turner gathers flowers for the arrangements) you can relax with a pre-dinner drink on the terrace. The food is richly sastisfying, with a mainland European flavour emanating both from the menu and the French staff. Sister hotel to the Casterbridge in Dorchester, page 45.

Whitley, Wiltshire

Top Lane, Whitley, Wiltshire
SN12 8QX

Tel (01225) 709 131
Fax (01225) 702 276
e-mail
enquiries@thepeartreeinn.com
website www.thepeartreeinn.com

Nearby Lacock Abbey, Bath
Location off B3353 just off West
Hill Road with ample car parking
Food breakfast, lunch and dinner
Price ££
Rooms 5 doubles all with bath and
shower; all rooms have phone, TV,
wi-fi **Facilities** restaurant, bar, garden
Credit Cards MC, V
Children accepted
Disabled 1 room is accessible
Pets not accepted
Closed Christmas Day and Boxing
Day **Proprietors** Martin and Debbie
Still

The Pear Tree Inn
Pub-restaurant-with-rooms

It's a pleasant change to go upstairs to a bedroom of unexpected quality: our reporter found theirs two or three cuts above the norm. It wasn't especially large, but there was a comfy bed; good sheets; two armchairs; a big-enough desk. It was nicely decorated in warm-but-neutral colours in harmony with the old building. The price of this double was £105 including breakfast: reassuring – you can pay £160 for much less.

Downstairs is given over to a cross between restaurant and pub, pleasingly designed, not too rustic, not too self-consciously contemporary. Note the artful collage of old farm implements. Martin and Debbie Still had to extend the old farm house to create extra space for the restaurant area and the open-roof extension with big windows is very successful, looking out on to a well thought out garden and patio.

Despite a string of accolades, and the usual gushing reviews in guides who take money for an entry, we didn't get over-excited by the food: it's competent cooking at its price. And there are reports of worryingly slow service.

Don't expect an especially personal welcome: through the front door you report straight to the bar where they're friendly, but often busy. Beyond the garden, the surroundings are nothing special. Still, a useful address in the Melksham area.

Williton, Somerset

Williton, Somerset
TA4 4QW

Tel (01984) 632306
Fax (01984) 634639
e-mail thewhitehouse@stefan-roberts.orangehome.co.uk

Nearby Exmoor, Cleeve Abbey; Quantock Hills.
Location on A39 in centre of town; with ample car parking
Food breakfast
Price ££
Rooms 10 double and twin, all with bath; all rooms have phone, TV
Facilities sitting room, bar, dining room **Credit cards** AE, DC, MC, V
Children accepted
Disabled access difficult **Pets** accepted by arrangement
Closed Never **Proprietors** Alison and Stefan Roberts

White House
Bed-and-breakfast

Dick and Kay Smith ran the White House in Williton for more than 30 years as a renowned restaurant with rooms, but since our last edition there has been a change of ownership and of function. Alison and Stefan Roberts moved here from the tiny channel island of Sark in December 2006, to take on the new challenge of running a very comfortable bed-and-breakfast, and have already proved very popular.

They have totally refurbished the place since their arrival. Bedrooms are now done out in cream linens with rich chocolate-brown velvet throws, and furniture is a mix of mexican pine and leather, the latter predominating in the communal areas. They have added a family suite in the main house, and further bedrooms are found in the converted stables and coach house. Mediterranean plants in the garden include figs and palms in large pots.

Alison says they are very keen to remain very hands-on – they run the b&b on their own, with Stefan preparing a generous full breakfast each morning, using locally-sourced ingredients.

Plans for the future include continuous improvements to the house and converting two barns into self-catering apartments. Reports welcome.

Wookey Hole, Somerset

Glencot Lane, Wookey Hole,
Wells, Somerset BA5 1BH

Tel (01749) 677160
Fax (01749) 670210
e-mail relax@glencothouse.co.uk
website www.glencothouse.co.uk

Nearby Wookey Hole caves, Wells,
Bath, Cheddar Gorge, Mendip Hills
Location in own grounds with
ample private car parking
Food breakfast, lunch, dinner
Price £££-££££
Rooms 15; all double, but 3 can be
twin; 3 rooms have shower only, rest
bath and shower; all rooms have
phone, TV, DVD/CD player
Facilities bar, restaurant, garden,
fishing, sauna, cinema, billiards, heli-
pad
Credit cards AE, MC, V
Children accepted **Disabled** not
suitable **Pets** accepted by arrange-
ment **Closed** never
Proprietors Ioana and Martin
Miller, Carey Ravden

Miller's at Glencot House
Country hotel

A hint of what's to come is the oriental carpet on the tarmac *outside* the front door. This place is not merely furnished with antiques, it's an Alladin's cave, *designed* with them: it's so crammed with interesting furniture and objects that you could spend a weekend pondering them, one by one. Witty, quirky visual statements come at you so fast you might start pinching yourself, like Alice in Wonderland. A pair of stuffed peacocks admire each other in the drawing room; dime bars sit in big glass jars; ceramic glove moulds line a mantle piece; a bowl of dolls' heads sits dottily on a shelf; a portrait hangs crooked by the fireplace – ask the owner, Martin Miller, why and he will say he knows, but can't tell you. It's stimulating, yet gracious, comfortable and intimate. The grounds are pretty special too, with a waterfall and a broad stream widening into a little lake where the trout rise and where a wi-fi boathouse is planned. Bedrooms range from small-but-reasonably-priced to spacious and expensive. Food is 'British-fusion'. The building itself is a Victorian-Jacobean mansion: stolid compared with what goes on inside. Glencot House was a conventional B & B; before Martin Miller (formerly editor of the Miller's antiques quides) and Ioana took it over. See also their well-known London hotel, page 112.

Yeovil, Somerset

Barwick, near Yeovil, Somerset
BA22 9TD

Tel (01935) 423902
Fax (01935) 420908
e-mail
reservations@barwick7.fsnet.co.uk
website
www.littlebarwickhouse.co.uk

Nearby Brympton d'Evercy;
Montacute House.
Location 2 miles (3 km) S of Yeovil
off A37; car parking
Food breakfast, lunch, dinner
Price ££
Rooms 6 double and twin, all with
bath or shower; all rooms have TV,
hairdryer, phone **Facilities** sitting
room, dining room, bar/private din-
ing room; garden
Credit cards MC, V
Children welcome over 5
Disabled access difficult
Pets accepted
Closed 2 weeks Jan **Proprietors**
Emma and Tim Ford

Little Barwick House
Restaurant-with-rooms

Emma and Tim Ford have built up a reputation for fine food at this restaurant
with rooms in Somerset. Tim is one of
Britain's finest chefs: he trained at Sharrow
Bay and spent time in several top hotels
refining his art. Previously he was head chef
at Summer Lodge in Evershot, but he and
his wife Emma, who was front-of-house
there, have now been running Little
Barwick for almost a decade.

Locally-sourced meat, game and fish
provide the cornerstone of Tim's cooking
(our inspector enjoyed pink roasted rump
of Dorset lamb with aubergine caviar and
black olive sauce), while the lunch menu is
a simpler variation of the dinner menu. The
wine list is extensive, including many wines
by the glass or half bottle.

Little Barwick has featured in these
pages for years, recommended for its
friendly informality, and this has remained
the case through changes of ownership.
The Fords have completed a programme
of redecoration that has freshened up
both the interior and exterior of this lovely listed Georgian dower house. The dining
room has recently been redecorated with
a Farrow and Ball stripe wallpaper.
Bedrooms remain cheerful with fresh
flowers, real coffee in cafetières and home-
made shortbreads.

Zennor, Cornwall

Treen, Zennor, Cornwall
TR26 3DE

Tel (01736) 796928
Fax (01736) 795313
e-mail
enquiries@gurnardshead.co.uk
website www.gurnardshead.co.uk

Nearby Tate Galley at St Ives, South
West Coast Path, Trengwainton
Garden, Minnack Open Air Theatre
Location on the B3306 between St
Ives and Land's End; ample car
parking
Food breakfast, lunch, dinner
Price ££
Rooms 7; 4 double, 3 twin, all with
shower. No phones or TV in the
rooms, but available on request.
Hairdryers also available on request.
Facilities bar, dining room, garden
Credit cards MC, V
Children accepted
Disabled no special arrangements
Pets dogs only **Closed** never
Proprietors Charles and Edmund
Inkin

The Gurnard's Head
Seaside inn

An early 17th century coaching inn, The
Gurnard's Head stands on the
windswept coastal road that runs between
St Ives and Land's End. Brothers Charles
and Edmund Inkin's motto is 'the simple
things in life done well' and they reckon on
applying this to all aspects of The Gurnard's
Head, as also to their other establishment,
the Felin Fach Griffin in Wales (page 143).

The Gurnard Head's stunning location
and views of the Atlantic makes it popular
with walkers, tourists and anyone looking
for peace, although the sounds and smells
from the neighbouring farm may not be for
urban-outdoor types. The bedrooms are
simple and tastefully decorated, with hand-
made beds and good linen. Each room is
lined with old books and local pictures and
maps — you might be staying with friends.

With the Atlantic 500 metres away, locally caught fish is a highlight of the seasonal
menu. At lunchtime, there's a chalkboard
menu offering broths and soups, stews,
sandwiches, homemade pork pies and fish
and chips. In the evening, local produce
crops up in dishes such as smoked Cornish
pilchards, 'The Gurnard's fish stew' and
porcini cannelloni. Well-chosen, affordable
wines or local real ales and cider. Too good
to be true? Our reporter's reply: 'Except for
the quibble about the farmyard smells, it
really is that good.'

Battle, East Sussex

Telham, Battle, East Sussex,
TN33 0TT

Tel (01424) 774338
Fax (01424) 775351
e-mail littlehemingfoldhotel@tis-cali.co.uk
website www.littlehemingfold.co.uk

Nearby Bodiam Castle; Great
Dixter; Rye; Sissinghurst.
Location 1.5 miles (3 km) SE of
Battle, off A2100; in 40-acre garden,
with trout lake, fields and woods;
ample car parking
Food breakfast, light lunch, dinner
Price ££
Rooms 13 double, 1 family room; 10
with bath; all rooms have phone, TV,
electric blankets; 4 rooms have log-
burning stoves **Facilities** 2 sitting
rooms, dining room, bar; garden,
boating, trout-fishing, tennis, croquet **Credit cards** AE, MC, V
Children accepted over 9
Disabled access difficult **Pets**
accepted **Closed** 1 Jan to 13 Feb
Proprietors Paul and Allison Slater

Little Hemingfold
Farmhouse **Country hotel**

Don't be misled by the word 'farmhouse': apart from the setting there is
not much that is agricultural about this
substantial, rambling building, part 17thC,
part early Victorian. The house has a
peaceful setting in 40 acres of farm and
woodland; it is surrounded by gardens, and
overlooks a pretty 2-acre trout lake (the
Slaters are happy to lend fishing rods).
Inside, intriguing nooks and crannies give
the house a special charm. The two sitting
rooms and the cosy dining room all have
log fires. So do four of the bedrooms, all
individually furnished, and accommodated
in the converted coach house and stables,
grouped around a flowery courtyard. This
is one of the most dog-friendly hotels in
the guide – six rooms are especially suited
to people travelling with animals.

Allison and Paul emphasize fresh ingredients in their traditional cooking, though we
have received mixed reports from visitors
about the food. One reader writes: 'the beef
we ordered for dinner was quite the best
ever and the puddings most unusual and
delicious...on Sunday, after a walk through
their lovely grounds, we indulged in a huge
breakfast, which was again superb'. After we
went to press we heard that the future is
uncertain here – it's on the market, but will
keep running until sold, so it's still worth
enquiring if you want to stay here.

Bepton, West Sussex

Bepton, Near Midhurst,
West Sussex GU29 0JB

Tel (01730) 819000
Fax (01730) 819099
e-mail reservations@parkhouse.com
website www.parkhousehotel.com

Nearby Petworth; Goodwood;
Cowdray Park; Chichester.
Location in countryside, on the
B2226 just N of Bepton village, 3
miles (5 km) SSW of Midhurst;
ample car parking
Food breakfast, lunch, dinner; room
service
Price £££
Rooms 15, 10 double, 2 family
rooms in main building, all with
bath; 2 cottages; all rooms have
phone, TV, hairdryer, fax/modem
point **Facilities** dining room, sitting
room, bar; garden, swimming pool,
tennis, croquet, putting green, 6-
hole pitch and putt course **Credit
cards** DC, MC, V **Children** welcome **Disabled** specially adapted
ground-floor bedroom **Pets** accepted by arrangement **Closed** never
Proprietor Seamus O'Brien

Park House
Country hotel

Park House has been in the O'Brien family for over 50 years, and has always
retained the atmosphere of a private country house – thanks first to the careful attention of Ioné O'Brien, and now to Seamus.

A 16thC farmhouse with Victorian additions, the hotel, with its cream-painted
roughcast walls, at first looks rather sub-
urban. Inside, however, the elegant public
rooms strike a very different note. The
honesty bar, festooned with mementoes
and photographs of polo players (Cowdray
Park is close at hand) is admirably well-
stocked, while the drawing room, particularly appealing at night, gleams with polished parquet floor, velvet-backed alcoves
filled with books and china, yellow walls,
and table lamps which cast a golden glow.

Bedrooms are traditional; best are the
two in the annexe, one of which has a private patio. The dinner menu has been
expanded (it used to be amazingly limited)
and features traditional English food. Lunch
can be as simple as sausage and mash or
oxtail pie. We would welcome comments on
the food.

Ship Street, Brighton, East Sussex
BN1 1AD

Tel (01273) 718588
Fax (01273) 718599
e-mail
reception.brighton@hotelduvin.com
website www.hotelduvin.com

Nearby seafront, The Lanes,
Brighton Pier.
Location from A23, take Kings
Road to Middle street, then turn
right into Ship Street, valet car park-
ing
Food breakfast, lunch, dinner
Price ££–£££
Rooms 37, 34 twin/double, 3 suites,
all with bath; all rooms have TV, CD
player, radio, minibar, trouser press,
hairdryer **Facilities** bar, restaurant,
wine cellar, walk-in cigar humidor,
billiards, courtyard with pergola
Credit cards AE, DC, MC, V
Children welcome **Disabled** access
possible
Pets not accepted **Closed** never
Manager Lora Strizic

Hotel du Vin
Town hotel

Down a narrow cobbled street, tucked
back from the seafront, a collection
of part gothic-styled buildings make up this
member of the stylish du Vin micro-chain
(others include Bristol, page 40, Winchester,
page 134 and Harrogate, page 245). In the
main building, bizarre gargoyles watch over
a double height hall and a heavily carved
staircase. Just through the reception area,
you can sink into the cosy leather armchairs or brown velvet sofas in the bar and
enjoy a drink and a cigar. Black and white
photos of celebrities and their favourite
smokes line the walls, while wooden seag-
ulls swoop and perch on the beams in the
high timbered ceilings. Through glass windows and doors, you can see the Bistro,
done out in wine-related pictures, floor-to-
ceiling windows and bunches of dried
hops. Bedrooms are each sponsored by
and named after a wine house. Those facing
the central courtyard (with a pretty vine-
covered pergola) have chalky blue-green
wood siding, beach-house style, and inside,
are decorated in soft blue and sand tones.
In the bathrooms, scroll top baths are
mounted in driftwood and old railway
sleepers. Two suites have telescopes for
spying boats out at sea.

We have reservations about the hotels du
Vin under their new ownership – see Bristol,
page 40 – and would welcome reports.

Bucklers Hard, Hampshire

Bucklers Hard, Beaulieu,
Hampshire SO42 7XB

Tel (01590) 616253
Fax (01590) 616297
e-mail res@themasterbuilders.co.uk
website
www.themasterbuilders.co.uk

Nearby New Forest; Beaulieu;
Lymington.
Location overlooking Beaulieu river
at Bucklers Hard, 2 miles (3 km) SE
of Beaulieu, 9 miles (14 km) SE of
Lyndhurst; ample car parking
Food breakfast, lunch, dinner
Price £££
Rooms 25 double, all with bath; all
rooms have phone, TV, hairdryer
Facilities sitting room, dining room,
yachtsman's bar; terrace, garden,
pontoon available **Credit cards** AE,
MC, V **Children** welcome
Disabled access difficult **Pets** not
accepted **Closed** never
Proprietors Jeremy Willcock and
John Illsley

Master Builder's House
Riverside hotel

The superbly sited Master Builder's Hotel had long been ripe for a carefully judged overhaul, and when its lease from Lord Montagu of Beaulieu came up some years ago for renewal, Jeremy Willcock and John Illsley, proprietors of the George in Yarmouth, Isle of Wight (see page 136) were just the right pair to step in. Lord Montagu's daughter, interior designer Mary Montagu Scott, undertook the redecoration, creating a straightforward traditional style with a maritime theme (plenty of old prints on the walls) in keeping with the spirit of Bucklers Hard, where some of Nelson's ships were built in the 18th century. Today it is a picturesque and popular marina, with a street of shipwrights' dwellings, a popular bar for visiting yachtsmen, and a maritime museum.

The 18thC Master Builder's House was lumbered some years back with an unsympathetic modern annexe, the Henry Adams Wing. Even the designer's best efforts cannot give the bedrooms here the character they lack, and although they are now comfortable and attractive, given their size, we feel they are somewhat ambitiously priced. Bedrooms in the main building have much more character. The sophisticated new reception area is an improvement on the old, and in the smart dining room, with views down to the river, 'modern classical' dishes are served.

Chichester, West Sussex

West Stoke, Chichester, West Sussex
PO18 9BN

Tel (01243) 575 226
Fax (01243) 574 655
e-mail info@weststokehouse.co.uk
website www.weststokehouse.co.uk

Nearby Kingley Valley national
nature reserve, Bow Hill, West
Witterings, Goodwood House
Location off A286 on Downs Road
in village of West Stoke before the
church, with off road car parking
Food breakfast, lunch, dinner
Price £££
Rooms 7 double/twin all have bath
some shower; all rooms have
TV/DVD player, phone, hairdryers,
wi-fi internet
Facilities restaurant, conference
room, garden, terrace, croquet
Credit cards AE, MC, V
Children welcome
Disabled access difficult
Pets accepted
Closed Christmas and Boxing Day
Proprietors Rowland and Mary
Leach

West Stoke House
Country hotel

Most of the ingredients of a charming small hotel are in place here. A large white Georgian house in real (but flattish) countryside on the edge of the South Downs; a well kept garden; well proportioned rooms, high ceilings; eclectic and quite stylish furnishings in the public rooms, including red leather armchairs, modest antiques (and some dull repro) with the old floorboards left bare; cleanly decorated bedrooms with neutral colour schemes. Opened in 2004 by Rowland and Mary Leach, with no experience in the hospitality business, it's a good example of the new breed of relaxed hotel underpinned by professionalism. We enjoyed Rowland's friendly welcome, and his dress sense: ungoverned hair, shorts and elastic sided 60s Chelsea boots. He's got the basics right – comfortable beds, good cotton sheets, quality bath fittings – without burning money.

This is a restaurant with rooms, so hopes were high for the dining room. However, we rate the food no better than what you'd expect for the price. Service, when we visited, was worryingly slow: 46 minutes for two main courses to arrive. When we asked the manager how long the desserts might take, the response was a cheeky line in guest management we hadn't heard before: "We never rush things here."

Cranbrook, Kent

Cranbrook, Kent TN17 3NR

Tel (01580) 712220
Fax (01580) 712220
e-mail clothhalloast@aol.com

Nearby Sissinghurst; Scotney Castle
Gardens.
Location in countryside 1 mile (1.5
km) E of Cranbrook on road to
Tenterden, before cemetery; in
grounds of 5 acres; ample car parking
Food breakfast, dinner by arrangement
Price ££
Rooms 3 double, 2 with bath, 1 with
shower; all rooms have TV and
hairdryer **Facilities** sitting room,
dining room; 2 terraces, garden,
heated outdoor swimming pool,
summer house, croquet **Credit
cards** not accepted
Children accepted by arrangement
Disabled access difficult **Pets** not
accepted **Closed** Christmas
Proprietor Katherine Morgan

Cloth Hall Oast
Manor house guest-house

Lovers of Mrs Morgan's previous guest-
house will be happy to know that,
although no longer running our long-time
favourite Old Cloth Hall, she has simply
moved to the nearby Cloth Hall Oast.
With 20 years of experience to support
her new venture, Mrs Morgan describes it
as "just as nice as the other – if not better"
and it is already receiving positive reviews.

The house is situated on a 5-acre estate
that is hidden from the road, slightly isolated and very quiet. A large pond with fish
and a pretty tree in the middle provides a
lovely view from lawn chairs on the half-
moon shaped decking. For sunny summer
days, you can enjoy a swim in the heated
pool or simply relax in the nearby summer
house. Two terraces with outdoor patio
furniture, a superb croquet lawn and a pergola in the garden complete the picture.

The interior of Cloth Hall Oast is just as
special as her previous place. The dining
room, open to three galleried floors that
include a grand piano, showcases a stunning custom-made chandelier. The bedrooms feel light and warm and one has a
whirlpool bath. The sitting room has a fireplace that's perfect for curling up beside
on a cool evening. We would welcome
comments on the food.

Cuckfield, West Sussex

Ockenden Lane, Cuckfield,
West Sussex RH17 5LD

Tel (01444) 416111
Fax (01444) 415549
e-mail reservations@ockenden-
manor.co.uk
website www.hshotels.co.uk

Nearby Nyman's; Sissinghurst;
Wakehurst Place; Gatwick;
Brighton.
Location 2 miles (3 km) W of
Haywards Heath close to middle of
village, off A272; in 9-acre grounds,
with ample car parking
Food breakfast, lunch, dinner
Price £££
Rooms 20 double, 2 single, all with
bath; all rooms have phone, TV,
hairdryer
Facilities sitting room, bar, dining
room; terrace, garden
Credit cards AE, DC, MC, V
Children welcome
Disabled no special facilities **Pets**
not accepted
Closed never **Proprietors** Sandy
and Anne Goodman

Ockenden Manor
Manor house hotel

A telling comment from a recent inspector: 'Anne Goodman oversees the decoration herself, so gives it the personal touch, rather than simply splashing out on the finest.' She has made many changes for the better here since taking over this attractive 16th/17thC manor house.

Bedrooms are spacious and individual (and crammed with giveaways); a superb master suite with sombre panelling relies on reds and greens to give a feeling of brightness. Several of the bathrooms are notably spacious, and they are equipped with Molton Brown toiletries. The main sitting room, though lavishly furnished, has a personal feel. Staff are friendly and obliging. (A notice in the hotel states that whatever a hotel's character and charm, it is only as good as its staff.)

Dinner, which is served in the oak-panelled restaurant with painted ceiling and stained glass windows, is another highlight. Food is based on local produce, with vegetables and herbs from the garden.

Although Ockenden Manor is popular with business people, it is a human, comfortable hotel. 'Hidden away behind trees and a high wall; quiet; good value', says our inspector.

East Grinstead, West Sussex

Vowels Lane, near East Grinstead,
West Sussex RH19 4LJ

Tel (01342) 810567
Fax (10342) 810080
e-mail info@gravetyemanor.co.uk
website www.gravetyemanor.co.uk

Nearby Wakehurst; Nyman's
Gardens; Glyndebourne
Location 4.5 miles (7 km) SW of
East Grinstead by B2110 at
Gravetye; in 30 acre grounds with
ample car parking
Food breakfast, lunch, dinner, room
service
Price ££££
Rooms 17 double, 1 single, all with
bath; all rooms have phone, TV,
hairdryer, wi-fi; 2 rooms have air-
conditioning
Facilities 2 sitting rooms, bar, din-
ing room; terrace, garden, croquet,
trout fishing
Credit cards AE, MC, V **Children**
welcome over 7 **Disabled** ramp
access but no adapted rooms **Pets**
not accepted (1 mile from kennel)
Closed never **Proprietors** Andrew
Russel and Mark Raffan

Gravetye Manor
Manor house hotel

The country house hotel, now so much a part of the tourist scene in Britain, scarcely existed when Peter Herbert opened the doors of this serene Elizabethan house over 40 years ago. After his retirement since our last edition, Andrew Russel and Michelin-starred chef Mark Raffan took the helm. Standards in every department remain unflaggingly high. Service consistently achieves the elusive aim of attentiveness without intrusion, while the ambitious food is about the best in the county. A recent visitor, who has known the hotel for 30 years, remained as impressed as ever: 'A sleek operation that doesn't compromise.' However, another commented on 'lots of wealthy-looking people in sunglasses and strange-looking jogging suits'.

The pioneering gardener William Robinson lived in the house for half a century until his death in 1935. Great care is taken to maintain the various gardens he created; Robinson was also responsible for many features of the house as it is seen today – the mellow oak panelling and grand fireplaces in the calm, gracious sitting rooms, for example. Bedrooms – all immaculate – vary in size from the adequate to the enormous, and prices range accordingly.

East Hoathly, East Sussex

East Hoathly, Sussex BN8 6EL

Tel (01825) 840216
Fax (01825) 840738
website www.oldwhyly.co.uk

Nearby Glyndebourne, Charleston
Farm House, East Sussex National
Golf Course, Batemans.
Location just off A22 S of Uckfield
on road to Halland, ample car park-
ing
Food breakfast, dinner
Price ££
Rooms 3 double and twin, 2 with
bath, 1 with shower **Facilities** sitting
room, dining room; terrace, garden,
croquet, hard top tennis court, heat-
ed swimming pool, lake, walking
paths **Credit cards** not accepted
Children welcome **Disabled** access
difficult **Pets** by arrangement
Closed never **Proprietor** Sarah
Burgoyne

Old Whyly
Country house guest-house

Driving up to Old Whyly in the spring-
time is magical; owner Sarah
Burgoyne has planted 4,000 tulip bulbs and
at the right season, the lawn is ablaze with
colour. Set in 40-acre grounds, with a
duck-dotted lake, well-maintained gardens
and walks that take in the nearby 600-acre
stud farm, this Grade II listed 18thC
manor has an enviable setting

Once you cross the well-gravelled drive
and climb the front steps, you will be welcomed in Sarah's (and her dog, Noodle's)
antique-filled home. The impressive family
painting collection lines the walls, including
a full-length portrait of Sarah herself. The
sitting room has a roaring fire with inviting
furniture – perfect for admiring the china
collection or just reading a book.
Bedrooms are spacious and comfortable.
However, one of the best reasons to stay
at Old Whyly is the food. Sarah, a passionate cook who trained in Paris, prepares
excellent dishes and, although many of her
customers tend to eat at Glyndebourne,
Sarah is more than happy to provide dinner.

Breakfast includes honey from Sarah's
bees kept in the orchard and eggs from
the hens that wander about on the lawn.

Fletching, East Sussex

Fletching, near Uckfield,
East Sussex TN22 3SS

Tel (01825) 722890
Fax (01825) 722810
e-mail info@thegriffininn.co.uk
website www.thegriffininn.co.uk

Nearby Sheffield Park;
Glyndebourne; Ashdown Forest.
Location in village 1 mile (1.5 km)
E of A275; with car parking
Food breakfast, lunch, dinner
Price ££
Rooms 12 double and 1 twin, 6 with
bath, 7 with shower; all rooms have
TV, hairdryer
Facilities bars, restaurant, bar bil-
liards; terrace, patio, garden
Credit cards AE, DC, MC, V
Children welcome **Disabled** 2
rooms on ground floor
Pets accepted in bar, but not in bed-
rooms or restaurant
Closed Christmas Day **Manager**
James Pullan

The Griffin Inn
Village inn

On our latest visit to the Griffin Inn, the
pub was packed, the dining room was
almost full and the kitchen was bustling.
Successful? Evidently. But still welcoming and
cosy? Definitely.

This 16thC village inn has been owned by
the Pullan family for 20 years and it main-
tains its winning combination of good food
(it can claim to be Britain's first gastro-pub)
and pretty bedrooms with beams, low ceilings and four-poster beds. Everything is a bit
uneven, quaint, on a small scale – but
endearing rather than cramped. Beds are
inviting and bathrooms are in an attractive
Victorian style, with funky porthole mirrors.
That said, some of the rooms were looking
a little tired on our last visit; but we imagine
that re-investment is on the way.

The pub has more beams, paneling, open
fires and hunting prints, while the old public
bar has been turned into the 'Club Room',
with sofas, armchairs and a backgammon
board. Good food is always at hand either in
the pub or in the restaurant, which uses
fresh seasonal ingredients and local organic
vegetables. Both menus change daily. The
wine list has over 100 wines, 70 percent of
which are priced at under £20 per bottle.

You can take your drink out to the garden overlooking Sheffield Park and enjoy
live jazz at the weekends. In summer, there's
a full-scale BBQ serving Pacific Rim dishes.

Littlestone, Kent

Coast Road, Littlestone,
New Romney, Kent TN28 8QY

Tel (01797) 364747
Fax (01797) 367156

Nearby Rye; Dungeness
Lighthouse; Sandwich.
Location in New Romney, take
Station Road to sea front, turn left,
and follow hotel signs for 1 mile; car
parking
Food breakfast, weekday sandwich
lunch, weekend light lunch, dinner
Price ££-£££
Rooms 10 double and twin, all with
bath or shower; all rooms have TV,
hairdryer
Facilities sitting room, dining room,
look-out room; terrace, garden, hard
tennis court, croquet, boules, beach
adjacent to golf course
Credit cards DC, MC, V
Children accepted over 14
Disabled access difficult
Pets not accepted
Closed Christmas **Proprietors**
Clinton and Lisa Lovell

Romney Bay House
Seaside hotel

The approach through sprawling
Littlestone is unpromising, particularly
in the dark when you don't know where
you're heading. But this dignified 1920s
house, built by Clough Williams Ellis for
American columnist Hedda Hopper, has a
superb position between the sea and
Romney Marsh. Clinton and Lisa Lovell
took over Romney Bay House in 2003, and
have kept the style of the interior much
the same, while upgrading the bathrooms.
The interiors are reminiscent of a small
hotel in Provence, with plenty of French
furniture and fabrics. This is a thoroughly
relaxed place: the cosy bar; the warm, fire-
lit sitting room packed with groups of comfortable, inviting chairs; breakfasts in the
pretty conservatory; drinks or cream teas
on the terrace in fine weather. Dinner is a
non-choice four course menu, planned
around the diners each evening and made
with local produce.

An upstairs 'look-out' room has the feel
of a beach house, with piles of towels for
swimming, wicker chairs and sea shells.
Bedrooms have creamy cottons, fresh
white bedlinen, bright checks, and
antiques; those on the first floor have full
length windows, allowing uninterrupted
views out to sea.

London

64-66 Ebury Street, London,
SW1W 9QD

Tel (020) 7259 8570
Fax (020) 7259 8591
e-mail info@bb-belgravia.com
website www.bb-belgravia.com

Nearby Buckingham Palace;
Victoria Palace Theatre, Cardinal
Place shopping centre, Royal Albert
hall
Location off Eccleston Street,
between Victoria and Sloane Square
tube stations; metered parking only
Food breakfast
Price ££-£££
Rooms 17; 8 double, 7 twin, 2 fami-
ly rooms, all with bath or shower; all
rooms have phone, flatscreen TV,
internet connection; hairdryers on
request
Facilities sitting room, breakfast
room, garden, bikes available
Credit cards AE, MC, V
Children welcome
Disabled one adapted single room
Pets not accepted
Closed never
Proprietor Penny Brown

B&B Belgravia
Town house hotel

Penny Brown opened B&B Belgravia in
2004 with the aim of revolutionising
bed and breakfast: providing modern, stylish accommodation, without sacrificing
affordability. And this is certainly not your
average B&B. Guests enjoy communal
areas such as the stylish sitting area with
24-hour coffee-making facilities; an open-
plan breakfast room/kitchen where your
full English is cooked to order in front of
you; and a garden so secluded and peaceful you can hardly believe it is just five minutes' walk from Victoria station. This quiet
setting, on a residential street lined with
handsome grade II listed Georgian town
houses, together with the charmingly
friendly staff, provides the homely atmosphere you might expect of a more conventional B&B.

Rooms are generously proportioned
and those on the lower floors benefit from
high ceilings and good light from floor-to-
ceiling windows. The decoration throughout is light, fresh, and modern and original
features such as cornicing and tiled floors
are found alongside modern frosted glass
panels and contemporary soft furnishings.

B&B Belgravia seems to have found a
winning formula. When we visited the
hotel was fully booked four months in
advance and there are now plans to
expand outside of London.

London

33 Beaufort Gardens, London
SW3 1PP

Tel (020) 7584 5252
Fax (020) 7589 2834
e-mail enquiries@thebeaufort.co.uk
website www.thebeaufort.co.uk

Nearby Harrods; Victoria and
Albert Museum.
Location off Brompton Road, just
W of Harrods; pay and display park-
ing in street
Food breakfast; room service
Price ££££
Rooms 29 double, twin, single and
suites, all with bath or shower; all
rooms have phone, TV, Sky, CD
player, air-conditioning, fax/modem
points, hairdryer; wi-fi, fax/answer-
ing machines on request
Facilities sitting room, bar **Credit
cards** AE, DC, MC, V
Children accepted
Disabled access difficult
Pets not accepted
Closed never **Proprietors** Ahmed
and Sarah Jajbhay

The Beaufort
Town bed-and-breakfast

Three Harrods doormen in a row gave
our inspector unerring directions for
the hundred-yard walk to The Beaufort,
part of a Victorian terrace overlooking a
quiet Knightsbridge cul-de-sac. Taken over
by Ahmed and Sarah Jajbhay, this is still one
of the few hotels in the world which surprises you with what doesn't appear later
on your bill. Feel like a glass of champagne?
No charge. Cream tea? Limo to or from
the airport? Light meal in your room? The
answer's still no charge. And, just when you
have been made to feel so good that you
want to give a tip, you fall victim to a no-
tipping policy.

All the rooms are different, some decorated in muted pastels, others following in
the cheerful footsteps of the public areas.
Each room has a CD player and portable
stereo and, for those who need added pro-
tection from the English weather, there are
also chocolates, shortbread, brandy and
umbrellas. And then there are the flowers.
Plenty of them. Many are real, but most are
hanging on the walls as part of the enormous collection of English floral watercolours. Noted for the friendliness of its
staff, the Beaufort has many faithful regulars.

Camberwell Church Street,
London SE5 8TR

Tel (020) 7703 5984
Fax (020) 7385 4110
e-mail info@churchstreethotel.com
website www.churchstreethotel.com

Location in busy high street near
Camberwell Green; parking in nearby residential street with permits
(£5) from reception.
Nearby South London Gallery, Oval
cricket ground, clubs, London Eye
20 minutes by bus, also County Hall
(Saatchi Gallery); leisure centres
Food breakfast
Price ££
Rooms 31; 25 double, 6 single; all
doubles except 3 have own bath, 3
have shared bathroom; all rooms
have TV, hairdryer; most have flat-
screen TV, DVD, air-con **Facilities**
breakfast 24-hour room-bar, with
honesty bar; tapas restaurant
Cards AE, MC, V **Disabled** not
suitable **Children** welcome; under
six, free in parents' room **Closed**
never **Proprietors** Jose and Mel
Raido

The Church Street Hotel
City hotel

The conventional name and restrained
exterior give no hint of what's inside. In
reception, a gold painted altar for the desk;
colourful ikons on the walls; French tiles on
the floor. Swirly patterned carpets lead you
upstairs; lurid religious paintings hang in the
passages; custom-made brown bedroom
doors have iron studs. The signals are a little
confusing, but hip-60s-Latin-American with
a contemporary twist more or less sums it
up. Your bedroom is likely to burst with
colour: our reporter's was cobalt blue with
a comfortable hand-made wrought-iron
bed, painted crucifixes in high alcoves and
hand-painted Mexican tiles in the bathroom.

Spanish-Greek brothers José and Mel
Raido created this place from a former family property, wanting to do something
refreshing and affordable – and they have.
Their success is borne out by the generally
youthful, cool crowd from all over the world
that you'll meet in the walnut-panelled
breakfast room/bar. A tapas bar is promised
in the basement; otherwise it lacks a separate public sitting area. Located in noisy,
multi-ethnic Camberwell, just along from
the Green, but Oval tube, with fast access to
the centre, is just around the corner.
Nothing like anywhere else in Britain.

2 Warringtom Crescent, Little
Venice, London W9 1ER

Tel (020) 7286 1052
Fax (020) 7286 1057
e-mail rescollonade@theetoncollec-
tion.com
website www.theetoncollection.com

Nearby Little Venice.
Location 1-minute walk from
Warwick Avenue tube, 3 car parking
spaces in garage, £15 per night, must
be pre-booked
Food breakfast, dinner, 24 hr room
service
Price £££
Rooms 43; 35 double, 5 twin, 3 single, most with shower, some with
bath; all rooms have TV, stereo,
phone, minibar, safe, hairdryer,
trouser press, iron **Facilities** sitting
room, restaurant with terrace **Credit
cards** AE, DC, MC, V **Children**
welcome **Disabled** not suitable **Pets**
by arrangement **Closed** Christmas
Manager Michael Kahn

The Colonnade
Town house hotel

Set in Little Venice, with its canals and bridges, The Colonnade manages to overcome the trappings of a large hotel to provide a private place to stay. The building itself occupies two Victorian town houses that were built in 1865 as private resi-dences. In the late 1800s, it was used as a girls' school and, in the early 1900s, it became a maternity hospital. Alan Turing, creator of the first computer and the man who solved the Enigma code, was born here, and you'll find a suite named after him. When the building later became a hotel, Sigmund Freud stayed here while waiting for his house in Hampstead to be finished. In his suite, a bed sits in a gallery above a sitting room with enormous floor-to-ceiling win-dows. In the JFK Suite, you can sleep in the four-poster bed built for President Kennedy's state visit in 1962. The rest of the bedrooms are done out in three smart colour schemes: black and gold, green and gold or red and gold. In the sitting room, comfy sofas, attractive stripy chairs, an open coal fire and complimentary sherry, port and lollipops offset the strange artificial topiary.

In the basement, the achingly hip Enigma bar and restaurant serves contemporary Mediterranean fare. Was that snakeskin-tex-tured paneling we spotted beside the bar?

10 Monmouth Street, London
WC2H 9HB

Tel (020) 7806 1000
Fax (020) 7806 1100
e-mail covent@firmdale.com
website www.firmdale.com

Nearby Covent Garden; Royal
Opera House; West End theatres.
Location in fairly quiet street
between Shaftesbury Avenue and St
Martin's Lane; metered parking or
public car park nearby
Food breakfast, lunch, dinner; room
service
Price ££££ **Rooms** 58; 46 double
and twin, 6 suites; 6 single, all with
bath; all rooms have phone, TV,
video, CD player, fax/modem point,
air-conditioning, minibar, hairdryer
Facilities drawing room, restaurant,
bar, library, work-out room, beauty
treatment room, screening room,
meeting rooms **Credit cards** AE,
MC, V **Children** accepted **Disabled**
access possible, lift/elevator
Pets not accepted **Closed** never
Proprietors Tim and Kit Kemp

Covent Garden
Town hotel

The group of seductive London hotels
owned by Tim and Kit Kemp includes
six sprinkled across the city. They began
with Dorset Square (no longer in their
ownership, or the guide) and then opened
several more similar town house hotels,
before becoming more expansive here in
Covent Garden, but without losing any of
their previous assurance. The latest addition is Haymarket Hotel.

Monmouth Street is an attractive, quiet
street ideally placed for theatre and media-
land. The building was formerly a French
hospital, which Tim and Kit (she is responsible for all the decoration) have transformed
into a hotel that at once feels glamorous, yet
welcoming and not in the least intimidating.
A stunning drawing room stretches across
the first floor, with a well-stocked drinks-
and-snack bar at one end, where guests can
help themselves. On the ground floor is a
small bar/bistro, serving tasty, simply cooked
dishes; or you can order from the well-bal-
anced room service menu.

Bedrooms all look different, although
each possesses a matching fabric-covered
mannequin (the hotel is a favourite with
models), and they all have superb granite
bathrooms. One bedroom has a musical
theme, another a memorable four-poster
bed (reputedly the largest in London). The
cosy attic rooms are also delightful.

189 Queen's Gate, London
SW7 5EX

Tel (020) 7584 6601
Fax (020) 7589 8127
e-mail reservations@gorehotel.com
website www.gorehotel.com

Nearby Kensington Gardens; Hyde
Park; Albert Hall; Harrods.
Location just S of Kensington
Gardens; metered parking and pub-
lic car park nearby
Food breakfast, lunch, dinner
Price ££££
Rooms 50; 44 double, 6 single or
twin, all with bath or shower; all
rooms have phone, TV, DVD, mini-
bar, hairdryer, safe, wi-fi
Facilities library/sitting room, bar,
restaurant
Credit cards AE, DC, MC, V
Children welcome
Disabled access possible, lift/eleva-
tor **Pets** not accepted **Closed** never
Proprietors Edward Bracken and
Con Ring

The Gore
Town house hotel

In 1990 the team who opened Hazlitt's (see page 106) bought this Victorian town house (long established as a hotel) set in a wide tree-lined street near Kensington Gardens, and gave it the Hazlitt treatment: bedrooms furnished with period antiques, walls enlivened with pictures, and they recruited a young and friendly staff, trained to give efficient but informal service.

It has character by the bucketload; walls whose every square inch is covered with prints and oil paintings; bedrooms fur-nished with antiques, each with its own style – a gallery in one room, Judy Garland's bed in another. There is also an impressive dossier in each room describ-ing what to do locally – 'put together with verve and a feel for what the guest might really want'. The panelled bar on the ground floor is a popular rendezvous for non-residents as well as guests. Across the hallway is Bistro 190 (same owners, same style) which opens from 7.30 am to 11.30 pm and, and as well as breakfast, offers lighthearted modern dishes with an inter-national spin.

Restaurant 190, which is famous for its ways with fish, is stylish with rosewood panels and deep red velvet chairs.

Since our last edition it has changed hands, so reports would be welcome.

6 Frith Street, Soho, London
W1D 3JA

Tel (020) 7434 1771
Fax (020) 7439 1524
e-mail reservations@hazlitts.co.uk
website www.hazlittshotel.com

Nearby Oxford Street; Piccadilly
Circus; Covent Garden; theatres.
Location in Soho, between Oxford
Street and Shaftesbury Avenue; pub-
lic car parks nearby
Food breakfast; room service
Price ££££
Rooms 23; 19 doubles (1 twin), 1
suite, 3 singles; all with bath; all
rooms have phone, TV, fax/modem
point, hairdryer, safe,minibars
Facilities sitting room **Credit cards**
AE, DC, MC, V
Children welcome **Disabled** not
suitable **Pets** accepted by arrange-
ment
Closed never **Proprietors** Peter
McKay and Douglas Blainel

Hazlitts
Town house hotel

There is no quarter of central London
with more character than Soho; and
there are few places to stay with more
character than Hazlitt's, formed from
three Georgian terraced houses off Soho
Square. The sloping, creaking floorboards
have been retained (it can be an uphill walk
to your bed), and the rooms decorated
with suitable antiques, busts and prints.
Recent restoration work has revealed
original fireplaces and Georgian paneling
that's nearly 300 years old. The bedrooms,
named after some of the people who visited or stayed in the house where the
eponymous essayist himself lived, are
delightfully different from most London
hotel rooms, some with intricately carved
wood headboards, one with a delightful
four-poster, all with free-standing bath tubs
and Victorian fittings in the bathrooms.

As befits an establishment with such literary connections, Hazlitt's is particularly
popular with visiting authors, who leave
signed copies of the works when they
depart. Sadly, the dresser in the little sitting
room in which they are kept is now locked
to protect the books, which had a habit of
going missing. Continental breakfast is
served in the bedrooms, as well as light
dishes such as pasta and filled baguettes. A
hotel for people who like their comforts
authentic, yet stylish.

162 Chiswick High Road, London
W4 1PR

Tel (020) 8742 1717
Fax (020) 8987 8762
e-mail reservations@highroad-house.co.uk
website www.highroadhouse.co.uk

Nearby Hampton Court Palace,
Twickenham, Richmond, Kew
Gardens
Location on Chiswick High Rd
(A315) with no parking but hotel can
feed your meter. Nearest tube
Turnham Green
Food breakfast, lunch, dinner, room
service
Price £££
Rooms 14; 13 standard doubles, 1
superior; all have showers, superior
has bath; all rooms have phone
TV/DVD player, wi-fi, phone,
hairdryer **Facilities** dining room,
bar, games room, tv plasma room,
brasserie **Credit cards** AE, DC,
MC, V **Children** accepted **Disabled**
one adapted room **Pets** not accepted
Closed never **Proprietor** Nick
Jones

High Road House
City hotel

You can hope that a hotel owned by Nick Jones (proprietor of Soho House and Babington House) is going to be interesting and this doesn't disappoint. The decoration is city chic but doesn't feel cold: the colours bring the place to life and add an air of cosiness. The bar and dining room are buzzy, with masses of light and are not so cramped that you think that your next door neighbour can hear your thoughts. The food is traditional English with French twists, but nothing too pretentious.

Downstairs in the basement is a fantastic space painted in deep red with retro furniture which can be a nightclub; a place for meetings; a place for private sports parties (big plasma screen); a children's activity area or a place for chilling out and playing pool or mini football.

The bedrooms are, as you would expect, very cool (maybe a bit too white) with comfy beds, delicious Cowshed toiletries in the bathrooms and very quiet. All the windows are triple glazed, which is just as well as there is a very busy yet fun, trendy road outside.

This a great hotel for all ages; and it is especially popular with mothers and children – activities for the latter are supervised by minders, while mothers have a massage, a hair appointment or a facial.

55 Hanger Lane, London
W5 3HL

Tel (020) 8991 4450
Fax (020) 8991 4451
e-mail sri@hotel55-london.com
website www.hotel55-london.com

Nearby Heathrow (20 mins), Ealing Common, Central London (20 mins), North Ealing Tube
Location on A406 Hanger Lane, parking for 5 cars, ample space behind hotel in NCP
Food breakfast, lunch, dinner
Price ££
Rooms 25; all double, all with shower, 5 with bath and shower; all rooms have phone, TV, hairdryer, air-con, internet connection, safe
Facilities bar, garden, garden room
Credit cards AE, MC, V
Children welcome (but no extra beds provided)
Disabled 2 suitable rooms
Pets not accepted **Closed** never
Proprietor Sanjay Tohani

Hotel 55
City hotel

This young hotel had only been open a year when we went to press. It's well placed for Heathrow: the Piccadilly line (North Ealing) is right behind the hotel, and takes you in without a change.

Sri, the charming and helpful manager, greets you as you step through the automatic doors. Straight through the ground floor and you are in the chic bar area, with walls clad in leather, low seating and a plasma screen. But the real joy of this place is the garden room leading on to a landscaped garden – rare in London. It's surprisingly quiet, considering the hotel is on a busy road and the tube is so close. You can have your continental breakfast in the garden room, read the papers or have a light lunch. However, the kitchen wasn't fully functional as we went to press, so guests were choosing from menus of nearby restaurants, and getting the food brought to their table.

The bedrooms and bathrooms are small, but nicely done in neutral shades. They too are refreshingly quiet (double glazing): the ones overlooking the garden are particularly peaceful. If climbing stairs is an effort, (there's no lift) then flop on to the orthopaedic mattress (in every room) while sipping your environmentally friendly water. Plenty of business people here – which does affect the atmosphere.

London

159 Knightsbridge, London
SW1X 7PD

Tel (020) 7584 6274
Fax (020) 7225 1635
e-mail reservations@thekghotel.com
website www.thekghotel.com

Nearby Hyde Park; Victoria and
Albert Museum; Harrods, Harvey
Nichols.
Location near junction with
Brompton Road, opposite
Knightsbridge Barracks; car park in
Raphael Street
Food breakfast; drinks
Price £££
Rooms 28; 5 double, 4 twin, 7 sin-
gle, 12 suites, all with bath; all rooms
have phone, flat-screen TV, air-con-
ditioning, hairdryer, safe **Facilities**
sitting room, office area, wi-fi
throughout
Credit cards AE, DC, MC, V
Children welcome
Disabled 2 accessible suites; lift/ele-
vator **Pets** not accepted **Closed**
Christmas eve and Christmas day
Proprietors Marler family

The Knightsbridge Green

City hotel

Owned by the same family as the St
Enodoc (see page 69), the
Knightsbridge Green is a comfortable yet
affordable hotel halfway between Harrods
and Harvey Nichols. The Marler family
keep their prices lower than comparable
hotels in the area by steering clear of pricy
frills. There are no minibars, no restaurant,
no breakfast room (breakfast is served in
the large bedrooms) and no health club
(guests can use the one at the Berkeley for
a fee). There are, however, tea and coffee
making facilities in all of the rooms, an ice
machine and bar service (11am to 8pm).

Despite employing a charismatic manager, Paul Fizia, the Marlers are still very
much involved with the day-to-day running
of the hotel, and it shows. It has a cared-
for feel, and a host of regular guests use it
as a *pied-à-terre*. Downstairs the decoration is refreshingly modern: the entrance
in cool mint-green, the large sitting areas
in shades of green and blue. The attractive,
well-lit bedrooms are all different, with
bold printed fabrics, modern furniture and
spotless marble bathrooms. Some rooms
have pretty window seats, one has a sleigh
bed, another a four-poster, and suites have
sofa beds, so are ideal for families. Staff are
friendly, and they serve an excellent full
English breakfast with freshly squeezed
orange juice and bacon from Harrods.

London

28 Basil Street, London SW3 1AS

Tel (020) 7589 6286
Fax (020) 7823 7826
email reservations@lhotel.co.uk
website www.lhotel.co.uk

Nearby Knightsbridge; Hyde Park;
Buckingham Palace.
Location between Sloane Street and
Harrods; public car park opposite
and at Capital Hotel, if available
Food breakfast, lunch, dinner
Price ££££
Rooms 12; 8 std/exec doubles, 3
deluxe, 1 suite; all with bath and
shower; all rooms have phone, flat
screenTV with integrated web
access, digital radio, minibar, safe,
air-con **Facilities** lounge, restau-
rant/bar, honesty bar **Credit cards**
AE, DC, MC, V **Children** welcome
Disabled access difficult (steps), but
has 1 ground floor room and lift/ele-
vator **Pets** accepted by arrangement
Closed restaurant only, Sun lunch
and dinner **Proprietor** David Levin
Manager Isabel Murphy

The Levin
City hotel

This impressively-situated hotel, in the
heart of Knightsbridge, opened in late
2007. Formerly L'Hotel (long in the guide),
owner David Levin has renewed its appeal
with a multi-million pound renovation.

The stylishness strikes you as you walk in
– everything is 'designer' and top quality –
hand-blown ice-blue crystal chandeliers by
Refer and Star, George Smith chairs, a green
pony skin love seat by Christopher Guy.
Whether or not the names matter to you,
the effect is impressive and everything is
immaculate. Bedrooms are beautifully designed,
with contrasting colours and textures. Fabric-
covered back-lit headboards give the rooms
a cosy feel. The non-uniform room shapes of
this old building have been imaginatively put
to use, with sofas built into large bay windows. Original fireplaces add further character. Bathrooms are a fair size, with Italian
marble and under-floor heating: stylish and
spotlessly clean.

Attention to detail is superb, with all the
technical wizardry you could want and also
– uniquely, we believe – a mini-champagne-
cocktail-bar in each room, with champagnes,
mixers and a book of cocktail recipes.

Despite its design credentials, The Levin
has a friendly atmosphere and manages to
avoid pretentiousness. It is hard to find fault
with the place – though equestrians may bri-
dle at the pony skin love seat.

London

26-28 Trebovir Road, Earl's Court,
London SW5 9NJ

Tel (020) 7370 0991
Fax (020) 7370 0994
e-mail info@mayflower-group.co.uk
website www.mayflower-group.co.uk

Nearby Earl's Court exhibition centre; Natural History and Science Museums; Victoria & Albert Museum; Knightsbridge, Chelsea
Location just off Earls Court Road, near corner with Nevern Square
Food breakfast
Price £££
Rooms 48; 34 double/twin, 4 single; all rooms have phone, TV, wi-fi
Facilities sitting room, lounge, business centre; garden
Credit cards AE, MC, V
Children welcome
Disabled access not possible
Pets not accepted
Closed never
Manager Faisal Saloojee

The Mayflower
City hotel

Trudging past the dire Earl's Court budget hotels en route to The Mayflower, you will feel relief at the sight of its smart, freshly painted façade. No disappointment, either, once inside: to the left, an airy bar/sitting room, with a bird trilling in its cage; to the right, a spacious, calm, sophisticated reception area.

Our reporter was booked into a mid-range double, priced at a modest £95, and therefore ready for a tiny bedroom. In fact, it was tiny, but perfectly formed. In a clever move that makes this budget address feel both hip and characterful, The Mayflower's owners have enlivened the rooms with Oriental artefacts, carved wooden cupboards and mirrored bedheads, silk cushions and velvet bedspreads, plus attractive wooden blinds and sweeping curtains at the windows. Give them individual doors instead of the tacky, basic ones that are there now and they would be even more special.

The imaginative breakfast in the airy basement breakfast room came as 'no surprise', and as our reporter left she reflected that the Mayflower stands out 'like an Aladdin's lamp in a junk shop amongst budget central London hotels.'

London

111a Westbourne Grove, London
W2 4UW

Tel (020) 7243 1024
Fax (020) 7243 1064
e-mail enquiries@millersuk.com
website www.millersuk.com

Nearby Portobello Road Market;
Notting Hill Gate; Kensington
Gardens; Kensington High Street.
Location on first floor above restau-
rant on corner of Westbourne Grove
and Hereford Road (entrance in
Hereford Road); car parking on
meters
Food breakfast
Price £££
Rooms 8 double and twin, all with
bath; all rooms have phone, TV
Facilities sitting room, library
Credit cards AE, MC, V
Children accepted **Disabled** not
suitable
Pets not accepted **Closed** never
Proprietors Martin and Ioana
Miller

Miller's Residence
Town guest-house

If you are an antique lover who thinks
your house is as full as it can be, a stay at
Martin Miller's London hotel (he was the
editor/author of the much respected
Millers Antiques Guide) will be an educa-
tional as well as a comfortable experience.
Only local knowledge or skilful map-reading will bring you to the hotel's bright red
door in Hereford Road. The oriental rugs
and prints on the stairs do a poor job of
preparing you for the eclectic (and some
might say eccentric) splendour of the large
first-floor drawing room. It is not so much
full of antiques as stacked with them, and
you can't help feeling that the addition of
just one more snuff-box might cause a
perilous situation. Lit in the evening by
dozens of candles (helped here and there
by a little electricity), a stay at Millers is an
entirely unique experience.

Your welcome from the staff couldn't be
warmer, and the bedrooms (all named
after poets and up more stairs on the second floor) are elegantly, if less dangerous-
ly, furnished, each in a style appropriate to
its poet. Breakfast, taken at one large table,
is a do-it-yourself affair and there is a
tremendous choice of restaurants within
easy walking distance – but don't forget
your key as the front door is always
locked. See also page 86 for Miller's sister
hotel in Somerset.

London

16 Sumner Place, London
SW7 3EG

Tel (020) 7589 5232
Fax (020) 7584 8615
e-mail reservations@ numbersix-teenhotel.co.uk **website** www.num-bersixteenhotel.co.uk

Nearby South Kensington muse-ums; Knightsbridge; Kings Road.
Location off Old Brompton Road; no private car parking
Food breakfast; room service
Price £££
Rooms 42 double, all with bath/shower; all rooms have phone, TV, minibar, hairdryer, safe, umbrellas, wi-fi
Facilities sitting room, bar, conser-vatory; small garden
Credit cards AE, DC, MC, V
Children accepted
Disabled access possible, lift/eleva-tor **Pets** not accepted **Closed** never
Manager Kate McWhirter

Number Sixteen
Town guest-house

Number Sixteen is one of London's most characterful luxury bed-and-breakfast establishments. The original building has spread along its early Victorian South Kensington terrace, to encompass four adjoining houses – all extensively refurbished in the last few years.

Public rooms and bedrooms alike are brimful of pictures, including a huge eye-catching abstract in the reception room. Downstairs there are always big bowls of fresh flowers – sweet peas or roses per-haps – and the large rear patio garden is well kept and full of colour. Inside, the dec-oration is richly traditional and harmo-nious. A series of small sitting rooms with Victorian moulded ceilings, polished antiques and luxurious drapes, lead to an award-winning conservatory, from where, on summer days, you can sit and admire the profusion of flowers outside.

Bedrooms are generously propor-tioned, comfortable and stylish, largely fur-nished with period pieces or reproduc-tions; some have French windows opening on to the garden. Breakfast is served in your room or in the public areas. The hotel has no dining room but there are plenty of restaurants on the Old Brompton Road nearby.

181-183 Cromwell Road, London
SW5 0SF

Tel (020)7 244 2000
e-mail enquiries@therockwell.com
website www.therockwell.com

Nearby Kensington High Street,
Earl's Court, South Kensington,
Heathrow (30 minutes on under-
ground) **Location** on Cromwell
Road. Pay parking behind hotel 8.30
am to 6.30 pm and (usually) free
spaces after 6.30. NCP car park in
Holiday Inn - details from reception.
Food breakfast, lunch, dinner
Price £££ **Rooms** 40; 27 double, 13
single, all with shower only, air conditioning, telephone, voicemail, flat
screen satellite TV, free broadband,
safe, minibar **Facilities** bar, dining
room, garden, reception sitting area,
conference room, laundry service,
24-hour room service **Credit cards**
AE, DC, MC, V **Children** welcome
Disabled no specially adapted rooms
but some rooms on ground floor;
lift/elevator **Pets** not accepted
Closed never **Proprietor** Anna
Swainston

The rockwell
Town hotel

We must declare an interest: one of the
backers of The rockwell, a new
London hotel opened in 2006, is architect
Michael Squire, neighbour and sailing cronie
of the guide's publisher. How to write about
it without bias? Some years ago, Squire and
his partners acquired two large, adjoining
houses at the impersonal west end of the
Cromwell Road, opposite the Cromwell
Hospital, and first thought of making them
rooming houses for students. Then, unexpectedly, they got permission for change of
use. Overcoming their worries about the
location, they spent serious money turning
it into a contemporary hotel. The bedrooms, though created out of a variety of
spaces, and very comfortable, seemed at
first a little too much like conventional city
hotel rooms for this guide. But, staying the
night, they grew on us, with their beautiful
oak fittings and large beds with fine sheets.
Most are far from being boxes. Fairly priced,
too. And we found the corridors and con-
necting parts unusually well lit and congenial. But the essential charm we seek came
home when we had drinks in the attractive
garden followed by dinner in the cosy but
coolly decorated little dining room.
Imaginative, carefully prepared food, relaxed
but friendly service and again, fair prices.
Londoners could do a lot worse than eat
out here (see above left for tips on parking).

Peter's Lane, Cowcross Street,
London EC1M 6DS

Tel (020) 7336 0931
Fax (020) 7336 0932
e-mail reservations@rookery.co.uk
website www.rookeryhotel.com

Nearby The City; St Paul's;
Smithfield; Farringdon tube station.
Location in pedestrian street in
Clerkenwell, near Smithfield and
City; parking in nearby public car
park
Food breakfast, room service
Price ££££
Rooms 33; 29 double, 3 single, 1
suite, all with bath; all rooms have
phone, fax/modem points, TV, mini-
bar, hairdryer, safe, wi-fi
Facilities conservatory; terrace
Credit cards AE, DC, MC, V
Children accepted **Disabled** 4 bed-
rooms on ground floor **Pets** accept-
ed by arrangement
Closed Christmas **Proprietors**
Peter McKay and Douglas Blaine

The Rookery
Town hotel

Opened by the owners of the imaginative Hazlitt's and the Gore (see pages
106 and 105), this homely little hotel full of
old curiosities and flights of fancy is in a
traffic-free alleyway among the restaurants
of fashionable Clerkenwell. Created from a
row of converted listed Georgian cottages,
it is packed with character and 'time-warp'
detail: wood panelling; period shutters; open
fires; flagged floors; even a special creaky
sound put into the treads of the new stairs
to make them seem old. Pretty bedrooms
have little half-shutters, fresh Egyptian cotton sheets, summer and winter duvets.
Minibars and 'workstations' are discreetly
hidden behind antique doors. Bathrooms
are delightful, with Victorian fittings,
exposed copper pipes and wainscotting.
The suite, on two floors, has a rococo
French bed, attendant blackamoor and an
Edwardian bathing machine; an electronical-
ly controlled panel shuts off the upper floor
for business meetings.

A conservatory, with open fire and leather
chairs, serves as a day room, opening on to a
tiny terrace garden. Breakfast, continental, is
on trays: fresh orange juice, coffee and croissants prepared and baked by the hotel's own
pâtissier. We visited recently and enjoyed the
vaguely Dickensian atmosphere as much as
ever. Try nearby Portal restaurant in St John
Street – good Portuguese food.

5 Sumner Place, London SW7 3EE

Tel (020) 7723 2244
Fax (0870) 705 8767
e-mail hotel@the sumner.com
website www.thesumner.com

Nearby Oxford Street shopping,
West End, Hyde Park.
Location on Upper Berkeley Street,
2 streets north of Marble Arch, 5
mins walk from Marble Arch tube;
NCP metered parking on street
Food breakfast
Price £££
Rooms 20 double/twin; all with
shower, 2 with bath; all rooms have
LCD TV, air conditioning, hairdry-
er, minibar, wi-fi/cable broadband
Facilities sitting room, dining room
Credit cards AE, DC, MC, V
Children accepted over 6 **Disabled**
bedrooms on ground floor, lift/ele-
vator **Pets** not accepted **Closed**
never **Proprietors** Palgan family

The Sumner
Town bed-and-breakfast

The Palgan family, who ran Five Sumner
Place (long in the guide) until it closed,
completed renovations of this Georgian
town house in 2006, when it opened as The
Sumner. The results of their £1.5m invest-
ment are impressive – the place is immaculate and stylishly done, without being over-
designed. The amiable young manager Peter
Palgan says they wanted to find a balance
between comfort and design, and they seem
to have found it.

The hotel's staff are charmingly friendly
and the place has a very comfortable and
friendly feel – Peter says they want their
guests to feel that they are coming back to
a private home (albeit a rather grand one).

The stylish sitting room is particularly
striking – its high Georgian ceilings and original cornicing are complemented with a
beautiful wooden floor, muted colours and
warm browns, chunky dark wood furniture
and inviting, deep sofas.

Bedrooms are generously proportioned,
particularly those on the ground and first
floors, which have very high ceilings. The
'deluxe' rooms are very stylish, and the one
our inspector saw had a huge walk-in shower. Bathrooms are spotless: white-tiled, with
a block of turquoise colour. The 'executive'
and double rooms are also a good size,
though perhaps less individually decorated
than the 'deluxe'. Reports welcome.

9-11 Sydney Street, London,
SW3 6PU

Tel (020) 7376 7711
e-mail
info@sydneyhousechelsea.com
website
www.sydneyhousechelsea.com

Nearby Harrods, Victoria & Albert
Museum, Natural History Museum
Location between Fulham Road and
Kings Road; no parking but two
NCP car parks nearby (corner of
Sydney St & Kings Road, Sloane
Avenue)
Food breakfast, 24 hour room serv-
ice (limited after 10pm)
Price ££££
Rooms 21 double, plus 'room at the
top'; all have shower, 11 have baths.
All have telephone, flat-screen TV,
DVD player, hairdryer, combination
safe and internet access **Facilities**
sitting room, bar, breakfast room
Credit cards AE, DC, MC, V
Children welcome **Disabled** not
suitable **Pets** not accepted**Closed**
never **Proprietor** Andrew
Brownsword

Sydney House Chelsea
Town guest-house

On a handsome residential street,
announced only by a subtle name-
plate, Sydney House could be a private
residence – clearly a draw for its many
regular guests, some of whom stay weekly
while in London on business.

Andrew Brownsword, owner of Gidleigh
Park (page 42) and Bath Priory, bought this
elegant grade II listed Georgian town
house in 2002, totally refurbishing it.
Original features are found alongside
sophisticated, modern decoration and furnishings. Neutral colours dominate the
reception/sitting area, where a large palm,
modern tapestries and matching cushions
in the suede-covered chairs add splashes
of colour.

Bedrooms are smart and fresh, with
clean, light bathrooms. The 'room at the
top', set on the seventh floor, is perhaps
surprisingly small, but leads out on to its
own generously-sized private terrace, with
wooden table and chairs and an area
heater – so you can take in the impressive
views over London year-round.

The staff at Sydney House are immacu-
lately presented, professional and courteous but seemed to be feeling the strain of
too many visitors. We wondered whether
the high volume of guests might take its
toll on the interior, or on the service.
Reports welcome.

London

Twenty Nevern Square, London
SW5 9PD

Tel (020) 7565 9555
Fax (020) 7565 9444
e-mail
hotel@twentynevernsquare.co.uk
website
www.twentynevernsquare.co.uk

Nearby Earl's Court Exhibition
Centre, Natural History Museum,
Victoria and Albert Museum.
Location 2-minute walk from Earl's
Court tube station, with 4 car park-
ing spaces on secure lot, £17.50 per
night, must be pre-booked
Food breakfast, 24 hr room service
Price ££
Rooms 20; 6 single, 14 double or
twin, all with shower or bath; all
rooms have TV, stereo, phone,
hairdryer
Facilities restaurant, sitting room
Credit cards AE, DC, MC, V
Children accepted
Disabled access difficult
Pets not accepted **Closed** never
Manager Sulaiman Saloojee

Twenty Nevern Square
Town house hotel

Peace and tranquility aren't two words
usually associated with London but,
just around the corner from bustling Earl's
Court, Twenty Nevern Square is suprising-
ly calm and cosy. Set across from a graceful private square, this town house hotel is
compact rather than cramped and intimate rather than uncomfortable.

Decorated in a combination of colonial
and italian influences, rooms have a feeling
of understated luxury. Natural fabrics have
been used throughout; silk curtains, wood-
en floors and hessian carpets blend nicely
with muted walls and smart patterned
bedspreads. One hundred metres of silk
has been used in decorating the Chinese
room, with oriental-print cushions and
floor-to-ceiling white and navy drapes and
a unique hand-carved cabinet resembling a
temple. Four bedrooms have delightful
'sleigh' beds and two others have terraces
that look down into local backyard gardens. Bathrooms are brick, smart and done
out entirely in marble.

Breakfast is served downstairs in the the
conservatory-style restaurant. In the small
sitting room, two lovebirds in a wicker cage
twitter happily to themselves. After our
visit to Twenty Nevern Square, we felt pretty content, too.

St Johns Square, 86-88 Clerkenwell
Road, London, EC1M 5RJ

Tel (020) 7324 4444
Fax (020) 7324 4456
e-mail info@thezetter.com
website www.thezetter.com

Nearby Farringdon tube, Barbican,
Old Spitalfields Market, Liverpool
St Station
Location Location: off A5201
Clerkenwell road; NCP parking
around the corner (residents at hotel
get discount)
Food breakfast, lunch, dinner
Price £££-££££
Rooms 59; all doubles with shower;
all rooms have phone, TV,
CD/DVD players, hairdryers, safe,
air-con, w-ifi **Facilities** restaurant,
sitting room, terrace with tables, 2
board rooms with private kitchen
Credit cards AE, MC, V **Children**
accepted **Disabled** 1 room **Pets** not
accepted **Closed** hotel: never;
restaurant closed over Christmas and
New Year **Proprietors** Mark
Sainsbury and Michael Benyan

The Zetter
Town hotel

This is one of the new breed of eco-
friendly hotels gaining popularity in
London. Water is pumped from its own
bore hole, supplying the rooms and air
conditioning. When it gets too hot, the sky-
lights in the glass atrium pop open for ven-
tilation; the room keys control the lights, so
no energy is wasted when you leave.

The bar, restaurant and terrace are all
done out in kitsch, retro style which manages, thankfully, not to be garish. The
restaurant is wonderfully light thanks to
the floor-to-ceiling windows. The food is
best described as 'modern Mediterranean';
note the selection of cocktails.

The bedrooms are stacked over 4/5
storeys, clustered around the central atrium: quite a dizzying sight from the ground
floor. Their colours might not be to everyone's taste: neon pinks, greens and blues –
but they are all of a fairish size and peaceful. Complimentary hot water bottles. The
seven roof-top suites have great views
from their private balconies.

The Zetter room service is self service:
located near the bedrooms on each floor
are vending machines. Swipe your room
card, and they give you tea, coffee, wine
and snacks, adding the cost to the bill.

Lymington, Hampshire

High Street, Lymington,
Hampshire, SO41 9AA

Tel (01590) 677123
Fax (01590) 677756
e-mail
sales@stanwellhousehotel.co.uk
website www.stanwellhouse.com

Nearby New Forest; Beaulieu; Isle
of Wight.
Location on High Street, close to
the quay and marina; public car
parks nearby
Food breakfast, lunch dinner
Price £££
Rooms 27; 12 double, 8 twin, 4 luxury suites; 3 four-posters; all with
bath, 1 with shower; all rooms have
phone, plasma TV, hairdryer
Facilities conservatory, bar, dining
room, bistro, seafood restaurant;
garden **Credit cards** AE, DC, MC,
V **Children** welcome **Disabled**
access difficult **Pets** accepted **Closed**
never **Proprietors** Robert Milton
and Victoria Crowe

Stanwell House
Town hotel

Until a recent reincarnation, Stanwell
House Hotel was a fading Georgian
landmark in the prettiest part of
Lymington's attractive High Street. When
Jane McIntyre took over in 1995 the place
was transformed: an Italianate stone-
flagged courtyard now stretches the length
of the building, affording inviting views from
the street of a glass-roofed sitting room
strewn with velvet cushions; on one side of
the entrance is a smart country clothing
shop, Stanwells, on the other a new
seafood restaurant in simple 17thC style –
dark walls, oak settles, pewter plates and a
trompe l'oeil fireplace.

The candle-lit restaurant – steel chairs
upholstered in purple, cerise, pink and
deep red velvet, swathes of silk curtains –
and the bedrooms in the main house are
theatrical, not to say over the top.
Dramatic walls, rich hangings and piles of
white cushions vie for attention. The bedrooms in the extension are a lesson in
how to make undistinguished rooms look
pretty and welcoming. The place attracts a
laid-back youngish clientèle.

As we went to press, Stanwell House
had just been taken over by Robert Milton
and Victoria Crowe, who have already
redecorated, aiming to make the place
smarter. Readers' comments welcome.

Petworth, West Sussex

Petworth, West Sussex
GU28 0JF

Tel (01798) 342346
Fax (01798) 343066
e-mail info@old-station.co.uk
website www.old-station.co.uk

Nearby Petworth.
Location just S of Petworth off
A285, ample parking
Food breakfast
Price ££–£££
Rooms 10 doubles, all with bath; all
rooms with TV, radio, hairdryer
Facilities breakfast room, sitting
room; terrace
Credit cards AE, MC, V
Children accepted over 10
Disabled by arrangement
Pets not accepted
Closed Christmas
Proprietors Gudmund Olafsson and
Catherine Stormont

The Old Railway Station

Bed-and-breakfast

If you've ever dreamed about stepping back in time and taking a great rail journey, now you can do just that – in West Sussex. The Old Railway Station provides unique accommodation in either the original Petworth Railway Station building, dating from 1892, or in one of four Pullman carriages.

The station building, now Grade II listed, is both impressive and welcoming. The former waiting-room, which now contains the breakfast room and sitting-room, has 20-foot vaulted ceilings, original ticket office windows and, in winter, a roaring log fire. In the summer, you can enjoy breakfast on the terrace, which was the station platform.

At the other end of the platform sit four Edwardian Pullman carriages, just like the ones used by the Orient Express.

Because of the obvious space constraints, bedrooms and bathrooms are narrow, but very long. Original furnishings, marquetry in the walls and antique luggage and clocks all add to the charm, though bathrooms are modern. Beds are large – almost as wide as the carriages – and inviting.

Inside the main building are two bedrooms, one at the top of a book-lined spiral staircase (the library). Both are spacious and well-fitted out and one has an original stained glass window in the bathroom that overlooks the waiting room. Some recent visitors found it expensive.

Reading, Berkshire

26 The Forbury, Reading,
Berkshire, RG1 3EJ

Tel (08000) 789789
Fax (0118) 959 3061
e-mail info@theforburyhotel.co.uk
website www.theforburyhotel.co.uk

Nearby Abbey Ruins, Blakes Lock
Museum
Location off A329 in centre of town
just off Valpy street with valet park-
ing
Food breakfast, lunch, dinner
Price ££££
Rooms 24; 15 superior doubles, 4
luxury, 4 suites, 1 grand suite (4 of
doubles can be twins) 23 rooms have
bath and shower, 1 has just shower;
all rooms have TV, phone, hairdryer,
wi-fi **Facilities** cinema, library, sit-
ting room, grand salon **Credit cards**
AE, MC, V **Children** accepted
Disabled 1 room **Pets** not accepted
Closed never **Proprietor** Toby
Hunter

The Forbury
City hotel

Our inspector wrote: 'I am reclining on
a *chaise longue* draped with a fur
throw. Warmed by a cosy fire in the marble
hearth, lulled by the voice of José Gonzalez
on the Bang & Olufson entertainment system, which includes a plasma TV screen that
tracks you as you move around the room.'

'I have just emerged from a soak in an
oval glass bath designed for two, where the
water slid from the wall in a sheet and tiny
pinpricks of coloured lights twinkled in the
mosaic ceiling above. Music plays; candles
flicker, the towels are large and fluffy, the
bathrobe velvety. The shower doubles as a
steam sauna.'

The Forbury was built, in grand Queen
Anne style, as County Council headquarters
in 1912. Latterly it was used as serviced
offices until its present owner, property
developer Toby Hunter, decided to create a
hotel with – and this is astonishing, given the
scale of the place – just 24 bedrooms. It feels
intimate and could claim to be one of
Britain's sexiest bolt-holes. Its lofty principal
room (described so lyrically above) was once
a council chamber, but is now serenely quiet
and stunningly decorated.

Some minor quibbles: the staff, though
committed, were learning the ropes when
we visited; the food is perhaps a little predictable; and there's more character in the
hotel's design than in its surroundings.

Ringlestone, Kent

Ringlestone Hamlet, near
Harrietsham, Maidstone, Kent
ME17 1NX

Tel (01622) 859911
Fax (01622) 859740
e-mail
bookings@ringlestonehouse.co.uk
website www.ringlestone.co.uk

Nearby Leeds Castle; Sissinghurst;
Canterbury; Rochester; Rye.
Location in hamlet; off A20,
between Harrietsham and
Wormshill; car parking
Food breakfast, lunch, dinner
Price £££
Rooms 3 double and twin, all with
bath; all rooms have phone, TV, CD
player, hairdryer, minibar, trouser
press
Facilities dining room, sitting room;
garden, terrace
Credit cards AE, DC, MC, V
Children accepted
Disabled access difficult **Pets** not
accepted **Closed** Christmas
Proprietors Mike Millington-Buck
and Michele Taylor

Ringlestone House
Country house bed-and-breakfast

Affable Mike Millington-Buck (he used to run Leeds Castle) had this secluded little hamlet up on the downs buzzing with projects, when our last edition went to press. The centrepiece, a 16thC inn, once used as a hospice for monks, with warm, traditional, oak-beamed bars offering good food, home-made pies, English fruit wines, and French house and chateaux wines, has since been taken over by Shepherd Neame.

Ringlestone House – the converted, tile-hing Kentish farmhouse over the road from the inn – remains in the hands of Mike and his daughter Michele Taylor, and continues to provide very comfortable lodgings. One entry in the Visitor's Book remarks 'You've thought of everything'. Indeed, these are delightful rooms, with cream natural fabrics, French rustic furniture, pretty white embroidered sheets and pillow cases and spotless bathrooms with power showers, but it is the thoughtfulness here that impresses. Summer and winter duvets, a whole tea-set in your room so you can invite friends in, a washing machine and ironing board on the landing, three kinds of breakfast, including a tray in your room, and a housekeeper, Jane, to look after any other needs. Reports welcome.

Rushlake Green, East Sussex

Rushlake Green, Heathfield,
East Sussex TN21 9QJ

Tel (01435) 830553
Fax (01435) 830726
website
www.stonehousesussex.co.uk

Nearby Battle; Glyndebourne.
Location just off village green 3
miles (4.5 km) SE of Heathfield, in
large grounds with ample car parking
Food breakfast, lunch by arrangement, dinner
Price £££
Rooms 6 double and twin, all with
bath; all rooms have phone, TV,
hairdryer, wi-fi
Facilities sitting room, library, dining room; billiards, snooker; gardens, croquet, fishing, shooting
Credit cards MC, V
Children welcome over 9
Disabled access difficult **Pets**
accepted in bedrooms only
Closed Christmas to 6 Jan
Proprietors Peter and Jane Dunn

Stone House
Country house hotel

Our latest reporter enthusiastically agrees with everything we have said about Stone House in the past. It is Peter and Jane Dunn's ancestral family home, a glorious 16thC manor house. The delightful Jane ('old world and lovely manners') does what she enjoys most – cooking, and looking after her guests individually. Her relaxed and friendly demeanour belies a very sure touch, and Stone House is run with great competence – which means it is much in demand for house parties, Glyndebourne visitors (luxury wicker picnic hampers can be prepared), shooting weekends and even small executive conferences. They have recently created a Victorian walled vegetable garden and an 18thC-style rose garden. Wine has become a hobby for Peter and Jane, and they are justly proud of their wine list.

Bedooms are beautifully decorated; two have fine antique four-posters and are particularly spacious (the bathrooms can double as sitting rooms). Televisions are hidden so as not to spoil the period charm. An excellent place in which to sample authentic English country living at its most gracious – log fires and billiards, woodland walks and croquet – together with the atmosphere of a home. A favourite of the guide for many years, we have had consistently good feedback.

Rye, East Sussex

98 High Street Rye, East Sussex
TN31 7JT

Tel (01797) 222114
Fax (01797) 224065
e-mail stay@thegeorgeinrye.com
website www.thegeorgeinrye.com

Nearby Camber Sands, Great
Dixter Gardens, Bodiam castle,
Hastings Old Town, Sissinghurst
castle gardens
Location off A259 in centre of town
with no car parking
Food breakfast, lunch, dinner
Price £££
Rooms 5 junior suites, 14 deluxe
doubles, 7 can be twin; all rooms
have bath and shower; all rooms
have phone, TV, CD, DVD,
hairdryer, wi-fi **Facilities** ballroom,
restaurant, private dining room,
courtyard garden, bar
Credit cards AE, MC, V
Children accepted **Disabled** access
difficult **Pets** not accepted
Closed never **Proprietor** Alex and
Katie Clarke

The George in Rye
Seaside hotel

The George is a Rye institution enjoying a new life. In 2005 it was bought by Katie Clarke and her husband Alex. They lived with swirly carpets and partition walls for a year "to get the feel of the place" then attacked, closing for eight months and reopening with stunning results.

At one end of the entrance hall, panelled walls and a huge hearth create a cosy sitting area, while the other side shows the hotel's contemporary face, with psychedelic portraits of the Beatles adding warm splashes of colour. By contrast, the sprawling bar at the back is somehow less inviting – the panelled sitting room is perhaps has a better ambience for pre-dinner drinks.

Katie, a set designer, is responsible for the 24 delicious bedrooms, designing much of the furniture herself. A warren of stairs and corridors leads to the rooms, each different, demonstrating her confident eye for colour as well as comfort.

The dining room, though elegant, doesn't have quite the allure of the bedrooms or lobby. However, ex-Moro chef Rod Grossman's food is memorable. If the 2003 Pinot Noir from Sandhurst Vineyard in Kent is on the winelist, try it. They're making every effort to provide quality at affordable prices here – long may it last.

Rye, East Sussex

Mermaid Street, Rye, East Sussex
TN31 7ET

Tel (01797) 222828
Fax (01797) 222623
e-mail jeakeshouse@btinternet.com
website www.jeakeshouse.com

Nearby Great Dixter; Ellen Terry
Museum, 1066 country.
Location in centre of Rye; private
car parking nearby
Food breakfast
Price ££
Rooms 11; 7 double and twin, 1 sin-
gle, 2 family rooms, 1 suite; 9 rooms
with bath, 1 with private bath across
hall; all rooms have TV, phone
Facilities dining room, sitting room,
bar **Credit cards** MC, V
Children accepted over 8
Disabled access difficult **Pets** by
arrangement **Closed** never
Proprietor Jenny Hadfield

Jeake's House
Town house bed-and-breakfast

This splendid 17thC house – or rather three houses turned into one – has been lovingly restored to make a delightful small hotel: a verdict confirmed by many readers, who return time after time. It is the domaine of Jenny Hadfield, who used to be an operatic soprano, and although the place is essentially a charming small hotel, she has lent it a certain theatrical quality. Originally built as a wool store in 1689, it later became a Baptist school and, earlier this century, the home of American writer Conrad Potter Aiken, when it played host to many of the leading artistic and literary figures of the time.

The beamed bedrooms, which come in various shapes and sizes, overlook either the old roof-tops of Rye or Romney Marsh. Bedsteads are either brass or mahogany (some are four-poster), bedspreads lace, furniture antique. There are plenty of thoughtful extras in the rooms. Downstairs, a galleried ex-chapel makes the grandest of breakfast rooms. A roaring fire greets guests on cold mornings, and Jenny will serve you either a traditional breakfast or a vegetarian alternative. There is a comfortable parlour with a piano and a bar, with books and pictures lining the walls. 'Situated on the street in Rye (the cobbled Mermaid Street) within walking distance of all the sights,' says our inspector. This will suit our older readers.

St Leonards-on-Sea, East Sussex

9 Eversfield Place,
St-Leonards-on-Sea, TN37 6BY

Tel (01424) 460109
e-mail info@zanzibarhotel.co.uk
website www.zanzibarhotel.co.uk

Nearby Hastings old town, Hastings
Fort
Location on seafront near Warrior
Square, just off A21; permit parking
at the front of the hotel
Food breakfast
Price ££-£££
Rooms 8 double, all with
shower/bath; all rooms have
flatscreen TV with freeview, DVD,
hairdryer, ironing board, iron, tea
and coffee making facilities, fridge
with milk/water
Facilities sitting room, garden, hon-
esty bar
Credit cards DC, MC, V
Children welcome
Disabled access difficult
Pets small dogs only
Closed never
Proprietor Max O'Rourke

Zanzibar
Seaside town house hotel

The somewhat run-down seaside town
of St Leonards-on-Sea is not over-
whelmed with hotels worth writing about,
but this stylish and relaxed place stands out.
Zanzibar occupies a Victorian seafront
town house which has been restored and
modernised by its enthusiastic and hands-
on owner, Max O'Rourke. On arrival, along
with your complimentary glass of champagne you are given a parking permit, a
key, and advice on where to go if you want
to explore. The ethos here is very much
'make yourself at home', though the
friendly staff are always on hand.

Zanzibar's eight rooms are individually
themed around a region of the world and
the decoration and furniture subtly reflect
this, adding a unique character to each without going over the top. Every bathroom has
a special feature – in 'Antarctica' where our
inspector stayed, it was a combined show-
er/sauna. Breakfast is ordered the previous evening and delivered hot to your
room, or the grand salon. Choices include
kippers, poached eggs, smoked salmon and
a 'full English' – all fresh and delicious.

Max says: "the best thing about Hastings
and St Leonards is that there isn't that much
to do", and the steady stream of (mostly)
Londoners coming to Zanzibar for a refreshingly calm, relaxing break, seem to agree.

Seaview, Isle of Wight

Priory Drive, Seaview, Isle of Wight
PO34 5BU

Tel (01983) 613146
Fax (01983) 616539
e-mail enquiries@priorybay.co.uk
website www.priorybay.co.uk

Nearby Osborne House; Bembridge
Maritime Museum; Cowes.
Location in own grounds with private beach, on B3330 S of Seaview
between Nettlestone and St Helens;
ample car parking
Food breakfast, lunch, dinner
Price ££-££££
Rooms 18 double and twin, all with
bath; all rooms have phone, TV,
hairdryer; also 10 self-catering cottages
Facilities drawing room, sitting
room, bar, 2 dining rooms; garden,
6-hole golf course, tennis, swimming
pool, private beach, sailing, fishing,
windsurfing,**Credit cards** AE, MC,
V **Children** welcome **Disabled**
access possible **Pets** not accepted
Closed never **Proprietors** Andrew
and James Palmer

Priory Bay Hotel
Seaside hotel

When Andrew Palmer's motorboat
broke down on the sweeping private beach of Priory Bay, he stumbled on
an old-fashioned hotel with extensive
grounds that he never knew existed,
despite a lifetime of holidaying in the area.
He bought it, and with the help of a talented friend, Annabel Claridge, effected a
stunning transformation, opening in summer 1998. Bedrooms are decorated with
charm and freshness, each different, some
seaside simple, others more dramatic. The
house itself has a colourful history and a
quirky hotch-potch of styles with a Tudor
farmhouse at its core and a Norman tithe
barn in the grounds. Memorable details
include the Gothic church porch brought
from France in the 1930s, the Tudor fireplace depicting the Sacrifice of Isaac, and
the delightful Georgian murals of pastoral
island scenes in the dining room. Less lovely are the grounds – or so we thought last
time we visited – and the scattered
oubuildings, some barrack-like. The highlight is the wonderful sweep of beach
where children can be kept happy for hours
(this is an extremely child-friendly hotel).
Dinner, on our visit, was very good.

Reports welcome.

Seaview, Isle of Wight

High Street, Seaview, Isle of Wight
PO34 5EX

Tel (01983) 612711
Fax (01983) 613729
e-mail reception@seaviewhotel.co.uk
website www.seaviewhotel.co.uk

Nearby Osborne House; Flamingo
Park; Bembridge.
Location near the beach in seaside
village 3 miles (5 km) E of Ryde; car
parking
Food breakfast, lunch, dinner; room
service
Price ££
Rooms 27; 16 double, 11 twin, all
with bath/shower; 2 suites both with
bath; 2 self-catering cottages; all
rooms have phone, satellite TV,
hairdryer **Facilities** sitting room, 2
dining rooms, 2 bars **Credit cards**
AE, DC, MC, V **Children** welcome
Disabled new wing has disabled
facilities **Pets** not accepted in hotel
Closed never **Proprietor** Brian
Gardener

Seaview Hotel
Seaside town hotel

If you like breezy, old-fashioned English
seaside resorts, you will love sailing-mad
Seaview, and probably this hotel, which
also acts as the central pub of the village.
The Seaview was run enthusiastically by
the Hayward family for more than 20
years, until it was bought by Brian
Gardener in 2003. Since then a whole new
wing has been built, adding a further seven
rooms, and greatly improving disabled
facilities. The whole hotel has been thoroughly refurbished and redecorated, with
Keech Green Interiors designing the bedrooms in the new wing. We are told that
Brian's aim when taking over the Seaview
was to create a place which was on a par
with the most stylish London boutique
hotels, but by the sea.

There are two public bars, towards the
rear of the building, and two restaurants,
both serving the same menu. One, called
the Sunshine Room, but actually painted
blue, is an airy room with a contemporary
feel. The other is more formal, with a nau-
tical bar. New chef Graham Walker, who
worked in several Michelin-starred restaurants before coming here, uses locally-
caught seafood. We would welcome comments on the food and on whether the high
standards and personal service enjoyed
here previously are being maintained.

Sidlesham, West Sussex

Mill Lane, Sidlesham
West Sussex, PO20 7NB

Tel (01243) 641233
e-mail enquiries@crab-lobster.co.uk
website www.crab-lobster.co.uk

Nearby Chichester, Selsey Bill,
Bosham, Pagham harbour walk and
nature reserve
Location on B1245 south of
Chichester
Food breakfast, lunch, dinner
Price £££
Rooms 4 double; 1 with shower
only, 3 with bath; 2-bed self-catering
cottage
Facilities bar, dining room, terrace,
garden; internet connection
Credit cards AE, MC, V
Children accepted
Disabled access possible to restau-
rant only
Pets not accepted
Closed never
Proprietor Sam Bakose

The Crab and Lobster
Restaurant with rooms

The landscape surrounding The Crab
and Lobster is enchanting: salt marsh
and woodland interlaced with watery
creeks stretching across Pagham Harbour
to the distant sea. Despite its spanking
new interior, this 350 year-old building
offers, with its slate floors, cream painted
or bare brick walls and open fire, sophisticated charm.

There are four bedrooms. Our inspector stayed in one under the eaves – smartly decorated with white walls and black
beams, but too small and awkward a space,
perhaps, to justify its £140 price tag. The
telescope was a thoughtful touch, though
the business-like, wall-mounted plasma TV
seemed out of place and detracted from
the cosy hideaway feel. The elegant bathroom has a velvet chaise longue (great
touch), but was lacking in shelf space.

But these are niggles. The Crab and
Lobster is a stylish waterside hideaway,
and what's more the food is excellent.
Dinner was a great success: local crab and
lobster, superbly dressed, plus sea bass
that had been brought to the door that
day by a local fisherman, a fine mushroom
risotto with wild ceps and a couple of bottles of Sancerre – perfect.

The Royal Oak in nearby East Lavant is
under the same ownership (01243 527434).

Stockbridge, Hampshire

Village Street, Longstock,
Stockbridge, Hampshire SO20 6DR

Tel (01264) 810612
Fax (01264) 811078
e-mail info@peatspadeinn.co.uk
website www.peatspadeinn.co.uk

Nearby Stockbridge, Romsey,
Winchester, Test Valley fishing and
fisheries
Location in sleepy village centre
with off road car parking
Food breakfast, lunch, dinner
Price ££
Rooms 6 doubles, all with bath
shower; all rooms have phone, TV,
hairdryer, minibar
Facilities bar, dining room, court-
yard, lounge, terrace, in-house sport-
ing agents
Credit cards MC, V
Children over 10
Disabled access difficult
Pets not accepted
Closed Christmas Day and Boxing
Day **Proprietors** Lucy Townsend
and Andrew Clark

Peat Spade Inn
Village inn

'A charming mix of traditional and new,
rustic and efficient' says our reporter.
If the interior photo looks familiar, then you
are right: the place owes much to the Hotel
du Vin mini 'chain'. Lucy and Andrew, who
acquired this old Test Valley fishing inn in
2004 and reopened it in 2006 having completely reconceived it, used to work with
Robin Hutson, the founder of Hotel du Vin
and of course with Robin's co-director and
sommelier, Gerard Basset. Robin remains
their mentor; Robin's wife Judy did the interior decoration and Basset masterminded
the wine list.

The bar-dining area is rustic-smart with
clean white napkins on scrubbed pine tables;
the food OK – ambitious but given the
prices perhaps in some respects not quite
there; our reporter's room – restful browns
and greens and wide oak floor boards in the
bathroom, excellent cotton sheets on a
thoroughly comfortable bed – homely, restful, comfortable. Lucy and Andrew, as befits
Thatcher lovers and Blair haters ('If he
comes through the door, I'll turn him away')
are attacking this, their first venture, as proprietors with proper commitment and to
prove it Lucy has learned to fly fish and shoot clays.
Ask about their fishing weekends for
novices and experts, individuals and compa-
nies. Ghillies and tutors to order.

Ventnor, Isle of Wight

Hambrough Road, Ventnor,
Isle of Wight, PO38 1SQ

Tel (01983) 856333
e-mail info@thehambrough.com
website www.thehambrough.com

Nearby Botanic Gardens, St
Lawrence, Bonchurch
Location off the A3055 on
Hamborough road with car parking
Food breakfast, lunch, dinner
Price ££-£££
Rooms 7; 2 suites, 5 doubles, 6 with
bath and shower 1 with shower only;
all rooms have phone, TV, CD,
DVD, hairdryer, wi-fi
Facilities bar, private dining room,
chefs table, spa treatments, restau-
rant, garden
Credit cards MC, V
Children accepted
Disabled access difficult
Pets not accepted
Closed never
Proprietor Jo Dos Santos

Hambrough Hotel
Seaside hotel

Ventnor, a world away from the Isle of
Wight's north coast, is a pretty
Victorian cliff-top town with winter gardens, an esplanade, a sandy beach and a
shack selling crab and lobster. The
Hambrough stands mid-way between the
High Street and the seafront, overlooking
the Cascade Gardens and the little harbour. It has seven spacious bedrooms, a
restaurant, a small sitting room and a bar. It
doesn't aim to do too much, but what it
does, it hopes to do well, and at a fair price.

By and large, it succeeds. The restaurant
is making waves locally and the set-menu
six-course 'gourmet dinners', well chosen
wines included, are a notably good deal at
£45 a head when we went to press, as are
the lunches at £14.95 for three courses. A
serious kitchen (complete with "chef's
table" from where guests can watch the
action) opens off an all-white dining room.

Our inspector had absolute quiet in her
spacious room: muted colours, large bed
with cotton waffle, sofa facing the window,
DVDs, minibar, espresso machine. Her only
quibbles: the service, though professional,
lacked warmth; and the overall feel of the
house is more stylish rather than truly
characterful.

Wickham, Hampshire

The Square, Wickham, Hampshire
PO17 5JG

Tel (01329) 833049
Fax (01329) 833672
e-mail info@oldhousehotel.com
website www.oldhousehotel.co.uk

Nearby Portsmouth (ferries); South
Downs; Winchester, Chichester.
Location 2.5 miles (4 km) N of
Fareham, on square in middle of vil-
lage; car parking
Food breakfast, lunch, dinner
Price ££
Rooms 15 double, all with bath; all
rooms have TV, phone, hairdryer
Facilities sitting room, 3 dining
rooms, bar
Credit cards AE, MC, V
Children accepted **Disabled** access
difficult **Pets** not accepted
Closed never **Proprietor** John
Guess

Old House
Village hotel

The Old House, a stalwart of the guide
for many years, possesses much that
we look for: an interesting setting – at a
corner of the main square of one of the
finest villages in Hampshire; a superb building – Grade II listed early Georgian; a
delightful secluded garden; an immaculately kept and welcoming interior, with
antiques and 'objets' arranged to the best
possible effect; and an attractive restaurant, created from the original timber-
framed outhouse and stables.

Nothing is over-stated. Bedrooms vary
considerably – some palatial, others with
magnificent beams, one or two rather
cramped – but again a mood of civilized
comfort prevails. Our reporter remarked
on the imposing carved bar and the attractive beame d dining room. However, times
are changing for the Old House, and it has
changed hands several times in recent
years. New owner John Guess arrived in
2007, and began redecorating, with the aim
of continuing improvements. The decorations, the ambience and even the French
regional menu have happily stayed largely
the same and so, it seems, does the warmth
of welcome. A reader writes: 'lovely bedrooms... staff excellent... food delicious...
they deserve to do well as so much thought
is put into providing a lovely experience.'

Winchester, Hampshire

14 Southgate Street, Winchester, Hampshire SO23 9EF

Tel (01962) 841414
Fax (01962) 842458
e-mail reception.winchester@hotel-duvin.com **website** www.hotelduvin.com

Nearby Cathedral; Venta Roman Museum; Winchester College.
Location in the town centre, a minute's walk from the cathedral; ample car parking
Food breakfast, lunch, dinner; room service
Price £££
Rooms 23; 22 double and twin, 1 suite, all with bath; all rooms have phone, TV, CD player, minibar, hairdryer
Facilities sitting room, dining room/breakfast room, private dining room, bar, wine-tasting cellar; garden, boules **Credit cards** AE, DC, MC, V **Children** welcome
Disabled several bedrooms on ground floor **Pets** not accepted
Closed never **Manager** Phil Lewis

Hotel du Vin
Town house hotel

There is still an alluring buzz in the air at this stylish, affordable Georgian town house, flagship of the Hotel du Vin mini-chain – even though it's been taken over by Malmaison, a large hotel group (see also pages 40, 91 and 245). This was the original Hotel du Vin and it's got panache. The wood-floored, hop-garlanded Bistro sets the tone: staffed by a charming bunch of mainly French youngsters, it has the intimate, slightly chaotic yet professional air of the genuine article. Start with a bucket of champagne in the voluptuous mirrored and muralled bar, then choose a bottle from the inventive, kindly priced wine list to go with the inventive, sunny, Modern English food.

The bedrooms and bathrooms are every bit as appealing, with fresh Egyptian cotton bedlinen, CD players, capacious baths and huge showers. For maximum quiet, ask for a Garden Room, or splash out on the sensuous Durney Vineyards suite with a four-poster draped in maroon velvet, a black slate double shower and murals depicting famous paintings of nudes. A continental 'Breakfast in Bed' is available as part of the room service. There is also a loftily proportioned sitting room, its walls decorated with *trompe l'oeil* panelling in delicious shades of caramel and pale green.

Winchester, Hampshire

75 Kingsgate Street, Winchester,
Hampshire SO23 9PE

Tel (01962) 853834
Fax (01962) 854411

Nearby Cathedral; Venta Roman
Museum; Winchester College.
Location next door to College, on
corner of Canon Street; small court-
yard garden with some car parking
Food breakfast, lunch, dinner
Price ££
Rooms 14, 9 double with bath, 2
twin with bath, 2 single with shower;
all rooms have phone, TV, wi-fi
Facilities sitting room, 2 bars, patio
Credit cards AE, MC, V
Children welcome over 14
Disabled access difficult
Pets welcome
Closed Christmas Day **Managers**
Kate and Peter Miller

Wykeham Arms
Town inn

'Enormously charming; tons of person-
ality,' confirms our latest reporter.
Tucked away in the quietest, oldest part of
the city, with Winchester College only
yards away and the Cathedral also close by,
this is primarily a well-frequented local
pub, and a first-rate one: 250 years old with
four cosy bars furnished with old school
desks, one engraved with the Winchester
motto, Manners Makyth Man. Interesting
objects – old squash rackets, peculiar walking sticks – line the warm brick-red walls.
This quirky character runs to the bedrooms, which are small in proportion and
low-ceilinged, but each furnished in its own
style with a personal feel, and adapted to
accommodate all the usual facilities.

   Breakfast is served upstairs, over the pub,
in a pleasant straightforward English country breakfast room with Windsor chairs and
a fine collection of silver tankards. Hearty
pub food at lunch time and an *a la carte*
menu in the evenings; real ales and an
impressive list of over 100 wines, changed
regularly, 20 served by the glass. Outside is a
cobbled courtyard. Over the road is the
'Saint George' annexe with seven pleasant
bedrooms and a suite with a 'folly' bedroom
in the old College Bakehouse.

Yarmouth, Isle of Wight

Quay Street, Yarmouth, Isle of Wight PO41 OPE

Tel (01983) 760331
Fax (01983) 760425
e-mail res@thegeorge.co.uk **website** www.thegeorge.co.uk

Nearby Yarmouth Castle (adjacent); Newport 12 miles; ferry terminal.
Location in town, close to ferry port overlooking Solent; long stay car park 3-min walk
Food breakfast, lunch, dinner; room service
Price £££
Rooms 17; 13 double and twin, 2 suites, 2 single, all with bath; all rooms have phone, TV, hairdryer
Facilities sitting room, restaurant, brasserie; garden, private beach, 36 ft motor yacht available for charter
Credit cards AE, MC, V
Children welcome over 8
Disabled access difficult **Pets** accepted by arrangement **Closed** never **Proprietors** Jeremy and Amy Willcock and John Illsley

George Hotel
Seaside town hotel

In many ways the George is a perfect hotel: an atmospheric building in the centre of a breezy and historic harbour town, with welcoming rooms, a buzzing brasserie with tables spilling across the waterfront garden, and a quieter, more formal restaurant where good, inventive food is served. When they took over the peeling and faded 17thC former govenor's residence, owners John Illsley (former bass guitarist of Dire Straits) and Jeremy and Amy Willcock took great care to restore and renovate with sympathy. A panelled and elegantly proportioned hall sets the scene, leading to a cosy wood-panelled sitting room with thick velvet drapes at the windows, an amusing mid-Victorian evocation of the George above the fireplace and a roaring log fire in winter. Across the hall is the dark red dining room, and beyond the central stairs, the Brasserie and garden, where you can eat in fine weather.

Upstairs, the bedrooms are all inviting and all different: one has a four-poster; another is a light and pretty corner room; two have wonderful teak-decked balconies with views across the Solent. (The hotel has its own motor yacht for outings.) 'It's a sheer pleasure,' writes a satisfied reader, 'to hop on the ferry at Lymington, alight at Yarmouth, and settle in to the George for two or three days.'

Aberaeron, Cardigan

Pen Cei, Aberaeron, Ceredigion
SA46 0BA

Tel (01545) 570 755
Fax (01545) 570 762
e-mail info@harbour-master.com
website www.harbour-master.com

Location off A487 in centre of town
on the quay; with ample car parking
Food breakfast, lunch, dinner
Price ££
Rooms 9; 1 suite, 6 double, 2 single
all with bath and shower (1 with
hand held); all rooms have TV,
DVD player, hairdryer, some have
phone and wi-fi
Facilities dining room, bar
Credit cards MC, V
Children accepted in the cottage
Disabled access to rooms difficult
Pets not accepted
Closed Christmas day
Proprietors Menna and Glyn
Heulyn

Harbourmaster
Seaside inn

Back in the 1950s, an eccentric resident
of Aberaeron decided to give each of
her five properties a different brightly
coloured coat of paint. The idea caught on,
and today the purpose-built Regency harbour town is an uplifting riot of colour,
where The Harbourmaster Hotel makes a
splash all its own with a brilliant cobalt
blue external livery. Opened in 2005, it is,
as you would expect, a former harbourmaster's residence.

The ground floor is given over to eating
and drinking, with a curving bar, informal
dining room and inventive menu featuring
local produce, including the day's catch,
Welsh black beef and tapas. At breakfast,
freshly baked bread or Welsh laverbread.

The light, tasteful interior decoration
manages to be contemporary 'cool' as well
as homely; an eyecatching feature is the listed spiral staircase. Upstairs there are seven
bright, modern bedrooms, fine for a
stopover. Best is the one at the top, from
where the harbourmaster once kept an
eye on all three harbours under his control
in Cardigan Bay. No children under five.

Brechfa, Carmarthenshire

Brechfa, Carmarthenshire
SA32 7RA

Tel (01267) 202332
Fax (01267) 202437
e-mail info@wales-country-hotel-co.uk **website** www.wales-country-hotel.co.uk

Nearby Kidwelly Castle; Llansteffan Castle; Brecon Beacons, National Botanical Gardens of Wales.
Location 10 miles (16 km) NE of Carmarthen, on B4310, in village; with ample car parking
Food breakfast, dinner
Price ££
Rooms 5; 3 double, 1 twin, 1 4-poster, all with bath; all rooms have widescreen TV, DVD, minibar, hairdryer **Facilities** sitting room, dining room, restaurant, 2 bars, microbrewery; garden **Credit cards** MC, V **Children** welcome over 12 **Disabled** not suitable **Pets** by arrangement **Closed** rarely
Proprietors Stephen Thomas and Annabel Viney

Ty Mawr
Country hotel

Firmly at right angles to the main street of this tiny village on the fringe of Brechfa Forest, and by the River Marlais, Ty Mawr has a pretty garden and fine views of the surrounding wooded hillsides. It was bought in 2004 by Stephen Thomas and Annabel Viney, who completely refurbished it while preserving the oak beams, stone walls and tiled floors that proclaim the building's three and a bit centuries' tenure of this glorious spot. The public rooms are cosy and cheerful and include an immaculate bar with smart pine fittings, and a comfy, chintzy sitting room with an open log fire. The long slate-floored restaurant looks out on to the garden and, candle-lit in the evenings, is where the chef's skill in the kitchen shows in earnest: fresh, usually Welsh, ingredients are assembled without undue fuss but with plenty of imagination. The wines are well-chosen and offered at eminently reasonable prices. Upstairs, the bedrooms are bright, comfortable and pleasantly rustic, and breakfast in the morning answers to appetites ranging from the merely peckish to the downright ravenous. The flowers in the garden tubs are quite impressive, but it's worth remembering that the National Botanical Garden of Wales is nearby. Reports welcome.

Builth Wells, Powys

Cwmbach, Newbridge-on-Wye
Builth Wells, Powys, LD2 3RT

Tel (01982) 552493
e-mail post@the-drawing-room.co.uk
website www.the-drawing-room.co.uk

Nearby Elan Valley walks, Brecon Beacons, Cambrian and Black Mountains
Location off A470 in Builth Wells with ample car parking
Food breakfast, dinner
Price ££££
Rooms 3 doubles, 2 with bath, 1 with shower; all rooms have TV/DVD player, internet **Facilities** dining room, 2 sitting rooms, garden
Credit cards MC, V **Children** not accepted **Disabled** not suitable **Pets** not accepted **Closed** Sun, Mon except bank holidays – best to ring and check **Proprietors** Colin and Melanie Dawson

The Drawing Room
Restaurant-with-rooms

This is one of Wales's growing group of exceptional restaurants with rooms, where commitment and attention to detail are second to none. Colin and Melanie Dawson have converted a Georgian house on the main road (not completely silent, though little traffic at night) into a small restaurant, two sitting rooms and three guest bedrooms named after Colin's grand-children Phoebe, Otis and Oliver. The bed-rooms are contemporary in style, one deco-rated bright red and quite masculine, the other two more feminine. They are not large, but perfectly formed and whilst lounging in the bath (one of them is a slipper bath) you can watch the hill sheep grazing opposite.

Colin and Melanie have decorated this property beautifully and with great attention to detail. Although the sitting rooms are small you don't mind as they are immacu-lately furnished with comfy sofas, chairs, roaring fires and interesting objets d'art. However, the emphasis here is on the food – pleasant as it is to get good bedrooms too. Both Colin and Melanie are chefs, and their food wins many plaudits. When we visited the menu included a ragout of sea bass, salmon and black bream with langoustine, fennel and leeks as well as a fillet of local Welsh beef. Make sure you book well in advance as this place is getting booked up very quickly as its reputation grows.

Crickhowell, Powys

Crickhowell, Powys NP8 1BW

Tel (01873) 810408
Fax (01873) 811696
e-mail bearhotel@aol.com **website**
www.bearhotel.co.uk

Nearby Brecon Beacons; Offa's
Dyke; Hay-on-Wye.
Location in town centre on A40
between Abergavenny and Brecon;
ample car parking
Food breakfast, lunch, dinner, bar
snacks
Price ££
Rooms 35 double and twin with
bath or shower; all rooms have
phone, TV, hairdryer **Facilities** sit-
ting room, 2 dining rooms, bar; gar-
den
Credit cards AE, MC, V **Children**
accepted
Disabled 2 ground-floor bedrooms
Pets accepted
Closed Christmas Day; restaurant
only, Sun
Proprietors Judith and Steve
Hindmarsh

The Bear
Town inn

It really doesn't matter what route you
take into Crickhowell as, like most other
travellers for the last 500 years or so,
you're bound to end up at The Bear.
Owned and very much run by Judith
Hindmarsh and her son Steve, it's one of
those versatile places that can turn itself
into whatever you want: if you feel like a
drink, it's an excellent bustling pub shining
with polished brass and pewter. If you feel
like an informal meal, you'll be given an
excellent one in either bar or in the oak-
beamed and flag-floored kitchen restaurant. If you want something more upmarket, all you need do is move to the smaller, smarter à la carte restaurant that looks
out into the courtyard (flower-filled in
summer). Here, provided you are more
than eight years old, you will find flowers
on the table and food open to interna-
tional influences, prepared with an imagination and a lightness of touch that belies
the traditional trappings outside.

If you need a hotel, The Bear can comfortably surpass your expectations as well:
the bedrooms are a mixture of sizes and
of styles – old and new – but all are furnished and equipped to uncompromisingly
high standards. Finally, if you need to
escape the hurly-burly, there is a quiet,
beamed sitting room.

Crickhowell, Powys

Crickhowell, Powys, NP8 1RH

Tel (01874) 730371
Fax (01874) 730463
e-mail calls@gliffaeshotel.com
website www.gliffaeshotel.com

Nearby Brecon Beacons national park, River Usk, Abergavenny
Location off A40 in own large grounds with ample car parking
Food breakfast, lunch, dinner
Price ££-££££
Rooms 23; 2 luxury doubles, 6 large doubles, one 4 poster, 10 standard, four small doubles (14 can be twins); all rooms have shower, some have bath; all rooms have phone, TV, hairdryer; some have DVD player
Facilities dining room, sitting room, drawing room, conference room, conservatory, garden, terrace, fishing
Credit cards MC, V
Children welcome
Disabled 1 ground floor room in cottage 4 **Pets** not accepted **Closed** Jan **Proprietors** James and Susie Suter, Nick and Peta Brabner

Gliffaes
Country house hotel

We've known about Gliffaes for many years and hesitated to put it in the guide despite its fine reputation because it seemed a little large (21 bedrooms), a little imposing (quite a grand Victorian-Italianate country pile); but above all not especially relaxed or personal. Then we dropped in by chance one day in 2006 and changed our minds.

It's a superb example of a family-run (now third generation) country house hotel: a stunning location; caring, hands-on management; unpretentious yet with high standards. There's a friendly buzz, and the young family team of Brabners and Suters really do seem to be good with people. You will probably take away memories of the lovely views from the terrace, grounds falling steeply to the rushing Usk; and of the large grounds with exotic plantings. You might also catch a memorable fish: the hotel has two miles of highly regarded salmon and trout fishing on the Usk.

The decoration is traditional yet stylish. Most of the homely-smart country house style bedrooms are spacious. Dinner is a smartish occasion – guests change, but into 'country casual' clothes, not black tie. The food is good, much of it from local suppliers. Tea is the most lavish spread you are likely to see for a while.

Eglwysfach, Powys

Eglwysfach, Machynlleth, Powys
SY20 8TA

Tel (01654) 781209
Fax (01654) 781366
e-mail info@ynyshir-hall.co.uk
website www.ynyshir-hall.co.uk

Nearby Llyfnant valley;
Aberystwyth.
Location 11 miles (18 km) NE of
Aberystwyth, just off A487; ample
car parking
Food breakfast, lunch, dinner
Price £££–££££
Rooms 9; 5 doubles, 4 suites, all
with bath and shower; all rooms have
phone, TV, hairdryer **Facilities** sitting room, dining room, bar, conservatory in 1 room
Credit cards AE, DC, MC, V
Children accepted over 9
Disabled 1 ground-floor room
Pets accepted in 1 bedroom
Closed Jan
Proprietors Rob and Joan Reen

Ynyshir Hall
Country house hotel

The Reens have been at Ynyshir Hall for some years now and, happily, seem to know what they are about. Since our last publication they have been taken over by the Von Essen group, not always good news in our opinion. We've assumed they are being left alone to run the place their own way. Both Reens are ex-teachers, Joan of geography, Rob of design and art – and his paintings now decorate the walls of the whole house. Given Rob's background, you might well expect the decoration of the hotel to be rather special, too – and you would not be disappointed. The colour schemes are adventurous, the patterns bold, the use of fabrics opulent, the attention to detail striking. The bedrooms are named after famous artists, which is paralleled in the colour schemes and fantastic replicas of Matisse, Hogarth and Monet that Rob has created. The new ownership means extra cash for refurbishment, so changes are expected.

The white-painted house dates from the 16th century, but is predominantly Georgian and Victorian. It stands in 12 glorious acres of landscaped gardens next to the Dovey estuary. The Michelin-starred food is adventurous but not over-complex – modern British – based on fresh local ingredients, especially fish, game, shellfish and Welsh lamb.

Felin Fach, Powys

Felin Fach, Brecon, Powys
LD3 OUB

Tel (01874) 620111
Fax (01874) 620120
e-mail
enquiries@eatdrinksleep.ltd.uk
website www.eatdrinksleep.ltd.uk

Nearby Hay Bluff, Pen y Fan,
Brecon Beacons and Black
Mountains, Brecon, Hay-on-Wye,
Llangorse Lake (sailing and wind-
surfing)
Location edge of village with off-
road car parking
Food breakfast, lunch, dinner
Price ££-£££
Rooms 7, all doubles; all rooms have
bath, extra beds for children, phone,
some TV **Facilities** bar, dining area,
grassed outdoor drinks area, croquet,
local activities booking service
Credit cards MC, V **Children**
accepted **Disabled** no special facilities
Pets accepted **Closed** Mon lunch; 3
days at Christmas **Proprietors**
Charles and Edmund Inkin, who also
run the Gurnard's Head, page 88.

The Felin Fach Griffin
Country inn

The location is uninteresting, beside a busy-ish road, and you might think this is any old Welsh pub. But there's a clue it may be something different: the exterior is painted a mellow ochre, the colour seen all over Tuscany. Inside, you'll be struck by the layout: right by the bar is a pair of squashy leather sofas where you flop with the papers. A log fire is raised above floor level, radiating heat in two directions, into the bar and the adjacent dining room. Tongue-and-groove panelling is painted a brilliant blue. Nooks and crannies are filled with books.

The food is distinctly above average for the price (wild mushroom risotto and sherry butter £9.95; or Welsh minute steak with braised leeks £9.95), and won an award in 2007 for providing good food for families. Home-made soda bread arrives on a simple wooden board. There's a choice of 11 interesting wines by the glass, including *prosecco*. When we visited in 2006 we noticed the whacky-looking chef with a ring in his nose. The Griffin can claim to be Wales's original gastropub. Off the main dining room there's another smaller one with two tables seating eight (great for a party) in front of the Aga, where the day's fresh stocks simmer.

Upstairs are seven fresh, but perhaps boxey bedrooms with homey decoration, again using bright colours.

Llanarmon, Denbighshire

Llanarmon Dyffryn Ceiriog
Nr Llangollen, North Wales
LL20 7LD

Tel (01691) 600 665
Fax (01691) 600 622
e-mail gowestarms@aol.com
website www.thewestarms.co.uk

Nearby Chirk Castle, Ceiriog
Valley, Rhaeadr waterfall, Erdigg
Hall, Llangollen
Location on B4500, 7 miles SW of
Llangollen situated in centre of
hamlet, surrounded by countryside
with ample car parking at the rear
Food breakfast, lunch, dinner
Price £££
Rooms 15 rooms; 2 suites, 1 four
poster, 11 doubles, 1 twin, all with
bath some with shower; all rooms
have phone, TV/DVD player,
hairdryers
Facilities dining room, bar, garden
Credit cards MC, V
Children welcome
Disabled 1 accessible room
Pets accepted **Closed** never
Proprietors Grant Williams, Lee
and Sian Finch

The West Arms
Country inn

A traditional, unspoilt inn with above average food and simple but comfortable bedrooms (try one of the character rooms which have pretty brass or four poster beds.) They are perhaps a little feminine, but decorated in a comfortable, unpretentious country style. You should get a warm welcome, and the mood will be helped along by flagstones and roaring inglenook fires surrounded by old blackened beams with traditional brasses on display. Our inspector found the dining room quite lacking in atmosphere, however the bar seemed the place to be for informal eating and drinking with the locals or alternatively the beer garden which has truly spectacular views over the Welsh hills and valleys.

Heartening food comes from the reputable chef Grant Williams, who had been there 15 years as we went to press – a long time in this business, so there's probably a happy team here.

The West Arms is located in a natural spot for an inn, where three cattle drovers' tracks converge on the way to the markets at Oswestry, Chirk and Wrexham. Wonderful walking in the Berwyn Hills or Ceiriog Valley is a must if staying here.

Llanddeiniolen, Gwynedd

Llanddeiniolen, Caernarfon,
Gwynedd, LL55 3AE

Tel (01248) 670 489
Fax (01248) 670 079
e-mail enquiries@tynrhos.co.uk
website www.tynrhos.co.uk

Nearby Snowdonia; Bangor; Conwy
Castle; Llandudno dry ski slope.
Location from the A5 turn on to the
A4244 , then take the B4366 after
the roundabout
Food breakfast, lunch, dinner
Price ££
Rooms 3 courtyard rooms, 10 in
main house with bath and shower; all
rooms have TV; some have wi-fi
Facilities dining room, restaurant,
sitting room, bar, conservatory; cro-
quet, garden, helipad **Credit cards**
AE, MC, V **Children** accepted
Disabled access to ground-floor
rooms and public rooms **Pets**
accepted by arrangement **Closed**
never **Proprietors** Janet and Martin
James

Ty'n Rhos
Country hotel

Janet and Martin James are the proud owners of this rather unusual place at
Llanddeiniolen, near Caernarfon. Ty'n Rhos
('house on the heath') was a farm with 72
acres when it was first bought in 1972. Over
the years, it has been transformed into a
stylish small hotel with a relaxed rural
atmosphere. Entering, you will be struck by
the conservatory, which has magnificent
views over the well-tended gardens and
rolling countryside beyond. Next door is a
cosy little bar that serves canned beers,
wine and soft drinks. Next door is the dining room, which is light and airy and again
offers spectacular views. The chefs pride
themselves on using local fresh fish, meat
and vegetables, and herbs straight from their
garden in summer, and offer hearty traditional Welsh or more continental breakfast.

The bedrooms are all individually furnished with quality fabrics and furnishings,
some with fantastic views; they vary in size.
Outside the main building are three courtyard rooms, one especially suitable for those
with walking difficulties. There are also two
self-catering cottages. The other big plus
here is the location, with everything you'd
expect of a Wales hotel – historic castles
and towns, dry skiing, seaside and serious
mountain walks nearby.

Llandrillo, Denbighshire

Llandrillo, near Corwen,
Denbighshire LL21 0ST

Tel (01490) 440264
Fax (01490) 440414
e-mail tyddynllan@compuserve.com
website www.tyddynllan.co.uk

Nearby Bala Lake and Railway;
Snowdonia.
Location 5 miles (8 km) SW of
Corwen off B4401; with ample car
parking
Food breakfast, lunch, dinner
Price £££
Rooms 12 double and twin, 10 with
bath, 2 with shower; all rooms have
phone, TV, radio
Facilities sitting room, bar, restaurant; croquet, fishing
Credit cards MC, V **Children** welcome **Disabled** 1 suite suitable
Pets accepted in bedrooms by
arrangement **Closed** never
Proprietors Bryan and Susan Webb

Tyddyn Llan
Restaurant-with-rooms

A firm favourite with readers since our first edition, this Georgian stone house near Llandrillo is decorated with elegant flair, period antiques and fine paintings, creating a serene ambience. Tyddyn Llan is very much a home, despite the number of guests it can accommodate. There is a major extension to the building, cleverly complementary to the original, using slate, stone and cast-iron.

A reader writes: 'No intrusive reception desk; spacious sitting rooms furnished with style; dining room shows great flair; bedrooms well equipped with original pieces of furniture; small but modern and very pleasing bathrooms; peaceful, comfortable stay, warm atmosphere provided by attentive hosts'. Fiona Duncan, our series editor, visited recently and observed: 'Bryan Webb should have a Michelin star for his instinctive cooking.'

Bryan and his wife Susan offer diners with a new angle on Welsh country house food with inventive and well-planned small menus using quality local ingredients, plus an impressive wine list.

The place is surrounded by large, beautiful grounds.

Promenade, 17 North Parade,
Llandudno, Conwy LL30 2LP

Tel (01492) 860330
Fax (01492) 860791
e-mail sales@osbornehouse.co.uk
website www.osbornehouse.co.uk

Nearby dry ski slope; Conwy Castle;
Bodnant Gardens; Snowdonia
Location on seafront opposite pier
and promenade gardens; off-road car
parking
Food breakfast (in room), lunch,
dinner
Price £££
Rooms 6 suites, all with phone,
bath, walk-in shower, TV, DVD,
fridge, free broadband internet
Facilities bar, 'bistro' restaurant, sit-
ting area in reception, outdoor
drinks area
Credit cards AE, DC, MC, V
Children not under 12, not in par-
ents' room
Disabled not suitable
Pets not accepted
Closed one week at Christmas
Proprietors Maddocks family

Osborne House
Town hotel

There's virtually no mobile signal in the charmingly old-fashioned resort of Llandudno, but that's part of its appeal. Between the unspoilt beaches and the backdrop of mountains, life goes at a gentle pace. Summer here means strolling along the Promenade with an ice-cream cornet, pausing to watch Punch and Judy. In a plum position on the Prom, Osborne House fits its surroundings perfectly.

The Maddocks family have lavished attention on it. The public rooms are glamorous enough, but it's the six gorgeous suites, all with sea views and private parking spaces, that really impress, and are kindly priced considering the wealth of antiques, pictures and porcelain in each one, and the marble bathrooms with splendid roll top baths. Some might find it all a bit over the top, certainly very Victorian, but downstairs the public spaces have plenty of modern touches including a sleek bar with two large plasma TV screens competing for attention. 'The Café,' a bistro-café, reckons on serving good food in a rather grand Victorian surroundings, but in an informal style – no set hours, okay to have just one course, and eat at the bar, a table or on a sofa.

Osborne House will suit younger readers better than our other Llandudno entry, St Tudno, page 148.

Llandudno, Conwy

Promenade, Llandudno,
Conwy, LL30 2LP

Tel (01492) 874411
Fax (01492) 860407
e-mail sttudnohotel@btinternet.com
website www.st-tudno.co.uk

Nearby dry ski slope; Conwy Castle;
Bodnant Gardens; Snowdonia
Location on seafront opposite pier
and promenade gardens; parking for
12 cars and unrestricted street park-
ing
Food breakfast, lunch, dinner
Price £££
Rooms 19; 12 doubles and twins, 4
family, 2 suites, 1 single, all with
bath or shower; all rooms have
phone, TV, fridge, hairdryer
Facilities 2 sitting rooms, dining
room, bar, garden, indoor swimming
pool **Credit cards** AE, DC, MC, V
Children welcome
Disabled not suitable, lift/elevator
Pets accepted by arrangement
Closed never **Proprietor** Martin
Bland

St Tudno
Seaside hotel

Martin Bland is meticulous in attending
to every detail of this award-winning
seafront hotel, which he has been improving for almost 30 years now. He could not,
however, improve on its location: right on
Llandudno's dignified promenade, opposite
the carefully restored Victorian pier and
sheltered from inclement weather by the
Great Orme headland. Each of the nineteen
rooms have been individually decorated in
bright, cheerful colours with matching fabrics and furnishings: most have spectacular
views of the sea. Thoughtful extras such as
complimentary wine and fresh flowers add
to the comfort. The two sitting rooms facing the Promenade are delightfully Victorian
yet surprisingly light and spacious, perfect
for reading or indulging in afternoon tea.

The air-conditioned Garden Room
Restaurant is light and inviting, and suits its
name with a profusion of plants and cane-
backed chairs. The seasonal menu with daily
changing carte, based on the best local
ingredients, deserves serious study in the
comfortable bar, and – though it's not
cheap – the cooking is right on target. If
you over-indulge, you can try to recover
your figure by pounding up and down the
lovely covered pool, decorated with
murals. All of this would be difficult to
resist even without the bonus of the hotel's
young and helpful staff.

Llanfairpwllgwyngyll, Anglesey

Penmynydd, Llanfairpwllgwyngyll,
Anglesey LL61 5BX

Tel (01248) 715005
Fax (01248) 715005
e-mail post@neuaddlwyd.co.uk
website www.neuaddlwyd.co.uk

Nearby Beaumaris, Conwy,
Caernarfon Castles; Plas Newydd;
Bodnant Gardens; Snowdonia
National Park
Location down drive in own
grounds with off road car parking
Food breakfast, dinner
Price ££-£££
Rooms 4; 3 double, 1 twin bedded;
all rooms have bathroom, TV, DVD
and CD players **Facilities** drawing
room, dining room
Credit cards MC, V
Children not under 12
Disabled no specially adapted rooms
Pets not accepted
Closed Sun and Mon, except for
bank holidays
Proprietors Susannah and Peter
Woods

Neuadd Lwyd
Country guest-house

Our reporter, Fiona Duncan, wrote:
'It's difficult to pigeonhole this place.
If you say it's a guest-house in the middle
of farmland on remote Anglesey, connota-
tions of nylon sheets, dour rooms, old har-
ridans and stodgy food cloud the mind.
And yet... the room in which I am dozing,
tucked under a goose-down duvet on a
deep mattress, is one of the most attractive hotel bedrooms I can recall, equipped
with flat-screen TV, DVDs, digital radio,
walk-in shower and separate bath (no
phone though). All the furniture, the beds,
beaded throws and cushions, pictures,
lamps, even the clock on the mantelpiece,
are new and carefully chosen, lending the
feel of a swish bedroom in a luxury hotel.'

Susannah Woods, who trained at
Ballymaloe Cookery School and is the
chef, spent 20 years as a midwifery sister
before deciding, with her husband, Peter,
to restore this early Victorian rectory. You
could be happy here just relaxing, walking
and enjoying the scenery, but there's also
plenty to do: a stroll around Beaumaris
Castle perhaps, or you could drive 20 minutes to Holyhead, buy a £14 return ferry
ticket and spend the day in Dublin. You'll
be back in time for the excellent dinner.

Llansanffraid Glan Conwy, Conwy

Colwyn Bay, Conwy, LL28 5LF

Tel (01492) 580611
Fax (01492) 584555
e-mail info@oldrectorycountry-house.co.uk **website** www.oldrectorycountryhouse.co.uk

Nearby Bodnant Gardens; Betws-y-Coed; Llandudno.
Location on A470 half a mile (1 km) S of junction with A55; ample car parking
Food breakfast, dinner
Price £££
Rooms 6 double, 5 with bath, 1 with shower; all rooms have phone, TV, hairdryer, tea and coffee making facilities **Facilities** sitting room, dining room; garden
Credit cards MC, V **Children** accepted over 5 **Disabled** 2 ground-floor rooms **Pets** in coachhouse only
Closed Dec to Feb **Proprietors** Michael and Wendy Vaughan

The Old Rectory
Country rectory

This pretty former Georgian rectory, home of the owners, enjoys an exceptional elevated position, standing in two-and-a-half acres of flowery gardens with lovely sweeping views across the Conwy Estuary to Conwy Castle and Snowdonia beyond. Most of the bedrooms, two of which are in a separate building, share this view. The rooms, despite the modern appliances, have an old-fashioned feel about them, with ponderous beds, mostly either half tester or four-poster, in walnut, mahogany and oak. Downstairs is an elegant panelled drawing room decorated with the Vaughans' collection of Victorian watercolours.

The couple's progression as hoteliers, and particularly Wendy's as a chef, has been remarkable. An ex-nurse with no culinary training whatsoever, she began by cooking for parties of visiting American tourists. As they started to take in bed-and-breakfast guests and then graduated to fully fledged hotel, so Wendy's culinary skills improved and they now hold several awards for their food, including three rosettes, six Good Food Awards and a Conde Nast Restaurant for Wales award. Wendy still produces a delicious and imaginative three-course dinner each night unaided, except for help with the washing up and the vegetable chopping (from Michael, who oversees the wine list to complement her food).

Llanthony, Gwent

Llanthony, Abergavenny, Gwent
NP7 7NN

Tel (01873) 890487
website
www.llanthonyprioryhotel.co.uk

Nearby Offa's Dyke; Brecon
Beacons; Hay-on-Wye.
Location off A465 from
Abergavenny to Hereford, take
mountain road heading N at
Llanfihangel Crucorney; with ample
car parking
Food breakfast, lunch, dinner
Price £
Rooms 4 double and twin
Facilities dining room, bar; garden
Credit cards not accepted **Children**
accepted over 10
Disabled access not possible **Pets**
not accepted
Closed Oct to Easter (open week-
ends) **Proprietor** Geoffrey Neil

River Wye

Llanthony Priory
Country Inn

Far into the Black Mountains, on the west
bank of the Afon Honddu and overlooked by Offa's Dyke to the east, Llanthony
Priory lies high and remote in the Vale of
Ewyas. The most spectacular approach is
southwards from the sloping streets and
busy bookshops of Hay-on-Wye.

One of the earliest Augustinian houses
in Britain, it was endowed by the de Lacy
family, but by the time of Henry VIII's dis-
solution of the monasteries had fallen into
disuse. The Prior's quarters survived
amongst the ruins and are now used as the
hotel. Gothic horror enthusiasts will be
delighted not only by the setting but also
when they learn that the highest of the
bedrooms can only be reached by climbing
more than 60 spiral steps up into the
south tower.

This is not a hotel for the fastidious or
the faint-hearted: it is a long way from anywhere and much used by walkers attracted
to the stunning country that surrounds it.
Unless you plan to arrive on foot yourself,
you should remember that your fellow
guests may have had their appetites sharp-
ened by fresh air and their critical faculties
dulled by fatigue. However, the chance to
sleep in this unique piece of history (with a
four-poster and half-tester available) and to
wake up to the view from the tower also
comes with a very modest price tag.

Nant Gwynant, Gwynedd

Nant Gwynant, Gwynedd,
LL55 4NT

Tel (01286) 870211
website www.pyg.co.uk

Nearby Bodnant Gardens;
Caernarfon, Beaumaris and Harlech
Castles; Isle of Anglesey; Blackrock
Sands.
Location take the A5 to Holyhead,
as you enter Capel Curig, turn left
on to the A4086. 4 miles (6 km) on
the hotel is on a T junction with the
lake in front of it
Food breakfast, lunch, dinner, tea
Price ££
Rooms 15 double, 1 single; 6 with
private bathroom, 1 ground floor
annexe room with bathroom, 5 pub-
lic bathrooms **Facilities** sitting
room, dining room, smoke room,
bar, sauna, natural swimming pool,
games room, fishing
Credit cards MC, V **Children** welcome **Disabled** 1 ground-floor room
Pets by arrangement **Closed** Nov to
Dec and mid week until the 1st of
March **Proprietors** Jane and Brian
Pullee

Pen-y-Gwryd Hotel
Climbing hostel

A pilgrimage place for climbers: this is
the home of British Mountaineering,
where Edmund Hillary and his team set up
their training base before the assault on
Everest in 1953. Still in the same friendly
family after 58 years, the charming old
coach inn, set high in the desolate heart of
Snowdonia, is just the sort of place you
dream of returning to after a day out-
doors: simple, unsophisticated, warm and
welcoming, with good plain home cooking,
including wickedly calorific puddings.

In keeping with the purpose of the place
the bedrooms are simple with no frills, not
all of them have *en suite* bathrooms, but
they all have fluffy towels and warm
embroidered bedding and linen; the best
room is in the annexe and has a grand four-
poster bed. One of the bathrooms houses
a vintage Victorian bath that looks deep
and inviting. For the less intrepid walkers
there is still plenty to see in the vicinity, as
it is littered with castles and gardens.

After a hard day on the hill you can soak
your aching muscles in the natural pool in
the garden or unwind in the sauna. For children (or playful adults) there is a games
room with a dart board and table tennis.

Penally, Pembrokeshire

Penally, near Tenby, South
Pembrokeshire SA70 7PY

Tel (01834) 843033
Fax (01834) 844714
e-mail info@penally-abbey.com
website www.penally-abbey.com

Nearby Tenby; Colby Woodland
Garden; Upton Castle, Pembroke
Castle
Location in village 1.5 miles (2.5
km) SW of Tenby; with ample car
parking
Food breakfast, dinner
Price £££
Rooms 12 double and twin with
bath; all rooms have phone, TV,
fax/modem point, hairdryer
Facilities sitting room, billiards
room, dining room, bar, indoor
swimming pool; garden **Credit
cards** AE, MC, V **Children** accept-
ed **Disabled** access possible to 2
ground-floor bedrooms
Pets not accepted
Closed never **Proprietors** Steve and
Elleen Warren

Penally Abbey
Country house hotel

Ever since the Middle Ages this has been
recognized as one of the spots from
which to appreciate the broad sweep of the
Pembrokeshire coast and National Park
from Tenby to Giltar Point. The links golf
course wasn't there, but the ruins of the
medieval chapel which gave this Gothic
country house its name are still in the
secluded and well-tended gardens. The windows and doors all have the characteristic
double curve arches. There is a comfortable
and well furnished drawing room with an
open fire, a welcoming bar far from the
world's woes and weather, and a tall, candle-
lit dining room for the well planned and
prepared dinners, which include a wide
choice of fresh Welsh produce. The bedrooms are well equipped: some you could
play cricket in and are furnished traditionally, some in quite a grand style. St Deiniol's
Lodge now houses a further five rooms,
decorated in more contemporary style.
Steve and Elleen Warren have made a smart
but easy and informal hotel that is child
friendly (babysitting on tap). Children are
welcome in the dining room for the (excellent) breakfasts, but an early supper sensibly
makes this a child-free zone in the evening.

We revisited recently and enjoyed
Steve's *bonhomie* and Elleen's food as much
as ever.

Penmaenpool, Gwynedd

Penmaenpool, Dolgellau, Gwynedd
LL40 1YB

Tel (01341) 422129
Fax (01341) 422787
e-mail relax@penhall.co.uk
website www.penhall.co.uk

Nearby Mawddach Estuary;
Snowdonia; Lake Vyrnwy,
Portmeirion.
Location off A493 Dolgellau-Tywyn
road; with ample car parking
Food breakfast, lunch, dinner
Price £££
Rooms 14 double and twin with
bath; all rooms have phone, TV,
hairdryer; superior and deluxe
rooms have minibar **Facilities** sitting
rooms, library, billiards room, 2 dining rooms, bar; garden, helipad, fishing **Credit cards** DC, MC, V
Children babes-in-arms and children over 6 accepted
Disabled access possible to restaurant **Pets** accepted in 1 room by
arrangement **Closed** 10 days in Jan
Proprietors Mark Watson and
Lorraine Fielding

Penmaenuchaf Hall
Country house hotel

Not far from the market town of
Dolgellau, Penmaenuchaf Hall's drive
winds steeply up a wooded hillside from
the south bank of the Mawddach Estuary
to this sturdy grey stone Victorian manor
house. Set on terraces in 21 acres of
grounds, the views across Snowdonia must
have been top of the list of reasons that
brought the original builder – a Lancashire
mill owner – to this peaceful spot at the
foot of Cader Idris. A rose garden and a
water garden add a charm of their own to
the beautiful setting.

Indoors, Mark Watson and Lorraine
Fielding have saved but also softened the
Victorian character of the house so that,
from the imposing main hall you are drawn
to the warmth and light of the ivory morning room, the sitting rooms and the library.
The same sympathetic treatment carries
through to the bedrooms – fine fabrics are
married with fine furniture and only the
beds are baronial. If you are not tempted
by the excellent walking in the surrounding hills, you can revive the skills of a mis-
spent youth in the billiards room or simply
doze in the sunny conservatory. A new
oak-panelled garden room restaurant,
Llygad yr Haul, has recently been added.
Reports welcome.

Pwllheli, Gwynedd

Pwllheli, Gwynedd, North Wales
LL53 5TH

Tel (01758) 612363
Fax (01758) 701247
e-mail gunna@bodegroes.co.uk
website www.bodegroes.co.uk

Nearby National Trust walks,
Snowdonia, Bodmant Gardens
Location 1 mile west of Pwllheli on
the A497 Nefyn road; in own
grounds with ample car parking
Food breakfast, dinner (lunch on
Sundays)
Price ££
Rooms 11; 10 doubles, 1 single
(only shower); all doubles have bath
and shower; all rooms have phone,
tv, hairdryer **Facilities** restaurant,
garden **Credit cards** MC, V
Children welcome **Disabled** not
suitable **Pets** accepted **Closed** Dec,
Jan and Feb, and Mondays
Proprietors Chris and Gunna
Chown

Plas Bodegroes
Restaurant-with-rooms

Plas Bodegroes means Rosehip Hall – a
fittingly romantic name. It's a small
Georgian manor with a delicate frill of a
veranda, whose slim cast-iron columns are
smothered in wisteria, roses and wild
strawberry. The grounds feature a heart-
shaped swathe of lawn and a 200-year-old
avenue of beech trees. To one side, a long
red-and-white Danish pennant on a tall
flagpole flutters in the wind. Chef-propri-
etor Chris Chown's elegant wife, Gunna,
who looks after front of house is
Danish/Faroese.

Chris is the holder, since 1991, of one of
only two Michelin stars in Wales and Plas
Bodegroes is emphatically a restaurant-
with-rooms. The 11 bedrooms are cosy
and pretty, in Scandinavian style, all shapes
and sizes. The dining room is romantic,
too, with its clever use of mirrors, its elegant French doors on to the veranda and
its beautifully lit duck-egg blue walls.
Welsh lamb and Black beef feature prominently on the unpretentious menu, though
equal emphasis is given to fresh fish. The
wine list is interesting with gentle prices
and breakfast is exceptional. Plas
Bodegroes is off the beaten track on the
Lleyn Peninsula, with mystical Bardsey
Island at its tip, in almost completely
unspoilt countryside. Food and a setting of
this quality are hard to find at these prices.

Reynoldston, Nr Swansea

Reynoldston, Gower, near Swansea,
SA3 1BS

Tel (01792) 390139
Fax (01792) 391358
e-mail admin@fairyhill.net
website www.fairyhill.net

Nearby Weobley Castle; Gower
Peninsula; Heritage Centre;
Swansea.
Location 12 miles (19 km) W of
Swansea, 1 mile (1.5 km) NW of vil-
lage; in 24-acre park and woodland,
with ample car parking
Food breakfast, lunch, dinner
Price £££-££££
Rooms 8 double with bath and
shower; all rooms have phone, TV,
DVD player, CD player, iPod con-
nector, wi-fi **Facilities** sitting room,
bar, 2 dining rooms, conference
room; croquet, garden
Credit cards MC, V **Children**
accepted over 8
Disabled access possible to restau-
rant only **Pets** not accepted
Closed 24 to 27 Dec; 1 Jan for 3
weeks **Proprietors** P. Davies and A.
Hetherington

Fairyhill
Restaurant-with-rooms

Our latest inspection confirmed that
standards were being well maintained in this quiet and utterly civilized
retreat situated in the heart of the Gower
Peninsula and only about 25 minutes from
the M4, since the current owners took
over in late 1993.

Set in 24 acres of grounds – with walled
garden, orchard, trout stream and lake, and
much of it still semi-wild – the three-
storey Georgian building has a series of
spacious, attractively furnished public
rooms on the ground floor, leading to the
dining room.

Paul Davies, one of the proprietors, is
executive chef, with the kitchen under the
guidance of James Laurence. They enjoy
producing seasonal menus and make
excellent use of traditional local specialities such as Gower lobster and crab,
Penclawdd cockles, Welsh lamb and laverbread. The extensive wine list, cellared in
the old vaults of the house, includes wine
from Wales. Most bedrooms overlook the
large park and woodland, and are comfortable and well-equipped – they even have
CD players, on which to play your choices
from the hotel's large and catholic collection of disks.

We've received one worryingly negative
reader's report, but trust this is a one-off.
More reports would be welcome.

Skenfrith, Monmouthshire

Skenfrith, Monmouthshire,
P7 8UH

Tel (01600) 750235
Fax (01600) 750525
e-mail enquiries@skenfrith.co.uk
website www.skenfrith.co.uk

Nearby Brecon Beacons National
Park, Ross-on-Wye, Hereford,
Abergavenny
Location off minor road on edge of
village in own grounds; ample off
road car parking
Food breakfast, lunch, dinner
Price ££-£££
Rooms 8, all double; all with bath,
phone, TV
Facilities bar, dining room, function
room, small garden
Credit cards AE, MC, V
Children accepted, but not for
evening meals unless over 10
Disabled not suitable
Pets accepted (fee)
Closed never
Proprietors Janet and William
Hutchings

The Bell at Skenfrith
Country inn

Though contemporary and cosy rarely coincide, this is one place that convincingly combines the two. Tucked into the fold of a hill in the Welsh Marches, it has all the ingredients for a winter break that metropolitans could wish for: a huge inglenook radiating heat, surrounded by sofa, settle and rocking chair; a candle-lit, flagstone dining room serving locally sourced modern British dishes, along with a well-organised wine list; and eight delightful, simple-sophisticated bedrooms.

Converted in 2001 by Janet and William Hutchings, the formerly run-down inn stands on the Monnow River close to Skenfrith Castle in an unchanged village. There are wonderful walks from the door, including the 18-mile Three Castles Walk, which is demanding but possible in a single day. If you want to do it in two days, the staff, if not too busy, will pick you up at the end of the first day. When you get back, you could have a Jersey cream tea to ease your sore feet.

Garden enthusiasts should note The Bell's midweek spring offer of two nights' dinner, bed and breakfast combined with absorbing themed lectures and a tour of the historic gardens at nearby Llanover Garden School (from £260 per person).

Talsarnau, Gwynedd

Talsarnau, Gwynedd, Wales
LL47 6YA

Tel (01766) 780200
Fax (01766) 780211
e-mail maes@neuadd.com
website www.neuadd.com

Nearby Portmeirion; Ffestiniog
Railway; Harlech Castle.
Location 3 miles (5 km) NE of
Harlech, up small road off B4573;
ample car parking
Food breakfast, lunch, dinner; room
service
Price £££
Rooms 15 double and twin, all with
bath or shower; all rooms have
phone, TV, fax/modem point,
hairdryer
Facilities sitting room, conservatory,
dining room, bar; terrace, garden,
helipad **Credit cards** MC, V
Children welcome
Disabled 3 ground-floor rooms,
lift/elevator **Pets** accepted in some
coach house bedrooms **Closed** never
Proprietors Lynn and Peter
Jackson, Peter Payne

Maes-y-Neuadd
Country hotel

If you haven't been to Maes-y-Neuadd
before, you run the risk of running out of
confidence in your own map-reading skills
as the little road from the coast winds up
and up through woods. Fear not and press
on, for the journey will be worth it. You
will arrive outside a stone-built slate-
roofed manor that is only a century or so
younger than Harlech Castle, creeper-clad
in parts, and if the time is right you can
look back across the water to see the sun
set behind the Lleyn peninsula. It may be
Snowdonia outside, but inside it is definitely deep-pile all the way. Chintzes in the
drawing room, leather in the bar and, in
the pale and elegant dining room, master-
pieces from the kitchen of Peter Jackson
(chef and co-owner) all combine to make
this a seriously comfortable hotel.

Much of the fresh produce comes from
Maes-y-Neuadd's own garden (the gardeners get a credit). Menus are set, with choices for each of the possible five courses
until pudding when you reach 'Diweddglo
Mawreddog' (the grand finale), which
means you get them all. When you are
shown to your room, take note of how
you got there as the upstairs corridors are
all similar. The reverse is true of the smart,
variously-sized bedrooms, which are individually decorated and furnished.

Three Cocks, Powys

Three Cocks, near Brecon, Powys
LD3 0SL

Tel (01497) 847215
Fax (01497) 847339
e-mail info@threecockshotel.com
website www.threecockshotel.com

Nearby Brecon Beacons; Hay-on-Wye; Hereford Cathedral; Black Mountains.
Location in village, 11 miles (18 km) NE of Brecon on A438; ample car parking
Food breakfast, lunch, dinner
Price ££
Rooms 7 double and twin, 6 with bath/shower, 1 with shower
Facilities sitting room, reception room with TV, dining room, breakfast room; large garden
Credit cards MC, V **Children** welcome
Disabled access difficult
Pets not accepted **Closed** Jan
Proprietors Roy and Judith Duke

Three Cocks
Village inn

The building is a charming ivy-covered 15thC coaching inn in the Welsh hills, constructed around a tree (still in evidence in the kitchen) and with its cobbled forecourt on the most direct route from Hereford to Brecon. Inside, carved wood and stone walls continue the natural look of the exterior, with beams and eccentrically angled doorways serving as proof positive of antiquity. The charmingly friendly and enthusiastic Dukes took over in 2006 and continue to draw people great distances to the warm welcome and roomy restaurant with its lace-covered tables. There are plenty of places where you can sit in peace, and residents have a drawing room of their own, in keeping with its public oak-panelled counterpart but with more light, stone and fabric in evidence. There is now also a coffee shop, leading on to the extensive gardens, serving refreshments and light lunches.

Bedrooms are modest but comfortable and well equipped, with dark oak furniture and pale fabrics. The food is honest, hearty British fayre, making full use of the wealth of local sources, including the Black Mountain Salmon Smokery, as well as local cheeses and meats. Roy uses local merchant Tanners as his wine cellar, importing an eclectic range of wines from around the world.

Ashbourne, Derbyshire

Mappleton, Ashbourne, Derbyshire
DE6 2AA

Tel (01335) 300900
Fax (01335) 300512
e-mail
reservations@callowhall.co.uk web-site www.callowhall.co.uk

Nearby Chatsworth House; Haddon Hall; Hardwick Hall.
Location 0.75 mile (1 km) N of Ashbourne off A515; with ample car parking
Food breakfast, lunch Sun or on request, dinner Price £££ Rooms 16; 15 double and twin, 1 suite, all with bath or shower; all rooms have phone, TV, hairdryer
Facilities sitting room, dining rooms, bar; garden, fishing Credit cards AE, DC, MC, V Children welcome Disabled 1 specially adapted room Pets accepted by arrangement Closed Christmas Day, Boxing Day, New Year's Day
Proprietors Emma and Anthony Spencer

Callow Hall
Country house hotel

The Spencers have been 'foodies' for generations. They have been master bakers in Ashbourne since 1724, and one of the highlights of staying at this fine Victorian country house hotel is its excellent dining room. As well as growing many of their own ingredients, the Spencers also smoke and cure meat and fish themselves – arts that have been passed down through the family.

Set in extensive grounds at the entrance to the Peak District National Park, the hotel overlooks the stunning landscape of the Dove valley. Public rooms and bedrooms are done out in an appropriate and not too flamboyant country-house style. The walls of the entrance are guarded by stags' heads and the flag-stoned floor is scattered with Persian rugs. In winter an open fire crackles, while guests dine in the glow of the deep-red dining room, and in the drawing room, comfy sofas and chairs provide plenty of space for relaxing. Carved antiques and family heirlooms mingle with period repro furniture. Ask for a decent-sized room when you book: one or two are on the small side for the price. Staff are helpful yet unobtrusive, and the Spencers are hands-on owners, with Emma front of house and Anthony in charge of the kitchen.

Ashford-in-the-Water, Derbyshire

Fennel Street, Ashford-in-the-
Water, Bakewell, Derbyshire,
DE4 1QF

Tel (01629) 814275
Fax (01629) 812873
e-mail riversidehouse@enta.net
website
www.riversidehousehotel.co.uk

Nearby Chatsworth; Haddon Hall;
Bakewell.
Location 2 miles (3 km) NW of
Bakewell off A6, at top of village,
next to Sheepwash Bridge; with
ample car parking
Food breakfast, lunch, dinner
Price £££
Rooms 14; 1 executive suite, 13
double/twin, all with bath/shower;
all rooms have phone, TV, hairdryer
Facilities 2 sitting rooms, conserva-
tory, bar, 2 dining rooms; garden
Credit cards AE, DC, MC, V
Children welcome over 16
Disabled access possible to 4 rooms
Pets not accepted **Closed** never
Proprietor Penelope Thornton

Riverside House
Country hotel

Nestling in one of the Peak District's
prettiest villages, this stone-built, ivy-
clad house, has an idyllic setting in its own
secluded grounds, bordered by the river
Wye. The village is aptly named – on our
inspector's visit during a spate of heavy
rain, the river was threatening to
encroach, but the hotel's manager was
coping admirably, sandbags at the ready,
with the possibility of a flood alert.

Penelope Thornton (of the Thornton
chocolate family), who took over the hotel
in 1997, has instituted a refreshingly plain
style, entirely in keeping with the house's
Georgian origins. A large plant-filled conservatory leads into a cosy snug with a
recessed carved-oak mantelpiece and
open fire. There is an elegant, comfortable
sitting room and a variety of well-equipped
bedrooms of different sizes. Rooms in the
newer Garden wing overlook the river.

Crucial to Riverside is its reputation for
fine food, which is served in two intimate
dining rooms. Chef John Whelan creates
imaginative dishes such as *mille-feuille* of
marinated salmon with beetroot confit, and
celery and wild mushroom strüdel; he also
offers an intriguing selection of cheeses –
Lincolnshire Poacher, Belineigh Blue and
Gubbeen. Coffee is accompanied by a little
box of locally made Thorntons chocolates.

Baslow, Derbyshire

Baslow, Derbyshire DE45 1SP

Tel (01246) 582311
Fax (01246) 582312
e-mail info@cavendish-hotel.net
website www.cavendish-hotel.net

Nearby Chatsworth; Haddon Hall;
Peak District.
Location 10 miles (16 km) W of
Chesterfield on A619; with ample
car parking
Food breakfast, lunch, dinner
Price £££
Rooms 23 double with bath; all
rooms have phone, TV, minibar,
hairdryer
Facilities sitting room, dining room,
bar, garden room; garden, putting-
green, fishing **Credit cards** AE, DC,
MC, V **Children** welcome
Disabled access difficult
Pets not accepted
Closed never **Proprietor** Eric
Marsh

The Cavendish
Country house hotel

The Cavendish doesn't sound like a personal small hotel. But the smart name is
not mere snobbery – it is the family name
of the Duke of Devonshire, on whose glorious Chatsworth estate the hotel sits (and
over which the bedrooms look). And nei-
ther the hotel's size nor its equipment
interferes with its essential appeal as a polished but informal and enthusiastically run
hotel – strictly speaking an inn, as Eric
Marsh is careful to point out, but for practical purposes a country house.

Outside, the solid stone building is plain
and unassuming. Inside, all is grace and
good taste: the welcoming entrance hall
sets the tone – striped sofas before an
open fire, elegant antique tables standing
on a brick-tile floor, while the walls act as
a gallery for Eric Marsh's eclectic collection of more than 300 pictures. The whole
ground floor has recently been remodelled, and a café-style conservatory added.
Bedrooms are consistently attractive and
comfortable, but vary in size and character
– older ones are more spacious.

The elegant restaurant claims to have a
'controversial' menu. It is certainly ambitious and highly priced, but it met the
approval of recent guests who described
the food as 'unsurpassed – we were spoilt
to death!' The Garden Room is less formal.

Bourton-on-the-Water, Gloucestershire

High Street, Bourton-on-the-Water,
Gloucestershire, GL54 2AN

Tel (01451) 822 244
Fax (01451) 810 126
e-mail reception@dialhousehotel.com
website www.dialhousehotel.com

Nearby Burford, Blenheim, Upper
and Lower Slaughter
Location in the heart of the village
with large hotel car park
Food breakfast, lunch, tea, dinner
Price ££
Rooms 13 rooms, (2 twins)
Facilities bar, sitting-room, garden
Credit cards all major
Children not ideal
Disabled a garden room is accessible
by wheelchair
Pets garden room only
Closed rarely
Proprietors Adrian and Jane
Campbell-Howard

Dial House
Country hotel

The Dial House attracts a certain type of client (the upwardly mobile *Daily Telegraph* reader) and that type of client will like it very much. This is a place to forget boardroom worries; and wives (or girl-friends) will enjoy being 'pampered'. A hand-painted sign outside describes it as 'An oasis of peace and tranquillity.' In the summer, Bourton-on-the-Water can be crowded, so the neat garden behind the hotel gives guests a place to escape the hordes.

The place is spotless. Rooms are furnished comfortably with antiques and top-quality repro. The walls are hung with hand-blocked paper in handsome patterns. Bathrooms have roll-top free-standing baths, lots of Penhaligon's toiletries and piles of thick white towels. New arrivals are greeted with fruit and chocolates. A small bar downstairs caters for most tastes. A sitting-room for residents has a log fire in winter and brightly coloured modern chairs, for the owners are careful not to let this honey-coloured 17th century house become too old-fashioned. The two dining-rooms are likewise furnished in modern restaurant style and Jamie Forman, a Michelin 'Rising Star', has devised menus cleverly combining traditional dishes (steaks, smoked salmon) with modern trends (local sourcing, crushed potatoes, *boudin noir*). Colour supplement living *par excellence*.

Broad Campden, Gloucestershire

Broad Campden, Chipping
Campden, Gloucestershire
GL55 6UU

Tel (01386) 840295
Fax (01386) 841334
e-mail info@malt-house.co.uk
website www.malt-house.co.uk

Nearby Hidcote Manor; Sezincote
Garden; Snowshill Manor; Court
Barn Museum; Stratford-upon-
Avon; Cotswold villages;
Cheltenham.
Location 1 mile (1.5 km) SE of
Chipping Campden; with ample car
parking
Food breakfast
Price ££
Rooms 7; 6 doubles, 1 suite, all with
bath and shower; all rooms have TV,
DVD, hairdryer, tea and coffee mak-
ing facilities, wi-fi **Facilities** 2 sitting
rooms, dining room; croquet **Credit
cards** AE, MC, V **Children** wel-
come if well behaved **Disabled**
access difficult **Pets** by arrangement
Closed Christmas **Proprietor** Judi
Wilkes

The Malt House
Country guest-house

It is easy to miss this 17thC Cotswold
house (in fact a conversion of three cottages) in a tiny picture-postcard hamlet
comprising little more than a cluster of
thatched, wistaria-covered cottages, a
church and a pub. Once found, the Malt
House is delightful – with low beamed
ceilings, antique furniture and leaded windows overlooking a dream garden, where
the resident cat potters contentedly
about. 'Beautifully done out and a peaceful,
charming atmosphere,' comments our latest reporter.

Since Judi took the Malt House over she
has decreased the number of bedrooms,
all of which overlook the gardens and pad-
dock and orchard beyond. They are individually decorated in tasteful neutral
shades (some with *toille de jouie*) and furnished with antiques and collections from
Judi's travels. The public rooms are
immensely comfortable, with log fires in
winter, but small, adorned with *objets d'art*
from India and other exotic destinations.
The accommodation includes a pleasantly
laid out garden suite with a private sitting
room and an entrance to the garden.
Guests breakfast in the beamed dining
room, with inglenook fireplace.

Dinner can be arranged for parties of
12 or more – usually if the whole house is
taken exclusively.

Burford, Oxfordshire

99 High Street, Burford,
Oxfordshire OX18 4QA

Tel (01993) 823151
Fax (01993) 823240
e-mail stay@burfordhouse.co.uk
website www.burfordhouse.co.uk

Nearby Cotswold Wildlife Park;
Blenheim Palace; Broadway.
Location middle of Burford High
Street; parking in street or free car
park nearby
Food breakfast, light lunch
Price ££
Rooms 8 doubles with bath and
shower; all rooms have phone, satel-
lite TV, DVD, wi-fi, hairdryer
Facilities sitting room, breakfast
room, courtyard garden
Credit cards AE, MC, V **Children**
welcome
Disabled 1 ground-floor room
Pets not accepted
Closed Jan **Proprietors** Jane and
Simon Henty

Burford House
Town house hotel

Without disturbing its historical integrity, Simon and Jane Henty have smuggled 21stC comforts into their 15thC Cotswold stone and black-and-white timbered house in the heart of Burford. The whole place positively gleams with personal care and attention, with fresh flowers, books and magazines in the smartly decorated, dark-beamed bedrooms, and their own belongings, including family photos, dotted amongst the public furniture. There are two comfortable and contrasting sitting rooms downstairs, one of which gives on to a walled and paved garden, as does the ground-floor bedroom. There is also that welcome reviver of the thirsty traveller, an honesty bar, and the welcome reviver of the wet walker, a drying room.

Upstairs there are six more bedrooms, three with four-posters and one of these also has a huge free-standing bath in it. Each thoughtfully organized room is full of character, and each has an immaculate bathroom. Breakfast (included in the price of the room) is an excellent production, taken in the dining room looking out on to the High Street. Dinner is not available in the hotel, but there are plenty of restaurants and pubs within easy walking distance.

Burford, Oxfordshire

Sheep Street, Burford, Oxfordshire
OX18 4LR

Tel (01993) 823155
Fax (01993) 822228
e-mail info@lambinn-burford.co.uk
website www.cotswold-inns-hotels.co.uk/lamb

Nearby Minster Lovell Hall;
Cotswold villages; Blenheim Palace.
Location in village; with car parking
for 6 cars **Food** breakfast, lunch,
dinner
Price £££
Rooms 17 double and twin with
bath or shower; all have phone, TV,
hairdryer, wi-fi **Facilities** 3 sitting
rooms, dining room, bar; garden
Credit cards AE, MC, V **Children**
welcome **Disabled** 3 ground-floor
bedrooms **Pets** dogs in room by
prior arrangement **Closed** never
Proprietors Cotswold Inns and
Hotels **Manager** Andrew Swan

The Lamb
Town inn

If you want some respite from Burford's summer throng, you won't do better than The Lamb, only a few yards behind the High Street, but a veritable haven of tranquillity – particularly in the pretty walled garden, a view endorsed by a recent inspection.

Inside the creeper-clad stone cottages, you won't be surprised to find traditional pub trappings (after all, The Lamb has been an inn since the 15th century), but you may be surprised to discover 17 spacious beamed bedrooms decorated with floral fabrics and antiques. All are different – 'Shepherds', for example, has a vast antique four-poster bed and a little attic-like bathroom, 'Malt' (in what was once the neighbouring brewery) has a smart brass bed and large stone mullion windows.

Since our last edition, the Lamb has been taken over by the Cotswold Inns and Hotels mini-chain. The only change has been the addition of a further two bedrooms and some refurbishment – they say they want to keep it as it is.

Head chef Sean Ducie produces the daily-changing meals. These are served in the dining room, looking on to the geranium-filled patio. Coffee can be taken in here, or in the sitting room or TV room, both of which have comfortable chairs and sofas grouped around open fires

Reports welcome.

Chipping Campden, Gloucestershire

The Square, Chipping Campden,
Gloucestershire GL55 6AN

Tel (01386) 840330
Fax (01386) 840310
e-mail reception@cotswolhouse.com
website www.cotswoldhouse.com

Nearby Broadway; Stratford on
Avon.
Location in main street of town;
parking for 12 cars
Food breakfast, lunch, dinner
Price ££££
Rooms 20; all doubles with bath; all
rooms have phone, TV, hairdryer
Facilities 2 sitting rooms, bar; cro-
quet
Credit cards AE, MC, V **Children**
accepted over 6
Disabled access difficult
Pets accepted
Closed never
Proprietors Ian and Christa Taylor

Cotswold House
Town hotel

Described by one reader as 'the place
to stay' in Chipping Campden,
Cotswold House can claim to be a very
popular hotel. Set in a fine street, the
building, dating from 1650, was renovated
in the late 1980s with great attention to
detail; then, in 1999, it was bought by new
owners Ian and Christa Taylor, realizing
their ambition of owning (rather than
being employed in) a hotel. They further
upgraded the rooms and added the new
coach house, where clean modern lines,
gas log fireplaces and broad exposed
beams definitely add to the place.
Thoughtful touches include flat screen TVs
that automatically swivel out over the bed,
heated bathroom floors, chrome bookrests
and small TVs in the bathroom. In the main
hotel, an impressive spiral staircase leads
to well-appointed rooms, which are a similar standard to those in the coach house.

You have the choice of two restaurants:
the relaxed brasserie and the formal dining
room. The menu might offer warm salad of
pigeon and wild mushroom with shallot
dressing; pork belly with roasted scallops
and pancetta crisps; toffee caramel mousse
and vanilla roasted pineapple. Alongside
the coach house, a Mediterranean-style
garden, attractively lit in the evening, is
perfect for an after-dinner stroll.

Clipsham, Rutland

Main Street, Clipsham, Rutland,
LE15 7SH

Tel (01780)410355
Fax (01780) 410000
e-mail info@theolivebranchpub.com
website
www.theolivebranchpub.com

Nearby Burghleigh, Belvoir Castle,
Rutland Owl and Falconry Centre
Location in the centre of Clipsham
Price ££-££££
Rooms 6 en-suite; all rooms have
TV, radio, tea and coffee making
facilities; most have DVD player,
broadband
Facilities DVD/CD library,
patio/gardens
Credit cards MC, V
Children welcome
Disabled fully wheelchair-accessible
room **Pets** accepted in ground floor
rooms **Closed** Christmas night,
Boxing day, New Year's day
Proprietors Sean Hope and Ben
Jones

Beech House
Bed-and-breakfast

The Beech House is where you sleep, but the Olive Branch began it all and the two, though divided by the road, are really indivisible. So good was the food in the pub (named to mark the end of a quarrel with a farmer; this is not an ordinary place) that rooms were needed to house those who had travelled to enjoy it. What looks like a pretty doll's-house was bought and six en-suite rooms were made, decorated with fashionable modern colours and furnished with a mix of rather striking antique and modern pieces. It is a thoughtful management that provides a fully wheelchair-accessible bathroom in the ground floor room and attention to the guests' needs and attention to detail are probably what won the combined establishments the Michelin Pub of the Year award in 2007. There are four types of tea in the bedrooms and fresh coffee for the cafetière; a Roberts digital radio (*de rigueur* in smart inns these days); DVDs and a choice of duvets or sheets and blankets. So far so homely. But the extra factor which this place seems to have in spades is what Michelin's men call 'star quality', the willing, informal, kind and efficient service you get from people who have put their hearts (and their savings) into a venture like this.

Corse Lawn, Gloucestershire

Corse Lawn, Gloucestershire
GL19 4LZ

Tel (01452) 780771
Fax (01452) 780840
e-mail enquiries@corselawn.com
website www.corselawn.com

Nearby Tewkesbury Abbey; Malvern
Hills.
Location 5 miles (8 km) W of
Tewkesbury on B4211; with ample
car parking
Food breakfast, lunch, dinner
Price £££
Rooms 18; 16 double and twin, 2
suites, all with bath; all rooms have
phone, TV, hairdryer **Facilities** 3
sitting rooms, bar, restaurant, 2
meeting rooms; garden, croquet,
tennis, indoor swimming pool
Credit cards AE, DC, MC, V
Children accepted if well-behaved
Disabled 5 ground-floor bedrooms
Pets accepted in bedrooms **Closed**
24 to 26 Dec **Proprietor** Baba Hine

Corse Lawn House
Country hotel

This tall, red-brick Queen Anne house,
set back across common land from
what is now a minor road, must have been
one of the most refined coaching inns of
its day. Should you arrive in traditional
style, you could still drive your coach-and-
four down the slipway into the large pond
in front of the house, to cool the horses
and wash the carriage.

Baba Hine has been here since the late
1970s, first running the house purely as a
restaurant, later opening up four rooms
and in recent years adding various extensions (carefully designed to blend with the
original building) to provide more and
more bedrooms as well as more space for
drinking, eating and sitting. Baba Hine is
now front of house, having handed over
the kitchen to Andrew Poole who, she
says, produces dishes just as good as hers.
The menu is an eclectic mix of English and
French, modern and provincial dishes, all
carefully prepared and served in substantial portions; there are fixed-price menus
(with a vegetarian alternative) at both
lunch and dinner as well as a *carte*, all
notably good value.

Bedrooms are large, with a mixture of
antique and modern furnishings and the
atmosphere of the house is calm and
relaxing. Breakfasts are a home-made
feast. A recent visitor was enchanted.

Crudwell, Wiltshire

Crudwell, Malmesbury
Wiltshire SN16 9EP

Tel (01666) 577194
e-mail info@therectoryhotel.co.uk
website www.therectoryhotel.com

Nearby Cotswolds
Location village of Crudwell on the
edge of the Cotswolds with car parking
Food breakfast, lunch, dinner
Price ££-£££
Rooms 12 doubles, all with bath and
shower
Facilities bar/sitting room,
Victorian walled garden, table tennis,
helipad, outer heated swimming pool
Credit cards AE, MC, V
Children welcome
Disabled not suitable
Pets dogs accepted
Closed never
Proprietors Jonathan Barry, Julian
Muggridge

The Rectory
Village hotel

A real find: this newly opened hotel is as soothing as it is professional. Assured, and stylishly simple, devoid of gimmicks, it's unaffected but excellent. Recently refurbished and reopened by its young and savvy new owners, The Rectory stands on the edge of the Cotswolds in the village of Crudwell. The entrance hall-reception area is homely as well as contemporary, with an arresting pair of lamp stands and tall, unadorned, half-shuttered windows. The well-stocked three-tier magazine rack invites you to flop on one of the traditionally styled sofas and the welcome from the owners is personal without being intrusive. Jonathan Barry trained with the Hotel du Vin group; Julian Muggridge had an art gallery and antiques business: a happy combination if ever there was one. The reception area opens on to a wide, light, flagstoned corridor, prettily decorated with side tables and mirrors. Opening off it are a lovely panelled dining room, elegant in its simplicity, and a warmly, eclectically decorated bar/sitting room. The dining room offers a short, interesting menu.

The 12 bedrooms could have been furnished and decorated just for this guide. Named after hills along the Cotswold Way, they are all different, attractive without being fancy, sensibly priced homes from home in which it's a pleasure to spend time.

Great Rissington, Gloucestershire

Great Rissington, Gloucestershire
GL54 2LP

Tel (01451) 820388
e-mail enquiry@thelambinn.com
website www.thelambinn.com

Nearby The Slaughters; Stow-on-the-Wold; Burford; Sudeley Castle.
Location 4 miles (6 km) SE of Bourton-on-the-Water, 3 miles (5 km) N of A40; with ample car parking
Food breakfast, lunch, dinner
Price ££
Rooms 14; 7 double, 1 twin and 6 suites, all with bath or shower; all rooms have TV, wi-fi
Facilities sitting room, bar; garden
Credit cards AE, MC, V
Children welcome
Disabled not suitable
Pets accepted in bedrooms by arrangement
Closed Christmas Day, Boxing Day
Proprietors Paul and Jacqueline Gabriel

Cotswolds

Lamb Inn
Country inn

If you follow the River Windrush as it rises westwards from Burford, and then roughly follow its curve from the north (where it has given Bourton-on-the-Water its name), you will arrive in Great Rissington, deep in the Cotswolds. Overlooking gently rolling farmland and built from the local stone, the original elements of this inn are 300 years old. Taken over in the year 2000 by Paul and Jackie Gabriel, The Lamb is still very much a pub, indeed it is enough of a pub to merit a recommendation in a national guide to good beer. But it also now has two elements that many other inns lack – good board and lodging. Board comes in the shape of a surprisingly large – and comfortingly busy – restaurant. It does a roaring trade in traditional dishes freshly prepared from the best of local produce, often with a modern twist: the most popular of these is a half shoulder of lamb.

The bedrooms are bright, fresh and individually designed, and more than half have space for sitting as well as sleeping. All bathrooms have recently been renovated.

Hambleton, Rutland

Hambleton, Oakham, Rutland
LE15 8TH

Tel (01572) 756991
Fax (01572) 724721
e-mail hotel@hambletonhall.com
website www.hambletonhall.com

Nearby Burghley House;
Rockingham Castle; Stamford,
Belvoir Castle.
Location 2 miles (3 km) E of
Oakham on peninsula jutting into
Rutland Water; with ample car parking
Food breakfast, lunch, dinner
Price ££££
Rooms 17 double and twin with
bath; all rooms have phone, TV,
hairdryer
Facilities sitting rooms, 3 dining
rooms, bar; garden, swimming pool,
tennis, helipad; fishing, golf, sailing,
riding all nearby **Credit cards** AE,
DC, MC, V **Children** accepted
Disabled access possible, lift/elevator **Pets** by arrangement **Closed**
never **Proprietors** Tim and Stefa
Hart

Hambleton Hall
Country house hotel

If you're planning a second honeymoon, a break from work or a weekend away from the kids, this Victorian former shooting lodge in the grand hotel tradition is a sybaritic paradise, from which only your wallet and your waistline will suffer. The location is unrivalled, standing in stately grandeur on a wooded hillock, surrounded by manicured lawns, surveying the expanse of Rutland Water. The interior is sumptuous. In her design of the rooms, Stefa Hart uses rich, heavy fabrics, combining stripes and chintzes in some of the bedrooms, and showing a preference for delicate colours. The rooms still have their original mouldings and fireplaces and are furnished with fine antiques and paintings. Bedrooms with a view over the water are the most sought-after and expensive.

Many people are drawn here by the wizardry of Michelin-starred chef, Aaron Patterson. He works his magic on only the freshest of ingredients, whether Angus beef, sea bass or veal sweetbreads. One of the joys of staying here is that you can blow the cobwebs away with an exhilarating walk from the front door of the hotel as far as you want around Rutland Water, birdwatching as you go.

When we visited in 2007 we were as impressed as ever – and pleased to learn that the Harts are resisting pressure to add a spa, and opening a home bakery instead.

Hereford, Herefordshire

Castle Street, Hereford
HR1 2NW

Tel (01432) 356321
Fax (01432) 365909
e-mail info@castlehse.co.uk
website www.castlehse.co.uk

Nearby Hereford Cathedral,
chained library, Mappa Mundi, cider
museum, Offa's Dyke
Location In Hereford city centre on
Castle Street; valet parking
Food breakfast, lunch, dinner
Price £££-££££
Rooms 15; 10 suites, 1 deluxe dou-
ble, 4 singles; all with bath; all rooms
have TV, phone, video player, mini
hi-fi, fridge, safe
Facilities lounge, dining room, bar,
gardens, terrace
Credit cards AE, DC, MC, V
Children welcome
Disabled one adapted room
Pets dogs accepted, by prior
arrangement **Closed** never
Proprietor David Watkins

Castle House
Town house hotel

Life goes at a slower pace in this rural
part of England and Hereford is the ideal
county town: tight-knit, accessible and tranquil, yet with world-class attractions in its
fine cathedral and Chained Library. Castle
House is an elegant Grade II listed town
mansion whose charming gardens overlook
the old Castle moat. The cathedral and
shops are nearby, yet there is absolute
quiet: no traffic noise, just birdsong and the
quack of ducks. We can think of few loveli-
er, or better sited, city hotels in Britain.

Past the pillared entrance, you find an
impressive hall, with wooden central staircase and reception tucked neatly out of
sight. To one side: a panelled bar; to the
other, a spacious restaurant and sitting
room whose doors lead to the garden. All
the rooms are full of light. Upstairs are bedrooms of various shapes and sizes, some
optimistically described as 'luxury suites'
when 'spacious double' is more accurate.

The hotel was revamped in 2000 in a
style that might be described as 'continental bijoux' or 'faux posh'. We felt this was at
odds with the building and with Hereford
itself, but Castle House is a very good hotel.
The management is excellent and the food
imaginative. A 'tasting menu' at £49 per person, however, reiterates the hotel' s pretentious side, in a city and a county that are
among the least pretentious in England.

Kington, Herefordshire

Kington, Herefordshire HR5 3LH

Tel (01544) 230720
Fax (01544) 230754
e-mail martin@penrhos.co.uk
website www.penrhos.co.uk

Nearby Offa's Dyke Path; Hergest Croft Garden.
Location 1 mile (2 km) E of Kington on A44; in 6-acre grounds with ample car parking
Food breakfast, dinner
Price ££
Rooms 15; 2 4-posters, 2 suites, 11 double and twin, all with bath or shower; all rooms have phone, TV, hairdryer; fax/modem lead by arrangement
Facilities 2 sitting rooms, 2 dining rooms, bar; garden
Credit cards MC, V **Children** welcome
Disabled access easy **Pets** not accepted **Closed** never
Proprietors Martin Griffiths and Daphne Lambert

Penrhos Court
Organic country hotel

Penrhos Court is more a way of life than a hotel. In 1971 it was in such a parlous state that it was due for demolition. Martin Griffiths and Daphne Lambert have spent the last 30 years rolling the clock back, but perhaps not as far as 1280, when it was probably built. Now, as well as being a faithfully restored example of medieval architecture, it has been converted to an organic restaurant and hotel; Daphne, a professional nutritionist and chef of the restaurant for better than two decades, buys from other organic producers what she doesn't grow herself in her own kitchen garden, and runs organic cookery courses for those who want to become initiates. Menus change through the year to bring to the table the best of whatever is in season. It would be a misnomer to describe the place where you eat as 'the dining room', because it is self evidently a large beamed and galleried hall set with oak tables and lit through stained-glass windows.

The handsomely decorated and furnished bedrooms are all on the same scale, varying from the merely large to enormous. This is a relaxing, peaceful spot in unspoiled Border countryside and if you want to get back to nature without travelling too far, try the farm pond: there is a perpetual mini-wildlife programme running.

Langar, Nottinghamshire

Langar, Nottinghamshire
NG13 9HG

Tel (01949) 860559
Fax (01949) 861045
e-mail info@langarhall.co.uk
website www.langarhall.com

Nearby Belton House; Chatsworth;
Sherwood Forest; Lincoln
Cathedral.
Location in village behind church;
with ample car parking
Food breakfast, lunch, dinner
Price £££
Rooms 12 doubles; 1 room has
shower, all others have baths; all
rooms have phone, TV, hairdryer
Facilities sitting rooms, dining
rooms, bar; garden, croquet, fishing,
helipad **Credit cards** MC, V
Children welcome **Disabled** 1
ground-floor bedroom **Pets** accept-
ed by arrangement **Closed** never
Proprietor Imogen Skirving

Langar Hall
Country house hotel

After the death of Imogen Skirving's father,
a pre-war captain of Nottinghamshire
County Cricket Club and the last owner of
Langar Hall, she couldn't bear the thought of
losing the house, nor could she afford to keep
it on, except on the basis of sharing it with
guests. Thus was born the concept of Langar
Hall as a hotel and, despite burgeoning success, people who stay here feel more like
guests in a beautiful Georgian stuccoed country house rather than customers in a hotel.
The library appears to be totally unchanged,
with hundreds of books available to leaf
through with a drink or two before dinner. The
food is superb and the wine list well judged.

The best bedrooms are light and airy, with
furniture appropriate to the house that
Imogen wanted to save, and enjoy glorious
views of the Vale of Belvoir. For exercise, you
can play croquet or stroll round the village
church just behind the house. Best of all is
the friendliness of the hostess and her staff.
Imogen wanders around the dining room,
alighting at tables of single, bored business-
men and exchanging any sort of gossip, while
nothing is too much trouble for the chef or
staff. When our inspector realised, at 12.45
am, after an excellent dinner, that he had forgotten his sponge bag, an assortment of
toothbrushes, toothpaste and razors was
provided. We revisited in 2006 and enjoyed
the Imogen Skirving show as much as ever.

Leonard Stanley, Gloucestershire

Leonard Stanley, Stonehouse,
Gloucestershire GL10 3LU

Tel (01453) 822515
Fax (01453) 822515

Nearby Cotswold villages; Owlpen
Manor; Gloucester; Tetbury.
Location 4 miles (6.5 km) SW of
Stroud, 1 mile (2.5 km) off A419
between Leonard Stanley and King
Stanley; with ample car parking
Food breakfast, dinner by prior
arrangement
Price £
Rooms 1 double, 1 twin, 1 single, all
with bath or shower; all rooms have
TV, hairdryer, trouser press
Facilities sitting room, garden
room, dining room; garden
Credit cards not accepted **Children**
by arrangement
Disabled not suitable **Pets** not
accepted **Closed** occasional holidays
Proprietor Rosemary Reeves

Grey Cottage
Village guest-house

This stone-built cottage, owned by Rosemary Reeves, dates from 1834 and is spotless and pleasingly furnished. During renovation, original stonework and a tessellated hall floor were laid bare. The cottage is a very private guest-house with a cosy, cottagey atmosphere; there is no roadside advertisement and advance bookings only are accepted.

Generous home cooking includes such dishes as paupiettes of plaice with smoked salmon and lime and cumin sauce followed by prune and coffee mousse. An evidently discriminating New York couple give Grey Cottage a rave review: 'Even more than your guide promised. Beautiful garden with a 100-foot Wellingtonia, planted almost 150 years ago. The bedrooms and bathrooms are on the small side, but they are immensely cosy, with firm beds, reliable hot water, heated towel rails, trouser presses and fresh fruit. A thoughtful touch is the 'funny tales from Grey Cottage,' written by Rosemary, put by the bedside.'

The food is fresh, of high quality, and abundant. Rosemary is capable, charming and dedicated – but not intrusive. Unfortunately, most tourists end up paying more for accommodation nearer the principal sights hereabouts – but actually getting far less. Rosemary recently won the AA's Friendliest Landlady of the Year Award.

Little Malvern, Worcestershire

Little Malvern, near Malvern,
Worcestershire WR13 6NA

Tel (01684) 310288
Fax (01684) 311117
e-mail enquiries@holdfast-cottage.co.uk **website** www.holdfast-cottage.co.uk

Nearby Eastnor Castle; Worcester;
Hereford; Gloucester.
Location 4 miles (6.5 km) S of
Great Malvern on A4104; with
ample car parking
Food breakfast, lunch, bar meals,
dinner
Price £££
Rooms 8; 5 doubles, 2 twins, 1 single all with bath or shower; all rooms
have phone, TV, hairdryer
Facilities sitting room, bar, dining
room, conservatory; croquet
Credit cards MC, V **Children** welcome
Disabled access difficult
Pets accepted
Closed never
Proprietors Guy and Annie Dixon

Holdfast Cottage
Country hotel

'Cottage' seems to be stretching things somewhat – and yet, despite its size, this Victorian farmhouse does have the cosy intimacy of a cottage, and Annie and Guy Dixon create an atmosphere of friendly informality.

Inside, low oak beams and a polished flagstone floor in the hall conform to cottage requirement; beyond, headroom improves – though flowery decoration emphasizes the cottage status. Bedrooms are light and airy, with carefully co-ordinated fabrics and papers; some bathrooms are small. Outside, the veranda with its wistaria keeps the scale of the house relatively intimate. The garden – scarcely cottage-style – adds enormously to the overall appeal of the place, with its lawns, shrubberies, fruit trees and delightful 'wilderness'. Beyond is open farmland with spectacular views of the Malvern Hills.

The daily-changing menu is based on continental as well as traditional English dishes, using the best local and seasonal produce, as well as freshly prepared home-baked rolls and hand-made ice cream. Herbs are gathered from the garden to compliment the English fare, which is sometimes found alongside more unusual dishes such as guinea fowl.

Ludlow, Shropshire

73-74 Lower Broad Street, Ludlow, Shropshire SY8 1PH

Tel (01584) 876996
Fax (01584) 876860
e-mail phil@ross-b-and-b-ludlow.co.uk **website** www.ross-b-and-b-ludlow.co.uk

Nearby Ludlow Castle; Stokesay Castle; Berrington Hall; Ironbridge; Stiperstones; Stretton Hills.
Location in town centre near River Teme; car parking in street
Food breakfast
Price ££
Rooms 3 suites, all have sitting room and bath and shower; all rooms have phone, TV, hairdryer
Facilities sitting rooms, breakfast room; gardens **Credit cards** MC, V
Children accepted **Disabled** not suitable
Pets by arrangement **Closed** never
Proprietors Sally and Philip Maile

Bromley Court
Town bed-and-breakfast

Whether it's houses or horses that brought you to Ludlow, you'll find plenty of both – all thoroughbreds. The entire centre of Ludlow is listed Grade II (a bit too late for the castle, which is a ruin), and the racetrack brings people from far and wide. Another strong draw is the plethora of gourmet restaurants, several of them Michelin-starred, from which to choose.

In Lower Broad Street, Sally and Philip Maile have taken over the running of Bromley Court, three tiny Tudor cottages further along the road, Broadgate Mews, creating three suites, each on two levels and with a well-equipped breakfast bar. Each has its own front-down, with a delightful communal courtyard where guests can chat after afternoon tea or pre-dinner drinks if they feel so inclined.

The Mailes also run the Bull Hotel in the centre of town. Here, too, is where you need to come if you want an (excellent) cooked breakfast rather than something simpler at your breakfast bar. For lunch or dinner, take advice from the Mailes – they'll tell you which of the Michelin-starred restaurants is on song at the moment.

Malvern Wells, Worcestershire

Holywell Road, Malvern Wells,
Worcestershire WR14 4LG

Tel (01684) 575859
Fax (01684) 560662
e-mail reception@cottageinthe-
wood.co.uk **website** www.cot-
tageinthewood.co.uk

Nearby Malvern Hills; Eastnor
Castle; Worcester Cathedral.
Location 2 miles (3 km) S of Great
Malvern off A449; with ample car
parking
Food breakfast, lunch, dinner
Price £££
Rooms 31 double and twin with
bath or shower; all rooms have
phone, TV, hairdryer; 1 has air-con-
ditioning **Facilities** sitting room,
dining room, bar; garden
Credit cards AE, MC, V **Children**
welcome
Disabled ground-floor rooms in
annexe
Pets accepted in ground-floor rooms
and Beech House
Closed never **Proprietors** John and
Sue Pattin

The Cottage in the
Wood **Country hotel**

Three buildings and a family form this
glossy little hotel perched, very privately, in seven wooded acres, high above
the Severn valley and with a superb vista
across to the Cotswolds thirty-something
miles away (binoculars provided). There
are bedrooms in all three buildings, taking
the hotel over our usual size for this guide;
but the smartly furnished Georgian dower
house at its heart is so intimate, calm and
comfortable that we decided to relent.

A short stroll away is the rebuilt Coach
House, known as the Pinnacles, where
rooms are smaller but have the best views,
and Beech Cottage with four cottage-style
bedrooms. The family consists of John and
Sue Pattin, their daughter Maria, son
Dominic (head chef) and son in law Nick.
Apart from its food, the restaurant (modern English cuisine) has two other substantial qualities: windows that let you see
the view and a wine list that lets you roam
the world. Walkers can get straight out on
to a good stretch of the Malvern Hills and
for tourers the Pattins provide leaflets giving concise notes on everything that's
worth visiting for 50 miles (80 km)
around. For the rest of us, there's a very
well stocked bar and a free video library.

Moccas, Herefordshire

Moccas Court, Moccas,
Herefordshire HR2 9LH

Tel (01981) 500019
e-mail info@moccas-court.co.uk
website www.moccas-court.co.uk

Nearby Hay-on-Wye, Mappa
Mundi, Hereford Cathedral, Kilpeck
Church
Location in own extensive grounds
with ample private car parking
Food breakfast, dinner
Price £££-££££
Rooms 5; one double, 4 can be dou-
ble or twin; 4 rooms have bath, one
with private bathroom; all with TV,
one with DVD
Facilities sitting room, library, din-
ing room, music room, gardens
Credit cards AE, MC, V
Children unsuitable
Disabled not suitable
Pets not accepted
Closed Jan-Feb
Proprietors Ben and Mimi Chester-
Master

Moccas Court
Country hotel

'It's hard to think of anywhere more lovely to spend a night' writes our reporter. 'We arrived in the dark, something I'll repeat if I return, for in the morning each shuttered window of my heavenly bedroom and bathroom revealed a different view: first a little church; then the grounds filled with fine trees; the Wye flowing past green banks to the red Scar; the grassy terrace with stone steps and urns and wooded hillside beyond.'

Moccas Court was dilapidated and uncared for when Ben Chester-Master's family inherited it some years ago; restoration was recently completed by Ben and his wife Mimi, who have now made the place their home.

The house is at first imposing but quickly revealed as compact and elegant, with a wonderful oval staircase. There are five bedrooms for guests, who meet in the yellow library for drinks before dinner, eaten communally (unless you request otherwise). The dining room is a sensational circular room designed by Robert Adam, with original 18thC hand-painted wallpaper. Ben is the chef and he cooks beautifully.

Moccas Court is hard to pigeonhole: a private home, run on house-party lines, it has the luxury – and prices – of a serious hotel. Your mobile is unlikely to work, there's no internet, spa or gym, just the house, the setting and the river. Check the Moccas Court website before booking – it'll help you work out if it's for you.

Norton, Shropshire

Bridgenorth Road, Norton, Near Shifnal, Telford, Shropshire, TF11 9EE

Tel (01952) 730353
Fax (01952) 730 355
e-mail reservations@hundred-house.co.uk **website** www.hundred-house.co.uk

Nearby Telford, Chester, Ironbridge Gorge Museum, Severn Valley steam way, The Long Mynd (walk).
Location just off the M54 from junction 4, on the A442 between Telford and Bridgnorth, with car parking
Food breakfast, lunch, dinner
Price ££–£££ (min 2 night stay)
Rooms 10 double and twin, 1 single, all with bath; all have TV, phone, tea and coffee making facilities, hairdryer **Facilities** dining room, bar, brasserie; herb garden, beer garden
Credit cards AE, MC, V **Children** welcome **Disabled** some access in public rooms **Pets** well behaved dogs (£10 charge) **Closed** Christmas night **Proprietors** Henry, Sylvia and Stuart Phillips

Hundred House Hotel
Country hotel

"Quite extraordinary, a pleasant surprise around every corner" says one recent reporter. From the moment you pull in to the car park you don't quite know what to expect next. The building itself dates back to the 1500's, when it was the local court house, and the remains of the stocks and the whipping post can still be seen opposite. Push open the stained glass doors, and the atmosphere hits you: dim lighting, mellow wood floors, panelled walls, bouquets of dried herbs and flowers hanging from ceilings. The dining areas are spacious – the Hundred House caters for non-residential guests, but the tables are cosy and intimate, some in front of a large open fire, others tucked in various nooks. The menu is impressive and unusual, but cooked well with no corners cut. The bar is in the brasserie area and offers an impressive range of ales, with more little tables for a quick bite of lunch.

The bedrooms are, well, eccentric: swings in the 'superior' rooms; lively, floral decoration; and some very spacious bathrooms. The one single room in the house is a little cramped. The herb garden tended by Sylvia Phillips, is magical and is regularly used for marriage blessings. Elsewhere, you'll find relaxing sitting areas and a small pond. It is very much a family-run hotel, with parents and sons working together to create a memorable experience.

Oxford

92-94 High Street, Oxford
OX1 4BN

Tel (01865) 799599
Fax (01865) 799598
e-mail info@oldbank-hotel.co.uk
website www.oldbank-hotel.co.uk

Nearby Oxford colleges; Botanical
Gardens; Sheldonian Theatre.
Location in city centre, with ample
car parking
Food breakfast, lunch, dinner; room
service
Price £££-££££
Rooms 44; 42 double and twin, 2
suites; all rooms have phone, TV,
CD player, fax/modem point, air-
conditioning, safe, hairdryer
Facilities restaurant, bar, courtyard
Credit cards AE, DC, MC, V
Children accepted
Disabled 1 room is specially adapt-
ed, most other rooms have lift/eleva-
tor access **Pets** not accepted **Closed**
Christmas **Proprietor** Jeremy
Mogford

Old Bank Hotel
Town hotel

When this hotel opened in 1999 it was
Oxford's first 'contemporary' hotel,
but now it has been joined by the Malmaison
in an amazing conversion of the old Oxford
jail. Hardly a quintessential charming small
hotel, because of its size, but we still think
Old Bank Hotel is a good central Oxford
address. What was, until the 1990s, a venerable bank with a fine Georgian façade and an
Elizabethan core, is now a cool, sophisticated
hotel with a buzzing brasserie.

The building has much to recommend it.
The best bedrooms are graced with floor-
length windows or, in the Tudor part, beams
and deep window seats under lattice windows. All the rooms – and the bathrooms –
are impeccably decorated in the understated
chic-rustic style of the day (think taupe, think
beige, think cream). They feel elegant and luxurious, and, because they are new, pristine
and unsullied.

As well as a hotel, the Old Bank has
become the 'in' place to eat in Oxford. The
Quod Brasserie and Bar stretches across the
former banking hall ("weird to think that I
used to cash my cheques and see the bank
manager here", says one guest, a touch wist-
fully), and while hotel guests may yearn for a
relaxing sitting room of their own, most will
enjoy the buzz and bonhomie that emanates
from this always packed, Mediterranean-influ-
enced new meeting place.

Oxford

1 Banbury Road, Oxford OX2 6NN

Tel (01865) 310210
Fax (01865) 311262
e-mail info@oldparsonage-
hotel.co.uk **website** www.oxford-
hotels-restaurants.co.uk

Nearby Oxford colleges; Botanical
Gardens; Sheldonian Theatre.
Location 5 minutes' walk from city
centre, at N end of St Giles, close to
junction of Woodstock and Banbury
Roads; limited car parking
Food breakfast, lunch, dinner; room
service and afternoon tea
Price £££ **Rooms** 30; 25 double and
twin, 1 single, 4 suites, all with bath;
all rooms have phone, TV, hairdryer,
internet connection **Facilities** sitting
room, dining room, bar; terrace, roof
garden **Credit cards** AE, DC, MC,
V **Children** welcome
Disabled access difficult **Pets** not
accepted **Closed** never **Proprietor**
Jeremy Mogford

Old Parsonage
Town hotel

Talk about contrast. The two best
hotels in Oxford, Old Bank House
(see opposite), and this one are in the
same ownership – Jeremy Mogford. The
Old Parsonage is much more typical of
our guide, occupying a characterful, wistaria-clad house that has been owned by
University College since 1320. Compared
to its sleek, hip younger sibling, it seems at
first quaint and old-fashioned, yet there is
no themed olde worlde charm here,
despite the great age of the building.

The place has panache: the staff are
young and charming, the atmosphere
informal, and the laid-back bar/brasserie
(part sitting room, part dining room) has a
clubby, cosmopolitan feel. Here drinks and
a varied menu – salmon fish cakes, wild
mushroom tart, tarte tatin – are served all
day long. In fine weather, large white parasols
adorn the front terrace (the heavy, studded
front door, by the way, is three centuries
old), making a delightful place to eat lunch.
They also hold barbeques on the terrace
every weekend over the summer, and there
is live jazz every Friday evening throughout
the year (inside in the colder months).

Bedrooms – which tend to be on the
small side – are pretty and traditional in
feel, with pale panelling and unfussy chintz,
and marble bathrooms (with telephone).

225, Iffley Road, Oxford,
OX4 1SQ

Tel (01865) 249 200
e-mail rooms@theorchardhouseox-ford.co.uk
website www.theorchardhouseox-ford.co.uk

Nearby colleges, punting,
Ashmolean Museum, Oxford
Playhouse
Location about 1 mile from the city
centre, on bus route, with some off-
street parking
Food breakfast, picnic lunches by
arrangement
Price ££ (minimum two nights at
week-end)
Rooms 3; 2 doubles with shower, 1
twin with neighbouring shower
room; all rooms have TV, tea and
coffee making facilities, hairdryer
Facilities sitting room; garden
Credit cards MC, V **Children** over
12 **Disabled** ground floor room
accessible in wheelchair **Pets** not
accepted **Closed** two weeks over
Christmas/New Year **Proprietor**
Paul Ridley

The Orchard House
City bed-and-breakfast

The Orchard House is a short walk from the centre of Oxford, just past the Iffley Road track where Roger Bannister ran the first Four Minute Mile in 1954. Paul Ridley calls his establishment a Bed and Breakfast, but that is selling it short; we prefer 'micro boutique hotel'. It was built in the Arts and Crafts manner in 1903 for a painter whose studio has been adapted to provide a large, light living room in which the owner's col-lection of modern ceramics, tapestry and other artworks are shown and where the fortunate guests take breakfast. The possi-bilities range from an austere meusli and fruit, to a well done Full English (though Ridley is far too sophisticated to call it that). Typically, guests are parents of Oxford undergraduates, medicos visiting the two great teaching hospitals, or tourists. The hall and front room have heavy oak doors and decoration in tune with the Edwardian style of the exterior. The walled garden is a fur-ther attraction, enclosing old fruit trees and providing vegetables for the kitchen. There are only three bedrooms, two with attractive stone-floored bathrooms. Furnishing is sim-ple, comfortable and chosen with real taste. The Orchard House had only been open for three years when we went to press and looked sparkling new. A beacon of excel-lence in a city with rather dull alternatives.

Painswick, Gloucestershire

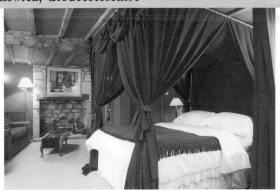

The Cross, Painswick,
Gloucestershire GL6 6XX

Tel (01452) 814006
Fax (01452) 812321
e-mail info@cardynham.co.uk
website www.cardynham.co.uk

Nearby Cheltenham; Chedworth
Roman Villa; Cirencester,
Gloucester, Sudeley.
Location in village, 3 miles (5 km)
N of Stroud; car parking on street
Food breakfast, Tues to Sat dinner
and Sun lunch
Price ££
Rooms 9; 6 double, 3 family, all with
bath or shower; all rooms have
phone, TV
Facilities sitting room, breakfast
room
Credit cards AE, MC, V **Children**
accepted **Pets** not accepted
Disabled not suitable **Closed**
restaurant only, Sun eve, Mon eve
Proprietor John Paterson

Cardynham House
Village bed-and-breakfast

Built with money from wool and from pale gold stone out of a local quarry, Painswick is a classic Cotswold town perched rather precariously on (and over the brink of) a steep hillside. If you're not paying attention you might quite easily walk past Cardynham House – a discreet sign above the venerable front door of this Grade II-listed flower-hung building, right on the street, is hardly enough to focus your attention when everything else around is so worth looking at. The real fun starts once you get inside. A cavernous open fireplace, flanked by a bread oven, warms a cosy drawing room which seems to metamorphose at some point into a conservatory.

Somehow, nine totally unique bedrooms have been created in this apparently mod-est-sized house, and each one is a triumphal exercise of imagination. Dotted with antiques and murals, each is decorated to a different theme and, even side by side in the same building, they all work unusually well. The most eccentric of all, air-conditioned because it hasn't a window to its name, has been got up like a desert pavilion. Another has its own private patio largely taken up with a covered plunge pool (heated, and with a powered current to swim against). Breakfast is taken in the restaurant that, on the evenings that it's open, serves Thai food.

Rhydycroesau, Shropshire

Rhydycroesau, Near Oswestry, Shropshire, SY10 7JD

Tel (01691) 653700
Fax (01978) 211004
e-mail stay@peny.co.uk **website** www.peny.co.uk

Nearby Erdigg; Llanrhaedar waterfall; Powys Castle; Pistyll Rhaedar waterfall
Location 3 miles (4.5 km) West of Oswestry on the B4580. Hotel is 3 miles (4.5 km)down on that road on the left
Food breakfast, dinner, light lunch on request
Price ££
Rooms 12 double; all with bath and shower; all rooms have TV, hairdryer, modem point, tea and coffee making facilities, phone
Facilities dining room, sitting room, bar, reading room; garden **Credit cards** AE, MC, V **Children** welcome **Disabled** 1 ground-floor room **Closed** 21st of Dec for 4 weeks **Pets** by arrangement
Proprietors Mr and Mrs Hunter

Pen-y-Dyffryn
Country hotel

Driving through the windy lanes cutting through the Shropshire hills from Oswestry, you can easily miss this attractive Georgian House tucked away off the main road. It nestles serenely among trees and green fields and you will be taken aback by the views that stretch (on a clear day) to the Welsh mountains. The dining room and sitting areas are decorated in warm, rich colours open log fires for the chilly winter evenings and are perfect, in the summer, for a sun-downer while watching the spectacular sunsets. If you prefer to drink or dine outside, there's a delightful little patio stretching round the side of the hotel.

The bedrooms are large and spacious, decorated in relaxing pastel shades, with large fluffy towels provided in all the *en suite* bathrooms (some with spa baths and Jacuzzis) and fresh flowers on arrival. Four of the bedrooms are in the coach house, which is ideal for guests with animals. They each have spectacular views and their own private little patio. The food is as you would expect: hearty and fresh-cooked, mostly with organic and local produce. The small bar by the entrance is staffed by helpful and friendly staff who can advise you on sightseeing, walking, or shopping in Wales or Shropshire.

Rowsley, Derbyshire

Rowsley, Derbyshire DE4 2EB

Tel (01629) 733518
Fax (01629) 732671
e-mail reception@thepeacocka-trowsley.com **website** www.thepea-cockatrowsley.com

Nearby Haddon Hall, Chatsworth, rivers Wye and Derwent
Location beside A6, between Matlock and Bakewell
Food breakfast, lunch, dinner; room service
Price £££
Rooms 16 doubles, one with four-poster, all en suite; all rooms have phone, TV, DVD player, tea and coffee making facilities, hairdryer
Facilities bar, conference rooms, private dining and restaurant, fishing, golf nearby
Credit cards AE, DC, MC, V
Children not child friendly (unfenced river) **Disabled** not suitable **Pets** dogs £10 per night
Closed never **Proprietors** Jenni and Ian MacKenzie

The Peacock at Rowsley

Country hotel

Just inside the door of the Peacock is a bowl of water for your dog. This is a sportsman's hotel, though an aesthete would be just as happy here; the pictures are outstandingly good. The River Wye — the only water in the country where wild rainbow trout breed naturally — is what the sportsmen come for. It is said to be the finest dry fly trout fishing in the land and the Head River Keeper from Haddon Hall is on hand to help you enjoy it. The Hall (Thornfield in BBC TV's *Jane Eyre*) is a nearby outing for days when the fish won't bite.

The Peacock, built in the 17th century, was once Haddon's dower house. Now it has all the comforts and convenience (wi-fi, DVDs) that modern visitors expect. Furnished with a mixture of old pieces and comfortable modern upholstery, there is an aura of antique furniture wax and wood smoke. Your dog will surely be allowed to snooze in front of the fire. In the bedrooms, fresh flowers, mahogany dressing tables and top-notch beds will make you feel at home. Uniformed staff are attentive and friendly — occasionally a little too much so for old-fashioned tastes. A great ledger in the hall records the fishermen's daily successes and disappointments. Whatever their luck on the river bank, they will not be disappointed in this handsome, well-run hotel.

Shipton-under-Wychwood, Oxfordshire

Shipton-under-Wychwood,
Oxfordshire OX7 6BA

Tel (01993) 830330
Fax (01993) 832136
e-mail relax@theshavencrown.co.uk
website www.theshavencrown.co.uk

Nearby North Leigh Roman Villa,
Breurn Abbey; Blenheim Palace.
Location in middle of village; with
ample car parking
Food breakfast, lunch, dinner
Price ££
Rooms 8; 7 double and twin, 1 fami-
ly, all with bath; all rooms have TV
Facilities restaurant, bar, medieval
hall, courtyard garden **Credit cards**
AE, MC, V **Children** welcome
Disabled 1 ground-floor bedroom
Pets accepted in bedrooms and bar
Closed never
Proprietor Philip Mehrtens

The Shaven Crown
Country house hotel

The Shaven Crown, as its name suggests,
has monastic origins; it was built in
1384 as a hospice to nearby Bruern Abbey,
and many of the original features remain
intact – most impressively the medieval
hall, with its beautiful double-collar braced
roof and stone walls decorated with tapestries and wrought ironwork. The hall forms
one side of the courtyard garden, which is
decked with flowers and parasols, and on a
sunny day is a lovely place in which to enjoy
wholesome pub lunches. Some of the bedrooms overlook the courtyard, others are
at the front of the house and suffer from
road noise – though this is unlikely to be a
problem at night.

Philip Mehrtens took over here after
moving from the Forest of Dean in 2004,
and set about refurbishing the public
spaces, and creating a new dining area.
Rooms are decorated sympathetically,
leaving the low ceilings, uneven floorboards, exposed beams and open fireplaces intact, and are furnished with
antiques and Jacobean furniture.

One of Philip's aims here is to make the
food as good as possible without over
charging, and to this end the menu is built
around fresh local produce, including daily
deliveries of fish. Dinner is taken in the oak-
beamed dining room which leads off the
hall. Reports welcome.

Stadhampton, Oxfordshire

Bear Lane, Stadhampton,
Oxfordshire OX44 7UR

Tel (01865) 890714
Fax (01865) 400481
website www.crazybearhotel.co.uk

Nearby Oxford City centre; Oxford
University.
Location leave the M40 at junction
7 onto the A329 at the petrol station
turn left then left again into Bear
Lane
Food breakfast, lunch, dinner
Price £££
Rooms 5 doubles, 10 suites, 2 cot-
tages, all with bath and shower; all
rooms have phone, TV, hairdryer,
DVD, CD **Facilities** 2 dining
rooms, bar; garden
Credit cards AE, MC, V **Children**
welcome **Disabled** 2 ground-floor
rooms **Pets** by arrangement **Closed**
1st week in Jan **Proprietor** Jason
Hunt

The Crazy Bear
Country hotel

Reception – a double-decker bus –
gives the first clue that you are about
to experience something different. The
public rooms consist of a beautiful old
beamed bar with a stuffed bear dangling
from the beams. A bottle-roofed dining
room serves traditional English food with
a twist of French; and an atmospheric Thai
restaurant had padded pink walls and a
leopard print carpet. The bedrooms in the
main building are only accessible by very
steep stairs and are all named after makes
of cigars. They are not particularly spacious, but are richly decorated with opulent fabrics giving a delightfully decadent,
wacky feel. Most of the bathrooms are
'wet' (shower not enclosed) in order to
achieve maximum space and this does
mean everything gets a little soggy. There
are more bedrooms in an outbuilding
reached through the lush, Italianesque gardens, with palm trees and pastiche statues.
These are more spacious, and are themed
(and named) by colour. An unusual touch
is the deep, modern bath at the end of
most of the beds: you can wallow while
watching TV, or mellow out listening to
music. Two cottages down the road can
also be used by guests, and the newly-
acquired farm supplies all produce – from
meat, cheese, herbs and bread – for the
kitchen. A one-off.

Stratford-upon-Avon, Warwickshire

58-59 Rother Street, Stratford-Upon-Avon, Warwickshire
CV37 6LT

Tel (01789) 267309
Fax (01789) 414836
e-mail caterhamhousehotel@btconnect.com
website www.caterhamhousehotel.co.uk

Nearby Royal Shakespeare Theatre; Shakespeare's Birthplace.
Location in centre of town; with car parking
Food breakfast
Price ££
Rooms 10 double and twin, all with bath or shower; all rooms have TV
Facilities sitting room, breakfast room, bar
Credit cards MC, V **Children** accepted
Disabled not suitable
Pets not accepted
Closed Christmas Day **Proprietor** David Young

Caterham House
Town bed-and-breakfast

Two Georgian houses have been knocked together to form this friendly B&B which, despite its central location – just a ten-minute walk from the Royal Shakespeare Theatre – has a surprisingly peaceful ambience. David Young took over ownership of Caterham House in 2003 from Dominique and Olive Maury, who had been here since the 1970s. He has since renovated the interior to a traditional English style, while making use of some of the furniture that was collected by his predecessors.

There is a small conservatory-style sitting room with an eclectic assortment of furniture, where generous teas and coffees are served each afternoon. Although there are no gardens, the sitting room opens out on to a small, colourful terrace.

You couldn't call the bedrooms huge, but all are spacious enough to accommodate a comfy chair, and each one is individually decorated. Breakfast is the only meal served, but guests can choose between a full English or continental with a variety of fruit compotes.

Reports would be welcome.

Tetbury, Gloucestershire

Near Tetbury, Gloucestershire
GL8 8YJ

Tel (01666) 890391
Fax (01666) 890394
e-mail reception@calcotmanor.co.uk
website www.calcotmanor.co.uk

Nearby Chavenage; Owlpen Manor;
Westonbirt Arboretum.
Location 3 miles (5 km) W of
Tetbury on A4135; with ample car
parking
Food breakfast, lunch, dinner
Price ££££
Rooms 34; 21 double and twin, 7
family suites, 6 family rooms, all
with bath or shower; all rooms have
phone, TV, hairdryer **Facilities** 2
sitting rooms, dining room; garden,
swimming pool, croquet, 2 all weath-
er tennis courts; playroom, Spa
Credit cards AE, DC, MC, V
Children welcome
Disabled 4 ground-floor bedrooms
Pets by arrangement **Closed** never
Proprietor Richard Ball

Calcot Manor
Country house hotel

This 15thC Cotswold farmhouse has been functioning as a hotel since 1984. Richard Ball took over Calcot Manor from his parents when they retired, and with a team of dedicated staff continues to provide the highest standards of comfort and service while preserving a calm and relaxed atmosphere. The lovely old house itself was a sound choice – its rooms are spacious and elegant without being grand – and the setting amid lawns and old barns, surrounded by rolling countryside, is all you could ask for.

Furnishings and decorations are carefully harmonious, with rich fabrics and pastel colours throughout. A converted cottage provides seven family suites, designed specifically for parents travelling with young children. For their entertainment, there's an indoor playroom.

Michael Croft is head chef of both the Conservatory Restaurant and the adjoining Gumstool Inn, which is more informal and moderately priced. In the restaurant, you might dine on asparagus, herb and lemon risotto, followed by seared sea bass served on parmesan mash with a spinach sauce, while in the inn, you could choose baked mature cheddar cheese *soufflé* and Gloucestershire Old Spot sausages with sage and red wine sauce.

Winchcombe, Gloucestershire

High Street, Winchcombe,
Gloucestershire, GL54 5LJ

Tel (01242) 602 366
Fax (01242) 604360
e-mail
reservations@wesleyhouse.co.uk
website www.wesleyhouse.co.uk

Nearby Sudeley Castle, Cheltenham
race course, Hailes Abbey (NT)
Location in the centre of the town,
parking in the street about 200m
away
Food breakfast, lunch, dinner
Price ££
Rooms 5 doubles, shower only; all
with TV; one with a small roof ter-
race/balcony
Facilities wine bar and grill, restaurant **Credit cards** AE, MC, V
Children welcome **Disabled** access
not possible **Pets** no dogs **Closed**
never **Proprietor** Matthew Brown

Wesley House
Restaurant-with-rooms

You don't go to Wesley House for spacious rooms, for fine antique furniture
or for its facilities. There are no telephones
or hairdryers in the bedrooms; no spas or
conference rooms. It doesn't even have a
place to park your car. As the smiling owner
put it, "We were built before the internal
combustion engine." And the five rooms,
which are small and furnished with old (not
antique) pieces, are squeezed into the old
town house where the original Methodist
once stayed. You go for the food, which is
excellent. The restaurant serves a short fine-
dining menu that would not disgrace a more
pretentious London restaurant. Portions are
generous, the price is modest (£35 for three
courses), the kitchen is skilled and the wine
list exemplary. Recorded music (Louis
Armstrong, Edith Piaf) was slightly intrusive. Next door there is a grill for simpler
meals. There were strawberries for breakfast, outstanding croissants and good
cafetière coffee. You will have slept well
because the beds are comfortable and the
town is quiet at night, but don't expect
luxury. Our inspector's shower room,
hardly larger than the loo on a train, was
scented with Champagne and Roses from
an aerosol. This is out of character (and
smells disagreeable). The rooms are *vin
ordinaire*, that is to say, inexpensive and fine
for everyday, but not for an occasion.

Woodstock, Oxfordshire

Market Street, Woodstock,
Oxfordshire OX20 1SX

Tel (01993) 812291
Fax (01993) 813158
e-mail enquiries@feathers.co.uk
website www.feathers.co.uk

Nearby Blenheim Palace; Oxford.
Location in middle of town; with
limited car parking
Food breakfast, lunch, dinner
Price £££
Rooms 20; 16 double and twin, 4
suites all with bath or shower (1 has
steam room); all rooms have phone,
TV
Facilities 2 sitting rooms, conservatory, bar, dining room, restaurant;
courtyard garden
Credit cards AE, DC, V **Children**
welcome
Disabled access difficult
Pets accepted by arrangement
Closed never
Manager Craig Webb

The Feathers
Town hotel

An amalgam of four tall 17thC town
houses of mellow red brick, now an
exceptionally civilized town hotel. One visitor was full of praise for the way the staff
managed to make a weekend 'entirely
relaxing, without intruding in the way that
hotel staff so often do'. Another, however,
was a little more negative about the pervasive tourist ambience in much-visited
Woodstock and the fact the hotel feels
'managed', with the owner notably absent.

The upstairs drawing room (with library
and open fire) has the relaxed atmosphere
of a well-kept English country home
rather than a hotel, with antiques, fine fabrics, an abundance of fresh flowers and a
refreshing absence of the ubiquitous Olde
Worlde. There is also a cosy study for
reading the papers or drinking tea. If you
want fresh air, there is a pleasant courtyard garden and bar. Bedrooms are spacious (on the whole) and beautifully decorated, comfortable yet still with the understated elegance that pervades the whole
hotel. Five further bedrooms are to be
found in the building next door, renovated
a few years ago. The elegant panelled dining room serves excellent food from
Simon Garbutt's interesting contemporary
menu. Recent refurbishments have updated the style of the rooms.

Worfield, Shropshire

Worfield, near Bridgnorth,
Shropshire WV15 5JZ

Tel (01746) 716497
Fax (01746) 716552
e-mail admin@the-old-vicarage.demon.co.uk **website**
www.oldvicarageworfield.com

Nearby Ludlow; Severn Valley
Railway; Ironbridge Gorge Museum.
Location in village, 8 miles (12 km)
W of Wolverhampton, 1 mile off
A454 , 8 miles (12 km) S of junction
4 of M54; in own grounds with
ample car parking
Food breakfast, lunch, dinner
Price ££
Rooms 14 double, 1 family, 2 rooms
with shower, 1 room with bath only,
all the rest have both; all rooms have
phone, TV, minibar, hairdryer
Facilities 2 sitting rooms, 3 dining
rooms, 1 with bar **Credit cards** AE,
DC, MC, V **Children** welcome
Disabled 1 specially adapted bed-
room **Pets** accepted in bedrooms
Closed Christmas
Proprietors David and Sarah
Blakstad

Old Vicarage
Country house hotel

When this substantial red-brick vic-
arage was converted into a small
hotel in 1981, every effort was made to
retain the Edwardian character of the
place – restoring original wood block
floors, discreetly adding bathrooms to
bedrooms, furnishing the rooms with
handsome Victorian and Edwardian pieces,
carefully converting the coach house to four
'luxury' bedrooms (one of which, 'Leighton',
has been specially designed for disabled
guests). Readers have praised the large, comfortable bedrooms, named after Shropshire
villages and decorated in subtle colours, with
matching bathrobes and soaps.

Attention to detail extends to the sitting
rooms (one is the conservatory, with glorious views of the Worfe valley) and the
three dining rooms. The award-winning
food (a daily changing menu with several
choices and impressive cheeseboard) is
English-based, ambitious and not cheap,
served at polished tables by cheerful staff.
There is a reasonably extensive wine cellar.

Beyton, Suffolk

The Green, Beyton, Bury St
Edmunds, Suffolk IP30 9AF

Tel (01359) 270960
e-mail manorhouse@beyton.com
website www.beyton.com

Nearby Bury St Edmunds;
Lavenham.
Location 4 miles (6 km) E of Bury
St Edmunds, signposted off A14;
with ample car parking
Food breakfast
Prices £
Rooms 4 double with bath or show-
er; all rooms have TV, hairdryer
Facilities sitting room, dining room;
garden
Credit cards not accepted
Children accepted over 5
Disabled 2 ground-floor rooms
Pets not accepted **Closed** never
Proprietors Mark and Kay
Dewsbury

Manorhouse
Country bed-and-breakfast

This B&B in a beautiful 15thC Suffolk longhouse is run full-time by husband and wife Mark and Kay Dewsbury and overlooks the village green. It's an elegant but down to earth place – the half-timbered rooms in the main house have been colourwashed and are filled with antiques, but outside, chickens have the run of the gravelled yard, garden and sometimes the vegetable garden too. All of them lay, and between them provide most of the eggs served for breakfast.

There's a great deal of space in which to spread out. The Ivory Room in the main house is suite-sized, with its own sitting area, and there are two more rooms – the Garden Room and the Dairy – in a converted barn at right angles to the house. The decoration is comfortably rustic: the Dairy has exposed brick and flint walls, the traditional building materials of the area, bright and cheerful furnishings and a walk-in power shower in the large bathroom. French windows open from the Garden Room on to a tiny paved area for sitting out in summer and contemplating the venerable old lichen-covered trees. The Dewsburys are excellent hosts – laid back and unflummoxed. For guests who fancy a stroll, there are a couple of pleasant pubs in the village.

Brancaster, Norfolk

Brancaster, Staithe, Norfolk
PE31 8BY

Tel (01485) 210 262
Fax (01485) 210 930
e-mail reception@whitehorsebran-caster.co.uk
website
www.whitehorsebrancaster.co.uk

Nearby Holkham Hall, Brancaster, Norfolk lavender, Burnham Market, Peddars Way
Location on A149 coast road with ample car parking
Food breakfast, lunch, dinner
Price ££
Rooms 15; 4 family rooms, 10 doubles (4 can be twin), 1 suite all with bath and shower; all rooms have phone, TV, hairdryer, wi-fi
Facilities dining area, sitting room, conservatory, restaurant, bar, garden, terrace
Credit cards MC, V **Children** accepted **Disabled** 2 rooms have access **Pets** well behaved dogs in 8 ground room floors **Closed** never
Proprietor Cliff Nye

The White Horse
Village inn

Cliff Nye, proprietor of The White Horse at Brancaster, is tired of reading in guides that from the outside, his building is not exactly charming – and rightly so, because as soon as you're inside, it's something else. First you walk into a bar area for non residents, with a local community atmosphere; this melts seamlessly into a more 'residential' area with reception desk and seating; and this gives way to the big, airy conservatory dining room with its scrubbed pine tables and extraordinary view out over a network of creeks and marsh across Brancaster Staithe to Scolt Head Island – surely one of England's most distinctive coastal panoramas. You could easily while away most of a morning or afternoon here, followed by lunch or dinner, and still not be tired of the view. Your room, either upstairs or in the extension with a turf roof, will be comfortable and cleanly decorated and furnished in a modern style with seaside colours and Lloyd Loom chairs. The food is good – no more or less than you'd expect for the price – though you might hope to find a somewhat wider range of seafood on the me nu. A lesson in how to transform what was a horrible old pub in a fabulous situation into thriving 21st century operation.

Burnham Market, Norfolk

The Green, Burnham Market,
North Norfolk, PE31 8HD

Tel (01328) 738777
Fax (01328) 730103
e-mail reception@hostearms.co.uk
website www.hostearms.co.uk

Nearby Houghton Hall; Holkham
Hall; Sandringham House;
Titchwell, Holme, Holkham and
Cley nature reserves.
Location in centre of village; with
ample car parking
Food breakfast, lunch, dinner
Price £££
Rooms 44; 37 doubles in main
house, 7 in Railway Inn, all with bath
or shower; all rooms have phone,
TV, hairdryer
Facilities sitting room, conservatory,
dining room, bar; garden
Credit cards MC, V **Children**
accepted **Disabled** ground-floor
bedrooms
Pets not accepted **Closed** never
Proprietors Paul and Jeanne
Whittome

The Hoste Arms
Village hotel

Overlooking the green in a village whose main claim to fame is that it was Admiral Nelson's birthplace, this handsome yellow-and-white 17thC inn has won a clutch of awards for its bedrooms, bar and restaurant. Downstairs, it positively buzzes with life in the evenings, when locals come here to drink and eat — in that order. The brasserie-style menu includes British, European and Oriental-inspired dishes.

The man responsible for its lively reputation, Paul Whittome, bought the Hoste Arms in 1989. Despite being deaf, he is a chatty, affable proprietor, whose wife Jeanne is responsible for the rustic-chic decoration. She clearly has a penchant for dramatic colour schemes, painting walls downstairs deep red, and using colourful plaids and eye-catching striped fabrics in the bedrooms. These vary in style and size; some have been criticized for being poky, so book carefully. Several are on the ground floor, three with small patios that lead on to the pretty walled garden, which provides a welcome refuge when the bar becomes too crowded. Changing art exhibitions mean that the walls are always packed with pictures. There have been major changes with the addition of new bedrooms and an eccentric "African Wing". More reports please.

Bury St Edmunds, Suffolk

Northgate Street, Bury St Edmunds,
Suffolk IP33 1HP

Tel 01284 761779
Fax 01284 768315
e-mail pott@globalnet.co.uk
website www.ouncehouse.co.uk

Nearby Cathedral; Abbey;
Gershom-Parkington Collection.
Location close to town centre; with
ample car parking
Food breakfast
Price ££
Rooms 5 double and twin with bath;
all rooms have phone, TV, hairdryer
Facilities 2 sitting rooms,
library/TV room, dining room; gar-
den **Credit cards** AE, DC, MC, V
Children welcome
Disabled access difficult **Pets** not
accepted **Closed** never **Proprietors**
Simon and Jenny Pott

Ounce House
Town house

Ounce House is a red brick, gable-
ended, three-storey house, set back
from the road a five-minute walk from the
abbey and pedestrianized shopping streets
in the centre of Bury St Edmunds.

The interiors are formal but homely
with drawing room and dining room decorated in calm colours; these are 'state-
ment' swagged and draped curtains, plenty
of lamps, *objets d'art* and interesting pictures. Most of the bedrooms are large and
one of the most attractive has pale yellow
walls, a crown arrangement over the bed-
head, two chintzy armchairs and a decorative chimneypiece. Since our last edition,
the Potts have opened up a further two
bedrooms, which are decorated in the
same homely style.

The owners, warm and open hosts, are
good at putting people at their ease.
Dinner is no longer served here, but there
are several good restaurants within walking distance, with which, as Mrs Pott put it,
it was hard for her to compete.

Guests have the use of the library, which
is more like a den, with a large leather
wing armchair, smaller easy chairs, an
upright piano, shelves packed with books
and an honesty bar. It is somewhere to go
with a friend for a long conversation, or to
watch TV.

Cley-next-the-Sea, Norfolk

Cley-next-the-Sea, Holt, Norfolk
NR25 7RP

Tel (01263) 740209
e-mail info@cleywindmill.co.uk
website www.cleymill.co.uk

Nearby Sheringham Hall; Cromer
Lighthouse; Holkham Hall.
Location 7 miles (11 km) W of
Sheringham on A149, on N edge of
village; with ample car parking
Food breakfast, dinner on request
Price ££
Rooms 9 double, all with
bath/shower
Facilities sitting room, dining room,
garden **Credit cards** MC, V
Children welcome
Disabled access difficult
Pets accepted **Closed** never
Proprietor Dr Julian Godlee
Manager Charlotte Martin

Cley Mill
Converted windmill

Imagine staying in a 'real' windmill. That is the sense of adventure that Cley Mill can induce even in the most world-weary. Memories of Swallows and Amazons or the Famous Five crowd in as you climb higher and higher in the mill, finally mounting the ladder to the look-out room on the fourth floor. Superb views over the Cley Marshes, a Mecca for bird-watchers.

The sitting room on the ground floor of the Mill is exceptionally welcoming – it feels well used and lived-in, with plenty of books and magazines, comfortable sofas, TV and an open fire. Bedrooms in the Mill feel rather like log cabins – much wood in the furniture and fittings. They are pretty rooms, with white lace bedspreads, and bathrooms ingeniously fitted in to the nooks and crannies.

Since our last edition, Cley Mill has changed hands. The new owner is Julian Godlee, a GP from Hertfordshire with roots on the Norfolk coast – the only bidder who wanted it to continue as a B&B. There has been maintenance and restoration, but the basic formula remains unchanged. A new bedroom has been added right at the very top of the windmill – reached by a steep ladder, it is only for the adventurous and fit, but the view makes it worthwhile. Try to book well in advance. See also our other windmill (page 36).

Fritton, Norfolk

Church Lane, Fritton, Norfolk
NR31 9HA

Tel (01493) 484008
Fax (01493) 488355
e-mail
frittonhouse@somerleyton.co.uk
website www.frittonhouse.co.uk

Nearby Somerleyton House and
Estate; Norfolk Broads; Gorleston
beach, Beccles, Southwold,
Aldeburgh, Walberwick
Location in own grounds with
ample private car parking
Food breakfast, lunch, dinner
Price £££
Rooms 9; all double, two can be
twin; all with bath or shower, phone,
TV, DVD, wi-fi
Facilities bar, dining room, sitting
room, private dining room, affilia-
tion with local leisure resort (swim-
ming, tennis, spa) **Credit cards** MC,
V **Children** welcome**Disabled** no
specially adapted rooms **Pets** small,
well-behaved dogs **Closed** never
Proprietor Hugh Crossley

Fritton House
Country hotel

This former 15thC smuggler's inn was turned into a hotel recently by 30-something Hugh Crossley, heir to the Somerleyton Estate of which it is a part. Interior design is by Hugh's sister Isobel, with many an old beam exposed to contrast with the mainly contemporary, easy-going feel of the place. It's as relaxed as a hotel gets, the tone set by Sarah, the young and infectiously enthusiastic manageress, but also by Hugh, who keeps a close eye and is always hatching a new plan. Ring for anything from your room – a cup of tea, a Mojito, even dinner – and it will be brought.

The nine bedrooms, with lovely bathrooms, are coolly comfortable with splashes of colour, boldly patterned fabrics and fresh flowers. They are furnished with a mix of Crossley family furniture and modern pieces. Downstairs there's a cosy sitting room, but the hub is the bar and restaurant, where locals come to eat. "Simple food, well cooked" is the aim. The wine list has an unusual selection of bottles for around £12.

Fritton House stands on the edge of a country park whose main feature is Fritton Lake, with rowing boats and other amusements. It's open to the public from April to October; for the rest of the year, and after five in summer, guests at Fritton House have the run of the place, free of charge. A great place to bring children.

Harwich, Essex

The Quay, Harwich, Essex
CO12 3HH

Tel (01255) 241212
Fax (01255) 551922
e-mail pier@milsomhotels.com
website www.the-pier-hotel.co.uk

Nearby Harwich sights including
Electric Palace Cinema, Ha'penny
Pier, Redoubt fort, golf
Location on quayside in old town;
own off-road car parking for 25 cars
Price ££
Food breakfast, lunch, dinner
Rooms 14; all doubles with own
shower or bath, phone, TV, wi-fi,
minibar **Facilities** 2 restaurants, bar,
terrace, sitting room, private dining
facilities, house party service, sailing
arranged on yacht or traditional
Essex craft **Credit cards** AE, DC,
MC, V **Children** accepted **Disabled**
specially adapted room and WC on
ground floor, access at rear of building **Pets** guide dogs only **Closed**
never **Proprietor** Paul Milsom

The Pier at Harwich
Seaside town hotel

Here's a good place for a weekend – if you like the sea, ships, and industrial seascapes. Picture-book pretty it isn't; atmospheric, absorbing and 'real' it most certainly is. The Pier, with its distinctive blue and white façade, designed to resemble a Venetian *palazzo*, was built in 1864 to accommodate overnight passengers from Harwich to the European mainland. It was from here, too, in 1620, that the Mayflower set sail for the New World, with a Harwich man at her helm.

There are two restaurants here: The Harbourside, relatively formal; and the Ha'penny Pier, a contemporary fisherman's wharf-style bar and bistro, for proper fish and chips, the chef's fish pie and daily spe-cials. Write your order on a notepad and hand it in at the bar. Check-in is at the bar, and bags are promptly taken to your room.

All the rooms are several cuts above what you would expect for the price (deep, white-sheeted beds, natural sea colours on tongue-and-groove panelling), but with only £10 each between a 'standard', a 'superior' and a 'deluxe' it pays to go for the largest – and get the view.

The Pier has been owned for nearly 30 years by the hands-on Milsom family. Like their other establishments, Maison Talbooth and Milsom's, it's a close-knit operation, with long-serving locals on the happy team.

Holkham, Norfolk

Park Road, Holkham, Norfolk
NR23 1RG

Tel (01328) 711008
Fax (01328) 711009
e-mail victoria@holkham.co.uk
website
www.victoriaatholkham.co.uk

Nearby Holkham Hall, Holkham
beach, Banham Zoo.
Location just off the B1105 on th
A149 near Wells; with ample car
parking
Food breakfast, lunch, dinner
Price £££
Rooms 11 double, 1 twin, 1 single,
all en suite except 1, all have bath,
some have hand-held showers; all
rooms have satellite TV, phone,
hairdryer
Facilities 2 dining rooms, 2 sitting
rooms, 3 bars; garden, 2 helipads
Credit cards MC, V
Children welcome **Disabled** 1
ground-floor room
Pets not accepted
Closed never **Proprietors** Viscount
and Viscountess Coke

The Victoria at
Holkham Country hotel

Part of the Holkham Estate owned by
the Earl of Leicester, The Victoria
(named after Queen Victoria, a year after
she became queen) is an eclectic and stylish blend of colonial furniture and fabrics.
Built in 1837 by Coke of Norfolk, the hotel
is a five-minute stroll from the beautiful
white sands of Holkham beach where
there are water sports. Viscount Coke, a
descendent of Coke of Norfolk, and his
wife Polly acquired the hotel some time
ago and undertook a major refurbishment.
One of its many successful outcomes is the
new conservatory.

Everywhere you turn your attention is
caught by some curious object or another,
since most of the furnishings and ornaments have been flown in from Rajasthan
there's a strong sense of the exotic. All of
the bedrooms are decorated individually
with flare and extremely good taste.
Although the rooms may look old they
have modern comforts such as seriously
comfy beds, big warm duvets and deep
baths for a serious soak.

The restaurant and bar area is very
much in keeping with the colonial feel,
slightly hard chairs, but beautiful wall hangings and views. The food is cooked and
presented to a high standard (don't overlook the fish and chips); and there's a long
wine list.

King's Lynn, Norfolk

Lynn Road, Grimston, King's Lynn, Norfolk PE32 1AH

Tel (01485) 600250
Fax (01485) 601191
e-mail
info@conghamhallhotel.co.uk
website www.conghamhallhotel.co.uk

Nearby Sandringham; Ely; Norwich.
Location 6 miles (10 km) NE of King's Lynn near A148; with parking for 50 cars
Food breakfast, lunch, dinner
Price ££££
Rooms 14; 11 double, 2 suites, all with bath, 1 single with shower; all rooms have phone, TV **Facilities** 2 sitting rooms, bar, dining room; garden, spa bath, tennis, croquet, putting **Credit cards** AE, DC, MC, V
Children welcome (over 7 in restaurant) **Disabled** easy access to restaurant **Pets** by arrangement (outside kennels) **Closed** never **Proprietor** Von Essen Hotels

Congham Hall
Country house hotel

'Quintessentially English' is how some guests describe their stay here. Practically everything about this white 18thC Georgian house, set in 40 acres of lawns, orchards and parkland, is impressive. The spacious bedrooms and public areas are luxuriously furnished and our reporter found the service to be solicitous and efficient and the staff helpful and welcoming. Cooking (in the modern British style) is adventurous and excellent, making much use of home-grown herbs. The restaurant is a spacious, airy delight, built to look like an orangerie, with full-length windows overlooking the wide lawns of the parkland, where the herb gardens are an attraction in their own right. Visitors stop to admire the array of 600 herb varieties and to buy samples, from angelica to sorrel. The restaurant doors open on to the terraces for pre-dinner drinks and herb garden strolls.

Personal attention is thoughtful. For walkers and cyclists, the hotel will arrange to collect luggage from guests' previous destinations and deliver it onwards too. It also keeps a book of special walks, devised by the previous owners, the Forecasts, and can arrange clay pigeon shooting on site, subject to availability. Taken over recently by Von Essen, so we wonder about the future. Reports welcome.

Lavenham, Suffolk

Market Place, Lavenham, Suffolk
CO10 9QZ

Tel (01787) 247431
Fax (01787) 248007
e-mail info@greathouse.co.uk
website www.greathouse.co.uk

Nearby Little Hall, Guildhall Priory
(Lavenham); Melford Hall;
Gainsborough's House, Sudbury.
Location 16 miles (26 km) NW of
Colchester, in middle of
village; with car parking
Food breakfast, lunch, dinner
Price £££
Rooms 4 family-size suites with
bath/shower, 1 standard double with
bath; all rooms have phone, TV, wi-
fi, minibar
Facilities sitting room/bar, dining
room; patio, garden
Credit cards MC, V
Children welcome **Disabled** access
difficult **Pets** welcome **Closed** Jan
Proprietor Régis Crépy

The Great House
Restaurant-with-rooms

The old timber-framed houses, the fine Perpendicular 'Wool Church' and the high street full of antiques and galleries make Lavenham a high point of any visitor's itinerary of the pretty villages of East Anglia.

The Great House in the market place was built in the heyday of the wool trade but was extensively renovated in the 18th century and looks more Georgian than Tudor – at least from the outside. It was a private house (lived in by Stephen Spender in the 1930s) until Régis and Martine Crépy turned it into a restaurant-with-rooms in 1985. The food (predominantly French) is the best for miles – 'stunningly good', enthuses one visitor (a fellow hotelier). If you can secure one of its five bedrooms it is also a delightful place to stay. All are different, but they are all light, spacious and full of old-world charm, with beams and antiques. Each has its own fireplace and sitting area, with sofa or upholstered chairs. The dining room is dominated by an inglenook fireplace that formed part of the original house. In winter, log fires blaze; in summer, French doors open on to a pretty stone-paved courtyard for drinks, lunch or dinner.

Lavenham, Suffolk

Water Street, Lavenham, Suffolk
CO10 9RW

Tel (01787) 247404
Fax (01787) 248472
website www.lavenhampriory.co.uk

Nearby Guildhall; 'Wool Church' of
SS Peter and Paul.
Location in centre of village beside
Swan; with ample parking
Food breakfast
Price ££
Rooms 6 double, 5 with bath, 1 with
shower; all rooms have TV, hairdry-
er
Facilities 2 sitting rooms, dining
room; garden
Credit cards MC, V
Children accepted over 10
Disabled not suitable
Pets not accepted **Closed** Christmas
and New Year
Proprietors Tim and Gilli Pitt

Lavenham Priory
Village bed-and-breakfast

Gilli Pitt runs Lavenham Priory with great flair, and the term B&B doesn't do it justice. It is a very special place: the beautiful Grade I-listed house dates from the 13th century when it was home to Benedictine monks, and has been restored in keeping with its later life as home to an Elizabethan merchant, complete with original wallpaintings, huge Tudor fireplace and sofas covered in cushions and throws. More important, however, is the warmth of the welcome from Gilli and her husband Tim, which stems from an enjoyment of sharing the main part of their home.

This is a place to enjoy, whatever the season. In summer the courtyard garden is fragrant with herbs, but in winter it's just as appealing to drink a hot toddy by the fire. The house is large, and as well as the Great Hall sitting room there's a smaller room (where shelves are stacked with board games) so more than one party can use the public rooms without feeling crowded. Each of the bedrooms has a superb bed, including a four-poster in the Painted Chamber and a solid cherrywood sleigh in the Gallery Chamber – worth a journey in their own right. Breakfast in the Merchants Hall is a feast, with fresh stewed and candied fruits, as well as the full English fry up.

Long Melford, Suffolk

The Green, Long Melford, Suffolk
CO10 9DN

Tel (01787) 312356
Fax (01787) 374557
e-mail enquiries@blacklion.net
website www.blacklionhotel.net

Nearby Long Melford church;
Melford Hall; Kentwell Hall.
Location in village 3 miles (5 km) N
of Sudbury, overlooking village
green; with car parking
Food breakfast, lunch, dinner
Price £££
Rooms 8 double, 1 suite, 1 twin, 1
family room; all have phone, TV
Facilities sitting room, 2 dining
rooms, bar, study
Credit cards AE, MC, V
Children welcome **Disabled** no
special facilities **Pets** accepted in
bedrooms **Closed** never **Proprietor**
Mr Craig Jarvis

The Black Lion
Country hotel

Long Melford is a famously attractive Suffolk village, and The Black Lion is at the heart of it, overlooking the green. It is an elegant early 19thC building, decorated and furnished with great sympathy, taste and lightness of touch. When owner Craig Jarvis took over some years ago, he reinstated its original name (the previous owners, the Erringtons, renamed it 'The Countrymen'), and transformed it into a hotel full of quirky character.

Each of the bedrooms is totally different, and all are impressively unusual. They range from the rather exotic to the more cooly romantic. The one our inspector stayed in had dark gold wallpaper, gold and brown embroidered bedspreads, exotic curtains, an ornate mirror and an oriental wardrobe.

Dinner can be eaten either in the comfortable bistro or the more formal, elegant dining room (both serve the same menu), and our inspector found it to be "absolutely delicious, first rate". Chef Annette Beasant's work with seasonal and locally produced ingredients, including her homemade bread and cream teas, have earned accolades recently. Reports welcome.

Morston, Holt, Norfolk
NR25 7AA

Tel (01263) 741041
Fax (01263) 740419
e-mail reception@morstonhall. com
website www.morstonhall.com

Nearby Sandringham; Felbrigg
Hall; Holkham Hall; Brickling.
Location 2 miles (3 km) W of
Blakeney on A149; with ample car
parking
Food breakfast, Sun lunch, dinner
Price ££££
Rooms 13 double and twin; all
rooms have phone, TV, CD player,
hairdryer **Facilities** 2 sitting rooms,
conservatory, dining room; garden,
croquet
Credit cards AE, DC, MC, V
Children welcome
Disabled 1 ground-floor bedroom
Pets accepted in bedrooms **Closed**
Jan, Christmas, Boxing Day
Proprietors Galton and Tracy
Blackiston

Morston Hall
Country hotel

Don't be put off by the rather severe-looking flint exterior of this solid Jacobean house on the North Norfolk coast. Inside, the rooms are unexpectedly bright and airy, painted in summery colours and overlooking a sweet garden, where a fountain plays in a lily pond and roses flourish. The *raison d'être* of Morston Hall is its dining room, the responsibility of Galton Blackiston, who shot to fame as a finalist in ITV's 'Chef of the Year'. He has since won huge acclaim for his outstanding modern European cuisine and, the icing on the cake, a Michelin star in 1999. His set four-course menu changes daily and might feature: confit of leg of duck on sautéed Lyonnaise potatoes with thyme-infused jus or grilled fillet of sea bass served on fennel duxelle with sauce vierge. The carefully-stocked wine cellar offers a comprehensive selection of (not overpriced) wines from all over the world. Galton and his wife, Tracy, also organize wine-tasting dinners and cookery lessons. He gives a number of half-day cookery demonstrations and runs two three-day residential courses each year. Most of the large bedrooms are decked out in chintz fabrics, with armchairs and all the little extras, such as bottled water, bathrobes and large, warm, fluffy towels.

Nayland, Suffolk

High Street, Nayland, near
Colchester, Suffolk CO6 4JF

Tel (01206) 263382
Fax (01206) 263638
e-mail reservations@whitehart-nay-
land.co.uk **website** www.whitehart-
nayland.co.uk

Nearby Colchester; Ipswich.
Location on the 314N of Colchester
in the High Street
Food breakfast, lunch, dinner
Price ££
Rooms 6 double with en suite bath
and shower; all rooms have TV,
phone, radio, hairdryer, modem
point, trouser press **Facilities** dining
room, small lounge, bar, private din-
ing room; garden
Credit cards AE, DC, MC, V
Children welcome
Disabled access difficult except in
public rooms
Pets not accepted
Closed 26th December to 9th Jan;
restaurant only, Mon **Manager**
Christine Altug

White Hart Inn
Country inn

'**A** great combination of old and new,'
says a recent report. Set in a cobbled
Suffolk village, the inn dates from the 15th
century, and was a popular halt for coaches to refuel and water. Nowadays good
food and comfortable rooms still draw
people in. Christine Altug, for many years a
shareholder in the business here, became
more hands on in 2006 and now acts as
the manager at the White Hart.

Breakfast, lunch and dinner are served in
the restaurant, which is not as hushed as it
first appears. Head Chef, Marcus Verberne,
has an impressive pedigree and it shows in
the beautifully presented food created
from local ingredients whenever possible.

The bedrooms epitomise the balance
between old and new: calm shades on the
walls contrasting with the bright, chic furnishings, sitting comfortably with the antique
elements, such as the old beams, which have
been preserved in most of the rooms. The
bathrooms are contemporary, adequately
equipped with large, fluffy towels.

Norwich, Norfolk

25-29 St Georges Street, Norwich,
Norfolk NR3 1AB

Tel (01603) 630730

Nearby Cathedral; Castle;
Guildhall; Bridewell Museum.
Location in city centre; with car
parking
Food breakfast, dinner
Price ££
Rooms 5; 3 double, 1 twin, 1 single,
all with bath; all rooms have phone,
TV, hairdryer **Facilities** sitting
room, dining rooms
Credit cards MC, V **Children**
accepted over 12
Disabled access possible to public
rooms **Pets** not accepted
Closed Christmas Day; restaurant
Sun, Mon
Proprietors Timothy Brown and
Robert Culyer

By Appointment
Restaurant-with-rooms

There is so much to see in Norwich and if you want to be in the thick of things, then this quirky establishment, in a 15thC merchant's house owned by Timothy Brown and Robert Culyer, might be the place for you. It is in St Georges Street, which runs parallel to Elm Hill, gloriously cobbled and lined with historic houses, and is ideally placed for seeing the sights.

As you enter through the kitchen, you are struck by the friendly atmosphere, which also pervades the five rooms that comprise the restaurant. They have some-what theatrical furnishings – heavy swagged curtains, rich night-time colours, crystal and silver glittering on impeccably laid tables. In this setting, you choose dishes from the large carte, such as fillet of beef, filled with a duxelle of tomatoes and mushrooms, wrapped in puff pastry, with a fresh garden mint and mustard sauce. Don't overdo it: otherwise you won't manage the magnificent cooked feast that goes by the name of breakfast the next morning.

The layout of the building seems more like a warren than a house. Appropriately, reception rooms and bedrooms, all with exotic and colourful decoration, are crammed with Victoriana and *objets trouvés*. It may not suit everybody, but it is thoroughly original and, as far as we're concerned, a breath of fresh air.

Norwich, Norfolk

Lodge Lane, Old Catton, Norwich,
Norfolk NR6 7HG

Tel (01603) 419379
Fax (01603) 400339
e-mail enquiries@catton-hall.co.uk
website www.catton-hall.co.uk

Nearby Cathedral; Castle; The
Broad; Norwich Castle.
Location 2.5 miles (4 km) NE of
Norwich, off B1150; with ample car
parking
Food breakfast, dinner by arrange-
ment
Price ££
Rooms 7 double, twin and family
with bath; all rooms have phone, TV,
hairdryer
Facilities sitting room, dining room;
garden
Credit cards AE, DC, MC, V
Children accepted over 12
Disabled not suitable
Pets not accepted **Closed** never
Proprietors Roger and Anthea
Cawdron

Catton Old Hall
Country house hotel

An impressive 17thC gentleman's residence, built from reclaimed Caen
stone, local flint and oak timbers, has been
transformed with great success into this
genteel family-run hotel. Though located in
an unprepossessing suburb of Norwich, it
has the twin advantages of being within
easy reach of the city centre, yet away
from the bustle. With its mullioned windows, beamed ceilings, inglenook fireplaces, polished antiques and warm colour
schemes, the interior feels intimate and
inviting. Owners Anthea and Roger
Cawdron are on hand to welcome guests
and pamper them during their stay, placing
books and glossy magazines by their beds,
and a tantalising array of soaps, bubble
baths, lotions and potions in the bathrooms. Named after former inhabitants of
the house, the bedrooms have been decorated boldly and with dash in country-
house style by Anthea, and the beds, some
of which are four-posters, are made up
with delicious Egyptian cotton sheets.

Anthea's talents also extend to the
kitchen, and if given prior notice she will
prepare an interesting dinner, using local
produce and herbs from the garden, according to – among others – old family recipes.

Snettisham, Norfolk

Old Church Road,
Snettisham, Norfolk
PE31 7LX

Tel (01485) 541 382
Fax (01485) 543 172
e-mail info@roseandcrownsnettisham.co.uk
website www.roseandcrownsnettisham.co.uk

Nearby Peddars Way, Houghton Hall, Holkham Hall, Sandringham, Norfolk Lavender, Brancaster, Burnham Market
Location off B1440, in centre of Snettisham village with ample car parking
Food breakfast, lunch, dinner
Price ££
Rooms 16; 1 twin, 15 doubles (4 can be split for twins); all rooms have phone, TV, wi-fi, air-con, hairdryers, irons **Facilities** 3 dining rooms, walled garden, bar, sitting room
Credit cards V **Children** welcome
Pets accepted **Disabled** 2 rooms have access **Closed** never
Proprietors Anthony and Jeanette Goodrich

Rose and Crown
Village inn

We like the way this inn keeps both locals and visitors happy. There are plenty of activities nearby, it is situated near an area of outstanding natural beauty, and it is far better value for money than its grander neighbours in nearby villages. The oldest part of the inn is the bar, originally built for workers who erected the local church, and where locals and visitors enjoy the beer and a wide selection of sandwiches whilst sitting by the open fire, then totter off to their rooms, minding the wonky old flagstones on the way.

On the way to your room, admire owner Anthony Goodrich's sporting prowess: his old school photos adorn the walls. The bedrooms are smallish, but done out in a fresh, sea-sidey way, with all the creature comforts you would expect. If you need a substantial lunch or dinner, head downstairs to one of the three dining rooms that provide fresh, locally sourced food, including beef from the salt marshes at Holkham, seafood from Brancaster and game from the gentlemen in wellies in the back bar.

Parents can rest assured that their children will be safe in the walled garden, sporting an impressive climbing frame and play area. They can be watched from the terrace or the attached dining room/sitting room. The Goodriches thoroughly deserve their Publicans' Pub of the Year award.

Southwold, Suffolk

High Street, Southwold, Suffolk
IP18 6EG

Tel (01502) 722186
Fax (01502) 724800
e-mail hotels@adnams.co.uk
website www.adnams.co.uk

Nearby 'Cathedral of the Marshes';
Dunwich Heath and Minsmere
nature reserves.
Location next to market square;
with car parking
Food breakfast, lunch, dinner
Price £££
Rooms 42 double, 25 in main hotel
and 17 garden rooms, all with bath
and shower; all rooms have phone,
TV, hairdryer
Facilities sitting rooms, dining
room, bar; garden, croquet
Credit cards MC, V **Children** wel-
come **Disabled** access possible,
lift/elevator **Pets** accepted in garden
rooms by arrangement
Closed never **Manager** Francis
Guildea

The Swan
Town hotel

One of the most welcoming rooms in
The Swan is the drawing room, with
its carved wood chimneypieces and archi-
traves, Murano glass chandeliers, chintzy
sofas and armchairs and relaxed atmosphere. On Sunday mornings the place is
full of newspapers and chat, with guests
and non-residents ordering coffee and
shortbread, and, on a fine day, the sun
pours in through the windows from the
market square. The Swan is ideal for a long
stay – the bedrooms at the front are
largest, though all, including the standard
rooms, are inviting and well-decorated in
smart, strong colours and with interesting
prints on the walls. Many have a view of
the sea, lighthouse or square. There are
also modern garden rooms, grouped
around a former bowling green, with large
picture windows which mean that, though
you can see out, everyone else can see in.

Staff are professional and helpful and
ensure that the hotel operates on a human
scale. It made us wish that there were more
places like this. Adnams Brewery owns The
Swan and its sister hotel, The Crown, down
the road. If you eat at The Crown, a cross-
billing system operates – just remember to
tell reception before you go.

Stoke by Nayland, Suffolk

Stoke by Nayland, Suffolk,
CO6 4SA

Tel (01206) 263245
Fax (01206) 264145
e-mail info@theangelinn.net
website www.theangelinn.net

Nearby Guildhall; Dedham Vale;
Flatford Mill; East Bergholt.
Location in village centre, on B1068
between Sudbury and Ipswich; small
car park for 20 cars
Food breakfast, lunch, dinner
Price ££
Rooms 6 double, 1 twin, all with
bath; all rooms have phone, TV,
hairdryer, wi-fi
Facilities sitting room, dining
rooms, bar; garden
Credit cards MC, V
Children accepted in 1 room
Disabled not suitable **Pets** accepted
Closed Christmas Day, Boxing Day,
New Year's Day **Proprietors**
Horizon Inns

Angel Inn
Village inn

A proper inn rather than a pub, with
spick-and-span bedrooms off a long
gallery landing upstairs, the Angel Inn has
been in business since the 16th century.
There are plenty of nooks and crannies in
the bar and a variety of seating in the series
of interconnecting public rooms. You'll find
sofas and chairs grouped together in the
lounge; and a dining room with its ceiling
open to the rafters, rough brick-and-tim-
ber-studded walls and a fern-lined well-
shaft 52 feet (16 m) deep. The bedrooms
are a fair size, individually and unfussily decorated, and are ideal for a one- or two-
night stop on a tour of Suffolk.

The public rooms downstairs have great
character, with interesting pictures and
low lighting, and are filled with the hum
and buzz of contented lunch and dinner
conversation. The food is excellent, with
local produce used where possible, including fresh fish and shellfish from nearby
ports, and game from local estates. Dishes
might include griddled hake with red onion
dressing, or stir-fried duckling with fine leaf
salad, Cumberland sauce and new potatoes. Service is informal, friendly and helpful. Children are not allowed in the bar, and
though flexible, there are rules about
young children eating in the dining room —
check when booking.

Ash Close, Swaffham, Norfolk
PE37 7NH

Tel (01760) 723845
e-mail enquiries@strattonshotel.com
website www.strattonshotel.com

Nearby Norwich; North Norfolk
coast.
Location down narrow lane between
shops on main street; with ample car
parking
Food breakfast, dinner
Price £££
Rooms 10; 5 double, 5 suites, all
with bath or shower; all rooms have
phone, TV, hairdryer **Facilities** 2
sitting rooms, dining room, bar
Credit cards MC, V
Children welcome
Disabled access difficult **Pets** wel-
come **Closed** Christmas
Proprietors Vanessa and Les Scott

Strattons
Country hotel

Strattons has long summed up every-thing we are looking for in this guide. Perhaps it's because Les and Vanessa Scott are such natural hosts who love entertaining; perhaps it's because of their artistic flair (they met as art students) or perhaps it's because they had a very clear vision of what they wanted to create when they bought this elegant listed villa in 1990. A reader writes: '20 out of 20 for staff atti-tude, value for money, quality of accom-modation… An absolute delight.'

Bedrooms, several of which have been upgraded, are positively luxurious. Plump cushions and pillows jostle for space on antique beds, books and magazines fill the shelves, and the same coordinated decora-tion continues into smart bathrooms — one resembling a bedouin's tent. The two beautifully furnished sitting rooms, *trompe l'oeil* hallway and murals painted by a local artist are equally impressive. Yet it is emphatically a family home and you share it with the Scott cats and children. The food is special, too. Vanessa, a cookery writer, continues to gain awards for her cooking. There are fresh eggs every day from their own chickens, and the daily changing menu is inventive and beautifully presented. It is cheerfully served by Les in the cosy basement restaurant.

Woodbridge, Suffolk

Dock Road, Ramsholt, Woodbridge,
Suffolk IP12 3AB

Tel (01394) 411229
Fax (01394) 411818

Nearby Felixstowe; Orford;
Aldeburgh.
Location off B1083, follow signs for
Bawdsey out of Woodbridge and
take right turn to Ramsholt Dock;
with ample car parking
Food breakfast, lunch, dinner
Price ££
Rooms 1 double with bath; has TV;
hairdryer on request.
Facilities dining room, bar; garden
Credit cards MC, V
Children welcome
Disabled not suitable
Pets accepted
Closed never
Proprietor Patrick Levy

Ramsholt Arms
Country pub-with-rooms

The Ramsholt Arms is one of only a few buildings visible for miles around on the shores of the Deben estuary. It's in the middle of nowhere, down a tiny track sign-posted 'Ramsholt Dock', branching off a lonely road through Breckland on the east side of Woodbridge. In fact, it is remarkable that there is a pub here at all. It's right on the water and at low tide waders walk the silvery, mirror-like surface of the mud. The interior is simply but artfully decorated and there are huge picture windows to capitalise on the view. Fashionable? Contemporary? No. Genuine? Yes. Patrick, the landlord, is a delightful, larger than life ex-merchant seaman.

There is just one (occasionally two) rather basic guest bedroom, simply furnished and decorated, and the bathroom is along the passage. But it is cheap, and has great views of the river. You wake up to the call of curlews or the slapping of halyards against masts.

Ramsholt's food is distinctly a cut above standard pub fare in terms of both choice and quality, and competetively priced: Glistening, fresh shell-on prawns; Orkney herrings; fishcakes; cauliflower soup. The Levys have made a big success of their isolated pub, and at summer weekend lunchtimes it is packed with visitors, arriving by land and water.

Breckland walk

Arkengarthdale, North Yorkshire

Arkengarthdale, nr Richmond,
North Yorkshire DL11 6EN

Tel (01748) 884567
Fax (01748) 884599
e-mail info@cbinn.co.uk
website www.cbinn.co.uk

Nearby North Yorkshire Dales
National Park, famous walks,
Location just N of Langthwaite and
Reeth in Arkengarthdale, Richmond
10 miles; with some car parking
Food breakfast, lunch, dinner
Price ££
Rooms 19; 14 double, 5 twin; all en
suite
Facitlities bar, restaurant
Credit cards MC, V
Children welcome
Disabled one suitable ground floor
room **Pets** not accepted
Proprietors Charles and Stacy Cody

Charles Bathurst Inn
Country inn

Charles and Stacy Cody took over this once derelict inn in Arkengarthdale during the 1990s and over a decade turned it into something special. It is very popular with Dales people, to whom it is important socially, and this may have made it a bit clannish, even self-satisfied. However, the CB Inn almost qualifies for a place in this guide just on the basis of the astonishing grandeur of the scenery with which it is surrounded. The bedrooms have glorious views. They are light and modern, with homely touches, some period furniture and all 19 have en-suite bathrooms. Downstairs, the ambience is darker and more masculine. The bar cleverly avoids the Widdecombe Fair style (much favoured by brewery chains), and yet still looks traditional. A large and tempting menu of locally-sourced dishes is painted on the vast mirror at one end of the room. Cask conditioned ales from Theakstons and Black Sheep refresh the weary, for this is walkers' country. The Inn is halfway along the Coast to Coast walk and those setting out from here can expect a hearty breakfast and good advice, well-made sandwiches for lunch and a Thermos of something warm.

Our inspector had reservations about the warmth of the welcome and attitude of staff, but we believe these arose from special circumstances. Reports welcome.

Barngate, Cumbria

Barngate, Ambleside, Cumbria,
LA22 0NG

Tel (015394) 36347
Fax (015394) 36781
e-mail info@drunkenduckinn.co.uk
website www.drunkenduckinn.co.uk

Nearby Lake walks, Ambleside,
Coniston.
Location After Ambleside, just off
the B5286 signposted to Hawkshead
– on the right is a directional sign to
the Duck, ample private car parking
Food breakfast, lunch, dinner
Price ££–£££
Rooms 17 double and twin, half
with bath, half with shower; all
rooms have TV, phone, modem
point, hairdryer **Facilities** dining
room, sitting room, bar; fly fishing;
great walking **Credit cards** AE, MC,
V **Children** welcome **Disabled** 2
rooms **Pets** not accepted **Closed**
never **Proprietors** Paul Spencer and
Stephanie Barton

Buttermere

Drunken Duck Inn
Country hotel

Situated in the heart of Lakeland amidst
sprawling hills and dales lies the Drunken
Duck, so named after a Victorian landlady
who found her ducks lying on the nearby
crossroads. Presuming them dead, she started to pluck them; but soon realized that
they were actually blind drunk, and not dead
in the slightest. This inn has real character
and charm. The bar/pub is delightful and
exactly as you would hope an old country
inn should look and feel, with old pictures,
prints and hunting memorabilia adorning the
walls. The menu in the bar and the dining
room is extensive, yet not over ambitious;
don't miss their home-brewed ale produced
at the back of the property; or choose from a
fine selection of wines (around 20 of them by
the glass). A recent reporter criticised the
fussy presentation of the food.

Ambling round the side of the inn you
will come across the 'deluxe' and
'supreme' rooms. Each is individually decorated with contemporary yet comfortable furniture and fabrics and the added
perk of private garden sitting areas and
even a balcony in the ever popular Garden
Room. The standard bedrooms in the main
house are also tastefully done out, if a little cramped.

Bassenthwaite Lake, Cumbria

Bassenthwaite Lake, near
Cockermouth, Cumbria CA13 9YE

Tel (017687) 76234
Fax (017687) 76002
e-mail info@the-pheasant.co.uk
website www.the-pheasant.co.uk

Nearby Bassenthwaite Lake;
Keswick.
Location 5 miles (8 km) E of
Cockermouth, just off A66; with
ample car parking
Food breakfast, lunch, dinner, bar
snacks
Price £££
Rooms 15; 11 double and twin, 3
suites and 1 single; all with bath and
shower; all rooms have flat-screen
TV, hairdryer, phone **Facilities** sit-
ting rooms, dining room, bar; garden
Credit cards MC, V **Children**
accepted over 8, but not in the bar or
dining room at night
Disabled access possible to public
rooms, Garden Lodge and 3 en suite
rooms **Pets** accepted in public rooms
and Garden Lodge rooms **Closed**
Christmas Eve and Day **Manager**
Matthew Wylie

The Pheasant
Country inn

'Still a very special place,' says our most
recent inspector. Nestled away behind
trees just off the A66, the Pheasant was
originally an old coaching inn, and there
are many reminders of this within, particularly in the little old oak bar, which is full of
dark nooks and crannies – a real piece of
history, little changed from its earliest
days. The building is a long, low barn-like
structure that has been exceptionally well
maintained. There is a small but well-kept
garden to the rear and grounds that
extend to 60 acres.

The three sitting areas are one of the
main attractions of the place. The two to
the front are low-ceilinged, with small windows and plenty of prints on the walls. The
third has an open log fire and a serving
hatch to the bar.

The grand refurbishment scheme was
undertaken in early 2000, and smaller, more
recent ones have seen the conversion of 20
old bedrooms into 15 larger, lighter, more
modern rooms. They are attractive and
individually decorated, partnered by *en suite*
bathrooms, and some have spectacular
views of the fells. The dining room has been
organized to make the best of its slightly
uncomfortable shape. The menu changes
daily and has won one Rosette and is close
to achieving its second. Service is outstandingly friendly.

Borrowdale, Cumbria

Borrowdale, Keswick, Cumbria
CA12 5UY

Tel (017687) 77247
Fax (017687) 77363
e-mail enq@leatheshead.co.uk
website www.leatheshead.co.uk

Nearby Derwent Water;
Buttermere; Castlerigg Stone Circle.
Location 3.5 miles (5.5 km) S of
Keswick, off B5289 to Borrowdale;
in garden with ample car parking
Food breakfast, dinner; half-board
obligatory at weekends
Price ££
Rooms 12 double and twin, 6 with
bath, 6 with shower; all rooms have
phone, TV, hairdryer **Facilities** 2
sitting rooms, dining room, bar; gar-
den
Credit cards MC, V
Children accepted over 9
Disabled 3 ground-floor rooms
Pets not accepted
Closed late-Nov to mid-Feb
Proprietors Roy and Janice Smith

The Leathes Head
Country hotel

Roy and Janice Smith are the resident owners of The Leathes Head in the beautiful Borrowdale valley. Originally built for a Liverpool ship owner, it is a Lakeland stone Edwardian house perched in its own wooded grounds near Derwent Water. Many of its period features, the plaster-work, the stained glass and a wood-pan-elled ceiling in the hall, are still there. It is informal enough to attract the walkers and climbers who return to the area year after year (even if it means carrying the newest additions to their families on their backs). Children are welcome (the hotel has all the necessary cots and high chairs) and can have a high tea in the evenings to give their parents the chance of a quiet dinner by themselves.

All the rooms are comfortably fur-nished (the largest being at the front) and most can squeeze in an extra bed. The three-acre grounds include lawns big enough and level enough to play boules or croquet – and flat areas are few and far between in this region. The real challenges are, of course, the fells beyond the gate and the hotel can help here too, with its extensive collection of walking guides.

Bowness-on-Windermere, Cumbria
LA23 3JP

Tel (015394) 43286
Fax (015394) 47455
e-mail kennedy@lindethfell.co.uk
website www.lindethfell.co.uk

Nearby Windermere Steamboat
Museum; Lake Windermere.
Location 1 mile (1.5km) S of
Bowness on A5074; with ample car
parking
Food breakfast, lunch, dinner
Price ££
Rooms 14; 12 double and twin, 2
single, 12 with bath, 2 with shower;
all rooms have phone, TV, hairdryer
Facilities 2 sitting rooms, dining
room, bar; garden, lake, croquet,
bowling green
Credit cards MC, V **Children**
accepted **Disabled** access possible to
ground-floor bedroom **Pets** not
accepted **Closed** 3 weeks in Jan
Proprietors Pat and Diana Kennedy

Lindeth Fell
Country house hotel

To stay at Lindeth Fell is like visiting a
well-heeled old friend who enjoys making his visitors as comfortable as possible,
who enjoys his food (but likes to be able to
identify what's put in front of him), is unrea-
sonably fond of good puddings, has a rather
fine wine cellar – and is justifiably proud of
the view from his house. Pat and Diana
Kennedy's establishment hits this mark
(they are always there to see that it does),
and, not unsurprisingly, their approach and
warm courteous welcome have been duly
rewarded with a faithful following.

Approached through trees, and set in
large mature gardens glowing with azaleas
and rhododendrons in spring, Lindeth
Fell's wood-panelled hall leads to a pair of
comfortable and attractive sitting rooms
and a restaurant where large windows let
in the tremendous view. Weather permitting, drinks and tea can be taken on the
terrace, and the same warm weather
might even allow for a game of tennis or
croquet. Upstairs, the rooms vary in size
and outlook. Both qualities are reflected in
their price but, as a general rule, the further up the house you go, the smaller the
room but the better the view. All the
rooms are comfortably furnished and
pleasingly decorated.

Bowness-on-Windermere, Cumbria

Crook Road, Bowness-on-
Windermere, Cumbria LA23 3JA

Tel (015394) 88600
Fax (015394) 88601
e-mail stay@linthwaite.com
website www.linthwaite.com

Nearby Windermere Steamboat
Museum; Lake Windermere; Beatrix
Potter's Hilltop
Location 1 mile (1.5km) S of
Bowness off the A5074; with ample
car parking
Food breakfast, lunch, dinner
Price ££-£££
Rooms 27 double and twin with
bath; all rooms have phone, TV,
hairdryer; wi-fi
Facilities sitting rooms, conservato-
ry, dining rooms, bar; terrace, gar-
den, veranda
Credit cards AE, MC, V
Children accepted
Disabled one specially adapted
room **Pets** not accepted **Closed**
never **Proprietor** Mike Bevans

Linthwaite House
Country house hotel

You could say of Mike Bevans that he
liked the view so much that he bought
the best place to see it from. It is our good
luck that he and his wife have also created
in this Edwardian country house a very
professionally-run hotel with a unique style.
The reception rooms are filled with palms,
wicker furniture and old curios as well as
antiques. Painted decoys, well-travelled
cabin trunks and oriental vases help to
evoke days of leisure and service in the far
reaches of the Empire. Service here manages to be crisp and amiable at the same
time: you are made to feel that you are on
holiday and not on parade. Whether you eat
in the richly coloured dining room or the
Mirror Room, the food has come from
Simon Bolsover's kitchen – well-thought-
out menus, beautifully presented. Bad luck,
though, if you're under seven: it's an early tea
for you, without the option.

Of the bedrooms, the best look directly
towards Windermere, some are in a modern annexe, and there is quite a variation
in size. They all have style though, with
thoughtful use of fabrics and furnishings
and bathrooms that are attractive rather
than utilitarian. Beyond the terraces outside are 14 acres of lawn, shrubs, woods
and a small lake.

Brampton, Cumbria

Brampton, Cumbria CA8 2NG

Tel (016977) 46234
Fax (016977) 46683
e-mail farlam@farlamhall.co.uk
website www.farlamhall.co.uk

Nearby Naworth Castle; Hadrian's
Wall; Lanercost Priory.
Location 3 miles (5 km) SE of
Brampton on A689, NE of (not in)
Farlam village; with ample car park-
ing
Food breakfast, dinner; light lunches
on request
Price ££££
Rooms 12 double with bath; all
rooms have phone, TV, hairdryer
Facilities 2 sitting rooms, dining
room; garden, croquet
Credit cards MC, V **Children**
accepted over 5
Disabled 2 ground-floor bedrooms
Pets welcome
Closed Christmas week
Proprietors Quinion and Stevenson
families

Farlam Hall
Country house hotel

'Charming family, quiet surroundings,
excellent food,' are the phrases that
encapsulate Farlam Hall. For more than 30
years now the Quinion and Stevenson
families have assiduously improved their
solid but elegant Border country house. It
has its roots in Elizabethan times, but what
you see today is essentially a large Victorian
family home, extended for a big family and
frequent entertaining. No coincidence that
it makes such a good hotel.

The dining room and public rooms are
discreet and the atmosphere is one of traditional English service and comfort. The
bedrooms vary widely, with some decidedly large and swish. Nevertheless, all are luxurious and charmingly done out, and some
have beautiful views of the grounds that
are home to a variety of llamas and sheep.

The chef, being one of the family, takes
pride in his food and it shows. The menu
changes daily (so guests staying for longer
than one night don't get bored) and there
is an impressive wine list that is overseen
by Mr Quinion, not to mention the extensive English cheese board or a choice of
deliciously unhealthy puddings.

Farlam Hall is well placed for the Lakes,
Dales and Northumberland Coast as well
as Hadrian's Wall.

Crosthwaite, Cumbria

Crosthwaite, near Kendal, Cumbria
LA8 8BP

Tel (015395) 68264
Fax (015395) 68264
e-mail
booking@crosthwaitehouse.co.uk
website
www.crosthwaitehouse.co.uk

Nearby Lake Windermere; Hill
Top; Sizergh Castle.
Location in countryside just off
A5074, 5 miles (8 km) W of Kendal;
with ample car parking
Food breakfast, dinner
Price £
Rooms 6; 5 double and twin, 1 sin-
gle, all with shower; all rooms have
TV **Facilities** sitting room, dining
room; garden **Credit cards** not
accepted **Children** welcome
Disabled access difficult **Pets**
accepted **Closed** late Nov to Feb
Proprietors Robin and Marnie
Dawson

Crosthwaite House
Country guest-house

White with damson blossom in the spring, Lyth Valley is a gentle land-scape with distant fells to remind you of where you are. Crosthwaite House is an attractive Georgian building with classic proportions and fine, tall rooms. Robin and Marnie Dawson are the relaxed owners who make their guests very welcome. There is an open fire in the comfortable sitting room, and a varied collection of books and games. You get the feeling that no-one would think you at all odd if, after a long walk and a hot shower, you just dozed off in front of the television until supper time.

Good hearty breakfasts are always there in the mornings in the wooden-floored dining room. There are six bright and sim-ply furnished bedrooms, each with their own shower room (although these can be something of a snug fit). Side windows have been let into the rooms at the rear of the house so that they can share the view with those at the front.

Crosthwaite House is now run as a bed and breakfast, and understandably so – Marnie says that after 40 years of cooking dinner for guests, "it's time to take life a lit-tle easier". The Punchbowl Inn (see next page) is a short stroll away, offering excel-lent dinners.

Crosthwaite, Cumbria

Crosthwaite, Lyth Valley
LA8 8HR

Tel (015395) 68237
Fax (015395) 68875
e-mail info@the-punchbowl.co.uk
website www.the-punchbowl.co.uk

Nearby Lake District National Park,
Grizedale Forst Park, Windermere,
Kendal
Location just N of the A5074
between Bowness and Levens
Food breakfast, luch, tea, dinner
Price ££
Rooms 9 doubles; all with bath and
shower
Facilities restaurant, bar, sitting
rooms **Credit cards** AE, MC, V
Children welcome **Disabled** not
suitable **Pets** not accepted
Closed never **Proprietors** Richard
Rose, Amanda Robinson, Paul
Spencer and Steph Barton

Punchbowl Inn
Country inn

The Punchbowl has had new owners since 2005. They have done it up in contemporary style, using mushroomy off-white shades from heritage paint makers. Tiny high-intensity downlighters make the free-standing roll-top bath and expensive taps glitter. Little bottles of as-it-were home-made shampoo and body lotion have hand-written labels. The power shower is excellent. The bath towels are enormous. The tongued and grooved wainscoting is painted Cooking Apple Green. More original is the old-style Roberts radio beside the bed tuned to Classic FM and playing when you first come in: perhaps a bit self-conscious, but not disagreeable.

Matthew Waddington's kitchen draws people from far and wide to eat quite luxurious and very imaginative dishes, made with great flair. William Nicholson's woodcuts of Twelve Sports, a polished refectory table with a bowl of fashionable green foliage and a dish of used corks give the room the air of a smart London restaurant, though the waitresses at the Punch Bowl are much nicer than their big city counterparts. The same dishes are obtainable in the bar for those who want to eat more informally. The surrounding countryside is lovely, the welcome genuine. A truly charming small hotel.

Dinham, Shropshire

Dinham, Ludlow, Shropshire,
SY8 1EH

Tel (01584) 874431
Fax (01584) 874431
website www.mr-underhills.co.uk

Nearby Martinier Falls, Ludlow
Castle, market in town, Shakespeare
festival.
Location at Market Square, turn left
at Castle Walls, on a lane called
Dinham Weir; limited off-road park-
ing
Food breakfast, dinner
Price ££
Rooms 6 doubles, with bath or
shower; 3 suites; all rooms have
phone, TV, hairdryer
Facilities dining room, small
lounge; garden
Credit cards MC, V
Children welcome
Disabled access difficult
Pets not accepted
Closed restaurant only, Tue
Proprietors Chris and Judy Bradley

Mr Underhill's at Dinham Weir **Restaurant-with-rooms**

As we approached this Michelin-starred restaurant-with-rooms at the end of the walk to Ludlow on the Mortimer Trail, we could almost have been reminded of many a similar place on the Lot or Dordogne. The paved garden, with its Mediterranean plants, is a sun trap looking on to the weir that breaks the flow of the River Teme below Ludlow Castle's walls. Here you can have breakfast or tea, or a glass of wine before an impressive dinner. Ludlow is now well known as a centre of haute cuisine: though this is the only Michelin-starred restaurant in the vicinity. The restaurant is sunny too, with a picture window overlooking the river. The no-choice (until pudding) menu, which is tailored to guests' needs, might include (to start) smoked haddock on spinach with a quail's egg in champagne *beurre blanc*; and local venison.

The six bedrooms are contemporary and stylish, if mostly compact, all with river views and cleverly shaped bathrooms. Three stylish suites, which offer more space, have been added in the neighbouring Millers House and the 'Shed' – a wooden-framed building situated where the Bradley's garden shed once stood. A great place, run on a personal scale.

Grasmere, Cumbria

Rydal Water, Grasmere, Cumbria
LA22 9SE

Tel (015394) 35295
Fax (015394) 35516
e-mail dixon@whitemoss.com
website www.whitemoss.com

Nearby Rydal Mount; Dove
Cottage.
Location 1 mile (1.5 km) S of
Grasmere on A591; with ample car
parking
Food breakfast; lunch and dinner
available for house parties and on
occasional weekends only
Price ££
Rooms 5 doubles, all with bath; 2-
bedroom cottage; all rooms have
phone, TV, hairdryer **Facilities** sit-
ting room, dining room, bar; garden,
fishing, free use of local leisure club
Credit cards AE, MC, V **Children**
older children welcome
Disabled access difficult
Pets accepted in cottage only
Closed Dec to Jan **Proprietors** Sue
and Peter Dixon

White Moss House
Country house hotel

Like many a parent, Wordsworth probably had to resort to bribery to per-
suade his son to fly the nest. Whether that
was the case or not, Wordsworth bought
him White Moss House and visited here
often. Built of grey Lakeland stone, now
creeper-clad, and set in a pretty, rose-rich
garden above the road from Grasmere to
Ambleside, Sue and Peter Dixon's small
hotel earned a disproportionately large
(but richly deserved) reputation for the
quality of its food and the scope of its cellar. The Dixons, wanting respite from long
working days, are now mostly running
White Moss House as a bed and breakfast.
They do, however, still offer dinner and
lunch for private house parties (they attract
many). They also serve lunch and dinner for
all comers on occasional weekends.

The whole house has comfort as its
watchword. Bedrooms are not vast, but all
are filled with a host of little touches ranging from fresh flowers to bath salts. The
two-bedroomed Brockstone Cottage is a
ten minute walk away up on the fellside, and
can be taken by one small party.

Great Langdale, Cumbria

Great Langdale, Ambleside,
Cumbria LA22 9JY

Tel (015394) 37272
Fax (015394) 37272
e-mail olddungeonghyll1@btcon-
nect.com **website** www.odg.co.uk

Nearby Lake Windermere;
Grasmere; Kendal.
Location 7 miles (11 km) NE of
Ambleside off B5343; in countryside
with ample car parking
Food breakfast, packed lunch, din-
ner, bar meals
Price ££
Rooms 14; 11 double, 3 single, 5
with shower
Facilities sitting room, dining room,
2 bars; garden
Credit cards AE, MC, V
Children welcome **Disabled** access
difficult **Pets** welcome
Closed 24 to 26 Dec **Proprietors**
Neil and Jane Walmsley

Old Dungeon Ghyll
Country hotel

Langdale is a magnificent valley in the centre of the Lake District, dominated by the Langdale Pikes. Walkers and climbers flock here to hike and scale some of the highest mountains in England (including the Scafell range). In 1885 the Old Dungeon Ghyll Hotel (then known as Middlefell) was run by John Bennett, a well-known guide for tourists. The historian G. M. Trevelyan bought it in the early 1900s and gave it to the National Trust. The horse-drawn 'charas' bringing visitors from Little Langdale over Blea Tarn Pass would stop at the top and blow their horn, a signal to get lunch or tea ready – the number of blasts matching the number of passengers. As an unofficial home for most of Britain's climb-ing clubs, the visitors' book was like a roll-call of the leading British climbers.

Neil and Jane Walmsley have been the proprietors since 1983 and have contin-ued to improve and develop this popular family hotel retaining as many old features as possible. The climbers were a pretty uncritical bunch (any kind of a roof was a luxury), but there is now a comfortable residents' sitting room with an open fire, a warm busy bar (open to the public) and a snug dining room offering wholesome uncomplicated food. There are fewer bath-rooms than bedrooms, although five of the rooms have their own showers.

Hawkshead, Cumbria

Near Sawrey, Ambleside, Cumbria
LA22 0JZ

Tel (015394) 36393
Fax (015394) 36393
e-mail mail@eeswyke.co.uk
website www.eeswyke.co.uk

Nearby Hill Top; Lake
Windermere; Grasmere.
Location in hamlet on B5285, 2
miles (3 km) SE of Hawkshead; with
car parking
Food breakfast, dinner
Price ££
Rooms 8 double and twin, 3 with
bath, 5 with shower; all rooms have
TV, hairdryer
Facilities 2 sitting rooms, dining
room;
Credit cards AE, MC, V **Children**
accepted over 8
Disabled 1 ground-floor room
Pets accepted in bedrooms
Closed Jan to Feb **Proprietors**
Richard and Margaret Lee

Ees Wyke
Country house hotel

Esthwaite Water, to the east of
Windermere, has been kept safely in
private hands, so has escaped the develop-
ment that has ravaged some of the other
Lakes. Ees Wyke, a gem of a white-painted
Georgian mansion, is perched above park-
like meadows that roll gently down to the
reed banks on the shore, punctuated here
and there by sheep and mature trees. As
well as unmarred views, Richard and
Margaret Lee have happily discovered the
secret of making people feel instantly at
home. No-one could be more relaxed
than Ruff the dog, whose speciality is imi-
tating the famous immovable object.

This is a well-kept house, with everything just so, even down to a plentiful sup-
ply of games and books for those
inclement days. In the dining room are
beautiful large windows to show off the
view (these are new since Beatrix Potter
stayed here for her holidays), Windsor
chairs and crisp white tablecloths. The dinners (Richard's department) run to five
generous and unhurried courses and the
price/quality ratio of the wine list is definitely tipped in your favour. The bedrooms
are attractive and generously proportioned, most with small but well-equipped
bathrooms, and comfortable enough to
allow you to build up the strength you
need to tackle the truly heroic breakfast.

Kirkby Lonsdale, Cumbria

Cowan Bridge, Kirkby Lonsdale,
Cumbria LA6 2JJ

Tel (015242) 71187
Fax (015242) 72452
e-mail info@hippinghall.com **web-site** www.hippinghall.com

Nearby Yorkshire Dales; Lake District; Settle to Carlisle railway.
Location on A65, 2.5 miles (4 km) SE of Kirkby Lonsdale; in 3-acre walled gardens with ample car parking
Food breakfast, lunch, dinner
Price £££-££££
Rooms 9 double/twin; 6 with bath/shower, 3 with shower; all rooms have phone, TV, hairdryer, CD player **Facilities** sitting room, dining room, breakfast room, conservatory with bar; garden, croquet, boules **Credit cards** AE, MC, V
Children welcome; over 12 in restaurant **Disabled** access possible
Pets accepted in one bedroom
Closed 2 weeks in Jan **Proprietor** Andrew Wildsmith

Hipping Hall
Country hotel

This place, long in the guide, underwent a major transformation since our last edition. The new owners have converted it from a small 'house party' country hotel into a contemporary restaurant-with-rooms. Former Young Chef of the Year Jason Birkbeck is in the kitchen, producing inspired dishes, using produce from the garden, that are still served in the spectacular beamed Great Hall. From the elaborately worded menu, you could choose Kittridding oxtail, glazed veal sweetbread and celeriac *purée*, followed by 'saddle of venison with black pudding ravioli, parsnip *purée*, creamed cabbage and juniper *jus*', or a fillet of 'line-caught' sea bass with 'hand-rolled' macaroni, wild mushrooms, spinach and autumn truffle.

Parts of the Hall date back to the 15th century when a hamlet grew up around the 'hipping' or stepping stones across the beck. After a strenuous day on the fells, you can relax in the bar-sitting area with open (gas-log) fire.

There are six cool, white bedrooms in the main house and three 'cottage' rooms across the courtyard.

Low Lorton, Cumbria

Low Lorton, near Cockermouth,
Cumbria CA13 9UP

Tel (01900) 77247 85107
Fax (01900) 77247 85107
e-mail nick@winderhall.co.uk **web-site** www.winderhall.co.uk

Nearby Derwent Water; Keswick;
Loweswater.
Location 3 miles (5 km) S of
Cockermouth, off B5289; with car
parking
Food breakfast, dinner
Price ££
Rooms 7 double and twin; all with
shower, 3 with bath; all rooms have
TV, hairdryer
Facilities sitting room, dining room;
garden
Credit cards MC, V **Children** wel-
come **Disabled** not suitable
Pets not accepted **Closed** Jan
Proprietors Nick and Ann Lawler

Winder Hall
Country guest-house

If you take the beautiful road from Keswick by the Whinlatter Pass, you will drop down towards Lorton into the prettiest countryside you could wish for. Winder Hall is a Grade II-listed Tudor manor, oozing character and charm. An inspector was recently greeted by the proprietors, Nick and Ann Lawler, plus young daughters spilling out of the door, and invited to enjoy some of the fantastic fell walks surrounding the property.

This is by no means a hotelly hotel: you get much more the feeling of being welcomed into the family home as a close friend. Dark oak panels cover the dining room walls, but light is abundant from the long low window overlooking the beautiful medieval herb garden and fells beyond. Nick is the chef and only uses local fresh produce in his Mediterranean/classic French dishes, and is looking to go completely organic in the next few years.

The drawing room and bedrooms are bright and airy, yet distinctly cosy. Of the six individually decorated bedrooms, only one has a vast fireplace and Priest's hole. But they all greet you with fresh flowers and home-made biscuits. Perfect for large parties wanting to take over the whole house or couples looking for a romantic weekend break to experience the beauty of the North.

Mungrisdale, Cumbria

Mungrisdale, Penrith, Cumbria
CA11 0XR

Tel (017687) 79659
e-mail themill@quinlan.evesham.net
website www.themillhotel.com

Nearby Derwentwater; Ullswater;
Hadrian's Wall.
Location 9.5 miles (15 km) W of
Penrith close to A66, in village; with
parking for 15 cars
Food breakfast, dinner
Price ££££ (including dinner)
Rooms 7 double and twin with bath;
all rooms have TV
Facilities sitting room, TV room,
games room, dining room; garden
Credit cards not accepted **Children**
welcome
Disabled access difficult **Pets**
accepted in bedrooms by arrange-
ment
Closed Nov to Mar **Proprietors**
Richard and Eleanor Quinlan

The Mill
Country hotel

This former 17thC mill cottage below
Skiddaw still has the millrace running
past it and is in very open, unspoilt countryside. Like Mungrisdale itself (which you
can travel through in three minutes), it is
by no means large, but manages to maintain a big reputation for its welcome, its
food and its thoroughly professional management. High season must test its capaci-
ty a little, but it has a substantial fan club
who come back year after year. The snug
dining room, where crazy stacks of candle
stubs and their accumulated drips, look
like small-scale models of spectacular limestone caverns, and where strangers actually talk to one another, is the scene both
for first-rate breakfasts and Eleanor
Quinlan's excellent five-course dinners.
How she manages to find time to bake the
bread as well is a mystery to one and all.

Wall space everywhere is almost entirely given over to the results of 30 years'
worth of oil and watercolour collecting by
the Quinlans. Some bedrooms are quite
small, but if you need more space there are
two bedrooms in the picturesque old mill
that share a sizeable sitting room. Popular
with bridge players, says John Quinlan. All
around are excellent walks for people of all
ages and any abilities. Don't mistake this
hotel for the neighbouring Mill Inn.

Newlands, Cumbria

Grange Road, Newlands, Keswick,
Cumbria CA12 5UE

Tel (017687) 72948
Fax (017687) 72948
e-mail info@swinsidelodge-hotel.co.uk **website** www.swinside-lodge-hotel.co.uk

Nearby Derwent Water;
Bassenthwaite Lake.
Location 3 miles (5 km) SW of
Keswick, 2 miles (3 km) S of A66;
with garden and parking for 10 cars
Food breakfast, dinner
Price ££££ (rate includes dinner)
Rooms 7 double, 4 with bath, 2 with
shower; all have TV, hairdryer
Facilities 2 sitting rooms, dining
room; garden
Credit cards MC, V
Children accepted over 12
Disabled not suitable **Pets** not
accepted
Closed over Christmas **Proprietors**
Eric and Irene Fell

Swinside Lodge
Country hotel

This attractive Victorian lakeland house occupies a picture-postcard setting by Derwent Water, far removed from the fleshpots of Keswick. Eric and Irene Fell took over here in 2004, and since then it has undergone some refurbishment, with all bathrooms being renewed.

The chef Clive Imber produces a daily changing menu around fresh, local ingredients, including beef and lamb from a local farm. Highlights include home made breads, soups and ice creams. Each evening dinner is followed by a hot pudding, cold dessert and a selection of Cumbrian cheeses. Wine comes from growers who use traditional methods.

As for the hotel itself, it is decorated with flair (not overdone) and you are trusted with good carpets and even better furniture. Everything that should be clean is clean, and everything else has been polished. The comfortable bedrooms are no different. The hotel's prime assets, though, are outside. Lying at the foot of Cat Bells as it does, there are walks of every description through genuinely unspoilt territory – and if you haven't the energy, you can always sit and look at it. All in all a relaxed, friendly hotel.

Reports welcome.

Sawrey, Cumbria

Near Sawrey, Ambleside,
Cumbria, LA22 0LF

Tel (015394) 36334
e-mail
enquiries@towerbankarms.com
website www.towerbankarms.com

Nearby Hilltop (NT), between
Esthwaite Water and Windermere
Location beside B5285 near Sawrey
with some car parking
Food breakfast, lunch, dinner
Price ££
Rooms 3; 2 doubles, 1 single; all with
showers and TV, tea and coffee mak-
ing facilities
Facilities bar, restaurant
Credit cards AE, DC, MC, V
Children welcome
Disabled not suitable
Pets accepted
Closed never
Proprietor Andrew Hutton

Tower Bank Arms
Country inn

Beatrix Potter pilgrims need look no
further. This simple inn, a short walk
from Hilltop (NT), where many of Miss
Potter's books were written, is surely
where Mr MacGregor allowed himself an
occasional dram and it is to be seen – dis-
tantly – in The Tale of Jemima Puddleduck
(p.43). It looks more like a cottage than a
pub, only the ticking clock over the porch
and a little blackboard announcing 'Bar
opens at 5 pm' suggesting otherwise. The
dining-room caters for many people staying in B&Bs in the village and the owner
wants the exterior to look unpretentious,
feeling that walkers with muddy boots or
those on budgets might otherwise be put-
off. For £7.50 they can enjoy dishes such as
Cumbrian Beef & Ale Stew ('with herby
dumplings and chunky chips'), in surroundings grander than one would expect at
that price, with Wedgwood china and linen
napkins. It is not a posh place or a large
one – two doubles and one single room –
but it is clean and tidy and the flagstoned
bar offers the comfort of a wood-fired
range and a number of good beers. Don't
come here expecting tea on the lawn or
room service. But if your imagination is
fired by a view of the street where Mrs
Tabitha Twitchet or the Sandy-Whiskered
Gentleman strolled, this is for you.

Seatoller, Cumbria

Seatoller, Borrowdale, Keswick,
Cumbria CA12 5XN

Tel (017687) 77218
Fax (017687) 77189
e-mail
enquiries@seatollerhouse.co.uk
website www.seatollerhouse.co.uk

Nearby Derwentwater; Buttermere;
Keswick.
Location 8 miles (13 km) S of
Keswick on B5289; ample car park-
ing
Food breakfast, packed lunch, din-
ner (not Tue)
Price ££
Rooms 10 double and twin, all with
bath
Facilities sitting room, library, din-
ing room, tea room, drying room;
garden
Credit cards MC, V **Children** wel-
come over 5 **Disabled** 2 ground-
floor bedrooms **Pets** welcome in
bedrooms **Closed** Dec to Feb
Proprietors Daniel Potts and Lynne
Moorehouse

Seatoller House
Country guest-house

It should be said at the outset that a stay at Seatoller House is something quite different from the run-of-the-mill hotel experience. You eat communally at set times, and to get the best out of the place you should take part in the social life of the house.

Seatoller House is over 300 years old and has been run as a guest-house for more than 100 years; the first entry in the visitors' book reads 23 April 1886. The long, low house, built in traditional Lakeland style and looking like a row of cottages, is in the tiny village of Seatoller, at the head of Borrowdale and the foot of Honister Pass. Bedrooms are in a tradi-tional country cottage style, and all have their own bathrooms (although some are physically separate from the bedrooms). The dining room is in a country-kitchen style, with a delightfully informal atmos-phere – one that spills over into the two sections of the low-ceilinged sitting room. Food is excellent; and if you are thirsty, just wander to the fridge, take what you like and sign for it in the book provided.

Several times a year the house is taken over by members of the Lakes Hunt, who enjoy running up and down the surround-ing fells in pursuit, not of foxes (the tradi-tional quarry) but of one another.

Ullswater, Cumbria

Ullswater, Penrith,
CA10 2ND

Tel (017684) 86514

Nearby Ullswater, Lake District
National Park
Location just off B5320, near
Pooley Bridge
Food breakfast, lunch, dinner
Price £££ (rate includes dinner)
Rooms 11; 8 double, 3 single
Facilities 4 sitting rooms, dining
room, 2 bars; garden
Credit cards not accepted
Children no special facilities
Disabled access to dining room pos-
sible; not to rooms
Pets accepted in rooms
Closed 1 Nov to Easter
Proprietor Mrs Baldry

Howtown Hotel
Country hotel

Howtown Hotel is the Real Thing. Instead
of pretending to be a charming private
house of some years ago, it actually is a
house that has been in the same family for
about a century. And little seems to have
changed – except the bathrooms, which are
modern and efficient. They are not en-suite,
but all are private and individual, usually just
across a passage. Downstairs, Toby jugs, brass
warming pans, the heads of foxes hunted in
the 1930s, and oil paintings make the hall
seem like a pre-war antique shop. Doors are
wood-grained in the old-fashioned way (no
Farrow & Ball paint here). The cosy little bar
with stained glass in the windows might be
the snug where the Swallows & Amazons'
uncle, Captain Flint, met his friends. The
Smoking Room opposite has succumbed to
modern diktat. Other public rooms are
grander, lighter, more like drawing-rooms.
The bedrooms are equally comfortable and
impressive. Presiding is Mrs Baldry, ably sup-
ported by a very capable management and
uber-friendly Poles. Nothing is too much
trouble. The place is as clean as a museum.
The scenery around is staggering. And they
sound a gong before meals.

Mrs Baldry says she doesn't like publicity,
and needs it still less. On the other hand,
we feel that not a few readers of this guide
will be just the right sort of guest for this
unique place.

Wasdale Head, Cumbria

Wasdale Head, Gosforth, Cumbria
CA20 1EX

Tel (019467) 26229
Fax (019467) 26334
e-mail wasdaleheadinn@msn.com
website www.wasdale.com

Nearby Hardknott Castle Roman
Fort; Ravenglass and Eskdale
Railway; Wastwater; Scafell.
Location 9 miles (14.5 km) NE of
Gosforth at head of Wasdale; with
ample car parking
Food breakfast, bar and packed
lunches, dinner
Price ££
Rooms 13; 7 double and twin, 3 sin-
gle, 3 suites, 11 with bath, 2 with
shower; all rooms have phone; also 6
self-catering apartments
Facilities sitting room, dining room,
2 bars; garden **Credit cards** AE,
MC, V **Children** accepted **Disabled**
2 ground floor rooms
Pets not accepted in public areas,
except bars **Closed** never **Landlord**
Howard Christie

Wasdale Head
Country inn

The Wasdale Head is in a site unrivalled
even in the consistently spectacular
Lake District. It stands on the flat valley
bottom between three major peaks – Pillar,
Great Gable and Scafell Pike (England's
highest) – and only a little way above
Wastwater, England's deepest and perhaps
most dramatic lake.

Over the last decade and a half, the old
inn has been carefully and thoughtfully
modernized, adding facilities but retaining
the characteristics of a traditional mountain inn. The main sitting room of the hotel
is comfortable and welcoming, with plenty
of personal touches. The pine-panelled
bedrooms are not notably spacious but
they are adequate, with fixtures and fittings
all in good condition. There are also six self-
catering apartments in a converted barn,
and three hotel apartments. The dining
room is heavily panelled, and decorated
with willow pattern china and a pewter jug
collection. Children under eight are not
allowed in here after 8pm. Food is considerably better than you would expect of a
mountaineering inn, served by young, friendly staff. There are two bars. The one for residents has some magnificent wooden furniture, while tasty bar food is served in the
congenial surroundings of the public bar,
much frequented by walkers and climbers.

Whitewell, Lancashire

Forest of Bowland, near Clitheroe,
Lancashire BB7 3AT

Tel (01200) 448222
Fax (01200) 448298
e-mail reception@innatwhitewell.com
website www.innatwhitewell.com

Nearby Browsholme Hall; Clitheroe
Castle; Blackpool.**Location** 6 miles
(9.5 km) NW of Clitheroe; with
ample car parking
Food breakfast, picnic lunch on
request, dinner, bar meals
Price ££
Rooms 15; 14 double and twin, 1
suite, all with bath; all rooms have
phone, TV, CD; some have minibar,
hairdryer, peat fire
Facilities dining rooms, bar; garden,
fishing **Credit cards** DC, MC, V
Children welcome **Disabled** 2
ground-floor rooms **Pets** welcome
Closed never **Proprietor** Richard
Bowman

The Inn at Whitewell
Country inn

Past and present come together with
great effect at this welcoming inn with
a glorious situation, on a riverbank plumb
in the middle of the Forest of Bowland. In
the 14th century it was a small manor
house where the Keeper of the Forest
lived. Today, some of the original architecture survives and rooms are furnished
with antiques, but modern comfort is the
order of the day, with, for example, videos
and hi-tech stereo systems in all the bedrooms. Most of these are spacious and
attractive, with warm lighting and prints
clustered on the walls; many contain an
extra sofa bed; a couple have four-posters.
To keep romance alive, you can book one
of the rooms with a fireplace and snuggle
up to a cosy peat fire while your favourite
CD plays on the Bang and Olufsen, or wallow in the deep vintage baths.

Food is an important consideration
here. English dishes feature predominately
on the menu – seasonal roast game or
grilled fish, followed by wicked home-
made puddings and a selection of farmhouse cheeses. Alternatively, bar meals are
on offer at lunchtime and in the evening.
Just past the bar is a small shop that sells a
great selection of wines, books, cheeses
and other bits and bobs. Be sure to check
the terms and conditions of the inn before
making a booking.

Windermere, Cumbria

Crook Road, near Windermere,
Cumbria LA23 3NE

Tel (015394) 88818
Fax (015394) 88058
e-mail hotel@gilpinlodge.co.uk
website www.gilpinlodge.co.uk

Nearby Windermere Steamboat
Museum; Holker Hall; Sizergh
Castle; Kendal; Grasmere.
Location on B5284 Kendal to
Bowness road, 2 miles (1 km) SE of
Windermere; with ample car parking
Food breakfast, lunch, dinner
Price £££
Rooms 14 double and twin with
bath; 6 suites; all rooms have phone,
TV, minibar, hairdryer
Facilities 2 sitting rooms, 4 dining
rooms; garden **Credit cards** AE,
DC, MC, V **Children** accepted over
7 **Disabled** access possible to
ground-floor rooms
Pets not accepted **Closed** never
Proprietors John and Christine
Cunliffe

Gilpin Lodge
Country house hotel

Just occasionally, whether by luck or judge-ment, you can arrive somewhere that tells you to congratulate yourself on your choice of hotel before you even step through the door: Gilpin Lodge is one of these happy places. John Cunliffe's grandmother lived in this Edwardian house for 40 years, and when he and his wife Christine came 25 years later, it had become a rather ordinary B&B. Now, with manicured grounds and gleaming paint, quite substantially and whol-ly sympathetically enlarged and set on a peaceful hillside with moor beyond the boundary, you are to some extent prepared for the warm welcome and deep-pile com-fort waiting for you inside. This is a highly professional and well-staffed operation, yet still driven by the enthusiasm of owners whose unmistakeable priority is the happi-ness of their guests.

If your tastes run to good pictures, fine fur-niture and immaculate service you will be happy; if they include excellent and imagina-tively presented food with more than the occasional touch of outright luxury (Gilpin Lodge holds a Michelin star) you will be hap-pier still; and if you want a large, thoughtfully decorated room, probably with its own sitting area, and a bathroom to talk about when you get home, then you're in luck.

Windermere, Cumbria

Holbeck Lane, Windermere,
Cumbria LA23 1LU

Tel (015394) 32375
Fax (015394) 34743
e-mail stay@holbeckghyll.com
website www.holbeckghyll.com

Nearby Lake Windermere.
Location 3 miles (5 km) N of
Windermere, E of A591; with ample
car parking
Food breakfast, light lunch, dinner
Price ££££
Rooms 19 double, all with bath; 4
suites; all have phone, TV, DVD,
hairdryer
Facilities 2 sitting rooms, 2 dining
rooms; garden, health spa, tennis,
croquet, putting
Credit cards AE, DC, MC, V
Children welcome
Disabled 3 lodge rooms
Pets accepted in bedrooms only
Closed 3 weeks Jan **Proprietors**
David and Patricia Nicholson

Holbeck Ghyll
Country house hotel

An award-winning hotel in a classic
Victorian lakeland house, ivy-clad with
steep slate roofs and mullioned windows –
plus oak panelling and art noveau stained
glass. Our latest reporter had a 'friendly welcome' and was impressed by its superb
position, providing both privacy from the
bustle of Windermere and grand lake views
from the immaculate gardens; also indeed
by the two comfortable sitting rooms, both
homelike and beautifully furnished.

The Nicholsons, professional hoteliers
both, took over in 1988 and have refurbished to very high standards in a traditional, slightly formal style – though proprietors and staff alike are friendly and
relaxed. Bedrooms and bathrooms are
beautifully and individually decorated, very
spacious, some with their own sitting
room. At the top of the house is a 'very
special' four-poster room. In the Lodge
nearby are six further rooms (four are self-
catering), with breathtaking views. The food
is a clear attraction: pre-dinner canapés are
served while you select from the inventive
daily-changing menu designed by head chef
Dave McLoughlin, winner of a Michelin
star. There is a jogging trail from which you
can spot deer and red squirrels.

Arncliffe, North Yorkshire

Arncliffe, Littondale, Skipton, North
Yorkshire BD23 5QE

Tel (01756) 770250
Fax (01756) 770250
website www.amerdalehouse.co.uk

Nearby Wharfedale; Grassington;
Pennine Way.
Location in a rural setting, 7 miles
(10 km) NW of Grassington, 3 miles
(5 km) off B6160; with ample car
parking
Food breakfast, lunch on Sundays,
dinner
Price £££
Rooms 10 double/twin; 4 with bath,
3 with showe, 3 with both; all rooms
have phone, TV, DVD, fax/modem
point, hairdryer
Facilities sitting rooms, bar, dining
room; garden **Credit cards** AE, DC,
MC, V **Children** welcome **Disabled**
not suitable **Pets** not acceptedinside
hotel **Closed** Jan-Feb **Proprietors**
Andrew and Caroline Middleton

Amerdale House
Country hotel

Amerdale House has long been in the
guide, but was taken over in October
2006 by Andrew and Caroline Middleton,
both trained chefs, who formerly ran the
Rose and Crown in Sutton-on-the-Forest
in York. Since then, they have redecorated
the whole place to make it brighter and
more neutral, using of some of the original
fixtures and fittings, while bringing it up to
date. The setting is one of the most seductive in all the Dales: on the fringe of a pretty village in a lonely valley, wide meadows
in front, high hills behind. We visited a few
years ago and were smitten with the location ('total peace and serenity') and the
comfortable and beautifully decorated
bedrooms and bathrooms.

Caroline is front of house, while
Andrew acts as head chef. As you might
expect from a hotel run by two chefs, the
emphasis is on the food, which is locally
produced. The restaurant is open to non-
residents. Dinner might include a starter
of haggis with leeks and roasted pepper
dressing, followed by rack of new season
spring lamb from Conistone Cold, with
red wine *jus*, then raspberry *crème brulée*.
There is a vaulted wine cellar, stocking an
abundance of Old and New World wines.

Amerdale House is usefully situated for
a number of Dales sights.

Bolton Abbey, North Yorkshire

Bolton Abbey, Skipton, North
Yorkshire BD23 6AJ

Tel (01756) 710441
Fax (01756) 710564
e-mail reservations@devon-
shirearms.co.uk **website**
www.devonshirehotel.co.uk

Nearby Castle Howard; Skipton
Castle; Brontë Parsonage; Harewood
House.
Location on B6160 just N of junction with A59; in grounds with
ample car parking
Food breakfast, lunch, dinner
Price ££££
Rooms 40; 37 double and twin, 1
family, 2 suites, all with bath; all
rooms have phone, TV, DVD,
hairdryer **Facilities** 3 lounges, conservatory, dining room, 2 bars, gym,
sauna, steam room, solarium, plunge
pool, indoor swimming pool; garden,
tennis, croquet, putting, helipad,
fishing **Credit cards** AE, DC, MC,
V **Children** accepted **Disabled**
access possible **Pets** accepted
Closed never **Manager** Eamonn
Elliott

Devonshire Arms
Country house hotel

As your helicopter whirls towards its
helipad, you can see that the moorland
of the Dales proper comes to within a mile
or so of the 17thC Devonshire Arms.
Follow the path down the bank of the
Wharfe, which gives the valley its name, for
the half mile from Bolton Abbey village to
the stone bridge and you're there. Owned
by the Duke and Duchess of Devonshire,
the hotel is doubly graced since it contains
antiques and paintings from Chatsworth,
the family seat; the Duchess has masterminded their placement and the design of
the interior. This is a hotel in two parts, old
and new. The elegant old wears its years
well and has happily grown out of exact
right angles. The new extension, which has
brought with it an indoor swimming pool,
gym and beauty salon, still has its sharp
corners, but is settling in well.

The dining alternatives cover a similar
spectrum. On the one hand is the quiet
comfort of the classical Burlington
Restaurant, which has been awarded a
Michelin star, and on the other a buzzy
blue and yellow brasserie with dishes to
suit most moods and a snappy wine list to
go with them. The bedrooms also come in
old and new varieties: the older win on
character and the newer score better with
their views.

Golcar, Huddersfield

Knowl Road, Golcar, Huddersfield
HD7 4AN

Tel (01484) 654284
Fax (01484) 650980
e-mail info@weaversshed.co.uk
website www.weaversshed.co.uk

Nearby Peak National Park;
Pennine Way.
Location 3 miles (5 km) W of
Huddersfield on A62 and B6111;
ample car parking
Food breakfast, lunch, dinner
Price ££
Rooms 5 double and twin with bath
and shower; all rooms have phone,
TV, fax/modem point, hairdryer
Facilities restaurant, bar; garden
Credit cards AE, MC, V **Children**
accepted
Disabled access possible **Pets** not
accepted **Closed** Christmas Day,
Boxing Day, New Year's Eve, New
Year's Day; restaurant only, Sun,
Mon, Sat lunch **Proprietors**
Stephen and Tracy Jackson

Weavers Shed
Restaurant-with-rooms

At first acquaintance Golcar would probably be dropped from just about anybody's list of places of outstanding natural beauty. But it has a fine secret – and the secret is the Weavers Shed. High on a hill, away from Huddersfield, in what started life in the 18th century as a cloth finishing mill and still has a fine flagged floor, is an excellent restaurant – and, what's more, you can sleep very comfortably indeed where you have just eaten.

Owner (and chef) Stephen Jackson and his collaborators in the kitchen are also keen market gardeners and have a plot which supplies many of their needs for fresh herbs, fruit and vegetables. Other elements of the menu are equally carefully chosen, with pork, for example, from traditional breeds and fish only featuring if the market is offering something worthwhile on the day. The style is modern British which, because of its simplicity, offers no hiding place for second-rate ingredients. Not surprisingly, the same sort of care has been taken with the wine list. The bedrooms are in the house next door. Built originally for the owner of the mill, it is a substantial building with light airy rooms, filled with a pleasing mixture of ancient and modern furniture and good-quality but unfussy fabrics. You won't forget breakfast.

Grassington, North Yorkshire

Summers Fold, Grassington, near
Skipton, North Yorkshire BD23 5AE

Tel (01756) 752584
Fax (07092) 376562
website www.ashfieldhouse.co.uk

Nearby Skipton Castle, Gordale
Scar, Janet's Foss, Ripon, Malham
Cove, Bolton Abbey
Location in Grassington, just NW
of main square; with ample car park-
ing
Food breakfast, dinner
Prices ££
Rooms 8 double and twin with bath
or shower; all rooms have TV,
hairdryer, wi-fi
Facilities 2 sitting rooms, 1 with bar,
dining room; garden
Credit cards MC, V
Children welcome over 10
Disabled not suitable
Pets not accepted
Closed two weeks each year
Proprietors Joe Azzopardi and
Elizabeth Webb

Ashfield House
Country guest-house

Grassington, and Wharfedale in general,
is a little-known Northern gem, especially for keen walkers. Tucked away off the
main street is Joe Azzopardi and Elizabeth
Webb's small private stone and slate hotel,
a peaceful sanctuary at the end of its own
yard. What's more, and unlike anywhere
else in Grassington, you can park your car
there. Oak and pine furniture, bare beams
and stone walls are combined with fresh
flowers and neat new furnishings.

An excellent four course dinner is
served in the pretty dining room each
evening. Joe presides over the kitchen,
making use of a great deal of fresh local
produce, and is assisted by Elizabeth.
Breakfast consists of an impressive array
of home-made produce – yoghurt, muesli,
granola and marmalade – together with
local bacon and own-recipe sausages.

The bedrooms are modestly sized with
fresh, clean decoration and their own
shower rooms. Since Joe and Elizabeth
took over here they have upgraded all of
the bathrooms and brought the whole
place up to date.

Beyond the house, insulated from the
bustle of the town, is a quiet walled garden
with a table and chairs where you can simply sit and enjoy the sunshine if the
prospect of a walk along the river seems
too testing.

Harome, North Yorkshire

Harome, Nr Helmsley, North
Yorkshire, YO62 5JE

Tel (01439) 770397
Fax (01439) 771 833
website www.thestaratharome.co.uk

Nearby Helmsley market town,
Castle Howard, Duncombe Park.
Location 2.5 miles SE of Helmsley
off the A170, ample car parking
Food breakfast, lunch, dinner
(restaurant in the Inn closed on
Mon) **Price** £££ **Rooms** 8 doubles, 3
suites, all with bath or shower; the
Farmhouse (sleeps 8); all rooms have
TV, DVD, CD, radio, hairdryer,
phone, tea and coffee making facilities **Facilities** dining rooms, breakfast room, bar, sitting room; garden
Credit cards MC, V **Children** welcome **Disabled** a couple of ground-
floor rooms **Pets** not accepted
Closed 1 week in winter, 1 week in
summer **Proprietors** Andrew and
Jacquie Pern

The Star Inn
Country hotel

'One of the most comfortable, relaxing nights I have spent in a hotel' says a recent inspector. Wellies and umbrellas wait by the front door of Cross House (the Inn's guest house) in case you feel like having a stroll around the beautiful countryside. The opulent sitting room is kept warm by the grand fire in the centre and once sat on the sofas with tea and seriously good cakes you can hardly make it to your room. When you do, you'll discover that they are immaculate, balancing the contemporary and the rustic perfectly with fantastic bathrooms (some with whirlpool baths) and music, DVDs and choco-lates and crisps to tide you over until supper.

Supper and lunch can be served in the Inn itself: just across the road. The pub and restaurant are bursting with charm and decorated in keeping with the 14thC thatched image, so expect old beams and secret little loft spaces in which to enjoy coffee after the Michelin-starred food cooked by Andrew. Upstairs the fairytale private dining room has been decorated by local artists. The small shop at the front of Cross House sells everything from silver jewellery to hams and cheeses. Black Eagle cottages (at the other end of the village) can accommodate small groups of friends. The Farmhouse, a short stroll from the main hotel, is also available for groups.

Harrogate, North Yorkshire

Prospect Place, Harrogate,
North Yorkshire, HG1 1LB

Tel (01423) 856800
Fax (01423) 856801
e-mail
info@harrogate.hotelduvin.com
website www.hotelduvin.com

Nearby central Harrogate, shopping, parks
Location opposite the Strav, five mins walk from railway station
Food breakfast, lunch, dinner
Price ££
Rooms 43, including 8 suites; all rooms have phone, TV, DVD player, CD player, hairdrrier, wi-fi
Facilities gym, pool table, walk-in humidor
Credit cards AE, MC, V
Children welcome
Disabled limited access
Pets not accepted
Closed never
Manager Robert Cooke

Hotel du Vin
Town hotel

This popular hotel in the heart of Harrogate – only three minutes' walk from Betty's famous teashop – would rather seem hip than genteel. If there is a slightly corporate feel about the Hotel du Vin it is forgivable because it goes with professionalism and means that the water is hot in the power shower, that the telephone will be answered quickly and sensibly and that your room will be spotlessly clean. An ironing board, two kinds of handmade crisps, a mock Hollywood 1930s electric fan and lifestyle magazines are thoughtfully provided in the room. There is a DVD player too. Colours are fashionable greys and browns. The wine theme runs through the hotel. You room may be called Ruinart or Mondavi and there are colourful pre-war aperitif posters in the corridors. Mid-week you may find guests in the hall, busy on laptops and mobiles, new 'professionals', not members of the old-fashioned professions. At the weekend people come to the outstanding bistro or to drink in the large and sophisticated champagne and claret bar (which sells beer too), or to play pool in the 'snug'. Or you may see a bride. Weddings, for which the hotel has a licence, are popular here. This is not a place for tea and scones; Harrogate is changing and Hotel du Vin has caught the zeitgeist. One of the more recently opened Hotels du Vin. See also pages 40, 91 and 134.

Hawes, North Yorkshire

Hawes, North Yorkshire DL8 3LY

Tel (01969) 667255
Fax (01969) 667741
e-mail
simonstonehall@demon.co.uk **web-site** www.simonstonehall.co.uk

Nearby Pennine Way; Wharfedale; Ribblesdale.
Location 1.5 miles (2.5 km) N of Hawes on Muker road; with ample car parking
Food breakfast, bar lunch, Sun lunch, dinner
Price £££
Rooms 18 double and twin with bath and shower; all rooms have phone, TV, wi-fi
Facilities bar, lounge, orangery, restaurant; garden, terrace
Credit cards AE, DC, MC, V
Children welcome
Disabled access possible to ground floor only **Pets** welcome **Closed** never **Manager** Caroline Billingham

Simonstone Hall
Country house hotel

Simonstone has undergone major refurbishment in the last few years, but still has the air of something special, helped by the friendliness of the staff. Outside, it is the same dignified, slightly forbidding, large Dales country house; but as you enter you will probably hear the lively chatter coming from the extensive bar area which is intended to re-create the hotel as a place that will attract local non-residents as well as overnight guests. To have this popular country pub within an essentially dignified old country hotel is something of a novelty – and not unpleasant. The pub is handsomely done out; bar meals and the range of wines by the glass are imaginative; waiters in black tie and apron, French bistro-style, bustle about. It gives the place an injection of life, but if you've come here for peace, or a romantic twosome, just walk down the corridor to the sitting room, hidden at the far end of the hall to provide guests with peace and quiet. Beyond is the panelled Game Tavern, serving lunch; dinner is served in the restaurant.

All bedrooms now have bathrooms with showers. The superior bedrooms are handsomely done out in country house style, some with sleigh beds, others with four-posters, many of them with fantastic views of the Dales. Prices have risen, some say unjustifiably, so we would welcome further reports.

Hawnby, Yorkshire

Hill Top, Hawnby, near Helmsley,
York Y06 5QS

Tel (01439) 798202
Fax (01439) 798344
e-mail info@innathawnby.co.uk
website www.innathawnby.co.uk

Nearby Rievaulx Abbey; Jervaulx
Abbey; North York Moors.
Location at top of hill in village 7
miles (11 km) NE of Helmsley; with
car parking
Food breakfast, lunch, dinner
Price ££
Rooms 9 double and twin with bath;
all rooms have phone, TV, hairdryer
Facilities sitting room/dining room,
bar **Credit cards** MC, V
Children accepted
Disabled access difficult **Pets** not
accepted (kennels nearby) **Closed**
Monday lunchtime; Christmas day
Proprietors Dave and Kathryn
Young

The Inn at Hawnby
Country hotel

After a spectacular drive through rolling valleys and the unspoilt stone village of Hawnby, you come across Dave and Kathryn Young's country inn, formerly The Hawnby Hotel. The 'village pub' façade hides an exquisite small hotel which was decorated with obvious flair by Lady Mexborough. The hotel used to be part of the 13,000-acre Mexborough estate and Lady Mexborough gave it much personal attention, refurbishing the Inn's six bedrooms which are named after colour schemes (Cowslip, Coral, Jade and so on), choosing Laura Ashley wallpaper and fabrics throughout the cosy rooms and immaculate bathrooms. Three further bedrooms are available just over the road, these ones named after stables.

Since our last edition the Youngs have tidied up the outside of the Inn and the gardens, as well as giving the public rooms and bedrooms some attention, aiming to make them altogether brighter and more welcoming. They have also turned their attention to the kitchen, hiring a new head chef who produces a full *a la carte* menu, all from scratch and using fresh, local produce.

Reports continue to heap praise on the Inn at Hawnby: 'This charming country hotel ... is an ideal base for touring North Yorkshire; a gem with fabulous views, home cooking and friendly service'.

Hunmanby, North Yorkshire

Stonegate, Hunmanby, North
Yorkshire YO14 0NS

Tel (01723) 891333
Fax (01723) 892973
e-mail staciedevos@aol.com
website www.wranghamhouse.com

Nearby Scarborough Castle; North
York Moors National Park.
Location behind church in village, 1
mile (1.5 km) SW of Filey; ample car
parking
Food breakfast, lunch, dinner
Price ££
Rooms 12; 11 double and twin, 1
single, 7 with bath, 5 with shower; all
have phone, TV, hairdryer **Facilities**
sitting room, dining room, bar; gar-
den
Credit cards AE, MC, V
Children welcome **Disabled** 1
adapted room
Pets by arrangement **Closed** never
Proprietors Peter and Stacie Devos

Wrangham House
Country house hotel

Wrangham House is a well-preserved
and elegant Georgian former vic-
arage set in an acre of wooded garden. The
main part of the house was built in the second half of the 18th century. The eponymous Francis Wrangham added a wing, now
housing the dining room, in 1803. Stacie
Devos and her husband Peter moved here
in 2005, and refurbished the kitchen, sitting
room, dining room and most of the bedrooms, as well as giving the gardens some
much-needed care and attention. Stacie
says the improvements are an ongoing project, the aim being to restore Wrangham
House to its former glory.

Peter is in charge of the kitchen and
produces a few set dishes (such as roast
rack of lamb), with the rest being based
around what fresh, local and seasonal produce is available, ranging from game to
locally caught fish and seafood – so there
is always something new on the menu.
Everything here is freshly made and Peter
and Stacie take pride in offering a personal and flexible service – guests on long
stays have the opportunity to influence the
menu by discussing their preferences with
Peter, and early dinners will be arranged
for families with young children.

Reports welcome.

Lastingham, North Yorkshire

Lastingham, North Yorkshire
Y062 6TH

Tel (01751) 417345/417402
Fax (01751) 417358
e-mail reservations@lastingham-
grange.com **website** www.lasting-
hamgrange.com

Nearby North York Moors;
Scarborough; Rievaulx Abbey.
Location at top of village, 7 miles
(10 km) NW of Pickering; ample car
parking
Food breakfast, lunch, dinner
Price £££
Rooms 12; 10 double, 2 single, all
with bath; all rooms have phone, TV,
hairdryer, wi-fi
Facilities sitting room, dining room;
terrace, garden
Credit cards MC, V
Children welcome
Disabled access to restaurant and
garden **Pets** accepted in bedrooms
by arrangement **Closed** Dec to mid-
Mar **Proprietors** Jane, Bertie and
Tom Wood

Lastingham Grange
Country house hotel

Lastingham Grange – a wistaria-clad former farmhouse – nestles peacefully in a
delightful village on the edge of the North
York Moors. Unlike many country house
hotels, it manages to combine a certain
sophistication – smartly decorated public
rooms, friendly unobtrusive service, elegantly laid gardens – with a large dash of informality, which puts you immediately at ease.
From the moment you enter, you feel as if
you are staying with friends. Recently, we had
this reaction from an inspector: 'Family feeling; very child friendly; charming rooms.–'

The main attraction is the garden. You
can enjoy it from a distance – from the
windows of the large L-shaped sitting
room (complete with carefully grouped
sofas, antiques and a grand piano) – or, like
most guests, by exploring. There is a beautifully laid rose garden, enticing bordered
lawns and an extensive adventure play-
ground for children.

Bedrooms are perfectly comfortable,
with well-equipped bathrooms, and have
been totally redecorated since our last
visit, when a reporter felt that they were
somewhat downbeat in places. Paul
Cattaneo and Sandra Thurlow produce
traditional English meals for the daily-
changing menu, prepared from fresh, local
ingredients. Reports welcome.

Leeds, West Yorkshire

42 The Calls, Leeds, West Yorkshire
LS2 7EW

Tel (0113) 244 0099
Fax (0113) 234 4100
e-mail
reservations@42thecalls.co.uk
website www.42thecalls.co.uk

Nearby Corn Exchange; Tetley's
Brewery; museums, galleries, shops,
West Yorkshire Playhouse.
Location Exchange quarter, over-
looking river Aire in central Leeds
Food breakfast, snacks
Price ££
Rooms 41; 31 double, 7 single, 3
suites, all with bath; all rooms have
phone, TV, fax/modem point, CD
player, minibar, hairdryer **Facilities**
sitting room, breakfast room, bar
Credit cards AE, DC, MC, V
Children welcome
Disabled one specially adapted
room, lift/elevator **Pets** by arrange-
ment **Closed** Christmas **Proprietor**
Sheikh Mohammed Bin Issa al Jaber

42 The Calls
Town house hotel

Expect the unexpected at 42 The Calls.
Through a small glass-porched entrance
and revolving doors, the sight of massive
beams, girders, ducts and grain chutes are,
one supposes, in keeping for an old corn
mill turned hotel.

In the bedrooms, fabrics and furniture
are traditional; some feature cleverly
designed desk lamps that are black ceramic shelves in the shape of the number 42.
A two-way serving hatch means that
breakfast can be placed straight into the
room, or shoes and laundry collected,
without disturbance. Every comfort has
been considered – a coffee machine, iron
and ironing board, CD player, DVD and
plasma screen TV; hot water bottles are
available and some rooms overlooking the
river have fishing rods. Suites are full of
character, with vast sitting rooms.

All this notwithstanding, we've had critical feedback in the last few years, citing
erratic, impersonal service and 'worn
edges'. We hope that the latest new owner
(see above) will reverse any decline.

Pateley Bridge, North Yorkshire

Wath-in-Nidderdale, Pateley Bridge, near Harrogate, North Yorkshire HG3 5PP

Tel (01423) 711306
Fax (01423) 712524
website
www.nidderdale.co.uk/sportsman-sarms

Nearby Wharfedale, Wensleydale; Fountains Abbey, Bolton Abbey.
Location 2 miles (3 km) NW of Pateley Bridge, in hamlet; with ample car parking
Food breakfast, bar lunch, dinner
Price ££
Rooms 11; 9 double, 2 twin with bath or shower; all rooms have TV
Facilities 3 sitting rooms, bar, dining room; fishing
Credit cards MC, V
Children welcome
Disabled easy access to public rooms **Pets** welcome by arrangement **Closed** Christmas Day, New Year's Day **Proprietors** Jane and Ray Carter

Sportsman's Arms
Country hotel

Our latest inspection confirms that the Sportsman's Arms is going from strength to strength. The long, rather rambling building dates from the 17th century, and the setting is as enchanting as the village name sounds; the River Nidd flows across the field in front; Gouthwaite reservoir, a bird-watchers' haunt, is just behind; glorious dales country spreads all around.

Jane and Ray Carter have been running the Sportman's Arms, with the help of a young enthusiastic team, for over 20 years now, and continue to make improvements. Bedrooms (two with four-posters) have been redecorated and are light and fresh, with brand-new bathrooms. Six more rooms, four with views across open countryside, have been created in the barn and stable block. All the public rooms have recently been refurbished as well.

And then there is the food. The Sportsman's Arms is first and foremost a restaurant, and the large dining room is the inn's focal point, sparkling with silver cutlery and crystal table lights. The lively menu embraces sound, traditional local fare, as well as fresh fish and seafood brought in daily from Whitby. To back it up, there is a superb wine list – and an extremely reasonable bill.

Ramsgill-in-Nidderdale, North Yorkshire

Ramsgill-in-Nidderdale, near
Harrogate, North Yorkshire
HG3 5RL

Tel (01423) 755243
Fax (01423) 755330
e-mail enquiries@yorke-arms.co.uk
website www.yorke-arms.co.uk

Nearby Harewood House; Newby
Hall; Fountains Abbey; Ripon
Cathedral.
Location in centre of village; take
Low Wath Road from Pateley
Bridge bordering Gouthwaite
Reservoir; with car parking
Food breakfast, lunch, dinner; room
service
Price ££££
Rooms 13; 11 double and twin, 2
suites, all with bath; all rooms have
phone, TV, hairdryer; some have
minibar
Facilities sitting room, games room,
dining rooms, bars; garden
Credit cards AE, DC, MC, V
Disabled not suitable **Pets** accepted
in some public rooms **Closed** never
Proprietors Frances and Gerald
Atkins

Yorke Arms
Restaurant-with-rooms

On the green in a pretty Nidderdale village, the creeper-clad Yorke Arms was
a fully-functioning pub for 150 years. Since
Frances and Gerald Atkins took over in
1997, it has evolved into a Michelin-starred
restaurant with rooms. You are greeted as
you enter by flagged floors, beams and, in
winter, open fires. There is also a reassuring
feeling of order: what should have been
polished has been polished, and what
should have been swept has been.

In the restaurant, wooden tables and a
wooden floor strewn with rugs keep the
techno-age at bay and serve as a showcase
for Frances Atkins' Michelin-starred daily
changing menu: traditional and modern
English dishes are her starting-point, but
she also draws on other cuisines from all
over the world. Old favourites such as
Yorkshire hot pot and halibut cheesy mash
usually make an appearance. The wine list is
comprehensive and sympathetically priced.

The bedrooms, which have all been
thoroughly refurbished, with stylish modern bathrooms, are comfortably furnished
and range in size (and price) from cosy to
a modest suite, 'Gouthwaite', which boasts
a sofa and armchairs.

Reeth, North Yorkshire

On the Green, Reeth, Richmond,
North Yorkshire DL11 6SN

Tel (01748) 884292
Fax (01748) 884292
e-mail inquiries@theburgoyne.co.uk
website www.theburgoyne.co.uk

Nearby Richmond Castle;
Middleham Castle.
Location 10 miles (16 km) W of
Richmond on B6270; with car parking
Food breakfast, packed lunch on
request, dinner; room service
Price ££
Rooms 9 double and twin with bath;
all rooms have phone, flat screen
TV, DVD player, hairdryer
Facilities sitting room, dining room;
garden, fishing
Credit cards MC, V
Children accepted over 10
Disabled access possible to ground-
floor room
Pets accepted by arrangement
Closed early Jan to mid-Feb
Proprietor Derek Hickson

Burgoyne Hotel
Village hotel

The Burgoyne Hotel stretches its late-Georgian length along the top of the sloping green in Reeth. If you turn round and look the other way, you'll see why: the Swale valley is extremely pretty, and with only the green in front of it, the Burgoyne has an uninterrupted view. Inside, time, money and taste have conspired to produce something of a masterpiece to which has been added the magic ingredient of a warm welcome. There are two elegant and richly furnished sitting rooms on the ground floor with Medieval touches here and there: stone coats of arms on the fireplaces and 'Gothic' oak doors. The restaurant, where the snowy napkins, the crystal and the silver stand out against the cool blues of the decoration, is a kind of inner sanctum where Paul Salonga's culinary art joins Derek Hickson's scientific (certainly encyclopaedic) understanding of wines.

The bedrooms, most of which face the valley, are beautifully appointed and deeply comfortable. Window seats offer pleasant perches for people who just want to sit and enjoy the view. Rather than hack space for bathrooms out of the well-proportioned rooms, one or two bathrooms are across the corridor — voluminous robes and slippers are provided for the short journey.

Ripley, North Yorkshire

Ripley, Harrogate, North Yorkshire
HG3 3AY

Tel (01423) 771888
Fax (01423) 771509
e-mail boarshead@ripleycastle.co.uk
website www.ripleycastle.co.uk

Nearby York; Fountains Abbey and
Studley Royal Water Gardens;
Ripley Castle
Location in village centre, 3 miles (5
km) N of Harrogate on A61; with
ample car parking
Food breakfast, lunch, dinner
Price ££
Rooms 25 double and twin with
bath; all rooms have phone, TV,
fax/modem point, hairdryer; minibar
on request
Facilities sitting room, dining
rooms, 2 bars; garden, tennis, fishing
Credit cards AE, MC, DC, V
Children accepted **Disabled** 1 spe-
cially adapted room, 8 ground-floor
rooms **Pets** accepted in some rooms
only **Closed** never **Proprietors** Sir
Thomas and Lady Ingilby

Boar's Head
Country house hotel

Anyone with a spare inn and enough
paintings and antique furniture to fur-
nish it could do worse than emulate Sir
Thomas and Lady Ingilby's successful renovation of the Boar's Head in Ripley. It is a
thriving establishment with helpful, pleasant staff who do not leave your comfort to
chance. There are bedrooms in the inn
itself, lighter more contemporary ones in
its cobbled courtyard, and across the road,
in the peace and quiet of Birchwood
House, are four of their six best rooms. All
have fresh flowers, pristine modern bathrooms and thoughtful decoration.

The public rooms are warm and welcoming, filled with period furniture;
seascapes and ancestors share the walls.
There is a choice for dinner: you can
either go to the relaxed bar/bistro (packed
when we visited) or the richer candle-lit
comfort of the restaurant to agonise over
a choice that includes crisp seabass with
squid ink noodles or supreme of guinea
fowl on a sweet pea *purée*. Fresh vegetables and game make seasonal appearances
from the Ingilby estate, presided over by
their castle.

Romaldkirk, County Durham

Romaldkirk, Barnard Castle, Co.
Durham DL12 9EB

Tel (01833) 650213
Fax (01833) 650828
e-mail hotel@rose-and-crown.co.uk
website www.rose-and-crown.co.uk

Nearby Barnard Castle; Egglestone
Abbey; High Force.
Location in centre of village, on
B6277, 6 miles (9.6 km) NW of
Barnard Castle; with ample carparking
Food breakfast, dinner, Sun lunch
Price ££
Rooms 12; 11 double and twin, 1
family, 9 with bath, 3 with shower;
all rooms have phone, TV, hairdryer
Facilities sitting room, dining room,
bar, brasserie, gun lockers, wi-fi
Credit cards MC, V **Children** welcome **Disabled** access possible to
courtyard rooms **Pets** accepted in
bedrooms
Closed Christmas Eve, Christmas
Day, Boxing Day **Proprietors**
Christopher and Alison Davy

Rose and Crown
Country inn

The Rose and Crown was built in 1733
in this very pretty light stone village. It
owes its original layout to the Saxons and
its name to the patron saint of the church
next door. Thoroughly renovated by
Christopher and Alison Davy some years
ago, the Rose and Crown has gone from
strength to strength. It is set in the centre
of the three-green village. The bar is comfortingly traditional: real ales, natural stone
walls, log fire, old photographs, copper and
brass knick-knacks. Excellent pub food is
served in the 'Crown Brasserie and Bar'.
More traditional four-course dinners,
English but imaginatively so, are served on
white linen in the oak-panelled dining
room and, when in season, often feature
local and organic produce, including moorland game, fresh fish from the East Coast,
and locally grown vegetables. Fresh bread
is baked every day.

There are seven comfortable bedrooms,
attractively decorated and furnished with
antiques, in the main building. Five more
have been added round the courtyard at
the back, and open directly on to it. All
come with fresh flowers. We revisited in
2007 and liked it as much as ever.

Winteringham, North Lincolnshire

Winteringham, North Lincolnshire
DN15 9PF

Tel (01724) 733096
Fax (01724) 733898
e-mail enquiries@winteringham-fields.com **website** www.winteringhamfields.com

Nearby Normanby Hall; Thornton Abbey; Lincoln.
Location in centre of village on S bank of Humber, 4 miles (6 km) W from Humber bridge off A1077; with ample car parking
Food breakfast, lunch, dinner; room service
Price £££
Rooms 10; 8 double, 2 suites, 7 with bath, 3 with shower; all rooms have phone, TV, hairdryer **Facilities** 2 sitting rooms, 1 dining room, conservatory; garden, helipad **Credit cards** AE, MC, V
Children welcome **Disabled** access difficult **Pets** accepted in courtyard rooms **Closed** Sun-Mon; Christmas, 1 week in April, 3 weeks in Aug, 1 week in Oct **Proprietors** Colin and Bex McGurran

Winteringham Fields
Manor house hotel

Halfway between Scunthorpe and the Humber bridge is one of Britain's gastronomic hotspots. Furthermore, you can sleep in great comfort no more than a few paces from the table. The hotel is in the middle of Winteringham, a quiet country village on the south bank of the Humber estuary. Colin and Bex McGurran have taken over here since our last edition, and Colin, the chef, is relishing the challenge of maintaining the very high culinary standards set by their predecessors, the Schwabs. Having lived and worked in such diverse places as Zambia, the UAE and France, Colin's influences are eclectic.

The rambling 16thC house is full of nooks and crannies and still has many original features such as exposed timbers and period fireplaces. These are set off by the warm colours of walls and fabrics and the antique furniture. The bedrooms are all uniquely decorated and have recently been renovated, and the bathrooms modernised. There are four in the main house (with not a single right-angle between them), three in the courtyard, one in a cottage round the corner, and two more made from a dovecote a couple of minutes away.

The McGurrans are adding a further dining room and two more sitting rooms, providing better disabled facilities.

From the fertile southern uplands bordering England, to the dramatic mountain ranges and barren coasts of the Highlands and Islands, Scotland is varied and often breathtakingly beautiful. Within a few hours' drive, the scenery changes from gently rolling hills, purple in summer with flowering heather, to majestic, craggy peaks. Visitors come to hike, climb, ski, play golf, fish in the lochs and rivers, and to explore Scotland's fascinating historical heritage and lively cultural life. Featured here are many of the most remote hotels in Britain: some on the edges of lochs or by the sea, others on islands or deep in the countryside. Our selection includes converted castles, country manors, farmhouses, ferry inns and crofts as well as town houses. Several are new to this edition of the guide. Visitors to the Scottish Borders might think of following the trail of Sir Walter Scott, staying at **Hundalee House**, a manor with exotic decoration (page 264); or the Arts and Crafts village hotel, **Skirling House** (page 268). In Dumfries and Galloway, where the land is rich and the sea warmed by the Gulf Stream, we recommend the friendly Victorian **Knockinaam Lodge** (page 267). Also in the west are two new hotels, the remote **Kilberry Inn** (page 265) and the dramatically-situated **Corsewall Lighthouse** (page 266). In Edinburgh, known for its historic buildings and annual Festival, we recommend **The Witchery by the Castle**, a wonderful 16thC building (page 261). New Edinburgh places are **Ingrams** (page 259) and **Windmill House** (page 260). In Glasgow, recent European Capital of Culture, we continue to recommend **One Devonshire Gardens** (page 262), though it is now part of the ubiquitous Hotel du Vin mini-chain.

Further north, in Argyll, where long fingers of sea and inland lochs probe the hills, you could spend a tranquil holiday at **Ards House** (page 276), **Ballachulish House** (page 272) or the ultimately secluded **Isle of Eriska Hotel** (page 280). New to this edition are **Boath House** near Nairn (page 271), and **The Ardeonaig Hotel**, on the southern shore of Loch Tay (page 283). There are two bed-and-breakfasts in the pretty Inverness-shire town of Fort William, **Crolinnhe** (page 277), and an old favourite, **The Grange** (page 278). To the east, **Minmore House** (page 279) is well placed for the Malt Whisky Trail, and solid Victorian **Struan Hall** is a recent discovery (page 269). If in search of true remoteness, you could choose relaxing **Summer Isles** (page 270), or one of the island hotels: **Three Chimneys** (page 274); or **Kinloch Lodge** on Skye (page 291); **Scarista House** on Harris (page 290) or **Burrastow House** on Shetland (page 295).

Edinburgh

34 Great King Street, Edinburgh
EH3 6QH

Tel (0131) 557 3500
Fax (0131) 557 6515
e-mail reserve@thehoward.com
website www.thehoward.com

Nearby Edinburgh Castle;
Holyrood Palace; Princes Street.
Location in New Town, E of
Dundas St; private car parking
Food breakfast, lunch, dinner; room
service
Price ££££
Rooms 18; 11 double and twin, 2
single, 5 suites; all rooms have
phone, TV, fax/modem point,
hairdryer
Facilities drawing room, bar, break-
fast room, restaurant, dining room,
drink service
Credit cards AE, DC, MC, V
Children welcome
Disabled access possible, lift/eleva-
tor **Pets** not accepted **Closed** never
Manager Johanne Falconer

The Howard
Town house hotel

The only indication that **34 Great King Street** is a hotel is the simple brass plate to the right of the front door. The location, a cobbled street in Edinburgh's New Town (new in the early 1800s, that is), could hardly be bettered, within walking distance of Princes Street and the Castle, but almost free of traffic noise.

The 1820s building, comprising three terraced town houses, displays all the elegance and sense of proportion one associates with the Georgian era. Push open the door, and willing service is immediately on hand, including directions to the hotel's own private car park. After checking in, the charming reception staff will ask if you'd like some tea and shortbread, thus reinforcing the sense of being a guest in a friend's house.

Public rooms are elegant and captivating, although the drawing room could do with better lighting. The breakfast room is graced by delightful Italianate murals, uncovered during restoration. Bedrooms are supremely comfortable.

Edinburgh

24 Northumberland Street,
Edinburgh EH3 6LS

Tel (0131) 556 8140
Fax (0131) 556 4423
e-mail info@ingrams.co.uk
website www.ingrams.co.uk

Nearby Princes Street, Castle, art
galleries, museums and central
Edinburgh shopping
Location on quiet side street with
own private car parking
Food breakfast
Price ££
Rooms 3; 1 double, 2 twin bedded; 2
have bath and shower, 1 with private
bathroom; all rooms have phone,
TV, hairdryer, wi-fi
Facilities dining room, laundry
Credit cards DC, MC, V
Children not under 14 **Disabled**
not suitable **Pets** not accepted
Closed Christmas **Proprietors**
David and Theresa Ingram

Ingrams
City bed-and-breakfast

This is a conventional but well-groomed B & B in a fine four-storey Georgian town house, with handsome entrance hall and staircase lit by an oval cupola. Everywhere, pleasing architectural features have been preserved, and it is beautifully furnished with David Ingram's collection of antiques – David is a well-known Edinburgh antiques dealer. It's been his, and his wife Theresa's home for many years. David is a welcoming host and local character with an impressive knowledge of Edinburgh's history and architecture.

The rooms are all comfortably and quietly furnished in period style with smart, up-to-date bathrooms. Despite the age of the house, nothing is tired and the housekeeping excellent – there's a full-time housekeeper with back-up, which makes a difference in this type of operation.

Breakfast, a 'sumptuous affair', is served by David Ingram in the elegant dining room (our inspectors appreciated the hall-marked Georgian silver): fresh fruit salad, home-made cordial, porridge and a full traditional cooked breakfast. David prides himself on his scrambled eggs and hand-made sausages. The Ingrams don't serve dinner, but you're within walking distance of a number of good restaurants; and guests have use of a fridge and microwave (likewise laundry facilities).

Coltbridge Gardens,
Edinburgh, EH12 6AQ

Tel (0131) 346 0024
Fax (0131) 346 0024
e-mail
windmillhouse@btinternet.com

Nearby The Scottish National
Gallery of Modern Art next door in
wooded grounds; waymarked river-
side walk; cental Edinburgh sights
and shopping.
Location in 2-acre grounds with
ample private car parking
Food breakfast
Prices ££-£££
Rooms 3; 2 double and one twin-
bedded; all rooms have TV, video
Facilities sitting room, garden.
Credit cards not accepted
Children accepted by arrangement –
cots available
Disabled not suitable **Pets** not
accepted **Closed** Christmas and
New Year **Proprietors** Michael and
Vivien Scott

Windmill House
City bed-and-breakfast

Looking for space, fresh air, and minimal traffic noise in Edinburgh? The answer is this spacious Georgian-style house, built 1999 in a unique and spectacular position overlooking the Water of Leith. The atmos-phere really is distinctly rural (the site was once used to graze sheep) despite it being only a mile – a 20-minute walk – from the city centre. The old restored windmill in the garden is home to a large family of badgers; the grounds have a weir and a waterfall.

Inside, there's an impressive staircase and galleried hall and an attractive drawing room with an open fire which guests can use. It's elegantly decorated throughout and the large, light and airy bedrooms are exceptionally comfortable. Bathrooms are warm, large and well equipped.

Michael and Vivien Scott are thoughtful hosts who will book you into the local restaurants and provide torches for those who wish to walk. Breakfast is 'substantial,' served in a charming dining room; our reporters enjoyed the fresh raspberries and blueberries.

Castlehill, The Royal Mile,
Edinburgh EH1 2NF

Tel (0131) 225 5613
Fax (0131) 220 4392
e-mail mail@thewitchery.com
website www.thewitchery.com

Nearby Edinburgh Castle, the Royal
Mile, Holyrood House.
Location at the gates of Edinburgh
Castle, public car park nearby
Food breakfast, lunch, dinner
Price ££££
Rooms 7 suites, all with bath; all
have TV, DVD, CD player, phone,
hairdryer
Facilities 2 restaurants, sister restau-
rant at Museum of Scotland
Credit cards AE, DC, MC, V
Children accepted
Disabled access difficult **Pets**
accepted by arrangement
Closed never **Proprietor** James
Thomson

The Witchery by the Castle Restaurant-with-rooms

It takes its name from the hundreds of witches burned at the stake nearby, but The Witchery is, thankfully, not macabre. However, it is gothic and, above all, luxuri-ous. Started some 30 years ago by James Thomson, it occupies a 16thC building at the gates of Edinburgh Castle and was pre-viously used as committee rooms for the General Assembly of the Church of Scotland. Entering from a close off the Royal Mile, you pass through a doorway still marked with the original merchant's initials and motto. Inside, candle-light reveals painted and gilded ceilings and walls covered in tapestries and 17thC oak paneling rescued from a fire at St Giles Cathedral. Gilded leather screens, red leather upholstery and antique church candlesticks add to the atmosphere.

Suites, either above the restaurant or in an adjacent building, are plush and opulent, with open fires, antiques, historic paintings and dramatic colour schemes, and have views towards the Old Town or over the Royal Mile.

You can eat either in the award-winning restaurant of the same name; in the Secret Garden, a terrace garden restaurant built behind the Witchery; or in The Tower, on the fifth floor of the National Museum of Scotland. If The Witchery is full, try its sister hotel, Prestonfield (0131 225 7800).

1 Devonshire Gardens, Glasgow
G12 0UX

Tel (0141) 339 2001
Fax (0141) 337 1663
e-mail info@onedevonshiregar-
dens.com **website** www.onedevon-
shiregardens.com

Nearby Cathedral, Hunterian
Musuem and other s ights.
Location 2 miles (3 km) from centre
at junction of Great Western and
Hyndland roads; ample free street
parking
Food breakfast, lunch, dinner
Price ££££
Rooms 38 double and twin, most
with bath; all rooms have phone, TV,
minibar, hairdryer; some have DVD,
fireplace
Facilities 3 drawing rooms, 2 restaurants, study, dining room, bar; patio
garden **Credit cards** AE, DC, MC,
V **Children** welcome **Disabled** not
suitable **Pets** accepted by arrangement **Closed** Christmas (call to
check) **Manager** Gary Sanderson

One Devonshire Gardens **Town house hotel**

This hotel is a marginal entry in the guide. It is large, expensive and now part of the Hotel du Vin/Malmaison chain. However, there is a shortage of interesting places to stay in Glasgow and it does have character, albeit of the formulaic, chic city hotel variety.

The place (actually three terraced hous-es in a row on the western side of the city) has an air of restrained luxury: in the pub-lic rooms ancestors gaze down from richly covered walls towards good antiques and plump upholstery. A pre-dinner drink by the drawing room fire should already have put you in a good mood before choosing between the House 5 restaurant or Amaryllis, a Gordon Ramsay restaurant. It is almost superfluous to add that the wine list – and the advice if you want it – are of matching quality.

The bedrooms are opulent: soft lighting, deep colours and heavyweight fabrics in some, pale and light-handed in others; all with fine furniture and sumptuous bath-rooms. Fresh fruit and flowers, your own CD-player and up-to-date magazines com-plete the picture. Staff are polite, discreet and attentive.

Gullane, East Lothian

Muirfield, Gullane, East Lothian
EH31 2EG

Tel (01620) 842144
Fax (01620) 842241
e-mail hotel@greywalls.co.uk **website** www.greywalls.co.uk

Nearby golf courses; beaches; castles; Edinburgh.
Location in village, 17 miles (27 km) E of Edinburgh off A198 to North Berwick; ample car parking
Food breakfast, lunch, dinner; room service
Price ££££
Rooms 23; 19 double and twin, 4 single, all with bath; all rooms have phone, TV, hairdryer **Facilities** 2 sitting rooms, library, bar, dining room, conservatory; garden, grass and hard surface tennis courts, croquet
Credit cards AE, DC, MC, V
Children welcome
Disabled bedrooms on ground floor
Pets accepted, but not in public rooms **Closed** Jan to Feb **Manager** Sue Prime

Greywalls
Country house hotel

Greywalls is a slick, expensive country house hotel, with – by our standards – quite a large number of bedrooms, but despite this we cannot resist including such a distinctive place. It is a classic turn-of-the-century house by Sir Edwin Lutyens, with gardens laid out by Gertrude Jekyll, and – more to the point for golf enthusiasts – it overlooks the tenth green of the famous Muirfield championship course.

The feel of Greywalls is very much one of a gracious private house, little changed in atmosphere since the days when King Edward VII was a guest. Furnished largely with period pieces, public rooms include an Edwardian tea room, a little bar well stocked with whiskies, and a particularly appealing panelled library. This is a delightful room – with no sense of a hotel about it – in which to curl up on one of the sofas either side of the fire, and leaf through one of the many books from the shelves. Dinner, served in a room overlooking the golf course, is elegantly presented and imaginative. Bedrooms are attractive, comfortable and well-equipped, particularly those in the original house rather than the new wing.

Jedburgh, Roxburghshire

Jedburgh, Roxburghshire TD8 6PA

Tel (01835) 863011
Fax (01835) 863011
e-mail
sheila.whittaker@btinternet.com
website www.accommodation-scot-land.org

Nearby Kelso, Dryburgh Abbey, Abbotsford; golf; fishing.
Location set in own grounds; ample car parking
Food breakfast
Price £
Rooms 5 double; all have TV, radio, hairdryer, tea/coffee kit
Facilities sitting room, dining room; garden
Credit cards not accepted
Children over 10
Disabled not suitable
Pets not accepted
Closed Nov to Mar
Proprietors Mr and Mrs Whittaker

Hundalee House
Bed-and-breakfast

Seeing the peaceful countryside around Jedburgh today, it is difficult to believe that this land has a history of violent confrontations between the Scots and English. Among the attractions are the Mary, Queen of Scots House, a ruined abbey, a museum dedicated to Victorian prison life and Ferniehirst Castle, the ancient seat of the Kerr family.

Not far away is Hundalee House. Set back in the hills, this 18thC limestone manor house has been home to the Whittakers for a decade. They created the fine large garden, putting in flowering shrubs, adding peacocks and digging a pond for koi carp. Inside, the taste is even more exotic, reflecting their time in Egypt. Egyptian motifs hang on the walls and Egyptian hounds guard the fireplace in the sitting room, which has fine views of the Cheviot Hills to the south. Bedrooms may not be luxurious but one has a four-poster bed. Two others share a bathroom; these offer notable value and are useful for a family. Sheila Whittaker does not serve dinner, but her breakfasts are 'cooked and copious,' according to one teenage visitor.

Kilberry, Argyll

Kilberry, Argyll
Scotland PA29 6YD

Tel (01880) 770 223
e-mail relax@kilberryinn.com
website www.kilberryinn.com

Nearby secluded beaches, distilleries, ferries to the surrounding islands,
Location on the B8024 between Tarbert and Lochgilphead
Food breakfast, lunch, dinner
Price ££
Rooms 4 double with shower; all rooms have TV, hairdryer, tea and coffee, books
Facilities restaurant
Credit cards MC, V
Children over 12 welcome
Disabled access to restaurant and 1 bedroom
Pets dogs accepted by arrangement
Closed Jan to Feb; Mon-Fri Nov to Dec; Mondays all year round
Proprietors Clare Johnson and David Wilson

The Kilberry Inn
Restaurant-with-rooms

This traditional whitewashed, red-roofed 'but 'n' ben' cottage had long been run as an inn before David Wilson and chef Clare Johnson, who used to run the renowned Anchorage Seafood Restaurant in the nearby fishing village of Tarbert, took it on and set about transforming it into a modern restaurant with rooms. Gone is the former cluttered, rustic, 'twee' look. It has been replaced with minimal and contemporary decoration, with cosy log fires, beams and quarried stone-walls, hung with art from local painters. The inn has four comfortable, tastefully decorated double bedrooms with showers, in adjacent buildings.

The focus in the restaurant is on fresh, locally produced ingredients – crab, lobster, langoustine, scallops and fish are all caught within a few miles of the inn, and meat is all reared nearby. Dinner might be potted Kilberry crab, followed by Sound of Jura monkfish with pepperonata and piquillo pepper dressing, then Isle of Mull cheddar with biscuits and chutney to finish.

The inn is situated on a remote single track road on the Kintyre peninsula, with stunning views of the surrounding lochs and islands, and David thinks this remoteness makes arriving an adventure in itself. Reports welcome.

Kirkcolm, Stranraer

Corsewall Point, Kirkcolm, Stranraer
Scotland, DG9 0QG

Tel (01776)853220
Fax (01776) 854231
e-mail info@lighthousehotel.co.uk
website www.lighthousehotel.co.uk

Nearby Stranraer – ferry to Ireland
Location remote; in own grounds
with ample private car parking
Food breakfast, lunch, dinner
Price ££
Rooms 11; 6 doubles, 5 suites, some
can be twin-bedded; all rooms have
phone, TV, DVD, hairdryer
Facilities 2 sitting rooms, restaurant, 20-acre grounds
Credit cards AE, DC, MC, V
Children accepted
Disabled one accessible room
Pets allowed in 2 of the suites
Closed never
Proprietor Gordon Ward

Corsewall Lighthouse
Lighthouse hotel

Remote – the last mile is down a track –
on a windswept promontory north of
Stranraer, this is a 200-year old working
lighthouse. The tower itself isn't part of the
hotel, but the structure at its foot, the former
lighthouse keeper's dwelling, houses
the restaurant, public areas and some of the
rooms. Other accommodation, including
the suites, are in separate buildings, none
more than three minutes from the hub.

Come here for a unique and romantic
experience, the generally light rooms and
dramatic seascapes, but not for style. It's
mostly done out comfortably, but in a conventional
way – you could hardly be anywhere
else but a hotel. Some of the smaller
rooms may not please perfectionists –
bear in mind it's an old building.

The food ('tremendous' says a reporter)
wins general approval. Service is thoughtful
and the welcome personal. 'Truly magical'
says one reporter of their experience
there. 'Nothing beats going out after dinner
to walk the shore and hear the waves
exploding on the rocks' says another.
Highland cattle graze the grounds. To climb
the lighthouse tower you need permission
in writing from the Northern Lighthouse
Board. Reports welcome.

Portpatrick, Dumfries & Galloway

Portpatrick, Dumfries & Galloway
DG9 9AD

Tel (01776) 810471
Fax (01776) 810435
e-mail reservations@knockinaam-lodge.com

Nearby Logan, Ardwell and Glenwhan Gardens, Castle Kennedy.
Location 3 miles (5 km) SE of Portpatrick, off A77; in grounds; ample car parking
Food breakfast, lunch, dinner
Price ££££
Rooms 10; 9 double with bath, one single with shower; all rooms have phone, TV, video, hairdryer
Facilities 2 sitting rooms, bar, dining room, garden; croquet, helipad
Credit cards AE, MC, V **Children** welcome
Disabled access easy, but no ground-floor bedrooms
Pets accepted, but not in public rooms **Closed** never
Proprietors Michael Bricker and Pauline Ashworth

Knockinaam Lodge
Country hotel

Galloway is very much an area for escaping the hurly-burly, and Knockinaam Lodge complements it perfectly (as well as being the ideal staging post for anyone bound for the ferry at Stranraer to Northern Ireland). Succeeding proprietors of the Lodge have had a reputation for fine food and warm hospitality, and the tradition is still maintained with the help of an enthusiastic staff and the present owner, David Ibbotson.

The house, a low Victorian villa, was built as a hunting lodge in 1869 and extended at the turn of the century. It was used by Sir Winston Churchill as a secret location in which to meet General Eisenhower during the Second World War. The rooms are cosy in scale and furnishings, the bedrooms varying from the stylishly simple to the quietly elegant. A key part of the appeal of the place is its complete seclusion – down a wooded glen, with lawned garden running down to a sandy beach. Children are welcome, and well catered for, with special high teas.

Since taking over in 2003, David has brightened up the place considerably, completely redecorating, as well as turning his attention to the grounds and painting the exterior. The restaurant now has a Michelin star, and the wine list has more than 540 bins. Reports would be welcome.

Skirling by Biggar, Lanarkshire

Skirling by Biggar, Lanarkshire
ML12 6HD

Tel (01899) 860274
Fax (01899) 860255
e-mail enquiry@skirlinghouse.com
website www.skirlinghouse.com

Nearby Peebles, New Lanark,
Edinburgh, Glasgow
Location off A702 to Edinburgh, on
A72 on the village green, private car
parking
Food breakfast and dinner
Price ££
Rooms 5; 4 double, 1 twin, all with
bath; all rooms have TV, DVD,
phone, hairdryer **Facilities** library,
drawing room, dining room, conser-
vatory; garden, tennis court, croquet
Credit cards MC, V **Children** wel-
come **Disabled** access possible **Pets**
by arrangement **Closed** Jan and Feb
Proprietors Bob and Isobel Hunter

Skirling House
Guest-house

Set in the centre of a peaceful Borders village, Skirling House was designed in
1908 by the Arts and Crafts architect
Ramsay Traquair. We are delighted to report
that owners Bob and Isobel are well aware
of the architectural gem they have on their
hands and, from the ornate wrought ironwork and decorative carvings to period
antiques, the Arts and Craft movement is
evident throughout. Lord Carmichael com-
missioned the house and, left over from his
family's art collection, is an impressive
16thC Florentine carved ceiling in the
drawing room. In keeping with the relaxed
atmosphere, you can sit back in one of the
comfy sofas or armchairs and admire the
ceiling, or simply cuddle up with a good
book beside the log fire.

Bedrooms, although very much in the
style of the place, have lovely views over the
three-acre garden. The grounds cover 115
acres and, with the surrounding rolling hills,
provide ample chance for a light stroll or a
more ambitious ramble. The menu, modern
and light in style, changes daily and the
Hunters use local produce as well as vegetables and herbs from the house gardens.

Located by one of the main routes to
Edinburgh, Skirling House makes a conven-
ient stop-over, but we think with its interesting design and tranquil setting, it makes
a worthwhile stopover.

Aboyne, Aberdeenshire

Ballater Road, Aboyne,
Aberdeenshire AB34 5HY

Tel (013398) 87241
Fax (013398) 87241
e-mail struanhall@zetnet.co.uk
website www.struanhall.co.uk

Nearby castle, distilleries, the
Grampians; fishing, golf.
Location in village; ample car park-
ing
Food breakfast
Price ££
Rooms 3 double; 1 single; all have
TV, radio, hairdryer, tea/coffee kit
Facilities sitting room, dining room;
garden
Credit cards MC, V
Children over 7
Disabled not suitable
Pets not accepted
Closed Oct to Apr
Proprietors Phyllis and Michael
Ingham

Struan Hall
Bed-and-breakfast

Looking at the solid mass of grey stone that is Struan Hall, we could hardly believe that its original site was five miles away. The house dates back to the 1800s, but in 1904 it was dismantled, moved stone by stone and rebuilt here. Set in 2 acres of grounds, with lawns and an Indian-style pavilion, a rockery and carp pool, Struan Hall makes a restful, comfortable base, whether guests are sightseeing, fishing, walking or playing golf.

Phyllis and Michael Ingham are accomplished hosts who have decorated their home to suit the Victorian atmosphere. Tartan carpets harmonize with the pine staircase, while the dining-room, where a communal breakfast is served, has a massive Victorian sideboard. Tiffany-style lamps light the hall.

Upstairs, the Scottish theme continues. The bedrooms are named after castles and have pine bedheads carved with Scottish motifs. Bathrooms, however, are right up-to-date. The Inghams do not serve dinner but are happy to recommend several pubs and restaurants in the town.

Achiltibue, Ross-shire

Achiltibuie, by Ullapool, Ross-shire
IV26 2YG

Tel (0185482) 622282
Fax (01854) 622251
e-mail summerisleshotel@aol.com
website www.summerisleshotel.co.uk

Nearby Ullapool; Inverewe
Gardens; beaches.
Location 10 miles (16 km) N of
Ullapool, turn left on to single track
road for 15 miles (24 km) to
Achiltibuie; hotel is close to village
post office; with ample car parking
Food breakfast, lunch, dinner
Price £££
Rooms 13; 11 double and twin, 2
suites, all with bath; all rooms have
phone, hairdryer; suites have TV
Facilities dining room, sitting room,
2 bars, sun room; fishing
Credit cards MC, V **Children** wel-
come over 6
Disabled access difficult
Pets dogs allowed in bedrooms but
not public rooms **Closed** mid-Oct to
Easter **Proprietors** Mark and
Geraldine Irvine

Summer Isles
Country hotel

'There is a marvellous amount of nothing to do' at Summer Isles. The
emphasis is on eating well, sleeping well
and relaxing in beautiful surroundings. 'Take
your Wellingtons, your sunglasses, your
dog, walking shoes, insect repellant, cam-
era, paint boxes, binoculars and comfy
clothes,' advise Mark and Geraldine Irvine,
whose family have owned this remote, cottagey, civilized hotel since the late 1960s.

The views across Loch Broom and the
Summer Isles are riveting, and the hotel's
public rooms make the most of them with
large picture windows. The decorations
and furnishings are simple and cosy, with a
touch of sophistication. There is a wood-
burning stove in the sitting room to keep
you warm, and modern art and photographs on the walls in the dining room. The
food is a major attraction – the Irvines
must be the holders of one of the fur-
thest-flung Michelin stars in the British
Isles, gained for the delicious and health-
conscious cooking of Chris Firth-Bernard,
featuring freshly-caught fish and shellfish
and home-grown fruit and vegetables.
Bedrooms are comfortable; best is the galleried Boathouse suite, which is stylish and
spacious, with a spiral staircase up to the
bedroom.

Auldearn, Nairn

Auldearn, Nairn, IV12 5TE

Tel (01667) 454896
Fax (01667) 455469
e-mail info@boath-house.com
website www.boath-house.com

Nearby Inverness, Nairn, Loch Ness, Balmoral Castle
Location off A96, near Nairn, ample parking--
Food breakfast, lunch, dinner
Price ££££
Rooms 8
Facilities 2 sitting rooms, restaurant, spa; golf, fishing, riding, clay shooting all available nearby
Credit Cards MC, V
Children welcome
Disabled one ground floor cottage, restaurant is accessible
Pets accepted by arrangement
Closed 2 weeks over Christmas
Proprietors Don and Wendy Matheson

Boath House Hotel
Country house hotel

This Grade A listed Georgian mansion was standing derelict until Don and Wendy Matheson found and fell in love with it in the early Nineties. Having restored the house to its former glory the Mathesons decided to open their home to guests, and have since made a great success of it.

Boath House has its own spa and eight guest bedrooms, all individually decorated in rich colours in a mix of contemporary and traditional styles. All have free-standing baths and separate showers, and two have four poster beds. It stands in 20 acres of grounds, including a 2-acre trout lake and Victorian walled garden.

The kitchen gardens provide many of the ingredients served in the award-winning restaurant. Charlie Lockley is head chef, and the focus is on organic, locally-produced and seasonal food. Local seafood is delivered daily, and meat and cheese come from a nearby farm. Wild food items, such as wild mushrooms and herbs, are also on the menu when in season, and even honey comes from the hotel's own hives – organic food is a real passion here.

The Mathesons are keen to foster a friendly, informal atmosphere and want their home to be "somewhere guests can relax and feel at ease", despite the grandeur of the house. We have heard great things about Boath House. Reports welcome.

Ballachulish, Argyll PA39 4JX

Tel (01855) 811266
Fax (01855) 811498
e-mail mclaughalins@btconnect.com **web-site** www.ballachulishhouse.com

Nearby Glencoe, Ben Nevis, West Highland Way; fishing, golf.
Location on hillside in own grounds; ample car parking
Food breakfast; dinner on request
Price ££
Rooms 8 double; all have phone, radio, hairdryer, tea/coffee kit
Facilities sitting room, dining room; garden, croquet, badminton, 9 hole golf course
Credit cards MC, V
Children over 10
Disabled unsuitable
Pets not accepted
Closed never
Proprietor Marie Mclaughalin

Ballachulish House
Seaside restaurant-with-rooms

Anyone wanting to immerse themselves in Scottish history should head straight for this 350-year-old country house, set in a valley with stunning views of Loch Linnhe and the nearby Morvern Hills. The present owner, Marie Mclaughalin, can tell you all about the chilling connections with the Glencoe Massacre (1692), as well as the Appin Murder (1752) that inspired Robert Louis Stevenson's novel, Kidnapped.

Despite its bloodthirsty past, however, Ballachulish House is a peaceful spot where good food, good wine and good company are the order of the day. Executive chef Darin Campbell is in charge of the kitchen, producing a daily changing menu around fresh, local produce. Much of this is also seasonal, such as wild mushrooms from the local woods and glens, and langoustines and scallops from Loch Linnhe. Since portions are ample, it is advisable to build up an appetite by walking, fishing or perhaps enjoying a game of badminton or croquet in the garden. The eight bedrooms are vast, with space for chairs as well as large beds.

Balquidder, Perthshire

Balquhidder, Lochearnhead,
Perthshire FK19 8PQ

Tel (01877) 384622
Fax (01877) 384305
e-mail monachyle@mhor.net
website http://mhor.net/hotel/

Nearby in the heart of Rob Roy
country.
Location on private estate; turn off
A84, 11 miles (17.5 km) N of
Callander at Kingshouse Hotel, then
follow single-track lane for 6 miles
(9.5 km); well-signposted; ample car
parking
Food breakfast, lunch, dinner
Price ££-££££
Rooms 14 double, all with bath or
shower; all rooms have phone, TV,
hairdryer **Facilities** sitting room,
bar, restaurant; terrace, garden, fishing, stalking **Credit cards** MC, V
Children well behaved children
accepted over 12 **Disabled** access
easy **Pets** accepted in 2 rooms
Closed Jan **Proprietors** Tom, Dick
and Melanie Lewis

Highland loch

Monachyle Mhor
Farmhouse hotel

A small, family-run farmhouse with a charm all its own. The setting is both serene and romantic – as well it might be: this was the family home of Rob Roy MacGregor, approached along the Braes of Balquhidder (described in Kidnapped) and set beside Lochs Doine and Voil.

Rob and Jean Lewis came here some 30 years ago from Monmouth and first farmed the 2,000-acre estate, then opened the building as a hotel as well. Since then Jean and Rob have moved to the South of France, but their children Tom, Dick and Melanie have taken over and expanded the business. A self catering cottage has been converted into suites, and the hotel now has a total of 14 individual and very stylishly-decorated rooms; five in the main house, and nine in the courtyard buildings. As well as the farm and hotel, the Lewises now also run a fish shop (Ben Ledi), The Scotch Oven bakery and the Old Library Tearooms.

Tom Lewis is the highly-praised chef, and the hotel's restaurant – situated in a light and airy conservatory overlooking the two lochs – is popular with locals and guests alike. Much of the produce comes from the farm, including lamb, beef and organic vegetables.

For a relaxing, country break in magnificent scenery and with memorable food, Monachyle Mhor would be hard to beat.

Colbost, Dunvegan, Isle of Skye
IV55 8ZT

Tel (01470) 511258
Fax (01470) 511358
e-mail
eatandstay@threechimneys.co.uk
website www.threechimneys.co.uk

Nearby Dunvegan Castle; the
Cuillins.
Location from Dunvegan take the
single-track B884 toward Glendale
for 5 miles (8 km); car parking
Food breakfast, lunch, dinner
Price £££
Rooms 6 suites, all with bath; all
rooms have phone, TV, DVD, CD
player, minibar, hairdryer **Facilities**
breakfast room; 2 dining rooms, bar,
garden
Credit cards AE, MC, V **Children**
welcome; early meal can be arranged
for very young children
Disabled 1 room specially adapted
Pets not accepted
Closed never **Proprietors** Shirley
and Eddie Spear

Three Chimneys
Seaside restaurant-with-rooms

For more than 20 years chef Shirley Spear and her husband Eddie have run Three Chimneys as an award-winning seafood restaurant in an idyllic seaside location in the far north-west corner of Skye. The good news is that you can now, having enjoyed yourself at dinner, stay the night – in style. The six suites created in a new building called the House Over-By, are luxurious, highly original – if understated – rooms designed to blend with the seascape and the changing light. Each contemporary, spacious and high-ceilinged room (some are on two levels) has direct access to the beach; bathrooms are heavenly. The view looks west to the Minch and sometimes to the misty islands of the Outer Hebrides on the horizon. Breakfast is served in a room overlooking the seashore and the islands in Loch Dunvegan.

Three Chimneys itself is a simple former crofter's cottage in which stone walls and exposed beams are mixed with modern furniture and fittings. As you would expect, the menu is a mainly fishy one – in the mornings you can watch the fishing boats set off to catch your dinner – but Highland beef, lamb and game are also a feature, and the puddings are just as good.

Comrie, Perthshire

Melville Square, Comrie, Perthshire
PH6 2DN

Tel (01764) 679200
Fax (01764) 679219
e-mail reception@royalhotel.co.uk
website www.royalhotel.co.uk

Nearby Loch Earn; The Famous
Grouse Distillery; Drummond
Castle.
Location in centre of Comrie, on
A85, about 25 miles (40 km)W of
Perth; limited car parking
Food breakfast, lunch, dinner; room
service
Price £££
Rooms 11; 8 double and twin, 3
suites, all with bath; all rooms have
phone, TV, fax/modem point,
hairdryer, safe
Facilities lounge, public bar, library,
2 dining rooms
Credit cards AE, MC, V **Children**
accepted **Disabled** access difficult
Pets accepted **Closed** never
Managers Jeremy and Teresa
Milsom

Royal Hotel
Town inn

All too often, town hotels, surviving on a diet of passing trade, show a distinct lack of enthusiasm and a rather blank face to the world; it's only occasionally that we find a new one that excites our interest. Comrie's Royal Hotel is such a one: from the moment you step inside, it feels right. Situated in the centre of this attractive little Highland town, and dating from 1765, it began life as a coaching inn, and earned its grand title after a visit by – who else? – Queen Victoria, accompanied by her servant, John Brown.

The atmosphere is homely, yet at the same time elegant and stylish, with log fires in the public rooms as well as squashy sofas, comfortable armchairs, antiques and oil paintings. There is a Brasserie for informal dining, as well as the main restaurant.

Recent visitors were delighted by their stay, and enthused about the freshness and prettyness of their rooms. All eleven have been individually planned and furnished with a cool eye for detail and design, and a touch of luxury (bathrobes and soaps). The hotel's modish makeover was the brainchild of owner Edward Gibbons, but it is managed by hands-on couple Jerry and Teresa Milsom.

Connel, Argyll

Connel, by Oban, Argyll PA37 1PT

Tel (01631) 710857
e-mail info@ardshouse.com
website www.ardshouse.com

Nearby Falls of Lora, ferries to the Hebrides, the Highlands.
Location overlooking water; ample car parking
Food breakfast
Price £
Rooms 4 double; all have TV radio, tea/coffee kit
Facilities sitting room, dining room; garden
Credit cards MC, V
Children not suitable
Disabled not suitable
Pets not accepted
Closed Christmas and New Year
Proprietor Margaret Kennedy

Ards House
Bed-and-breakfast

This pretty Victorian villa has uninterrupted views westward over the Firth of Lorn to the Morvern Hills. Sunsets are truly spectacular.

The house itself tends to ramble, as additions have been made over the years to the original cottage – the sitting room is conventional but comfortable with an log burning stove and a grand piano. The most recent owner, Margaret Kennedy, has retained the snug atmosphere, but no longer serves dinner (however there is a choice of restaurants nearby). Breakfasts are especially generous. You could choose not only the usual fresh fruit salad, muesli and yoghurt but also kippers, smoked salmon and scrambled eggs, pancakes and bacon with maple syrup, haggis on toast (with whisky if you want). All this is in addition to the full Scottish breakfast accompanied by potatoe scone.

Although the Oban to Tyndrum road runs right in front of the house, traffic is rarely heavy enough to disturb the peace. Special terms are available for short breaks.

Fort William, Inverness-shire

Grange Road, Fort William,
Inverness-shire PH33 6JF

Tel (01397) 702709
e-mail crolinnhe@yahoo.com
website www.crolinnhe.co.uk

Nearby Ben Nevis, West Highland
Museum; fishing, golf.
Location overlooking Loch Linnhe;
ample car parking
Food breakfast
Price ££
Rooms 3 double; all have TV,
hairdryer, tea/coffee kit
Facilities sitting room, dining room;
terrace, garden
Credit cards not accepted
Children over 12
Disabled not suitable
Pets not accepted
Closed Nov to Mar
Proprietor Flora MacKenzie

Ben Nevis

Crolinnhe
Bed-and-breakfast

Fort William has long been the jumping-off point for visitors to the Western Highlands. Active types come to climb Ben Nevis, Britain's highest peak, though the Nevis Range Gondola is an easier way to the top. The Great Glen, with its chain of narrow lochs along a valley, cuts away to the northeast. A short walk from the middle of Fort William, Crolinnhe has been the home of Flora MacKenzie since 1982. Having restored the Victorian house she is constantly redecorating in what is a 'smart', though perhaps slightly old-fashioned, style. This obviously suits the regulars who come here for the outdoor activities such as fishing, golf and hiking.

No doubt the 'breakfast at 8.30 am' rule also suits them. Guests decide the night before what they want, which helps the hosts, since 'the full works' can be a feast of porridge, followed by fresh Mallaig kippers or even haggis. More modest eaters can opt for fresh fruit or scrambled eggs.

Set on a hillside, Crolinnhe has truly spectacular views over Loch Linnhe, and although Mrs MacKenzie tells us she has no need nor desire to be in our guide, we think the view alone is reason enough to visit Crolinnhe.

Fort William, Inverness-shire

Grange Road, Fort William,
Inverness-shire PH33 6JF

Tel (01397) 705516
Fax (01397) 701595
e-mail jcampbell@grange-fortwilliam.com **website** www.the-grange-scotland.co.uk

Nearby Ben Nevis; 'Road to the Isles'; Loch Ness.
Location on outskirts; from town centre take A82 direction Glasgow, then turn left into Ashburn Lane; hotel is at top on left; ample car parking
Food breakfast
Price ££
Rooms 4 double and twin, 2 with bath and shower, 2 with shower; all rooms have TV, hairdryer **Facilities** breakfast room, sitting room; garden, sea loch close by
Credit cards by arrangement
Children not accepted
Disabled access difficult
Pets not accepted **Closed** mid-Nov to Easter **Proprietors** Joan and John Campbell

The Grange
Bed-and-breakfast

We were delighted to discover this outstanding bed-and-breakfast establishment on the outskirts of Fort William, run with great flair by Joan and John Campbell. A ten-minute walk from the fairly charmless town centre brings you to this late Victorian house, set in pretty terraced grounds overlooking Loch Linnhe.

A feminine touch is distinctly in evidence in the immaculate interior, which is decorated with admirable taste and a flair for matching fabrics with furnishings and fittings. First glimpsed, you might expect a stand-offish 'don't touch' approach from the owners, but nothing could be further from the truth at the Grange. Joan Campbell, responsible for the decoration, is naturally easy-going, with a great sense of hospitality.

All four bedrooms are superbly, and individually, decorated and furnished, their bathrooms lavish and luxurious – it all comes as rather a surprise. The Rob Roy room was the one chosen by Jessica Lange, who stayed here during the filming of Rob Roy, while the Terrace Room has, as its name suggests, its own terrace leading on to the gardens. Two of the bedrooms have Louis XV-style king-size beds; all four overlook the garden and Loch Linnhe. A delightful place.

Glenlivet, Banffshire

Glenlivet, Banffshire AB37 9DB

Tel (01807) 590378
Fax (01807) 590472
e-mail enquiries@minmorehousehotel.com **website** www.minmore-househotel.com

Nearby Glenlivet Distillery; Ballindalloch Castle.
Location on the B9008, next to the Glenlivet Distillery; in 4.5 acres garden with ample car parking
Food breakfast, picnic lunch on request, dinner
Price ££
Rooms 9; 7 double and twin, 2 suites, some with shower, all with bath; all rooms have phone, hairdryer **Facilities** sitting room, bar, dining room; garden, croquet lawn, tennis court **Credit cards** AE, MC, V
Children over 10
Disabled access difficult **Pets** by arrangement
Closed 25 Nov to 29 Dec
Managers Lynne and Victor Janssen

Minmore House
Country house hotel

We have always been impressed by the friendly, relaxed atmosphere at Minmore House, which continues to be generated by Lynne and Victor Janssen.

It is a solid mid-Victorian family home set in four-and-a-half acres of landscaped gardens. It stands adjacent to the famous Glenlivet whisky distillery, and was the home of George Smith, the distillery's founder. Not surprisingly, whiskey plays its part in the hotel, and the fine oak-panelled bar displays an impressive range of single malts. From the hotel, enthusiasts can follow the signposted Whisky Trail, visiting renowned Speyside whiskey distilleries.

'Proper' Scottish breakfasts, with kippers and smoked haddock, are on offer, as well as complimentary afternoon tea. In the award-winning restaurant, the four-course set dinners (with vegetarian options) have a Scottish bias. The hotel has a tranquil, relaxed atmosphere, with open fires in all the public rooms. With the exception of the two single rooms, the bedrooms and bathrooms are spacious. The Janssens are happy to arrange all manner of activities – golf, shooting, stalking, salmon and trout fishing, walking, and castle and distillery visits.

Isle of Eriska, Argyll

Isle of Eriska, Ledaig, Oban, Argyll
PA37 1SD

Tel (01631) 720371
Fax (01631) 720531
e-mail office@eriska-hotel.co.uk
website www.eriska-hotel.co.uk

Nearby Oban; Isle of Mull; Inverary Castle; Glencoe.
Location on private island connected by road bridge; from Connel take A828 toward Fort William for 4 miles (6 km) to N of Benderloch village, then follow signs; ample car parking **Food** breakfast, lunch, dinner **Price** ££££
Rooms 17; 12 double and twin, 2 single, 3 family rooms, all with bath; all rooms have phone, hairdryer
Facilities 3 drawing rooms, bar/library, dining room, indoor swimming pool, gym, sauna, garden; 6-hole golf course, driving range, tennis court, croquet, clay-pigeon shooting, watersports **Credit cards** AE, MC, V **Children** welcome **Disabled** access possible **Pets** accepted **Closed** Jan **Proprietors** Buchanan-Smith family

Isle of Eriska Hotel
Island mansion

A splendid hotel that has the twin advantages of seclusion, since it is set on its own remote island, and accessibility: it is connected to the mainland by a short road bridge. And for those who like to keep themselves occupied during their stay, its leisure centre, which includes a magnificent 17-metre heated swimming pool, and its sporting opportunities, will appeal.

Built in 1884 in grey granite and warmer red sandstone, in Scottish Baronial style, the Buchanan-Smith's hotel is a reminder of a more expansive and confident era. If it reminds you in feel, if not in appearance, of Balmoral, you will not be surprised to learn that the original wallpaper on the first-floor landing is also found in the royal castle. In fact the experience of staying here is very much like being in an old-fashioned grand private house, comfortable rather than stylish, with a panelled great hall, and roaring log fires and chintz fabrics much in evidence. In the library-cum-bar you can browse through the books with a malt whisky in hand, while excellent six-course dinners are served in the stately dining room. The handsome bedrooms vary in size and outlook. Since our last edition a further five rooms and two cottages on the island have been added.

Isle Ornsay, Isle of Skye

Isle Ornsay, Sleat, Isle of Skye
IV43 8QR

Tel (01471) 833332
Fax (01471) 833275
e-mail hotel@eileaniarmain.co.uk

Nearby Clan Donald Centre; Aros
Heritage Centre; Dunvegan Castle.
Location on water's edge, on estate
between Broadford and Armadale in
the S of the island, 20 mins drive
from Skye Bridge or Mallaig ferry
point; ample car parking
Food breakfast, lunch, dinner
Price £££
Rooms 16; 12 double, twin or triple,
4 suites; all with bath; all rooms have
phone, hairdryer **Facilities** sitting
room, 2 dining rooms; anchorage for
yachts
Credit cards AE, MC, V
Children welcome
Disabled access possible to suites
Pets accepted **Closed** never
Proprietor Sir Iain Noble

Eilean Iarmain
Seafront hotel

Hearing the soft lilt of the voices of the staff is one of the pleasures of a stay at this traditional Skye hotel, and a sure sign that you are in the Hebrides. This is a bi-lingual establishment, and the friendly and welcoming staff are fluent in both Gaelic and English.

The hotel is part of an estate belonging to Sir Iain and Lady Noble. Its three buildings are beautifully situated right on the water's edge, on the small rocky bay of Isle Ornsay, looking across the Sound of Sleat to the mainland Knoydart Hills beyond. If you are lucky, you may see otters on the shore.

The hotel's core is a white-painted Victorian inn, which comprises the reception area, two appealing dining rooms and six bedrooms. A further six bedrooms are in a building opposite, while the latest addition houses four split-level suites. All the rooms are traditional in character, hospitable and homely, with modern fittings and smart bathrooms. In each is a complimentary miniature bottle of whisky supplied from Sir Iain's distillery. The restaurant specializes in local fish, shellfish and game, and enjoys a local reputation.

Killiecrankie, Perthshire

Killiecrankie, By Pitlochry,
Perthshire PH16 5LG

Tel (01796)473220
Fax (01796) 472451
e-mail enquiries@killiecrankieho-tel.co.uk **website** www.kil-liecrankiehotel.co.uk

Nearby Pitlochry; Pass of Killiecrankie; Blair Atholl; Glamis.
Location in 4 acres, 3 miles (4.5 km) N of Pitlochry, just off A9 on the B8079; ample car parking
Food breakfast, lunch, dinner
Price ££
Rooms 10; 8 double and twin, 2 single, 1 suite, 8 with bath, 2 with shower; all rooms have phone, TV, hairdryer
Facilities sitting room, 2 dining rooms, bar, conservatory, garden
Credit cards MC, V
Children accepted
Disabled access possible
Pets not accepted **Closed** 3 Jan to 14 Feb **Proprietors** Tim and Maillie Waters

Killiecrankie Hotel
Country house hotel

A sensible, reassuring sort of establish-ment in a delightful setting that some-how encapsulates the modest Scottish country hotel. Built as a manse for a local clergyman in 1840, it stands at the foot of the Pass of Killiecrankie, formed by the River Garry slicing through the surround-ing granite hills, and it has its own attrac-tive grounds – a lovely place in which to relax and watch out for wildlife, including red squirrels and roe deer.

The ten straightforward yet comfort-able bedrooms are done out in country house fabrics and custom-made furniture and fittings finished in natural pine, lending them a somewhat Scandinavian air. An unexpected touch: beds are turned down each evening. The mahogany-panelled bar is a cosy, convivial place in which to gather for drinks, and a bright conservatory sec-tion is set for light lunches and imaginative bar snacks, including a selection of tapas. This is also where guests eat breakfast, overlooking the garden. In the main restaurant, chef Mark Easton, shortlisted for the Chef of Scotland award, prepares a large 'modern Scottish' menu. Special diets are also catered for.

Killin, Perthshire

South Loch Tay-side, by Killin,
Perthshire, FK21 8SU

Tel (01567) 820400
Fax (01567) 820282
e-mail info@ardeonaighotel.co.uk
website www.ardeonaighotel.co.uk

Nearby Loch Tay, Ben Lawers
mountains, Edradour distillery, Blair
Castle
Location on south shore of Loch
Tay, mid-way between Killin and
Kenmore
Food breakfast, lunch, dinner
Price ££
Rooms 25 double/twin, all with
bath/shower; all rooms have phone,
TV, hairdryer
Facilities 2 lounges, 3 restaurants,
bar, library; 13 acres of grounds
Credit cards MC, V
Children over 12 accepted
Disabled 2 specially adapted rooms
Pets well-behaved dogs, £10 per
night **Closed** never **Proprietors**
Pete and Sara Gottgens

The Ardeonaig Hotel
Country house hotel

A long, low gabled building, formerly a drover's inn, with views across Loch Tay to Ben Lawers, Ardeonaig gives the inn-with-rooms formula an interesting twist. South African owner Pete Gottgens asks visitors not to expect a luxurious hotel, but an inn with well above average service. The staff to guest ratio is high for this kind of operation, and the result is a feeling of well-being and unobtrusively looked after that often eludes grander places. He sees the place as an extension of his own house, and the Scottish Colonial ambience, as he describes it, is enveloping and cosy rather than smart or grand. To this end there are four down-stairs sitting areas all with open fires, so your chances of hibernating in peace with a book are good. The bedrooms, in calm colours, are comfortable, and there are no TVs: use the library instead, or get out on the loch to take advantage of the inn's own salmon fishing. Locally produced ingredients on the menu and, of course, an exclusively South African wine list.

Tweed Mill Brae, Kingussie,
Inverness-shire PH21 1TC

Tel (01540) 661166
Fax (01540) 661080
e-mail relax@thecross.co.uk **website**
www.thecross.co.uk

Nearby Aviemore; Loch Insh;
Highland Folk Museum.
Location from the traffic lights in
Kingussie town centre, take
Ardbroilach Rd for 300 m, then turn
left down Tweed Mill Brae; ample
car parking
Food breakfast, dinner
Price ££
Rooms 8 double and twin, all with
bath; all rooms have phone, TV, CD
player, hairdryer **Facilities** sitting
room, restaurant; garden
Credit cards AE, MC, V
Children well behaved children over
the age of 9 welcome
Disabled no special facilities; restau-
rant is accesible, rooms are not
Pets not accepted
Closed Jan (open for Hogmanay)
Proprietors David and Katie Young

The Cross
Restaurant-with-rooms

R uth Hadley's inspired cooking had long
made her and husband Tony's well-
established, award-winning restaurant-
with-rooms a must for gourmets. David
and Katie Young took over in early 2003
and, in their own words, believe "if it ain't
broke, don't fix it." And David should know
– he was a chief inspector for the AA. In a
secluded four-acre waterside setting, down
a private drive, the Cross is a modest former 19thC tweed mill, which houses nine
fresh and simple bedrooms as well as the
restaurant and a residents' sitting room.

Bedrooms are individually furnished,
and include canopied, twin and king-size
beds. One has a balcony overlooking the
Gynack, which flows alongside the mill, and
where you may sometimes see salmon
swimming and herons fishing.

The Youngs have also kept chef Becca
Henderson on in the kitchen, so the food
should continue to be good. We would
welcome comments.

Highfield, Muir of Ord, Ross-shire
1V6 7XN

Tel (01463)870090
Fax (01463)870090
e-mail info@thedowerhouse.co.uk
website www.thedowerhouse.co.uk

Nearby Inverness; Culloden; beaches.
Location 1 mile (2.5 km) N of Muir of Ord, 14 miles (22 km) NW of Inverness on the A862 to Dingwall; ample car parking
Food breakfast, dinner
Price £££
Rooms 4 double and twin, 3 with bath, 1 with shower; all rooms have phone, TV **Facilities** sitting room, dining room; garden
Credit cards MC, V
Children accepted by arrangement
Disabled 1 room
Pets accepted by arrangement
Closed up to a month, off-season
Proprietors Robyn and Mena Aitchison

The Dower House
Country house hotel

This former Dower House of a baronial home, which burnt down in the 1940s, was converted from thatched farmhouse to charming residence in the Georgian cottage ornée style in about 1800. It became a hotel, run by Robyn and Mena Aitchison as if it were a private house receiving paying guests, in 1989. Something of an oasis in the rugged landscape between the rivers Beauly and Conon, it is set in beautifully maintained mature gardens and grounds.

The elegant, red-walled dining room, with its highly polished mahogany tables, makes a stunning setting for evening meals, and Robyn's self-taught cooking, does not disappoint. Herbs and vegetables are from the garden, eggs from their hens, and meat, game and seafood are all local. The menu offers no choice, though it changes every day. The sitting room has comfortable chairs, flowery fabrics, plenty of books, an open fire and a bar concealed in a cupboard.

The five bedrooms vary in size and furnishings and are fairly simple. The largest is the most luxurious, with an enormous bed and spacious bathroom, while the suite looks on to the pretty garden. All the baths are traditional cast iron, with period fittings.

Pitlochry, Perthshire

Higher Oakfield, Pitlochry,
Perthshire PH16 5HT

Tel (01796) 473473
Fax (01796) 474068
e-mail info@knockendarroch.co.uk
website www.knockendarroch.co.uk

Nearby Blair Castle; Killincrankie
Pass; Loch Tummel.
Location close to town centre, 26
miles (41 km) N of Perth on A9;
ample car parking
Food breakfast, dinner
Price ££
Rooms 12 double and twin, all with
bath; all rooms have phone, TV,
hairdryer, radio
Facilities 2 sitting rooms, dining
room; garden
Credit cards MC, V
Children accepted over 12
Disabled access limited
Pets not accepted
Closed mid-Nov to 1 Mar
Proprietors Allan and Alison Inglis

Knockendarroch
Town mansion

Pitlochry is a particularly agreeable
Highland town, and Knockendarroch
House is the place to stay. Built in 1880 for
an Aberdeen advocate, it displays more
château-esque elegance than Scottish
Baronial pomp. It stands on a plateau
above the town, surrounded by mature
oaks (its Gaelic name means Hill of Oaks).

Furnished in careful good taste, the
house feels gracious and welcoming. There
are two interconnecting sitting rooms in
which to relax, with green ceilings, white
cornices, pastel green curtains and new
carpets – all very soothing. The dining
room is light and spacious, with many windows and some attractive furniture. The
cooking draws praise, but we would like
reports, please.

All the bedrooms have views; those
from the second floor are spectacular.
They are all well furnished and two have
small balconies.

Guests attending the famous Pitlochry
Festival Theatre (which began here at
Knockendarroch) are served an early dinner, and a courtesy bus is laid on to take
them to and from the town.

As we went to press, Knockendarroch
had just been sold, and the new owners
plan to continue running it as a hotel.
Reports welcome.

Port Appin, Argyll PA38 4DF

Tel (01631) 730236
Fax (01631) 730535
e-mail airds@airds-hotel.com **web-site** www.airds-hotel.com

Nearby Oban; Glencoe; 'Road to the Isles'; Ben Nevis.
Location between Ballachulish and Connel, 2 miles (3 km) off A828; ample car parking
Food breakfast, light lunch, dinner; room service
Price ££££
Rooms 8 double and twin, 3 suites, all with bath; all rooms have phone, TV, hairdryer **Facilities** 2 sitting rooms, conservatory, dining room, garden, shingle beach **Credit cards** MC, V **Children** accepted
Disabled no special facilities **Pets** accepted by arrangement
Closed last three weeks Jan
Proprietors Jenny and Shaun Mc Kivragan

Airds Hotel
Ferry inn

The owners of this old ferry inn on the shores of Loch Linnhe have very sensibly taken every advantage of its superb location: the dining room, the conservatory and many bedrooms face the loch. To capitalize further, they have also created, across the road, an attractive lawn and rose garden in which guests can sit and admire the view across the loch to the island of Lismore. The sunsets here are stunning.

Despite its fairly ordinary exterior, Airds Hotel is a smart and decorous establishment, impeccably run and maintained. The interior is elegant, with two sitting rooms prettily furnished with comfortable chairs, deep-pile carpets and open fires. Rooms are full of flowers and books, and paintings are in abundance. Each of the bedrooms is individually decorated and carefully furnished, with very comfortable bathrooms. Each day the dinner menu and wine list is left in your room, so that you can consult it at leisure, give your orders by late afternoon, and relax before dinner with an aperitif, confident that there will be no unnecessary delays. The dining room is somewhat formal and hushed, but the food, cooked by chef Paul Burns, is highly praised and often features such local delicacies as Lismore oysters, smoked salmon or venison.

Portree, Isle of Skye

Portree, Isle of Skye, IV51 9EU

Tel (01478) 612217
Fax (01478) 613517
e-mail info@viewfieldhouse.com
website www.viewfieldhouse.com

Nearby Trotternish peninsula.
Location on outskirts of town, 10
minutes walk S of centre; from A87
towards Broadford, turn right just
after national garage on left; with
ample car parking
Food breakfast, packed lunch,
dinner
Price ££
Rooms 11 double and twin, 10 with
bath; all rooms have phone, radio,
hairdryer **Facilities** sitting room,
dining room, TV room, washer and
tumble drier for guests
Credit cards MC, V **Children** welcome **Disabled** one specially adapted room on ground floor **Pets**
accepted, but not in public rooms
Closed mid-Oct to mid-Apr
Proprietors Hugh Macdonald

Viewfield House
Country guest-house

'It won't suit everyone,' writes our
reporter about Viewfield House, 'but
for those seeking an age gone by, the experience would be memorable.'

This is an imposing Victorian country
mansion, which, as the name suggests, has
some fine views from its elevated position.
The need for costly repairs to the roof
prompted Evelyn Macdonald, Hugh's grandmother, to open Viewfield House to
guests. The delight of it is that the distinctive character of the house was preserved;
and though you will not lack for comfort
or service, a stay here is likely to be a
novel experience. The house is full of colonial memorabilia: stuffed animals, and birds;
priceless museum relics; and a magnificent
collection of oil paintings and prints.

The rooms are original, right down to
the wallpaper in one instance (though all
but one now have *en suite* bathrooms in the
former dressing-rooms); there is a classic
Victorian parlour and a grand dining room
with a huge oak table. Guests are entertained
house-party style, although separate tables
can be used if they prefer not to dine communally – we admire this flexibility. Dinner is
no longer served, but a light supper can be
taken each evening between 7pm and 9pm.
Breakfast features a wide selection of cooked
items including Mallaig kippers, smoked haddock and porridge. Reports welcome.

St Andrews, Fife

St Andrews, Fife KY16 8PN

Tel (01334) 472003
Fax (01344) 475248
e-mail info@kinkell.com
website www.kinkell.com

Nearby St Andrews and its golf, university, cathedral.
Location in country, outside town; ample car parking
Food breakfast; dinner by request
Price ££
Rooms 3 double
Facilities sitting room, dining room; garden, tennis court, croquet lawn
Credit cards AE, MC, V
Children welcome
Disabled not suitable
Pets by arrangement
Closed never
Proprietors Sandy and Frippy Fyfe

Kinkell
Bed-and-breakfast

Quality accommodation is hard to find in or near the golfing paradise that is St Andrews. Close to the Old Course of the Royal and Ancient Golf Club, many bed-and-breakfasts do plenty of business with little or no effort, so it comes as a relief to find a comfortable home where the owners still take pride in offering traditional Scottish hospitality.

Part-Georgian and part-Victorian, Kinkell is a rambling house in a quiet setting of trees and fields running down to the shore. We like the cheerful informality of Sandy and Frippy Fyfe, frustrated restaurateurs who decided to offer bed-and-breakfast because they enjoy meeting guests from all over the world. In contrast to the rather grand dining room, bedrooms here are somewhat conservative, with the subdued colours of many family houses. The light twin-bedded room facing south still displays china models and porcelain painted by the owners' daughter. It is a pity that the only views of the gusty North Sea are from the small double room facing east. The tennis court and croquet lawn are an enjoyable bonus in fine weather.

Scarista, Isle of Harris

Isle of Harris, Western Isles
HS3 3HX

Tel (01859) 550238
Fax (01859) 550277
e-mail timandpatricia@scarista-house.com **website** www.scarista-house.com

Nearby beaches; golf; boat trips.
Location 15 miles (24 km) SW of Tarbert on A859, overlooking sea; in 2-acre garden, with ample private car parking
Food breakfast, packed/snack lunch, dinner
Price £££
Rooms 2 double, 1 twin, all with bath; 2 suites in Glebe House; all rooms have phone, hairdryer
Facilities library, 2 sitting rooms, dining room
Credit cards MC, V
Children welcome
Disabled no special facilities
Pets by arrangement **Closed** Christmas and Feb
Proprietors Tim and Patricia Martin

Scarista House
Island guest-house

Harris has little in the way of hotels, but Scarista would stand out even among the country houses of the Cotswolds.

The converted Georgian manse stands alone on a windswept slope overlooking a wide stretch of tidal sands on the island's western shore. The decoration is elegant and quite formal, with many antiques, but the atmosphere is relaxed and, by the open peat fires, conversation replaces television. The bedrooms, all with private bathrooms, have selected teas and fresh coffee, as well as home-made biscuits. Three of the bedroom are in the main house, with two refurbished suites available in The Glebe building, just behind the house.

Tim and Patricia Martin continue to maintain a high standard. They aim to be welcoming and efficient, but never intrusive, and to preserve that precious private home atmosphere.

One of Scarista's greatest attractions, particularly rewarding after a long walk over the sands, is the meals. The imaginatively prepared fresh local and garden produce and an impressive wine list ensure a memorable dinner in the candle-lit dining room.

Sleat, Isle of Skye, Highland
IV43 8QY

Tel (01471) 833214
Fax (01471) 833277
e-mail kinloch@dial.pipex.com
website www.kinloch-lodge.co.uk

Nearby Clan Donald Centre.
Location in 60-acre grounds, 6
miles (9.5 km) S of Broadford, one
mile (1.5 km) off A851; ample car
parking
Food breakfast, lunch by arrangement, dinner
Price ££
Rooms 14 double, all with bath; all
rooms have TV, radio, hairdryer
Facilities 3 sitting rooms, bar, dining room; fishing
Credit cards AE, MC, V
Children accepted **Disabled** access
reasonable – one ground-floor bedroom **Pets** accepted by arrangement
but not in public rooms
Closed Christmas **Proprietors** Lord
& Lady Macdonald

Kinloch Lodge
Country hotel

This white-painted stone house, in an isolated position with uninterupted sea views, at the southern extremity of the Isle of Skye, now known as the North House, was built as a farmhouse around 1700 and later became a shooting lodge. But it escaped the baronial treatment handed out to many such houses – 'thank goodness,' says Lady Macdonald, whose style is modern interior-designer rather than dark panelling and tartan. It has that easy-going private-house air. The guests' sitting rooms are comfortably done out in stylishly muted colours; there are open fires, and family oil paintings grace the walls. The dining room is more formal, with sparkling crystal and silver on polished tables.

Bedrooms used to be rather small, but have recently been reconfigured to give more space, and all now have en-suites, some with roll-top baths. The Macdonalds recently built the South House with accommodation for themselves and five more double rooms for guests. This new building is quite remarkable as it looks, both inside and out, as old as its 18th century neighbour, and includes a magnificent stone spiral staircase, as wells as a wealth of books, portraits and *objets d'art*.

The food at Kinloch Lodge is renowned – Lady Macdonald has written cookery books and gives cookery demonstrations.

Loch Lochy, by Spean Bridge, Inverness-shire PH34 4EB

Tel (01397) 712685
Fax (01397) 712696
e-mail info@corriegour-lodge-hotel.com **website** www.corriegour-lodge-hotel.com

Nearby Cawdor Castle; Urquhart Castle; Loch Ness; Glencoe.
Location on the road to Skye, between Spean Bridge and Invergarry, in own grounds, 17 miles (27 km) N of Fort William on A82; ample car parking
Food breakfast, dinner
Price ££
Rooms 9; 7 double and twin, 2 single, all with bath; all rooms have TV, hairdryer on request **Facilities** sitting room, bar, dining room, terrace, private beach and jetty, fishing, waterfall **Credit cards** AE, DC, MC, V **Children** accepted over 8 **Disabled** access possible **Pets** not accepted **Closed** Dec and Jan, weekdays Feb and Nov, open for New Year **Proprietors** Ian and Christian Drew

Corriegour Lodge
Lochside hotel

A former Victorian hunting lodge commanding outstanding views over Loch Lochy and set in six acres of mature woodland and garden within the 'Great Glen'. With its own attractive private beach and jetty on the loch, as well as a fishing boat and the services of a private fishing school at its disposal, this is an obvious choice for keen anglers, as well walkers and climbers, pony trekkers and sailors.

The reception hall at Corriegour Lodge is somewhat gloomy, but negative first impressions are quickly dispelled when the proprietor, Christian Drew, comes on the scene. Her friendliness and enthusiasm for the hotel she runs with her son, Ian, are infectious. The decoration throughout the rest of the hotel is cosy and pleasant, with a log fire in the sitting room and magical views over the loch from the large picture windows in the restaurant. Many of the comfortable bedrooms have the same view.

Food is an important element here, using local meat, fish and game. For pudding you could have cloutie dumpling with rum custard. The staff are genuinely friendly and willing to help.

More reports please.

Strachur, Argyll PA27 8BX

Tel (01369) 860279
Fax (01369) 860637
e-mail info@creggans-inn.co.uk
website www.creggans-inn.co.uk

Nearby Inverary town and castle; Loch Fyne; Loch Lomond.
Location on E shore of Loch Fyne; from Glasgow via Loch Lomond and the A83, or from Gourock by car ferry across the Clyde to Dunoon and the A815; ample car parking
Food breakfast, lunch, dinner
Price ££
Rooms 14; 13 double and twin, one suite, all with bath; all rooms have phone, TV, hairdryer **Facilities** 2 sitting rooms, bar, restaurant, garden, country sports
Credit cards MC, V
Children welcome
Disabled access difficult **Pets** not accepted **Closed** never **Proprietors** The MacLellan family

Creggans Inn
Lochside inn

Overlooking Loch Fyne, this former hunting lodge of the 3000-acre Strachur Estate was first opened as an inn some 40 years ago by Sir Fitzroy Maclean. His son, Sir Charles Maclean, set out to transform a fairly simple establishment into something rather more sophisticated, with high standards of modern comfort. The Robertson family took over and conducted refurbishment that included knocking out some walls to create larger (and fewer) rooms. As we went to press, the Inn had just been taken over by the MacLellan family, who plan to continue these improvements, starting with the lounge and dining room.

Head chef Calum Williamson remains, as does second chef Alex Dickson. The food here is excellent: drawing heavily on local products such as scallops and langoustines from Loch Fyne, it is light, inventive and delicious. The wine list is unusually good.

A major natural advantage is the position of the inn. The views over Loch Fyne and across the Mull of Kintyre to the Western Isles are breathtaking. Many parts of the Strachur Estate, including the private flower garden, are open to guests and a wealth of country activities is available, and well priced.

Reports would be welcome.

Strontian, Argll

Strontian, Argyll PH36 4HY

Tel (01967) 402257
Fax (01967) 402041
e-mail enquiries@kilcamblodge.com
website www.kilcamblodge.com

Nearby ferry to Isle of Mull and
Skye; Castle Tioram; Glencoe.
Location Corran ferry to Ardgour
from the A82 near Ballachulish, then
follow A861 to Strontian; in 19 acres
with ample car parking
Food breakfast, light lunch, dinner
Price £££
Rooms 10 double and suites, all with
bath; all rooms have TV, hairdryer,
phone **Facilities** 2 sitting rooms, bar,
restaurant, garden, private beach,
fishing, mountain bikes
Credit cards MC, V
Children welcome
Disabled no special facilities
Closed Jan
Pets accepted by arrangement, £5
per night **Manager** Phillip J.
Fleming

Kilcamb Lodge
Lochside hotel

There is a sense of adventure in travelling to a hotel by ferry, particularly
when it then involves a ten-mile journey,
first alongside a loch and then over a pass
through a steep-sided glen. Drop down
through the glen, pass through the small
village of Strontian, and there, in a romantic setting on the shores of Loch Sunart, is
Kilcamb Lodge.

Originally built in the early 18thC, with
Victorian additions, Kilcamb is a beautifully restored country house with ten bedrooms, some with a loch view. Set amidst
lawns and woodland, filled in spring with
the colours of rhododendrons, azaleas and
many wild flowers, it is a romantic and
calming bolthole, the perfect choice for
nature lovers: sea otters, seals, pine
martens, red and roe deer and golden
eagles can all be seen.

The ground floor public rooms are
pleasantly furnished with light and attractive pastel fabrics. There is a wonderful
Victorian wrought-iron staircase and a
large stained glass window. All the bedrooms are individually decorated and have
triple-lined curtains (it stays light very late
in summer). To cap it all, chef Mark
Greenaway has won awards for his
admirable cooking.

Walls, Shetland Islands

Walls, Shetland Islands, ZE2 9PD

Tel (01595) 809307
Fax (01595) 809213
e-mail burr.hs@zetnet.co.uk **web-site** www.users.zetnet.co.uk/burras-tow-house

Nearby Vaila Sound; Walls.
Location on sea, 2 miles (3 km) W of Walls; ample car parking
Food breakfast, light/packed lunch, dinner
Price ££
Rooms 5; 4 double and twin, one family suite, 4 with bath, 1 with shower; TV, hairdryer on request
Facilities dining room, 2 sitting rooms; boat for exploring area, civil wedding license
Credit cards AE, MC, V **Children** welcome
Disabled access possible; one room specially adapted
Pets accepted by arrangement
Closed Jan, Feb
Proprietor Pierre Dupont

Burrastow House
Seafront guest-house

On the remote west side of Shetland, at the end of the single track road, on a rocky promontory overlooking Vaila Sound and the Island of Vaila, stands this calm, solid 18thC stone house. It has been a guest-house since 1980, and for the last three years has been run with enthusiasm by Pierre Dupont. Peace, quiet, a love of nature and total informality are the keynotes here.

The original bedrooms in the compact main house are the ones to go for if you can. Both are large, and one has a second bedroom which is perfect for children. There are splendid beds in each: a four-poster in one and a half-tester, draped in blue silk, in the other. The newer bedrooms, in the recent extension, have less character, but they're comfortable. In the public rooms there are peat fires, books, an eclectic mix of furnishings and wonderful views from the windows; you may spy seals and otters. Pierre has made his mark with his natural, homely cooking, served in the cosy panelled dining room. Reports would be welcome.

With a temperate climate and a famously leisurely way of life, Ireland (also known in tourist literature as the Emerald Isle) is a place of contrasts and changing light, of mountains, lakes and rivers, lush pastures, bog and wild moorland, and 2,000 miles of coastline with small rocky coves, long sandy beaches, and some of the highest cliffs in Europe. In the most remote parts of the country, you can drive for miles without seeing anything but sheep. But if you want bright lights, music and good food, Ireland has any number of pubs that nightly celebrate the traditional Irish love of music and conversation, and excellent chefs to cook the abundant produce of their native land. Ireland also has a wealth of charming places to stay, and for this new edition of the guide, we have much expanded our selection mainly in Northern Ireland.

Northern Ireland

Shunned for years by travellers because of the troubles, Northern Ireland is now developing into a relatively popular destination. As we went to press, the troubles really did seem to be over. But, the overall quality of hotels is poor and for this reason, you are mostly better off in one of the characterful upmarket guesthouses. We found three such places to add to this edition: **Tyrella House** (page 299); **Newforge House** (page 301); and **The Moat Inn** (page 302). We were sorry to discover that in Belfast **The Old McCausland** has been taken over by the Malmaison chain: the hotel still occupies a fine old commercial building and it has some character, but this is of the slightly forced Malmaison variety (tel 028 9022 0200). A much more genuine alternative is **The Merchant**, now Belfast's top hotel, though certainly not a charming small hotel (tel 028 9023 4888). It is stupidly expensive, but has some character and style. If money is no object, give it a go: you'll be intrigued by the way it has been hewn out of the old Ulster Bank building – amazing dining room ceiling and world-class cocktail bar. **The Crescent Townhouse**, set in an elegant 19thC property, is another useful Belfast address (028 9032 3349). Other recommendations in Northern Ireland include **The Bushmill Inn** (page 298), just a mile from the famous Giant's Causeway, and **Grange Lodge** in Dungannon (page 300).

Irish Republic

The spectacular natural beauty of the Irish Republic is legendary, from the rich farmlands, woodlands, fertile valleys and golden beaches of counties Wicklow and Wexford in the east to the unspoilt coastlines of West Cork and Kerry, the romantic Lakes of Killarney, and the hills and lakes of County Sligo in the west. For a treat, try **Marlfield House** (page 335), in County Wexford; the romantic lakeside **Ard-na-Sidhe** (page 312) or **Temple House** (page 310). **Brownes Brasserie and Townhouse** stands out (page 326) among a surge of new hotels in the flourishing Georgian city of Dublin.

b12 Windsor Avenue, Belfast
BT9 6EE

Tel (028) 90661758
Fax (028) 9066 3227
e-mail ashrowan@hotmail.com

Nearby Ulster Museum; Botanic Gardens; Queen's University.
Location in residential street between the Malone and Lisburn roads; 1 mile
(1.6 km) S of the city centre; private car parking available
Food breakfast, dinner on request
Price ££
Rooms 5; 3 double/twin, 2 single, 3 with bath, 2 with shower; all with phone, TV, hairdryer, trouser press; safe on request **Facilities** sitting room **Credit cards** AE, MC, V
Children over 12 **Disabled** not suitable **Pets** not accepted **Closed** 22 Dec to 6 Jan **Proprietors** Sam and Evelyn Hazlett

Ash-Rowan Lodge
Town guest-house

Sam and Evelyn Hazlett were restaurateurs and love good food and feeding people. The generous breakfasts at this friendly, informal place keep you going throughout the day and there is a varied and interesting menu. The Hazletts' attractive Victorian family house stands in a residential road and the charming hosts are especially popular with classical musicians making guest appearances with the Ulster Orchestra, most probably because of the homely atmosphere.

Bedrooms are decorated in an individual style: they are all comfortable and full of bits and pieces, as is the entire house. All rooms have dressing gowns, and crisp Irish linens on beds. Prettier, quite spacious rooms at the top of the house have sloping attic ceilings, old white crocheted bedspreads, armchairs, plants, mixed colours. There are plenty of family 'things' in corridors and on landings: books, ornaments, a bird cage, old mirrors and porcelain, and dried flowers – fans of the modern minimalist style will not feel at home here, but it adds to the (not at all unpleasant) impression that you could be staying at your gran's house.

Due to its popularity among academics from the nearby university, you may find it is full, in which case Evelyn will recommend nearby Malone Lodge, which she describes as one of few guest-houses in Belfast, beside her own, which are up to scratch.

Bushmills, Co Antrim

25 Main Street, Bushmills, Co Antrim BT57 8QA

Tel (028) 2073 3000
Fax (028) 2073 2048
e-mail mail@bushmillsinn.com
website www.bushmillsinn.com

Nearby Giant's Causeway; Glens of Antrim; golf at Royal Portrush.
Location in main street of village on A2, 5 miles (8 km) E of Portrush; parking
Food breakfast, lunch, dinner
Price ££
Rooms 32; 28 double (22 twin); 24 with bath, 26 with shower; 4 singles with shower; all with phone, TV, with hairdryer, trouser press, computer socket
Facilities bar, restaurant, sitting rooms; terrace, garden
Credit cards AE, MC
Children welcome **Disabled** adapted bedroom **Pets** accepted; not in restaurant **Closed** never **Proprietor** Roy Bolton

The Bushmills Inn
Converted coaching inn

It is difficult to believe that chickens once lived on the first floor when this charming little inn, only a mile from the Giant's Causeway, was going through hard times. All that changed in 1987 when the present owners spotted the potential of the building. The oldest part – now the restaurant – dates back to the early 17th century when the nearby Old Bushmills Distillery was granted the world's first licence to distil whiskey. The entrance, through an archway from the street into the courtyard, leads to the front door in a little whitewashed round tower. Almost the first thing to be seen, once inside, is a glowing fire, which is always lit. A warren of attractive ground-floor rooms includes a small 'snug' – the original kitchen – with a roaring fire and old flagstones; the Victorian-style bar has gas lighting, leather chairs, dark wood panelling and a wooden floor. Bedrooms come in two varieties: older ones, furnished in comfortable cottage style are in the inn itself; newer ones in the Mill House extension – with river views – are larger, with natural wood panelling, rough white walls and their own sitting area. We visited just before going to press, and felt that rooms and food were overpriced, yet it is still very popular – especially with Americans, who perhaps sense a certain Wild West ambience.

Tyrella House. Downpatrick
Co Down

Tel (028) 4485 1422
e-mail tyrella.corbett@virgin.net
website www.hidden-ireland.com/tyrella

Nearby Mountstewart, Castleward
and Rowallane National Trust properties; walking in the Mountains of
Mourne; Royal County Down golf
course, Newcastle.
Location on the A2 Clough to
Ardglass road, just over 5 miles (8
km) from the turning at Clough;
gate lodge on right; private car parking.
Food breakfast; dinner on request, a
day's notice needed.
Price £
Rooms 3, all doubles with bath; tea
making facilities **Credit cards** AE,
MC, V **Children** not suitable
Disabled not suitable **Pets** dogs
accepted, but not in house; stable
available **Closed** Nov-1 March 1,
but parties of three couples visiting
together welcome at any time
Proprietor David Corbett

Tyrella House
Country house bed-and-breakfast

Staying at Tyrella (pronounced Ti-rulla) as David Corbett's guest is to experience in a genuine way the vanishing lifestyle of the Northern Irish landed gentry. It's a fine coun-try house, dating from the 18thC, in its own exclusive world down a longish drive, not another building in sight. The nicely propor-tioned rooms are on a human rather than an intimidating scale, and all around is the accu-mulated brown antique furniture and posses-sions of three generations of Corbetts. Don't expect immaculate paintwork or a trim drive; do expect a relaxed welcome, a large bed-room, a comfortable bed and the feeling of being in a home. David will greet you with tea if you arrive at the right time, and he can cook dinner (as we went to press, £25 for three courses), served on the one table in the graceful dining room. Note the rows of polo trophies on the mantelpiece. The food gets some pleasant compliments in the visitors' book. The house still stands in some 300 acres of its own, now used for equestrian events (David is a horseman) and has its own private beach, which guests can use. His rate of £45 per person for bed and breakfast is highly competitive if you consider that the same is being charged by owners of much less impressive places.

Grange Road, Dungannon, Co
Tyrone BT71 7EJ

Tel (028) 87784212
Fax (028) 87784313
e-mail stay@grangelodgecountry-
house.com
website www.grangelodgecountry-
house.com

Nearby Tyrone; Ulster American
Folk Park
Location in countryside 3 miles (5
km) S of Dungannon off the A 29 to
Armagh; parking available
Food breakfast, dinner
Price ££
Rooms 5; 3 doubles, 1 twin, 1 single;
1 with bath, 1 with hip-bath, 3 with
shower; all with phone, TV, hairdry-
er, tea/coffee making facilities
Facilities sitting rooms; gardens
Credit cards MC, V
Children over 12 **Disabled** not pos-
sible **Pets** welcome outside
Closed 20 Dec to 1 Feb
Proprietors Norah and Ralph
Brown

Grange Lodge
Country house

Our reporter was enchanted by the
setting – on a little hill in large and
lovely gardens – of this rambling, ivy clad,
Georgian house with later additions. But it
is the Grange Lodge table that has won
distinction and found it so many friends.
Norah Brown, who is self-taught, has several awards for her outstandingly good
cooking and she and her husband, Ralph,
are relaxed, easy-going, welcoming hosts.
Much of the fruit, vegetables and herbs she
uses are homegrown and sometimes a
second dining room is opened up to outside groups looking for her special talent
and dishes from her "best friend", the Aga.
Admirers praise the ageless quality of her
food and her sure touch; she says people
have just forgotten what real home cooking is. Her husband has the happy task of
bringing breakfast out from the kitchen:
try Mrs Brown's porridge with brown
sugar, cream and Bushmills whiskey,
rhubarb compote, soda bread and Ulster
grill with potato cake. The sitting room –
there's a 'den' with TV, too – is immaculate,
in elegant dark colours; most surfaces are
crammed with ornaments, family photos,
pewter and plates. Upstairs, ivy pushes at
the window panes of the bedrooms. Some
of Mrs Brown's biscuits are always to be
found on the hospitality tray.

Magheralin, Co Armagh

58 Newforge Road, Magheralin, Craigavon, BT 67 0QL

Tel (028) 9261 1255
e-mail enquiries@newforgehouse.com
website www.newforgehouse.com

Nearby more less in the middle of Northern Ireland, with Belfast half an hour away and the north coast and the Mountains of Mourne (SE) less than two hours' drive.
Location clearly signposted, just off A3, through Magheralin, 1st left onto Newforge Road, with ample private car parking
Food breakfast, dinner
Price ££
Rooms 6 doubles with bath/shower; all rooms have phone, TV, DVD player, hairdryer, wi-fi
Facilities drawing room, dining room; large garden **Credit cards** MC,V **Children** welcome **Disabled** access possible to dining room **Pets** not accepted **Closed** 3 weeks over Christmas and New Year
Proprietors John and Louise Mathers

Newforge House
Country guest-house

For Northern Ireland, this is about as sophisticated as a guest-house gets, in fact it's almost a small hotel. Instead of sharing the owner's home, you have the run of it, not least the graceful drawing room. John and Louise Mathers, the young owners, live in one outbuilding, while John's father has another. Six generations of Mathers (a linen family) have lived here; the latest bowed to the fact that it was too big and converted it to a guest-house, restoring it in the process. The Georgian interior has been respected, but the walls have that clean, smooth modern finish and there's an optimistic, airy atmosphere – windows are tall. The dining room has separate tables, so no communal dining. Another bonus: John is a trained chef, with a professionally fitted kitchen and the food is good: three courses (£27.50) with two choices at each course, ingredients fresh each day. There's a license, and a wine list. Give a day's notice for dinner.

Even the smallest of the six bedrooms, named after family members, is roomy, and all are individually decorated in the best of taste. In fact, they're as smart as many we've seen in chic city hotels. The spacious bathrooms gleam.

You're guaranteed a peaceful night here since the house stands well back from a quiet road just outside Newforge.

Templepatrick, Co Antrim

12 Donegore Hill, Templepatrick
Co. Antrim, BT41 2HW

Tel (028) 9443 2923
e-mail thelma@themoatinn.co.uk
website www.themoatinn.co.uk

Nearby Lough Neagh, Six-Mile
water valley; Templepatrick
Location off the M2 near to
Templepatrick
Food breakfast
Price ££
Rooms 2 doubles with shower; all
rooms have hairdryer, tea and coffee
making; ironing on request
Facilities drawing room, dining
room
Credit cards MC, V
Children welcome
Disabled access not possible
Pets not accepted
Closed Christmans and New Year
Proprietors the McCausland family

The Moat Inn
Guest-house

An enchanting place. With its roots as a 17th century inn, this sky blue and white house, with huge views from the upper floor, is the home of the McCausland family (he is a head teacher) and filled with music, pictures and good books. Thelma McCausland, full of warmth and energy, keeps two bedrooms for guests, with lovely Irish linen on the beds, and plenty of extra touches but no televisions ("we aren't the sort of people to have televisions in bedrooms"). One room is blue and charming, the other deep red, with a wooden ceiling, and striking. Both have bathrooms, with showers, *en suite*. Downstairs, the neat, pretty sitting room is at guests' disposal, as is the elegant dining room, with two white-clothed tables, one for each bedroom. Best of all, Thelma is a great cook: the smell of fresh baking fills the air and guests are treated to fresh cakes at tea and bread at breakfast (Irish soda bread a speciality). The house stands at the top of the hill in little Donegore next to the church. The McCauslands are a family who plainly know the important things in life, and it's a pleasure to spend time in their house. And only 40 minutes from Belfast.

Aghadoe, Co Kerry

Aghadoe, Lakes of Killarney,
Co Kerry

Tel (064) 31711
Fax (064) 31811
e-mail charming@indigo.ie **website**
www.killeenhousehotel.com

Nearby Killarney, 4 miles (6 km);
Muckross House; Gap of Dunloe;
lakes.
Location in countryside, 4 miles (6
km) from Killarney; parking available
Food breakfast, dinner
Price €€
Rooms 23; 8 championship, 15 standard; 8 with king-size double and
single; 2 double, 5 twin, 2 single, 6
double and single; 22 with bath, 1
with shower; all with phone, TV,
radio, hairdryer **Facilities** bar, sitting room; garden, terrace, tennis
court **Credit cards** AE, DC, MC,V
Children welcome if well-behaved
Disabled not possible **Pets** welcome
Closed 1 Nov to 1 Apr **Proprietors**
Michael and Geraldine Rosney

Killeen House Hotel
Country hotel

We had to visit a hotel with 'charming' as its e-mail address. And there it was: a charming small hotel, a rectory built in 1838 and given a bright new white front and architectural twiddly bits painted in red by Michael and Geraldine Rosney, who took it over in 1992. Michael is a jolly, amusing – and kind – person who used to manage the Great Southern Hotel in Killarney. He has created a warm, cosy, entertaining and lively little place, where he spoils his golfing clients and indulges their every whim. He sees them off in the morning and waits for their return in the evening, like an anxious parent. Then he is to be found in The Pub, 'possibly the only place in the universe that accepts golf balls as legal tender', where he dispenses Guinness and sympathy. Nothing is too much trouble for him: he puts phone messages in envelopes and distributes them himself. All this activity provides loads of fun for everyone, especially Michael, and you don't have to be a golfer to benefit from his generous spirit. Comfortable, spacious bedrooms are decorated in checks and plaids; there's a special one with a spa bath that he gives to regular guests as a 'thank you' for coming back again and again. Good showers; excellent food. Rozzers restaurant has been added recently, with chef Paul O'Gorman at the helm.

Aglish, Co Tipperary

Aglish, Borrisokane, Co Tipperary

Tel (067) 21129
Fax (067) 21200
e-mail bally@indigo.ie
website www.ballyc.com

Nearby Terryglass; Birr.
Location in 2 acres of garden, 0.5
mile (1 km) N of Borrisokane, sign-
posted on right; with ample car park-
ing
Food breakfast
Price €
Rooms 5; 3 double, 1 suite, 1 single,
all with bath
Facilities sitting room, dining room;
garden
Credit cards MC, V
Children welcome over 6
Disabled access difficult
Pets lodging available
Closed never
Proprietor John Lang

Ballycormac House
Converted farmhouse

Set amid north Tipperary farmland,
almost exactly in the middle of Ireland,
this is a 300-year-old-farmhouse which has
long been well known as a guest-house.
Since our last edition it has been taken
over from the previous owners, Herbert
and Christine Quigley, by John and
Cherrylyn Lang. Both keen riders and
huntsmen, they keep more than 30 horses
and ponies, and guests may go for rides
and participate in hunts with John. It's also
ideal for guests who simply wish to relax
and enjoy the Tipperary countryside, and a
family-sized hot tub is now available (albeit
at an extra charge) — either to help guests
relax or recover from a hard day's riding.

The Quigleys upgraded this pretty but
compact house, creating a warm and cosy
retreat. There are log fires in winter, and in
summer guests can see the organic herb,
fruit and vegetable gardens which provide
produce for meals. A full Irish breakfast is
served, including home-made preserves,
butter and fruit compote from the garden,
and freshly-baked scones. A large self catering building, Ballycormac Lodge, has been
added recently, sleeping up to 22 people.
Reports would be welcome.

Tipperary farmland

Ardara, Co Donegal

The Green Gate, Ardvally, Ardara,
Co Donegal

Tel (07495) 41546
website www.thegreengate.eu

Nearby Ardara (for tweed);
Glenveagh National Park.
Location 1 mile (1.6 km) from
Ardara, up a hill; with car parking
Food breakfast
Price €
Rooms 4; 2 double, 2 triple; all with
bath and shower
Facilities garden, terrace
Credit cards not accepted
Children welcome
Disabled access possible
Pets welcome in room
Closed never
Proprietor Paul Chatenoud

Donegal coastline

The Green Gate
Cottage bed-and-breakfast

This little place, a tiny farmhouse with stone outbuildings, owned and converted by a Frenchman who came to Donegal 15 years ago to write about "life, love and death", is bursting with charm. The book never got finished, but Paul Chatenoud, who left behind his musical bookshop and flat in Paris for a wilder existence on the top of a hill overlooking the Atlantic, has created what must be the most beautiful small B&B in Ireland. So much love and care has gone into this enterprise; he's done most of it with his own hands, from thatching the cottage roof to plumbing and whitewashing the four guest rooms. Simple they may be, but he thinks of everything: hot water bottles, a map in each room, and a bath in which you can rest your head back and gaze out of the window at the sky and the sea. His garden is filled with primroses, fuchsia and small birds, and he has planted hundreds, if not thousands, of orange montbretia up the lane. Breakfast is taken chez lui; in his own cosy kitchen he serves coffee/tea, cornflakes, bacon, eggs, sausage, toast and 22 types of home-made jam and marmalade – any time before 2 pm. And you get his delightful company. An English composer came for a night and was still there a week later. 'A treasure' says an entry in the visitor's book.

Ballingarry, Co Limerick

Ballingarry, Co Limerick

Tel (069) 68508
Fax (069) 68511
e-mail mustard@indigo.ie
website www.mustardseed.ie

Nearby Adare; Limerick, 18 miles
(29 km); Shannon airport, 33 miles
(53 km).
Location in 7 acres of gardens and
orchard on edge of village; car parking available
Food breakfast, snack lunch, dinner
Price €€€
Rooms 13; 8 double, 2 twin, 1 single, 2 suites; 8 with bath; 5 with
shower; all with phone, TV, hairdryer; 8 with trouser press; safe at
reception
Facilities gardens, terraces
Credit cards AE, MC, V **Children**
by arrangement **Disabled** possible
Pets by arrangement **Closed** Feb
Proprietor Dan Mullane

The Mustard Seed at Echo Lodge **Country house**

Dan Mullane won his spurs with a restaurant in a tiny thatched cottage in Adare, often called the prettiest village in Ireland. Now he's moved his chefs to a shiny new kitchen in a former convent a few miles away, where he's blissfully happy gathering herbs in the vegetable garden and master of a much larger domaine. Echo Lodge is painted yellow, and has blue pots on the doorstep; he's filled the niches left empty when the nuns moved out with figures of Buddha, to whose calming powers he lights candles in the evenings. His regulars are as happy as he is. 'Foodies' flock to his blue-walled dining room with the yellow laburnum outside the window. In season, you may well find a big dark pink peony on the table. Service is smooth, professional and busy. Mullane is very 'hands on'. It takes a brave man to keep the green baize door to the kitchen propped open: he does. Breakfast could be stewed prunes with an Earl Grey and lemon syrup, or porridge with cream and Irish whiskey. Among his many gifts, Dan can design a pretty bedroom, too. He likes French *toiles*, wallpaper striped like a Jermyn Street shirt, and fresh, gleaming white bathrooms; two of his most successful rooms are all in black and white. 'Is this paradise?' asks an Argentinian in the visitors' book.

Ballylickey, Co Cork

Ballylickey, Batry Bay, Co Cork

Tel (027) 50071
Fax (027) 50124
email ballymh@eircom **website**
www.ballylickeymanorhouse.com

Nearby Ring of Kerry; Killarney;
Bantry.
Location in gardens and grounds,
on N17 between Bantry and
Glengariff; car parking available
Food breakfast, lunch, dinner
Price€€€
Rooms 11; 7 suites, 4 double; all
with bath and shower, phone, TV,
hairdryer
Facilities 3 sitting rooms, restau-
rant; garden, terraces, swimming
pool **Credit cards** AE, DC, MC, V
Children welcome **Disabled** pool-
side cottage **Pets** not accepted
Closed end Oct to beginning Apr
Proprietors George and Christiane
Graves

Ballylickey Manor House **Country house hotel**

This Former Shooting Lodge, with romantic view of the sea from the front door, is a grande dame of the Irish country house hotel scene – the first to be accepted by the Relais and Chateaux group in 1967. So it has all the requisite comfort and style – and some extra very French touches added by Christiane Graves' talent with colours, fabrics and antiques. As a pri-vate family house, it was visited many times by the writer and poet, Robert Graves, uncle of owner George Graves, whose mother, Kitty, laid out the lovely gardens. Some rooms are in the main house; one has doors opening on to a little sheltered patio with table and chairs for sitting out; or you may choose simply to let in the sound of birdsong and the wonderful damp smell of the plants and foliage. You are even closer to nature in the blue-grey wooden cottages in the trees and shrubs by the swimming-pool. With the sound of French staff chattering away in the kitchen of the poolside Le Rendez-Vous restaurant – cov-ered in May with clouds of pink clematis – it is not hard to imagine oneself in a Relais and Chateaux in the South of France. Full marks should go to Mr Graves for his deci-sion – possibly an unpopular one with some guests – not to allow parking in front of the house, which wrecks the sea view, by placing obstacles on the gravel driveway.

Ballylickey, Co Cork

Ballylickey, Bantry, Co Cork

Tel (027) 50462
Fax (027) 51555
email info@seaviewhousehotel.com
website
www.seaviewhousehotel.com

Nearby Bantry; Beira Peninsula;
Ring of Kerry.
Location in countryside, just off
N71, 3 miles (5 km) N of Bantry; in
large grounds with ample car parking **Food** breakfast, lunch (Sun
only), dinner
Price €€€
Rooms 25; 15 double, 7 single, all
with bath/shower; 3 family with
bath; all rooms have phone, TV,
hairdryer **Facilities** 2 dining rooms,
2 sitting rooms, TV room, library,
bar; garden **Credit cards** AE, MC,
V **Children** welcome **Disabled** one
specially adapted room **Pets** accepted by arrangement **Closed** Nov-Mar
Proprietor Kathleen O'Sullivan

Sea View House
Country hotel

Kathleen O'Sullivan grew up in this white
Victorian house, a stone's throw from
Ballylickey Bay. In 1978 she turned it into a
successful small hotel. Her plan for an
extension, to give double the number of
rooms, was finally realized in 1990. 'Kathleen
is a delightful hostess,' writes a recent
reporter, and Sea View really is a 'very nice,
quiet comfortable hotel'.

The bedrooms are all similar in style,
beautifully decorated in pastel colours and
floral fabrics with stunning antique furniture
– especially the bedheads and wardrobes,
and matching three-piece suites, collected
or inherited from around the Cork area.
The rooms in the old part of the house are
more irregular and individual. All front
rooms have large bay windows and views of
the garden and sea (through the trees). The
'Garden Suite' downstairs is especially
adapted for wheelchairs.

There are two sitting-rooms – a cosy
front room adjoining the bar and a large
family room at the back. The dining-room
has been extended (though many regulars
do not believe it). Our reporter thought the
food 'excellent and generous'; breakfast was
'wonderful' with a big choice and traditional
Irish dishes, such as potato cakes. The menu
changes daily, and Kathleen is forever exper-
imenting with new dishes – roast smoked
pheasant on the day we visited.

Ballymacarbry, Co Waterford

Glenanore, Ballymacarbry, Co Waterford

Tel (052) 36134
Fax (052) 36540
e-mail hanorascottage@eircom.net
website www.hanorascottage.com

Nearby Dungarvan, 18 miles (29 km); Clonmel, 15 miles (24 km); Blackwater Valley.
Location in Nire Valley, 4 miles (6 km) out of Ballymacarbry; parking available
Food breakfast, packed lunch, dinner
Price €€
Rooms 10; all double/twin; all with Jacuzzi; all rooms with phone, TV, hairdryer; tea/coffee making facilities
Facilities garden, terrace, spa tub
Credit cards MC, V **Children** not accepted **Disabled** not possible **Pets** not accepted **Closed** Christmas week **Proprietors** the Wall family

Hanora's Cottage
Riverside guest-house

Changes have taken place since our last edition at award-winning Hanora's Cottage, built by a little bridge over the river in the beautiful Nire Valley for late owner Seamus Wall's great-grandmother. With the village school and church next door, the picturesque group of buildings and their setting made our inspector think of somewhere in the Pyrenees. The guest-house is a favourite with walkers, who come for the Comeragh Mountains and nearby forests and lakes. Mary Wall puts comfort high on her list and pampers her guests. She has added five new rooms and a spa tub in a conservatory-with-views, where guests may rest aching limbs and emerge refreshed for a candle-lit dinner in the new dining room. Food is prepared by the Walls' talented Ballymaloe-trained son, Eoin, and his wife Judith. In the new extension, brilliantly designed to fit with the rest of the building, Mary has put in a drying and boot room. Bedrooms are large, calm and peaceful, with thick carpets, and most have spa baths (superiors have double Jacuzzis). There are books by the beds, some Tiffany lamps, and quality bedlinen. The breakfast room looks out on to the little stone bridge and Seamus's renowned bread recipes are still being used. Plenty of fruit and freshly-squeezed juices, too. Ask for a front room if you want to fall asleep to the sound of the river.

Ballymote, Co Sligo

Mallymote, Co Sligo

Tel (07191) 83329
Fax (07191) 83808
e-mail stay@templehouse.ie
website www.templehouse.ie

Nearby Sligo, 12 miles (19 km);
Yeats Country; Lissadell House.
Location on 1,000-acre estate, 4
miles (6 km) from Ballymote; park-
ing available
Food breakfast, dinner
Price €
Rooms 6; 2 double, 2 twin, 2 family
rooms; 2 with bath, 3 with shower;
all rooms have hairdryer
Facilities garden, woodland, lake
fishing, boating
Credit cards MC, V
Children welcome, high tea in
kitchen for under-5s
Disabled access difficult
Pets dogs on leads (sheep); sleep in
car **Closed** 30 Nov to 1 Apr
Proprietors Roderick and
HelenaPerceval

Temple House
Country house

Is this a dream? It begins as you enter the
gates of what is a gentle, gracious world
of its own. In parkland filled with fat sheep,
this is a whopper of a Georgian mansion,
the home of the Percevals since 1665.
Much of what you see was refurbished in
1864; electricity was not put in until 1962.
To be overcome by awe and wonder
would be easy were it not for the charm
and kindness of Roderick and Helena
Perceval together with their children and
four dogs. Temple House is very much a
home, and they want it to be enjoyed.

Bedrooms, with marble fireplaces and
much of their original Victorian furniture,
seem to be the size of football pitches –
one is called the 'half-acre'. All the bedrooms and bathrooms have been revamped
since 2005, when Roderick and Helena
took over from Roderick's parents.

As shadows fall, you could take a walk to
the ruins of a 13thC Knights Templar castle
and a Tudor house down by the lake. The
family silver comes out for dinner – an experience in itself; delicious dishes and freshly-
baked bread. Guests dine together at a vast
mahogany table and the atmosphere is that
of a friendly house party. Big breakfasts.

Butlerstown, Co Cork

Butlerstown, Bandon, Co Cork

Tel (023) 40137
Fax (023) 40137
e-mail butlerstownhouse@gmail.com
website www.butlerstownhouse.com

Nearby Kinsale; Clonakilty;
Bandon; Cork.
Location in 10-acre grounds; with
car parking
Food self-catering
Price 1750 euros for 3 nights, 3995
euros for 1 week, 3-day minimum
stay
Rooms 1 self-catering apartment
with 5 double and twin rooms, all
with bath or shower **Facilities** sitting room, dining room, kitchen,
communications room, games room;
garden, terrace, croquet lawn
Credit cards MC, V **Children**
accepted **Disabled** not possible **Pets**
accepted by arrangement **Closed**
Christmas to early Feb **Proprietors**
Elisabeth Jones and Roger Owen

Co Cork coastline

Butlerstown House
Country house

Lis Jones and Roger Owen are an obviously happy couple who appear to be
over the moon with their escape from
South Wales to the lovely light and landscape of West Cork and the elegant spaces
of this delightful Georgian house. Their
pleasure is infectious and gives the place a
special warmth. The airy rooms are filled
with fine antiques – Roger is, usefully, a furniture restorer – and classic colours
enhance the simple lines and architectural
details of the house. A smart navy blue
front door leads into the hall with bifur-
cated staircase; ornate plasterwork in the
house takes the shape of scallop shells,
flowers, grapes, vine leaves and ribbon tied
into bows. Lis's bathrooms are a treat: she
likes brass taps, heated towel rails, blue-
and-white striped tiles. There's a four-
poster in one room and twin French
mahogany beds in another. The sitting
room has a view of the bluebell wood
where badgers roam at night; the dining
room has a long, polished table and Spode
on a Monmouth dresser; and there's an
aga in the huge kitchen. Some of the best
things about living in Butlerstown House,
say Roger and Lis, are the fresh air and the
stars in the West Cork night sky. The
house is now self-catering, accommodating
one group of up to ten adults.

Caragh Lake, Co Kerry

Caragh Lake, Killorglin, Co Kerry

Tel (066) 9769105
Fax (066) 9769282
e-mail ardnasidhe@liebherr.com
website www.killarneyhotels.ie

Nearby Killorglin, 4 miles (7 km);
Killarney, 21 miles (34 km); Dingle
peninsula; golf.
Location in lakeside gardens, 41/2
miles (7 km) from Killorglin; parking
available
Food breakfast, dinner
Price €€€
Rooms 20; 18 double/twin, 2 sin-
gle;18 with bath, 2 with shower; all
with phone, hairdryer; reception
safe; kettle on request; ironing room
Facilities gardens, terraces, boating,
swimming pool nearby
Credit cards AE, DC, MC, V
Children not suitable **Disabled**
downstairs room
Pets not accepted **Closed** 1 Oct to 1
May **Proprietor** Killarney Hotels
Manager Nuala Norton

Ard-na-Sidhe
Lakeside hotel

When we visited Ard-na-Sidhe (Gaelic
for Hill of the Fairies) there
appeared to be no-one about. The lovely
wooded prize-winning gardens, with paths
leading down to little grassy areas by the
lake where there are benches to sit on and
dream, were deserted. Most of the guests,
we were told, were out playing golf. These
golfing hotels are left like the Marie
Celeste during the day, and lucky non-
golfers may have the place to themselves.
This handsome Victorian stone house, festooned with creeper, was built by a Lady
Gordon and is so romantic that you can
be as fanciful as you like. It certainly feels
as if there are fairies about; indeed, behind
the house is a fairy hill, with passages said
to lead to a large cave. But these little
creatures do not like to be seen. All credit must be given to Killarney Hotels for
keeping the house quite uncommercialized
and unspoiled, and bringing in Roy
Lancaster to advise them on the gardens.
There are no facilities here, except natural
ones. But guests are given complimentary
use of the 25-metre pool and sauna at the
group's nearby sister hotels. Bedrooms
(spacious) are in the main house or in the
converted stables (very quiet and tranquil); all have impressive antiques and fabrics Lady Gordon might well have chosen
herself; excellent bathrooms.

Cashel, Co Tipperary

Main Street, Cashel, Co Tipperary

Tel (062) 62707
Fax (062) 61521
e-mail reception@cashel-palace.ie
website www.cashel-palace.ie

Nearby Rock of Cashel; Holycross
Abbey; Clonmel.
Location in gardens, set back off
road in town centre; with car parking
Food breakfast, lunch, dinner
Price €€€€
Rooms 23 (13 in house, 10 in
mews); 12 double, 7 twin, 4 single,
all with bath; all rooms have phone,
TV, hairdryer
Facilities sitting room, 2 dining
rooms, lift, garden, terrace
Credit cards AE, DC, MC, V
Children welcome
Disabled access possible **Pets** not
accepted **Closed** 24 to 30 Dec
Proprietors Pat and Susan Murphy

Cashel Palace Hotel
Converted bishop's palace

This exquisite 18thC former archbishop's
palace is in the historic market town of
Cashel, with its famous and dramatic Rock,
one of Ireland's most visited sites. The story
is that the Devil, in a hurry to fly on his way,
bit a chunk out of the Slieve Bloom
Mountains and dropped it here. From right
outside the hotel drawing room you may
follow the Bishop's Walk, which leads you
through the garden and a grassy meadow to
the Rock and its cluster of grey ruins. In the
garden are two mulberry trees planted in
1702 for the coronation of Queen Anne,
and the descendents of the original hops
planted by one of the Guinness family in the
mid-18thC (there's plenty of the 'black', velvety stuff in the Guinness Bar, with flagged
cellar floor and terracotta walls). There are
four-poster beds, fine antiques and pictures,
and spacious bathrooms – with towelling
gowns – and a magnificent early-Georgian
red pine staircase in the entrance hall with
'barley sugar' banisters. You have the choice
of two restaurants. On a recent visit we
were greeted at reception with a welcome
cup of tea and warm pastries, fresh from the
kitchen. We felt that some of the rooms
were perhaps lacking in charm and atmosphere, and the housekeeping could be better, but the exceptionally friendly and
knowledgeable staff are a great asset.
Reports welcome.

Cashel Bay, Co Galway

Cashel Bay, Co Galway

Tel (095) 31111
Fax (095) 31117
e-mail info@zetland.com
website www.zetland.com

Nearby Aran Islands; Connemara
National Park; Clifden, 14 miles
(22.5 km).
Location in gardens overlooking
Cashel Bay, on N340 to Roundstone
from Galway; car parking
Food breakfast, lunch, dinner
Price €€€
Rooms 20; 10 double; 10 twin; 9
with bath, 1 with shower; all with
phone, TV, radio, hairdryer
Facilities snooker room; tennis-
court; garden; shooting, fishing
Credit cards AE, DC, MC, V
Children welcome
Disabled ground-floor room **Pets**
dogs with baskets permitted in bed-
rooms **Closed** Dec to Feb
Proprietors John and Mona
Prendergast

Connemara National Park

Zetland House Hotel
Country house hotel

The brochure has pretty pictures of a little table laid with a pink cloth and sun-
light slanting through windows into antique-
filled rooms. But we think it is the charming
Prendergast family that brings regulars back
again and again for more of the Zetland
House experience. The setting happens to
be spectacular, in an area of outstanding
beauty, with views over Cashel Bay. Built in
the early 19thC as a shooting lodge, the
hotel is named after the Earl of Zetland,
who was a frequent visitor. Mona
Prendergast and her husband, John, who
trained at the Ritz in Paris, have been joined
by their children: son Ruaidhri has come
home after working in Lille in France; daughter Cliodhna is in the kitchen. No wonder
they've won an AA Care and Courtesy
Award. Nothing is too much trouble. Ask
Mona about the area, and she hurries off to
find for you a copy of a map she has printed
up, so she can show you the best route to
take or where to shop in Galway. Bedrooms
are delightful. The Green Room has its own
door to the garden, fresh, green trellis wallpaper, a marble washstand, and Edward
Lear's Book of Nonsense on the bedside
table. A fire is lit every morning in one of the
sitting rooms; there's an eye-catching collection of china plates. Annilan Lodge, a self
catering cottage in the grounds, has been
opened to offer a further five rooms.

Castlebaldwin, Co Sligo

Castlebaldwin, Boyle, Co Sligo

Tel (07191) 65155
Fax (07191) 65455
e-mail info@cromleach.com
website www.cromleach.com

Nearby Yeats Country; Lissadell House; Carrowkeel Cairns; Sligo.
Location in own farmland, near village of Ballindoon; car parking
Food breakfast, dinner; Sun lunch
Price €€€€
Rooms 10; all double/twin; all with bath and shower; all rooms with phone, TV, minibar, hairdryer, safe
Facilities sitting room, bar; garden, terrace, fishing, helipad
Credit cards AE, DC, MC, V
Children welcome; cot; private family dining room
Disabled not possible **Pets** dogs welcome **Closed** never **Proprietors** Christy and Moira Tighe

Cromleach Lodge
Restaurant-with-rooms

A small miracle: from modest beginnings as a bungalow with B & B for fishermen on Christy Tighe's family farm overlooking Lough Arrow, this unique little place has a string of coveted awards to its name. The modern design may not suit all tastes, but the Tighes were determined it should not be a blot on the green and beautiful landscape. So the building is long and low, under a slate roof, and looks as if it has grown out of the hillside. Ever-changing skies, still waters of the lake, cattle in the fields and blue-grey hills in the distance have a strangely calming effect. But the 'lodge' is no country bumpkin; the Tighes' renowned professionalism and standards of excellence are everywhere. Every room has the gorgeous view. Bedrooms are sophisticated and Moira Tighe's thoughtful touch much in evidence. The hairdryer is where it should be: on the dressing table. There are flowers and fruit; fresh milk for tea; chairs enticingly placed by the picture windows; every toilet requisite imaginable in the gleaming bathrooms. In the evenings, beds are turned down and curtains drawn. Christy knows about walks, archaeological sites and Yeats Country; Moira presides over her all-female classy kitchen. A special place, worth a special journey. The Tighes plan to more than double the number of rooms and add a spa. Reports welcome.

Castlegregory, Co Kerry

Cappatigue, Castlegregory,
Co Kerry

Tel (066) 7139196
Fax (066) 7139196
website www.theshorescountry-house.com

Nearby Tralee; Dingle; Killarney; golf at Ballybunion.
Location 1 mile (1.6 km) W of Stradbally on Connor Pass; with car parking
Food breakfast, packed lunch, dinner (Mon to Fri)
Price €
Rooms 6; 3 double, 2 twin, 1 triple, 3 with bath, 3 with shower; all rooms have phone, TV, hairdryer
Facilities sitting room; garden
Credit cards AE, DC, MC, V
Children welcome
Disabled ground-floor room available **Pets** not accepted
Closed 15 Nov 15 Feb **Proprietor** Annette O'Mahony

The Shores Country House **Country guest-house**

We heard glowing reports of The Shores – on the north side of the Dingle peninsula – on our travels, and of farmer's wife Annette O'Mahony's passion for looking after guests. She has more or less rebuilt her house to add on three extra rooms so that she can get her hands on some more people to cosset. The setting for the house is fabulous: just over the road in front is the 26-mile long sandy Brandon Bay beach; in five minutes, you can be in the sea. Towering up behind is Mount Brandon, the second highest mountain in Ireland. All rooms have sea views. One has its own balcony; there's a long balcony, too, for general use. And there's a library. Annette takes, as she says, "exceptional pride" in the interior decorating of the house, and there are all kinds of charming details in her rooms, such as writing desks, porcelain dolls, Laura Ashley papers and fabrics, cream and white bedlinen. Her style could loosely be described as Victorian. In her new cherry-wood kitchen she makes porter cake to accompany a welcome cup of tea on arrival, scrambles eggs and pours maple syrup over waffles for breakfast. Milk is from the farm. For dinner, there might well be beef raised on O'Mahony pastures, fresh salmon, prawns in garlic butter. Flasks of coffee and packed lunches hold you over through the day.

Clifden, Co Galway

Ballyconneely Road, Clifden,
Co Galway

Tel (095) 21384
Fax (095) 21314
e-mail ardaghhotel@eircom.net
website www.ardaghhotel.com

Nearby Kylemore Abbey;
Connemara National Park.
Location on coast road S of Clifden;
car parking
Food breakfast, bar lunch, dinner
Price €€€
Rooms 21; 16 double/twin, 3 suites,
2 family; 19 with bath, 4 with shower
only; all rooms with phone, TV,
radio, hairdryer; tea/coffee making
facilities; safe at reception
Facilities bar lounge, restaurant, sun
room; garden, terrace
Credit cards AE, DC, MC, V
Children welcome **Disabled** not
possible **Pets** accepted
Closed Nov to Easter or Apr 1
Proprietors Monique and Stephane
Bauvet

The Ardagh Hotel
Coast hotel and restaurant

This is so close to the sea you feel you could reach out and dip your toe in the water. The view from the restaurant over Ardbear Bay is fabulous: light and colours constantly change; sunsets are memorable. This small family hotel has an Alpine flavour that gives it considerable charm. Monique Bauvet's Dutch father bought the site and blasted a hole out of the limestone hillside for the blue and yellow, gabled, chalet-style building. She's the chef, housekeeper and gardener; her seafood chowder is a treat; her rooms are pristine (she's phasing out the flowery look for something more bright and contemporary); she made the garden among the rocks. Her husband, Stephane, can be found behind the front desk, or serving wine, and is always ready to help. They met in Switzerland and their hotel has a satisfying combination of friendliness and reliable, discreet efficiency. Locals frequent the downstairs bar lounge; Billie Holliday plays in the dining room; the son of the house plays football in the car park with the receptionist. Not all the well-equipped rooms have sea views; ask when booking. Tucked under the eaves, a sunny sitting room for residents has piles of magazines and a profusion of greenery. (In high season the coast road in front of the hotel could be busy.) We revisited before going to press and were pleased to find things as good as ever.

Clifden, Co Galway

Ballyconneely Road, Clifden,
Co Galway

Tel (095) 21460
e-mail info@mallmorecountry-
house.com **website** www.mallmore-
countryhouse.com

Nearby Clifden; Connemara
National Park; Kylemore Abbey.
Location a mile out of Clifden town
centre; in own 35-acre grounds on
Ardbear peninsula; car parking
Food breakfast
Price €
Rooms 6; 3 double, 1 twin, 1 family
room with 1 double and 2 singles, 1
with 1 double and 1 single; all with
showers and spring water, wi-fi;
hairdryers in most rooms
Facilities gardens and woodland
Credit cards not accepted
Children welcome; 20% discount
Disabled possible **Pets** not permit-
ted in rooms **Closed** 1 Nov to 1 Mar
Proprietors Alan and Kathleen
Hardman

Mallmore House
Country bed-and-breakfast

The Hardmans breed Connemara
ponies, for showing and dressage;
these hardy little natives are often kept
beside the drive to the family's lovingly
restored house with a cheery red front
door and late Georgian porch. The place is
stiff with historical interest: Baden Powell,
founder of the Boy Scouts, used to spend
his holidays here. Alan and Kathleen
Hardman came from The New Inn at
Tresco on the Isles of Scilly to work for
themselves and found the house in a
derelict state: only one room had been
used since the 1920s. From the back of the
house there is a lovely view through trees
over the bay to Clifden and out to the
Atlantic. You can walk down to the sea
through the orchard and past the old cottage. Rooms in this unusual and intriguing,
mainly single-storey house, with original
pitch pine floors, have a variety of views;
for water ask for Room 4. One room has
the original washbasin, and wallpaper with
a pattern of birds; another original wide
shutters, yellow paper, a Bonnard print and
spotless bathroom. Award-winning breakfasts are served in the dining room, which
also has its original shutters; tables have
pink cloths. On the menu: smoked salmon
pancakes; smoked mackerel; Irish bacon.
Very much a family affair; a daughter bakes
brown bread each evening.

Clifden, Co Galway

Beach Road, Clifden, Co Galway

Tel (095) 21369
Fax (095) 21608
e-mail thequay@iol.ie
website www.thequayhouse.com

Nearby Connemara National Park;
Galway, 50 miles (80 km).
Location on quay, 3 minutes by car
from Clifden town centre; car park-
ing in road
Food breakfast
Price €€
Rooms 14; 5 superkings, 9 double (4
twin); all with bath and shower; all
rooms with phone, TV, radio,
hairdryer; 6 with balcony
Facilities sitting room; garden, ter-
race
Credit cards AE, MC, V
Children welcome **Disabled**
ground-floor rooms Pets not accept-
ed **Closed** mid-Nov to mid-Mar
Proprietors Paddy and Julia Foyle

The Quay House
Town house

Paddy Foyle is a celebrated mover and
shaker in this rapidly-getting-very-hip
little seaside town, where he was born in
room 12 of Foyle's Hotel. He is also the
owner of the stylish Quay House, down on
the harbour wall where the fishing boats
tie up. A natural interior decorator, he has
the boldness and panache of a set designer: the house, built in 1820 for the harbourmaster, is a stage for his fanciful ideas
and outbursts of colour. You have the distinct sense you are in a producion of some
kind – is it an opera? a film? – as you pass
through the wondrous rooms. A favourite
theme is Scandinavian: washed-out, dis-
tressed paintwork; plenty of grey and
Nordic blue; wooden pannelling; striped
fabrics. One room is a riot of blue *tiolle de
Jouy*; there's a Napolean Room at the top of
the house; another has a frieze of scallop
sea shells. It's pretty; it's fun. But Paddy is a
restless pacer, always moving on, so expect
changes. He's already stuck a bay on to the
old flat-fronted house, brought the place
next door and turned it into studios.

On a recent visit we were once again
enchanted by the originality of the place,
and found Paddy as full of charm as ever. A
must if you are in this part of Ireland, and
well worth a detour.

Clifden, Co Galway

Clifden, Co Galway

Tel (095) 21035
Fax (095) 21737
e-mail enquiry@rockglenhotel.com
website www.rockglenhotel.com

Nearby Clifden; Connemara
National Park; Kylemore Abbey.
Location in own grounds by the sea,
1.5 miles (2 km) S of Clifden on the
N59 to Galway; with car parking
Food breakfast, bar lunch, dinner
Price €€
Rooms 26; 23 double and twin, 3
family, all with bath or shower; all
rooms have phone, TV, hairdryer
Facilities dining room, sitting room,
TV room, snooker; garden, croquet,
putting, tennis
Credit cards AE, DC, MC, V
Disabled ground-floor rooms avail-
able **Pets** not accepted **Closed** mid-
Jan to mid-Mar **Proprietors** Paedar
and Susan Nevin

Rock Glen Country House Hotel **Country hotel**

With clematis and Virginia creeper around the front door, Rock Glen is a proud winner of an award for the Most Romantic Hotel in Ireland and it is full of charm. The setting of this former shooting lodge, built in 1815, is glorious: in front of the hotel, a path through a meadow of long grass and wild flowers, leads to the shore-line. A yacht bobs about at anchor in the little bay. In the evenings, Connemara ponies and cattle come down to the water's edge. Rising up behind the hotel are the Twelve Pins mountains. With miles of sandy beach-es nearby and rugged countryside criss-crossed with drystone walls, it's a lovely place to walk, or simply to sit and quietly enjoy watching the ebb and flow of the tide. Hosts Paedar and Susan Nevin (who was born in Clifden) took over from John and Evangeline Roche in 2004. On a recent visit we were impressed with the food in the enchanting candle-lit dining room, where Fabrice Galand produces dishes with a strong Irish/French influence. The hotel was buzzing with people from the Connemara pony sales and the bar came alive in the evening, with a pianist and peat fires adding to the cosy ambience and jolly atmosphere.

Bedrooms are small but comfortable and well decorated. The Nevins are determined to make a success of it and have clearly worked very hard. Reports welcome.

Clones, Co Monaghan

Clones, Co Monaghan

Tel (047) 56007
Fax (047) 56033
e-mail mail@hiltonpark.ie
website www.hiltonpark.ie

Nearby Castle Coole and Florence
Court (National Trust); Armagh.
Location 3 miles (5 km) S of Clones,
near Clones Golf Club; in 500 acres
of parkland, woods, lakes; car parking
Food breakfast, dinner
Price €€€
Rooms 6; 5 double, 1 twin; all with
bath; all rooms have hairdryer, electric blankets and hot water bottles.
Facilities gardens; games room;
grand piano; pike and brown trout
fishing; rods; boating on lake
Credit cards MC, V **Children** over
7 by arrangement **Disabled** not possible **Pets** by arrangement **Closed**
end Sept to end Mar except for
group bookings **Proprietors** Johnny
and Lucy Madden

Hilton Park
Country house

In the Hidden Ireland group of country
houses taking paying guests is Hilton
Park – home of the Madden family since
1734 and remodelled in the Italianate
manner in the 1870s. It is grand, beautiful,
and most evocative of the great days of the
Irish country house. Johnny Madden
emerges out of his huge front door under
the portico to greet his guests. A wizard
with bacon, he prepares breakfast, which is
served in the old servants' hall below
stairs. He and his wife Lucy, a food writer
and accomplished cook, are memorably
delightful hosts. Their son Fred, who
trained as a chef in London, now joins Lucy
in the kitchen. Many family stories are to
be told about the guest bedrooms: one
was Johnny's when he was a child.

Little seems to have changed over the
years, though one of the rooms has been
renovated since our last visit. The wallpaper
in the Blue Room, with a four-poster bed
and stunning view down to the lake, was put
up in 1830. On our visit, the lace curtains
had just come out of a box opened for the
first time since 1927. Next door, a roll-top
bath, marble washstand, print of Landseer's
Hunters at Grass, and the scent of jasmine
from plants in pots arranged at the foot of
the tall window, all add to the grace and
charm. Lucy's dinner is by candle-light, with
fresh produce from her garden.

Cloyne, Co Cork

Cloyne, Middleton, Co Cork

Tel (021) 4652534
Fax (021) 4652534
e-mail barnabrow@eircom.net
website www.barnabrowhouse.ie

Nearby Youghal; Cork.
Location in 40 acres of gardens and woodland; car parking
Food breakfast, lunch, dinner
Price €€€
Rooms 19; 11 double, 4 twin, 4 family rooms; 2 with bath 17 with shower; all with phone, hairdryer
Facilities garden, terraces
Credit cards MC, V
Children welcome
Disabled ground-floor rooms
Pets accepted if well-behaved
Closed Christmas week **Proprietor** Geraldine Kidd

Barnabrow House
Country house and restaurant

Opened at the back gate, as it were, of nearby Ballymaloe, this could be called a 'cutting edge' country house. No faded chintzes or family portraits here. Semi-minimalist interiors, with bold, bright colours, moden design and vast expanses of gleaming wood floors look as if they have come out of glossy magazines. So many guests ask how they can achieve the Barnabrow look that owner/chef Geraldine Kidd has a list of suppliers ready and the Ironwoods Shop has been opened so that people can buy the African furniture and crafts that fill the house. The flooring, one learns, is teak from environmentally managed forests in Zimbabwe and the pointed, cone-shaped lamps in the restaurant can be bought in Cork. Behind the rejuvenated 17thC main house is a coach house with floors painted white and elsewhere much orange, pink and yellow; a rustic stone cottage; and restaurant with an outdoor timber terrace. Hens that are very free-range provide fresh eggs; organic produce for the table comes from the kitchen garden; Barnabrow even has its own spring for lashings of crystal-clear water.

Barnabrow House's main business is now weddings, but B&B is still available Sunday to Wednesday, and all week in the quieter months.

Dingle, Co Cork

Upper John Street, Dingle,
Co Kerry

Tel (066) 9151518
Fax (066) 9152461
e-mail info@pax-house.com
website www.pax-house.com

Nearby Killarney, 42 miles (68 km);
Mount Brandon; Tralee, 30 miles (48
km).
Location in countryside, half a mile
(0.8 km) out of Dingle town; signposted on N86; car parking
Food breakfast
Price €€€
Rooms 13; 8 double, 4 double and
single, 1 single; 5 with bath, 8 with
shower; all with phone, TV, radio,
hairdryer, trouser press, tea/coffee
making facilities
Facilities lounge, dining room; garden, patio, terraces **Credit cards**
AE, MC, V **Children** accepted
Disabled not possible **Pets** if well-
behaved **Closed** 1st Dec to 1st Mar
Proprietor John O'Farrell

Pax House
Guest-house

There is an abundance of wild fuchsia in
the hedgerows of the little lanes
around Pax House, high on a green hill
looking down over Dingle Bay. Before
breakfast, you can take an early walk down
to the shore, or, from the terrace, count
the cows coming out of the milking parlour of the farm below this rather odd
building that was once a retirement home.
John O'Farrell took over from the Brosnan-
Wrights in the summer of 2006, having
worked in the hospitality business for
more than 30 years, in such diverse places
as Switzerland, Thailand, America and
Spain. He has since repainted the house, all
bedrooms have fresh flowers, and a collection of original paintings, prints and sculp-
tures fill the house.

Most rooms have showers; cold taps produce water from the house's own spring
well. John serves a notably varied breakfast,
from a full Irish to pears in white wine,
honey and clove syrup, and kippers in a
lemon butter sauce. From the dining room
you can see the field on Sleahead that
starred in a film with Tom Cruise, and over
to the Ring of Kerry. The silence on the
green hill is blissful, but Dingle, a swinging little town, with its full share of traditional
music, pubs and restaurants, much frequented by celebs, is only a short walk away.

Donegal, Co Donegal

St Ernan's Island, Donegal,
Co Donegal

Tel (07497) 21065
Fax (07497) 22098
e-mail res@sainternans.com
website www.sainternans.com

Nearby Donegal Town, 2 miles (3 km); Sligo, 42 miles (67.5 km).
Location 2 miles out of Donegal on the N15; follow signposts; parking
Food breakfast, dinner
Price €€€
Rooms 6; all double/twin; all with bath/shower, 3 with full shower; all with phone, TV, radio, hairdryer
Facilities gardens, woodland and shore walks
Credit cards MC, V
Children not under 6
Disabled not possible **Pets** not accepted **Closed** end Oct to mid-Apr **Proprietors** Brian and Carmel O'Dowd

Saint Ernan's House
Island hotel

This small sugar-pink hotel on a wooded island caters for those who want peace and quiet and is tireless in striving for perfection. On a part of the Donegal coastline that has a natural serenity, the house was built in the 1820s by a nephew of the Duke of Wellington for his sick wife, who needed sea air to cure her of a debilitating cough. More recently a retirement home for clergy and a restaurant-with-rooms, it was bought in 1987 by banker Brian O'Dowd and his wife, Carmel, a teacher, who have gradually been restoring it to the country house it once was. The pursuit – and entrapment – of peace and quiet has produced a most pleasing and civilized result. And four-star comfort. From almost every window there is a view of mesmerising, still water, and Carmel has filled the house with antiques, pictures and pretty fabrics. The most coveted bedroom is the cosy attic, with views down over water and trees. The tone of the place is immediately set by the fact that there are no tables or chairs for sitting outside. The dress code prohibits sandals and shorts; there's no TV downstairs, either. A leisurely five-course meal in the evening rounds off the day. "A strange little breed" says Mrs O'Dowd, affectionately, of the peace and quiet aficionados. Wise, too.

Drinagh, Co Wexford

Drinagh, Wexford, Co Wexford

Tel (053) 58885/58898
Fax (053) 58885
e-mail killianecastle@yahoo.com
website www.killianecastle.com

Nearby Wexford; Rosslare;
Waterford Harbour; Kilmore Quay.
Location in farmland, 3 miles (5 km)
from Wexford; car parking
Food breakfast
Price €
Rooms 8; 3 double, 3 twin, 2 family;
6 with bath; 2 with shower; all rooms
with TV, hairdryer; iron in corridor;
tea/coffee making facilities under
stairs
Facilities garden; terrace; tennis
court; public telephone
Credit cards MC, V **Children** wel-
come **Disabled** not suitable **Pets** not
in house **Closed** 1 Dec to 1 Mar
Proprietors Jack and Kathleen
Mernagh

Killiane Castle
Farmhouse

Those who have already found Killiane
Castle tend to have that special expres-
sion worn by people who have a secret
they want to keep to themselves. For this is
a remarkable place and farmer's wife,
Kathleen Mernagh, a most charming and
thoughtful hostess. The Mernaghs' early
18thC house was built inside the walls of a
largely intact Norman castle, complete with
tower (now listed) and dungeon. From the
back rooms, you see the ruins of a small
chapel in a field and the marshes running
down to the sea. Down a leafy lane, miles
from the main road, it seems centuries away
from everywhere else. Twice a day, you can
hear the hum of machines as the cows file
in and out of the milking parlour. Kathleen
Mernagh, mother of five boys, loves what
she does and she does it extremely well.
Long before she married a farmer she
worked in hotel management. Our reporter
heard one guest say to another at breakfast
(Jack Mernagh serves his wife's dishes): "It's
just like a small hotel." Some bedrooms
overlook the weeping ash at the front of
the house; more interesting ones overlook
the courtyard and over the castle walls to
green countryside beyond. All are spacious,
well-equipped and comfortable. Happy
birds twitter and swoop over the rooftops
of this historic place, only a short drive
from Rosslare.

22 St Stephen's Green, Dublin 2

Tel (01) 638 3939
Fax (01) 638 3900
e-mail info@brownesdublin.com
website www.brownesdublin.com

Nearby Grafton Street; Trinity
College; Temple Bar.
Location overlooking St Stephen's
Green; car parking
Food breakfast, lunch, dinner
Price €€€
Rooms 11; 5 double, 2 twin/double,
3 single, 1 junior suite; all with bath;
all rooms with phone, TV, radio,
hairdryer, air-con, ISDN and fax
lines; iron and ironing board by
request;
safe in office **Facilities** drawing
room **Credit cards** all major
Children welcome **Disabled** possi-
ble **Pets** by arrangement **Closed**
Christmas Day
Proprietor Stein Group **Manager**
John Clarke

Brownes Townhouse
Restaurant-with-rooms

This classy B&B is decidedly not in the
minimalist mode of the smart new
Fitzwilliam (located nearby), more an ode to
Georgian Dublin: an elegant, listed townhouse on St Stephen's Green, only a few
doors down from the Shelbourne. Previous
owner Barry Canny spent more than £1m
on refurbishing what used to be the club-
house of The Order of Friendly Brothers of
St Patrick, founded in the 18thC to stop
duelling. It is sumptuous. Brownes has
recently been taken over by the Stein
Group, who have further renovated the
place, aiming to introduce modern comforts
without altering its character and charm.
Bathrooms have pink Alicante marble
counter tops; bedrooms have fax and ISDN
lines and 'laptop capability'. Some are on the
smallish side. The classic Georgian exterior
is untouched; inside great care has gone into
keeping to the style of the building. The
drawing-room has an Adam fireplace moved
from a floor above and the room's
mahogany door has been copied for all the
bedrooms. An ingenious front suite doubles
as an office, with a bed that folds away in the
wall to become bookshelves, and a boardroom table that breaks up into smaller
tables. The restaurant at street level has
been described as a bit 'fin-de-siècle Paris';
guests have it to themselves for breakfast.

70 Adelaide Road, Dublin 2

Tel (01) 475 5266
Fax (01) 478 2841
e-mail info@kilronanhouse.com
website www.kilronanhouse.com

Nearby Grafton Street; National
Gallery; Trinity College.
Location 5 minutes walk S of St
Stephen's Green; private, secure car
parking
Food breakfast
Price €€
Rooms 15; 11 double (8 twin), 2 sin-
gle, 2 family; all with shower; all
with phone, TV, hairdryer; safe and
free internet in reception
Facilities sitting room **Credit cards**
AE, DC, MC, V
Children over 10
Disabled no special facilities
Pets not accepted
Closed never
Proprietor Leon Kinsella

Kilronan House
Town guest-house

This veteran, reasonably-priced Georgian
guest-house in a quiet, leafy, residential
street near St Stephen's Green has been in
business for more than 35 years and is
perfectly situated for walking to some of
the city's most famous landmarks and shops.
A new owner has recently taken over and
refurbished the place, bringing it up to
date. Our reporter was impressed with
the warm, yellow walls and parquet floor
of the entrance hall and the welcoming
reception area tucked under the stairs.
Bedrooms are on four 'creaking' floors,
and it is a long climb to the top. Some are
on the small side. Colours tend to be yellow again, with elegant fabrics and pretty,
white-painted wrought-iron bedheads,
some pine furniture, heavy off-white curtains and the odd print on the walls. We
were told of one room – below ground
level – that was described as 'tiny', so it is
clearly advisable to check in advance
which rooms are available. The yellow sitting room has a big, gilt-edged mirror over
the fireplace, antique furniture and a chandelier. The yellow extends to the breakfast
room, with shining silver and crisp white
linens on the tables. The overall feel of the
place is old-fashioned, comfortable and
relaxed. Reports, please.

31 Leeson Close, Dublin 2

Tel (01) 676 5011
Fax (01) 676 2929
e-mail info@number31.ie
website www.number31.ie

Nearby St Stephen's Green;
National Gallery; Grafton Street,
Trinity College.
Location just off Lower Leeson
Street; 5 minutes walk from St
Stephen's Green; car parking
Food breakfast
Price €€€-€€€€
Rooms 20; 15 double (12 twin), 5
family; 17 with bath, 3 with shower;
all with phone, TV, DVD player,
hairdryer, wi-fi; safe at reception
Facilities sitting room, breakfast
room, conservatory; garden **Credit
cards** all major **Children** welcome
Disabled not suitable **Pets** not
accepted **Closed** never **Proprietors**
Noel and Deirdre Comer

Trinity College, Dublin

Number 31
Town guest-house

This is a very special and visually pleasing place: a mews house designed in the mid-1960s by controversial Dublin architect, Sam Stephenson, and the Georgian house across the garden that was acquired giving much more space. The delightful Noel and Deirdre Comer, former owners of Kilronan House (page 327), loved the originality from the outset. Only a plate on the wall with '31' on it indicates this is somewhere you may stay. The Stephenson building is modern and open-plan, with painted white brickwork and much glass, wood and stone; kilims hang on the wall. There's a little sunken sitting area, with a black leather sofa custom-built around the fire. French windows and wooden decking lead to the garden and the back of the Georgian house. Deirdre's generous and delicious breakfasts (homemade breads, jams, potato cakes, granola) are served in a white upstairs room on long tables with fresh flowers, sparkling silver, and white linen napkins. Five stylish bedrooms are in the mews house (two have patios). Fifteen more are in the Georgian house, with moulded ceilings and painted in National Trust colours. The Comers completed a thorough refurbishment in 2007, replacing all bathrooms and beds and bringing the place up to modern standards.

Dublin

12 South Frederick Street, Dublin 2

Tel (01) 617 0900
Fax (01) 617 0999
e-mail trinitylodge@eircom.net
website www.trinitylodge.com

Nearby National Art Gallery;
Temple Bar; Dublin Castle; the
Liffey.
Location a short walk from Trinity
College; with limited car parking
(with charge; booking essential)
Food breakfast
Price €€
Rooms 16; 8 double, 6 twin, 2 sin-
gle, all with shower; all rooms have
phone, TV, air-conditioning,
hairdryer, safe **Facilities** sitting
room
Credit cards AE, MC, V **Children**
welcome
Disabled not possible **Pets** not
accepted **Closed** 23 to 26 Dec
Proprietor Peter Murphy

Trinity Lodge
Town guest-house

Owner Peter Murphy opened this three-storey Georgian house in the heart of Dublin just off Nassau Street opposite Trinity College – in 1997 as an elegant, little guest-house that would not have any of the things he hates about hotels. So, guests are given individual atten-tion from the moment they step in through the blue front door and he places a candle in each room to give a special romantic glow to evenings. This is a handsome, listed building and in order to keep its character and symmetry, Peter chose not to put in a lift, or carve chunks out of rooms for bath-rooms. But, he's got almost everything else in the way of comfort and convenience, such as air-conditioning, trouser presses and personal safes. Colours are appropri-ately Georgian: green, deep red, yellow. There's a little sitting area in the entrance hall, with a window looking on to the street and some comfortable armchairs. Pictures in the house are by the Dublin artist, Graham Knuttel, who lives next door and whose work is very popular with Hollywood stars (he had a commission to paint a portrait for Robert de Niro). They are in bold bright colours and, as one of the staff observes, "have very suspicious-looking people in them, who don't want to look directly at you". You can walk easily to all the local sights from here

Dunkineely, Co Donegal

St John's Point, Dunkineely,
Co Donegal

Tel (07497) 37022
Fax (07497) 37330
e-mail castlemurray@eircom.net
website www.castlemurray.com

Nearby Donegal.
Location a mile (1.6 km) off the
main N56 from Donegal to
Killybegs, signposted in Dunkineely;
parking
Food breakfast, dinner
Price €€
Rooms 10 (9 with sea view); 5 dou-
ble, 5 twin; 2 with bath, 2 with show-
er; all with phone, TV, hairdryer,
tea/coffee making facilities
Facilities bar; garden, terrace
Credit cards MC, V
Children welcome **Disabled** not
possible **Pets** small dogs in rooms
Closed end Jan to beginning Feb
Proprietors Martin and Marguerite
Howley

Castle Murray House
Country restaurant-with-rooms

This charming little place has changed
hands since our last edition, with father
and daughter Martin and Marguerite
Howley now in charge. The setting of
Castle Murray House could be called magical. In front of the hotel, bright green fields
with low, drystone walls run down to the
sea and a small ruined castle on the point
is illuminated as night falls. Across the bay,
the sun goes down over the Slieve League,
the highest sea cliffs in Europe.

The restaurant is renowned for its local-
ly-caught seafood, including lobsters which
potter about in a tank by the raised, open
fire. Head chef Rem Dupuy creates 'French
dishes with an Irish touch' and the menu is
based on local, seasonal produce.

Up a pine staircase, bedrooms we felt
were a touch basic on our last visit have
since been redone, with modern bathrooms. The Howleys have also turned
their attention to the gardens and added a
new deck.

Reports welcome.

Galway, Co Galway

Killeen, Bushypark, Galway,
Co Galway

Tel (091) 524179
Fax (091) 528065
e-mail killeenhouse@ireland.com
website
www.killeenhousegalway.com

Nearby Galway city centre, 4 miles
(6 km); Connemara; the Burren.
Location in grounds, 4 miles (6 km)
from centre of Galway; car parking
Food breakfast
Price €€
Rooms 6; 4 double,1 twin, 1 triple; 5
with bath and shower; 1 with shower; all with phone, TV, radio,
hairdryer, tea/coffee making facilities, wi-fi **Facilities** drawing room,
dining room; garden
Credit cards AE, DC, MC, V
Children not suitable for children
under 12 **Disabled** not suitable **Pets**
not accepted **Closed** 1 week at
Christmas **Proprietor** Catherine
Doyle

Killeen House
Guest-house

What originality and imagination Catherine Doyle has shown in creating such charming quarters for guests in her fascinating early Victorian house. While the approach is somewhat dispiriting, through the outer suburbs of Galway and past new housing developments, once you get beyond the castellated gateway into the 25-acre garden and grounds, all that is forgotten in a trice. The interiors, packed with unusual antiques and bric-a-brac, are a feast for the eyes. The idea behind the bedrooms, Catherine explains, was 'to give everyone something different'. So, she has taken historical periods as themes: Regency; Victorian; Edwardian; Art Nouveau. But these are not artificial pastiches: they are comfortable, welcoming rooms that reflect the care Catherine puts into every aspect of running the house. (She writes the breakfast menu out by hand.) The detail goes right down to the sheets and hand towels. Each room has a reproduction radio, to fit in with the general style; each room even has its own pair of 'period' binoculars, for looking at birds when you take the path leading through the garden, past an old cottage, down to the shores of Lough Corrib. There is also the Garden Suite; modern, for a change, with bright blue and yellow carpet and painted chairs.

Glin, Co Limerick

Glin, Co Limerick

Tel (068) 34173
Fax (068) 34364
e-mail knight@iol.ie
website www.glincastle.com

Nearby Limerick; golf at
Ballybunion; Ring of Kerry.
Location on 400-acre estate, on
river's edge; with car parking
Food breakfast, dinner; room service
Price €€€€
Rooms 15; 14 double, 1 twin, 2 with
dressing rooms, all with bath; all
rooms have phone, TV, hairdryer
Facilities sitting room, dining room;
garden, tennis
Credit cards AE, DC, MC, V
Children accepted
Disabled not suitable **Pets** kennels
provided **Closed** end Nov to Feb
Proprietors Desmond and Olda
FitzGerald **Manager** Bob Duff

Glin Castle
Heritage house

One of the outstanding private houses of the world, this is the home of the 29th Knight of Glin, who represents Christie's in Ireland, and his wife who bears the charming title of Madam FitzGerald. On the banks of the Shannon, it is dreamy and beautiful, in pale stone and with castellations. As might be imagined with a title that goes back to the 14th century, it is filled with family history and lovely family things. Even when the Knight is at the castle, guests have the run of the house and garden. Friendly young staff are endlessly attentive. Glin exudes grace, and manages to be both grand and intimate at the same time. The entrance hall, which may have been used as a ballroom in the past, has Corinthian pillars and a plaster ceiling apparently untouched since the 1780s. In the reception rooms is a unique collection of Irish 18thC mahogany furniture. To go to bed, you take the flying staircase – the only one of its kind in Ireland – to the first floor. Some rooms have four-poster beds, and all have fabulous bathrooms.

You may tag along behind one of the guided parties to learn all about the place. A cosy little private sitting-room for guests has deep sofas round the fire, family photographs and after-dinner coffee. Be sure to make time for a walk to the walled garden.

Goleen, Co Cork

Gurtyowen, Toormore, Goleen,
Co Cork

Tel (028) 35324
Fax (028) 35324
e-mail fortviewhousegoleen@eir-
com.net **website** www.fortview-
house.ie

Nearby Goleen; Mizen Head; Schull
peninsula; Skibbereen; Bantry.
Location in countryside, 6 miles (10
km) from Goleen; car parking
Food breakfast
Price €
Rooms 5; 2 with 2 double, 2 with
double and single, 1 with double and
2 single; 1 with bath, 4 with shower;
all rooms with hairdryer
Facilities sitting room; garden, ter-
race **Credit cards** not accepted
Children over 6 welcome
Disabled not possible **Pets** not
accepted **Closed** 1 Nov to 1 Mar
Proprietor Violet Connell

Fortview House
Farmhouse bed-and-breakfast

This place is a labour of love, and it radi-
ates an appropriately warm glow.
Richard Connell built the newer part of
this house on the West Cork family dairy
farm himself, out of stone, and roofed it in
slate. The interior is the inspired work of
his delightful wife, Violet. With her own
ideas, and pictures from magazines, she has
created something so fresh, welcoming
and comfortable that it is hard to tear
oneself away. You can tell what's in store by
the two small bears in the retro pram in
the hall and the boxy blue-and-red chairs
in the sitting room. Violet's bedrooms are
named after wild flowers: periwinkle;
lavender; daffodil; fuchsia. In one, she has
hung straw hats on the wall. She has made
curtains out of striped mattress ticking
and stencilled a bathroom with sea shells.
In a family room with two single beds and
pretty patchwork quilts, she props teddy
bears up on the pillows as if they are waiting for new, young friends to come. The
beamed dining room has a long table, terracotta tiles, wood-burning stove, and old
pine furniture. Violet's breakfasts reflect
the same attention and care: eggs from the
Connell's own hens; freshly squeezed juices;
hot potato cakes, salmon and crème
fraîche. She has many admirers. Be sure to
book early.

Goleen, Co Cork

Goleen, Co Cork

Tel (028) 35225
Fax (028) 35422
e-mail suehill@eir.com.net
website www.heronscove.com

Nearby Mizen Head; Cork, 75 miles (120 km); Bantry, 25 miles (40 km); Skibbereen, 24 miles (39 km).
Location on Goleen Harbour; car parking
Food breakfast, lunch, dinner
Price €
Rooms 5; 1 double, 2 twin, 2 double with a single bed; 1 with bath, 4 with shower; all with phone, TV, CD/radio, hairdryer, electric blanket, tea/coffee making facilities; small fridge on request
Facilities terraces, garden
Credit cards AE, MC, V
Children by arrangement
Disabled not suitable
Pets not accepted
Closed Christmas and New Year
Proprietor Sue Hill

The Heron's Cove
Restaurant-with-rooms

A fisherman in a trawler brings Sue Hill's order to the door of her white-painted, waterside restaurant, which offers 'fresh fish and wine on the harbour' and, most likely, a view of a heron. It is an idyllic spot, on this rugged stretch of the West Cork coastline. It is not surprising to hear from Sue that some of her guests do not want to do anything but simply sit and watch the tide come in and go out again. Three of the bedrooms in this modern house open on to balconies overlooking the little sheltered cove, and from the terrace of the restaurant on the ground floor – which is open from May to October – there are steps down to the beach. Guests are clearly those who relish the peace and quiet.

Along the upstairs landing runs a long shelf with a row of books. Bedrooms are well-equipped. There are posters of Aix-en-Provence on the walls and Sue has turned the staircase into a gallery for local artists. She is also very switched on to IT and offers guests e-mail and fax facilities. It's only a short walk to the village of Goleen and Sue sends all visitors off on the spectacular drive to Mizen Head, which is Ireland's most southwesterly point.

Gorey, Co Wexford

Gorey, Co. Wexford

Tel (053) 942 1124
Fax (053) 942 1572
e-mail info@marlfieldhouse.ie
website www.marlfieldhouse.ie

Nearby Waterford; Kilkenny;
Wexford; Rosslare; beaches.
Location in 35-acre gardens and
woodland, 1 mile (1.6 km) out of
Gorey on Wexford road; with car
parking
Food breakfast, lunch, dinner
Price €€€€
Rooms 20; 18 double and twin, 2
single, all with bath, phone, TV,
hairdryer
Facilities sitting room, bar, dining
room, sauna; garden, terraces, ten-
nis, croquet
Credit cards AE, DC, MC, V
Children welcome; no under-10s in
dining room **Disabled** access possi-
ble **Pets** welcome **Closed** late-Dec
to late-Jan
Proprietors the Bowe family

Marlfield House
Country house hotel

A sign in the drive of this stunning
Regency house, once owned by the
Earls of Courtown and now a Relais and
Chateaux hotel (one of the best in Ireland),
reads: 'Drive carefully, pheasants crossing'.
Not only is this a preserve of all good
things for people, but it is pretty comfortable for animals, too. There's a little dog bas-
ket for a terrier beside the 18thC marble
fireplace in the semi-circular architect-
designed hall. Mary Bowe's peacocks, ban-
tams, ducks and geese are cherished and
indulged almost as much as her guests. This
is a gorgeous, overblown place, a feast for
the eyes because of Mary's passion for interior decoration. Her taste is reflected in
Waterford crystal chandeliers, little French
chairs, gilded taps and a domed conservatory dining room. Garlanded with awards –
Hostess of the Year, Wine List of the Year,
Best Breakfast, One of the World's Most
Enchanting Hideaways – the hotel has a tradition of warm hospitality and the Bowes'
daughters, Margaret and Laura, are now at
the helm. Bedrooms are sumptuous and
charming. Jewels in the crown are the State
Rooms, decorated with rich fabrics and fine
antique furniture: the French Room, with
marble bathroom, overlooks the lake; the
Print Room has views of the rose garden.
Outstanding food. We visited before going
to press and found it as impressive as ever.

Inistioge, Co Kilkenny

The Rower, Inistioge, Co Kilkenny

Tel (051) 423614
e-mail info@cullintrahouse.com
website www.cullintrahouse.com

Nearby Kilkenny, 19 miles (31 km);
New Ross, 6 miles (10 km); Jerpoint
Abbey; Waterford.
Location in wooded countryside, 6
miles (10 km) from New Ross; car
parking
Food breakfast, dinner
Price €–€€ (minimum stay 2
nights)
Rooms 6; 5 double/twin, 1 family; 2
with bath, 4 with shower; hairdryer
available; all rooms equipped with
hot water bottle
Facilities courtyard; gardens, terrace
Credit cards extra charge of 3 per
cent **Children** welcome **Disabled**
not possible **Pets** by prior arrangement **Closed** never **Proprietor**
Patricia Cantlon

Cullintra House
Country house

Patricia Cantlon is known for her long, leisurely, candle-lit dinner parties at the 200-year-old ivy-clad farmhouse where she was born. This is not for those with rigid eating habits. When our inspector called, Patricia had several important jobs to do before getting under way in the kitchen: sta-tion herself outside the front door with palette and brushes to finish off a painting; race off to the vet with one of her many cats. The day begins when a guest knocks on her door to alert her that people are up and about and waiting for breakfast (could be noon). Her informality and originality have won friends and admirers all over the world. They leave messages in the visitors' book such as 'Great fun'; 'The house, the sur-roundings, the food, and most of all Patricia, were a magnificent find'.

She has, indeed, created a bewitching retreat. The low-ceilinged house abounds in artistic extras such as the imaginatively-designed rooms in the green-roofed barn, and the conservatory, where Patricia lights banks of candles for pre-dinner drinks. There are log fires, long walks (there are 17 acres of woodland to explore), conversa-tions with cats and foxes, swimming with Patricia in the river. She's a natural hostess, with persuasive powers to make her guests feel they have entered a place that is not quite of this world. It works.

Innishannon, Co Cork

Innishannon, Co Cork

Tel (021) 4775121
Fax (021) 4775609
e-mail info@innishannon-hotel.ie
website www.innishannon-hotel.ie

Nearby Kinsale; Cork.
Location on banks of river, near village; with car parking
Food breakfast, lunch, dinner
Price €€
Rooms 13; 7double, 6 twin, all with bath and shower; all rooms have phone, TV, hairdryer **Facilities** dining room, sitting room, bar; garden, terrace, fishing, boating
Credit cards AE, DC, MC, V
Children welcome
Disabled ground-floor suite available **Pets** accepted in bedrooms
Closed mid-Jan to mid-Mar
Proprietors the Roche family

Innishannon House
Country hotel

This attractive, imposing 18thC house on the banks of the Brandon River has been delighting guests since seasoned hoteliers Conal and Vera O'Sullivan bought the place in 1989. However, it has recently been taken over by new proprietors the Roche family, who have refurbished the interior and given the walls an apparently much needed lick of paint. The Roches' son, David, is now manager. While maintaining the rustic country house style, the new owners have been redecorating the palce since they took over in 2004. No. 16 is a cosy attic room with an antique bedspread, No. 14 a fascinating circular room with small round windows and a huge curtained bed. The enormous suite has a Victorian bathroom.

Jean-Marc is still in change of the cooking – duck confit, fillet steak, smoked salmon – earning the place two rossettes. Dinner is served in the lovely pink dining room. Pre-dinner drinks are served outside in summer, or in the airy lounge or cosy bar. Innishannon is not the last word in seclusion or intimacy; there are facilities for conferences and wedding receptions.

We would welcome reports on how the new owners are doing.

Kenmare, Co Kerry

Castletownbere Road, Kenmare,
Co Kerry

Tel (064) 41252
e-mail muxnawlodge@eircom.net

Nearby Ring of Kerry; Beara penin-
sula; Killarney; Bantry Bay.
Location overlooking bay and sus-
pension bridge; 10 minutes walk to
town centre; car parking
Food breakfast; dinner on request
Price €
Rooms 5; 3 double, 2 twin; 2 with
bath, 3 with shower; all rooms with
TV, radio, hairdryer, tea/coffee mak-
ing facilities; trouser press available
Facilities garden, terrace, all-weath-
er tennis court
Credit cards not accepted **Children**
welcome **Disabled** not suitable
Pets welcome outside **Closed**
Christmas **Proprietor** Hannah
Boland

Muxnaw Lodge
Bed-and-breakfast

Kenmare is a market town at the head
of the sheltered Kenmare River estuary, with some handsome 19thC buildings.
A popular tourist centre, it has two busy
main streets with plenty of shops with
painted fronts selling woollen goods, and
two of the best hotels in Ireland. It is a
perfect kicking-off point for the road
around the gorgeous Ring of Kerry, which,
in the summer, can become a long traffic
jam, with nose-to-tail coaches. Allow a day
for it, and set up base camp at charming,
gabled Muxnaw Lodge, built in 1801, one
of the oldest houses in the town, set on a
hillside overlooking the suspension bridge.

Hannah Boland has created an attractive period style for her lovely old house,
with dark Laura Ashley wallpapers with little prints, brass beds and lovingly-polished
antique furniture. In the bedrooms, she
hides the modern electric kettles away in
wooden boxes so they don't spoil the general look. In a bathroom at the back of the
house, you may sit in the corner bath and
look at the sea. Breakfasts include yoghurt
with honey; fresh eggs from the butcher
are cooked on Mrs Boland's big red Aga in
the kitchen. Her apple tart is a resounding
success at dinner. She is such a delightful
hostess that guests may find themselves
getting away rather later than planned on
that trip around the Ring of Kerry.

Kilkenny, Co Kilkenny

16 Patrick Street, Kilkenny,
Co Kilkenny

Tel (056) 7765707
Fax (056) 7765626
e-mail res@butler.ie

Nearby Kilkenny Castle; cathedral;
Kilkenny Design Centre.
Location in gardens, in centre of
town; car parking
Food breakfast
Price €€
Rooms 13; 11 double, 2 twin; 1 with
bath, 12 with shower; all with phone,
TV, radio, hairdryer, trouser press;
some rooms have desks
Facilities garden, terrace
Credit cards all major **Children**
welcome
Disabled not possible **Pets** not
accepted **Closed** 24 to 29 Dec
Proprietors Kilkenny Civic Trust
Manager Gabrielle Hickey

Butler House
Town house

This tall, grand Georgian house was
once the dower house to Kilkenny
Castle, family seat of the Earls of
Ormonde. It has beautiful sweeping stair-
cases, plastered ceilings and marble fireplaces. In the 1970s, the house was refurbished in contemporary style by Kilkenny
Design, and the result is stunning. The lovely lines and spaces of the Georgian interi-
or have been enhanced by square, modern
furniture and neutral colours in carpets
and fabrics in the airy, uncluttered rooms.

The house has recently been refurbished, with large spacious rooms, oak furniture and muted colours. The effect, with
acres of white walls, is ordered, quiet and
restful. Safely lodged at Butler House, you
are right in the middle of Kilkenny, a busy
tourist centre, and you have your own
path to the castle that leads from the back
of the house through the formal walled
garden, and former stableyards, now converted to crafts workshops. Breakfast is
now served in the Kilkenny Design
Centre, a short stroll through the walled
garden. Morning coffee, biscuits and cake
(all very BH colours) are served on a pale
oak table in the entrance hall, which has
white columns and heavy cream curtains.
Superior bedrooms have bay windows and
garden and castle views. Butler House is
now run by the Kilkenny Civic Trust.

Kylemore, Co Galway

Kylemore, Co Galway

Tel (095) 41143
Fax (095) 41143
e-mail kylemorehouse@eircom.net
website www.connemara.net/kyle-
morehouse

Nearby Kylemore Abbey;
Connemara National Park; Clifden.
Location in garden and grounds, on
the N59 to Clifden; car parking
Food breakfast, packed lunches; din-
ner for groups
Price €
Rooms 7; 4 double, 2 twin, 1 single,
2 with bath, 5 with shower; hairdryer
on request
Facilities sitting rooms; garden; 3
private fishing lakes
Credit cards accepted
Children accepted
Disabled 1 downstairs room
Pets accepted if well behaved
Closed Oct to Easter **Proprietor**
Mrs Nancy Naughton

Kylemore House
Guest-house

Once the home of the poet Oliver St John Gogarty – who features in James Joyce's Ulysses – there's still a strong artistic flavour about this white house on the edge of Kylemore Lough, built for Lord Ardilaun in 1785. Owner Nancy Naughton says her regulars – mostly fishermen – don't want any changes; so the somewhat off-beat charm of the house seems to be unchanging. Something of a character herself, she has a strong aversion to TVs in bedrooms: "What will they be wanting with television?" she asks. Quite so: the pictures alone would keep anyone engrossed for hours. She has a portrait of Queen Henrietta Maria, said to be school of Vandyke (maybe he did the face himself?), some fine sporting prints and many more. In St John Gogarty's former library, with its unusual ceiling, is a suite of French painted furniture she bought in an auction in England. She says her fishermen don't care much where they sleep, but the bedrooms are spacious and filled with interesting pieces. Downstairs rooms have welcoming peat fires in beautiful fireplaces. The kitchen is always busy: Mrs Naughton making her home-made marmalade, brown bread and packed lunches.

Leenane, Co Galway

Leenane, Co Galway

Tel (095) 42222
Fax (095) 42296
e-mail stay@delphilodge.ie
website www.delphilodge.ie

Nearby Westport; Kylemore Abbey;
Clifden; golf.
Location by the lake in wooded
grounds on private estate; with car
parking
Food breakfast, lunch, dinner
Price €€€
Rooms 12; 8 double, 4 twin, all with
bath; all rooms have phone; hairdry-
er on request **Facilities** drawing
room, billiard room, library, dining
room; garden, lake
Credit cards AE, MC, V
Children welcome
Disabled 2 ground-floor rooms
Pets not accepted **Closed** mid-Dec
to mid-Jan
Proprietors Peter and Jane Mantle

Delphi Lodge
Fishing lodge

The 2nd Marquess of Sligo – who had
been with Byron in Greece – thought
this wild place as beautiful as Delphi, and
built himself a fishing lodge here in the mid-
1830s. When Peter Mantle, a former finan-
cial journalist, came across the house, it was
semi-derelict. Falling under the same spell,
he restored it with great care and vision,
and Delphi is one of the finest and foremost
sporting lodges in Ireland. Fishing is its main
business, but everyone is made welcome
here. Peter, a lively host and raconteur, runs
it like a friendly country house.

On our visit, on a misty April evening,
wood smoke was rising from the chimney, a
new delivery of Crozes Hermitage was
stacked up in the hall and Mozart was playing in the snug library overlooking the lake.
Among the guests were a couple of bankers
in their waterproofs, a novelist, and some
Americans from Philadelphia. Salmon are
weighed and measured in the Rod Room,
creating frissons of excitement and stories
for the communal dinner table; the ghillies
come in during breakfast to discuss
prospects for the day ahead. Bedrooms are
unfussy but pretty, with pine furniture; larger ones have lake views; bathrooms have
piles of fluffy, white towels. Book well ahead.
Our most recent inspector was impressed:
'a unique and stunning location; the absolute
country house experience.'

Lisdoonvarna, Co Clare

Lisdoonvarna, Co Clare

Tel (065) 7074025
Fax (065) 7074025
e-mail
ballinalackencastle@eircom.net
website www.ballinalackencastle.com

Nearby The Burren; Ballyvaughan;
Doolin Crafts Gallery.
Location in 100-acre grounds, 3
miles (5 km) S of Lisdoonvarna on
R477; car parking
Food breakfast, bar lunch, dinner
Price €€
Rooms 13; 2 king-size double, 4
standard double, 7 with double and
single bed; 10 with bath, all with
shower; all with phone, TV, radio,
hairdryer
Facilities sitting room, bar; garden
Credit cards MC, V **Children** wel-
come **Disabled** not suitable
Pets well-behaved dogs in room; not
in public areas **Closed** mid-Oct to
mid-Apr **Proprietors** Denis and
Mary O'Callaghan

Ballinalacken Castle Hotel **Country hotel**

This fascinating house, high on a green
hillside with uninterrupted Atlantic
views, was built as a 'villa' in the 1840s for
John O'Brien, MP for Limerick. Not only
does it have its own ruins of a 15thC
O'Brien stronghold, but the entrance hall
with cupola and green Connemara marble
fireplace remains more or less unaltered.
There is a newish, discreetish extension,
but main house bedrooms have large, dark,
old-fashioned pieces of antique furniture,
huge wardrobes, and original shutters.
From the bed in Room 4, you can see the
Aran islands; and Room 7 has a view of the
Cliffs of Moher. The lay-out is intriguing –
mostly on one floor.

Chef Michael Foley uses fresh local
ingredients to create dishes such as cannelloni of crab meat in a light salmon
mousse, with shellfish jus, and Barbary
duck with celeriac purree and Guinness
and fresh honey sauce. The dining room
has another cracker of a fireplace, turf fire,
original wood floor, pink tablecloths.
Nightcaps are served in the lounge bar,
and you can steep yourself in the history
of the place with locals and join in sing-
alongs on weekend evenings, when live
entertainment is laid on.

The O'Callaghans also offer self-catering
accommodation in nearby Gentian Cottage.

Lisdoonvarna, Co Clare

Lisdoonvarna, Co Clare

Tel (065) 7074026
Fax (065) 7074555
e-mail info@sheedys.com
website www.sheedys.com

Nearby The Burren; Ballyvaughan;
Doolin Craft Gallery.
Location in centre of Lisdoonvarna,
on edge of the Burren; car parking
Food breakfast, lunch, dinner
Price €
Rooms 11; 5 double, 6 twin; 9 with
bath, 2 with shower; all with phone,
TV, hairdryer; ironing board avail-
able
Facilities south-facing sun lounge,
seafood bar, sitting room, restaurant
Credit cards AE, MC, V
Children welcome **Disabled** not
possible **Pets** not accepted
Closed end Sep to Easter
Proprietors the Sheedy family

Sheedy's Restaurant & Hotel **Restaurant-with-rooms**

This small hotel was originally a farmhouse where the Sheedy family began
looking after visitors to this little spa town
(it has sulphurous springs) in 1855. John
Sheedy, ex-Ashford Castle head chef, has
come home to cook; his delightful wife,
Martina, looks after front of house and the
wine list and adds her taste for contemporary design. John Sheedy's food is highly
acclaimed and the restaurant has been
given a completely new look to complement his celebrated 'Modern Irish' cooking.
Walls are painted in a moody grey colour
called 'Muddy River'. Martina, who used to
work at Mount Juliet, has also transformed
the hotel, bringing in help from the nearby
Doolin Craft Gallery, renowned for sharp,
simple design in wool, crystal, linen and
tweed. The lobby heralds the exciting
shape of things to come, with shiny wood
floor, little curved reception desk, a bit of
exposed natural stone, paintwork in gentian blue and terracotta red.

Upstairs, bedrooms have been upgraded;
the priority is comfort, but with some modern design. A place to watch; reports, please.

Mallow, Co Cork

Mallow, Co Cork

Tel (022) 47156
Fax (022) 47459
e-mail info@longuevillehouse.ie
website www.longuevillehouse.ie

Nearby Mallow Castle; Anne's
Grove Gardens at Castletownroche.
Location on wooded estate, 3 miles
(5km) W of Mallow on Kilarney
road; ample free car parking
Food breakfast, dinner
Price €€€-€€€€
Rooms 20; 13 double/twin with
bath; 7 suites; all with central heat-
ing, TV, radio, phone, hairdryer
Facilities sitting room, drawing
room, bar, 2 dining-rooms; billiards,
table-tennis; fishing **Credit cards**
AE, DC, MC, V
Children welcome **Disabled** easy
access to public rooms only
Pets not accepted **Closed** 9 Jan to
16 Mar **Proprietors** the
O'Callaghan family

Longueville House
Country house hotel

One of the finest country house hotels
in Ireland: this elegant and imposing
pink listed Georgian house on a 500-acre
wooded estate on the Blackwater River has
a three-storey block in the centre built in
the 1720's, later wings, and a pretty Victorian
conservatory. Inside, it is full of ornate Italian
plasterwork, elaborately framed ancestral
oils and graceful period furniture. The drawing room overlooks lawns and rows of oaks
in the parkland; in the distance are the ruins
of the O'Callaghans' Dromineen Castle,
demolished under Cromwell, who dispos-
sessed the family. But, after 300 years, they
are back. Longueville House has everything,
including internationally-recognised chef
William O'Callaghan, who, according to one
leading food critic, cooks 'some of the finest
food in Europe'. Many of his ingredients
come from the estate farm, and he also produces a white wine from his own vineyard.
Bedrooms are comfortable and filled with
antiques. The ones at the front of the house
have the best views. A recent vistor says the
O'Callaghans are 'charming and informal',
and it is very easy to feel relaxed in their
beautiful house. The Presidents' Restaurant
is named after the portraits of Irish presidents that hang on the walls. The wine list is
superb, as is William's seven-course Surprise
Tasting Menu.

Millstreet, Co Waterford

Millstreet, Cappagh, Dungarvan,
Co Waterford

Tel (058) 68049
Fax (058) 68099
e-mail castlefm@iol.ie **website**
www.castlecountryhouse.com

Nearby Cappoquin, 5 miles (8 km);
Dungarvan; Waterford; Youghal.
Location in countryside, on a 120-
acre dairy farm, 9 miles (14 km)
from Dungarvon; car parking
Food breakfast, packed lunch,
dinner
Price €
Rooms 5 double all with bath/show-
er; all with TV, hairdryer; tea/coffee
making facilities **Facilities** gardens,
terraces
Credit cards MC, V **Children** wel-
come **Disabled** no downstairs rooms
Pets small dogs, with baskets,
accepted **Closed** 1 Nov to 14 Mar
Proprietors Joan and Emmett
Nugent

The Castle Country House
Farm guest-house

Regulars at this converted farmhouse,
within the keep of a small 15thC castle
on a rock among the lush green fields of the
Blackwater Valley, know what they like: the
Nugents have an 80 per cent repeat business. There is the walk down the drive that
was once an avenue of elms, through the
imposing front gates and along the lane to
the little stone bridge over the River Finisk.
The air is heavy with the scent of water and
grass, and you may be joined by Bob, the
house dog. You might have the bedroom in
the original tower known as Miss O'Keeffe's
Ballroom (in the 1700s the house belonged
to her family). Meals come from Joan
Nugent's farmhouse kitchen and are served
in the yellow dining room, with walls more
than five-and-half-feet thick and an original
15thC stone archway. Emmett Nugent can
nearly always be distracted from his tasks to
relate the history of his fascinating edifice.
He has made a path around the base of the
rocky mound, so visitors may make a circular tour; and he has also restored a clammy
dungeon where, he explains, guests like to
gather on warm evenings to enjoy a glass or
two and get up to some 'medieval' fun and
games. Joan also likes to hang her washing
there. You feel that somehow you are the
first to discover the comforting peace and
quiet of Castle Farm. The Nugents are
delightful, welcoming and thoughtful hosts.

Mountrath, Co Laois

Mountrath, Co Laois

Tel (0502) 32120
Fax (0502) 32711
e-mail roundwood@eircom.net
website www.roundwoodhouse.com

Nearby walking, horse-riding, fishing; Slieve Bloom mountains.
Location in countryside, 3 miles (5 km) N of Mountrath on Kinnitty road; with gardens and ample car parking
Food full breakfast, dinner
Price €€€
Rooms 10; 8 double (3 twin), 2 family rooms; all with bath; all rooms have central heating **Facilities** sitting room, study, dining room, hall, library; croquet
Credit cards AE, DC, MC, V
Children very welcome **Disabled** not suitable
Pets accepted by arrangement
Closed 3 weeks Jan and Christmas
Proprietors Frank and Rosemarie Kennan

Roundwood House
Country house

A recent reporter reacted very well to the Kennans' operation. The house is 'not in perfect repair, but for the type of place they run, this didn't seem to matter': it's a 'wonderful place, and the Kennans really are charming and informal hosts'. The perfectly proportioned Palladian mansion is set in acres of lime, beech and chestnut woodland. The Kennans have wholeheartedly continued the work of the Irish Georgian Society, who rescued the house from near-ruin in the 1970s. All the Georgian trappings remain – bold paintwork, shutters instead of curtains, rugs instead of fitted carpets, and emphatically no TV. Despite this, the house is decidedly lived in, certainly not a museum.

For Rosemarie's plentiful meals, non-residents sit at separate tables; residents must sit together – you don't have a choice – fine if you like to chat to strangers, not ideal for romantic twosomes. After-dinner conversation is also encouraged over coffee and drinks by the open fire in the drawing-room. You may well find the Kennans joining in.

Four pleasant extra bedrooms in a converted stable block are perhaps cosier and of a better standard than those in the main house. It's very child-friendly (the Kennans have six), with a lovely big playroom at the top of the house, full of toys.

Mulranny, Co Mayo

Rosturk, Mulranny, Co Mayo

Tel (098) 36264
Fax (098) 36264
e-mail stoney@iol.ie
website www.rosturk-woods.com

Nearby Westport, 18 miles (29 km); Achill Island, 11 miles (18 km); Newport, 7 miles (11 km).
Location 3 miles before Mulranny on the Newport/Achill road; in 5-acre grounds with car parking
Food breakfast, dinner
Price €
Rooms 4; 2 double, 2 twin; 2 with bath and shower, 2 with shower; radio on request; all with hairdryer
Facilities snooker room; tennis court, garden, woodland, beach
Credit cards not accepted **Children** welcome **Disabled** not possible
Pets welcome **Closed** 1 Dec to 1 Mar **Proprietors** Alan and Louisa Stoney

Rosturk Woods
Country guest-house

It is no surprise that word of Alan and Louisa Stoney's charming little complex among trees on the tidal, sandy shore of Clew Bay has spread so far. First of all it's a paradise for children – with the doorstep on the beach, so to speak. When the tide is out, you can walk across to an island and there is plenty to see in the way of wildlife. The Stoneys' adaptable newly-built family house was completed in 1991; an even newer self-catering cottage opened for business in 1999 and was booked – immediately – for the summer. But the buildings blend nicely into the leafy background, and with wood fires, wooden floors and lots of painted furniture, the house has an open, airy, seaside feel about it, which is instantly relaxing. Rooms are comfortable; some are up under the eaves.

Since our last edition things have changed here and the Stoneys are now only offering self catering accommodation in two cottages; one with three bedrooms and one with four. Reports welcome.

Co Mayo

Nenagh, Co Tipperary

Ardcrony, Nenagh, Co Tipperary

Tel (067) 38223
Fax (067) 38013
e-mail magaret@ashleypark.com
website www.ashleypark.com

Nearby Lough Derg; Limerick, 27
miles (43 km); Shannon.
Location on private estate, with
lake, 3.5 miles (6 km) out of Nenagh
on Borrisokane road; car parking
Food breakfast, dinner
Price €
Rooms 6; 3 double, 2 twin, 1 family;
3 with bath and shower, 3 with
shower; TV and hairdryer on
request
Facilities garden; lake, boat, fishing
rods, riding; public telephone
Credit cards not accepted **Children**
welcome
Disabled not possible **Pets** accepted
Closed never
Proprietor Sean Mounsey

The Shannon at Limerick

Ashley Park House
Country house bed-and-breakfast

A peacock was sitting, wailing, on the rail of the green veranda when we visited Ashley Park: one of the owner's beloved birds that are fed every morning in a ritual of the household. Mr Mounsey is insistent that nothing here should be like a hotel. He need have no fears on that front. This wildly atmospheric early 18thC house comes complete with ballroom, ruined chapel on an island on the lake, original stabling and farmyard in a more-or-less untouched state, and a scheduled Neolithic ring fort in the woods. The whole place is a nature reserve, too. Mozart is played at breakfast and Frank Sinatra at dinner. We were unable to see any bedrooms, as they were occupied by a sleeping film crew, but, like all the other rooms in the house, they are huge, as are the bathrooms with their Victorian fittings. The Irish President, Mary McAleese, has stayed in Room 2. Roses trail along the veranda that runs the length of the house and, to relax, you can sit and read in the octagonal Chinese Room. There are turf fires; Mr Mounsy's daughter, Magaret, bakes a delicious scone; fresh eggs can be ordered straight from the hen. Hotels just don't come like this.

Newmarket-on-Fergus, Co Clare

Newmarket-on-Fergus, Co Clare

Tel (061) 363739
Fax (061) 363823
e-mail info@carrygerryhouse.com
website www.carrygerryhouse.com

Nearby Shannon airport, 8 miles (13 km); Limerick, 20 miles (32 km); Ennis (32 km).
Location in gardens and grounds; car parking
Food breakfast, dinner
Price €€–€€€
Rooms 11; 6 superior double, 4 double, 1 twin, 1 family room; 10 with bath, 1 with shower; all with phone, TV; hairdryer on request
Facilities restaurant, bar, courtyard
Credit cards AE, DC, MC, V
Children over 12
Disabled access possible
Pets accepted
Closed 24 to 27 Dec **Proprietors** Niall and Gillian Ennis

Carrygerry Country House County house hotel

Being so conveniently close to Shannon airport – a ten-minute drive away – this could have settled for being a commercial hotel. But the kindness and warm hospitality of Niall Ennis and his wife, Gillian, have made this old manor house into a place to remember for those staying for either their first or last night in Ireland.

In gardens, woodland, and pasture Carrygerry, built in the 18th century with a gable end and a remarkable courtyard entered through an archway, was a private house until as recently as the 1980s. Gillian is passionate about her house and she has filled it with antiques and pretty things. The two cosy sitting rooms, either side of the front door, are delightful places to pass away the time, with blazing fires, deep sofas, striped cushions, oriental carpets, and rich, dark colours. The house really seems to come alive in the evenings, when it positively glows in candle-light. In the former coach house in the courtyard is a bar; some bedrooms are there, too. At the end of a flight or a long drive, this is a comfortable, welcoming traveller's rest.

Rathnew, Co Wicklow

Newrath Bridge, Rathnew,
Co Wicklow

Tel (0404) 40106
Fax (0404) 40338
e-mail reception@hunters.ie
website www.hunters.ie

Nearby Powerscourt Gardens;
Russborough House; Glendalough;
golf.
Location in gardens on River Vartry,
in countryside half a mile from
Rathnew; car parking
Food breakfast, lunch, dinner
Price €€€
Rooms 16; 15 double/twin, 1 single,
15 with bath, 1 with shower; all
rooms with phone, TV, hairdryer;
hot water bottle
Facilities gardens, terrace
Credit cards all major **Children**
welcome **Disabled** ground-floor
room **Pets** not accepted **Closed** 24
to 26 Dec **Proprietors** the Gelletlie
family

Hunter's Hotel
Coaching inn

The area around it is fast becoming part
of Dublin commuterland, but not much
changes here in this little island of constancy. In 1840, some Victorian travellers touring Ireland reported: 'We strongly recommend Mr Hunter's Inn at Newrath Bridge,
which is, according to our experience, the
most comfortable in the county.' The same
applies today. This is a delightful, proudly
old-fashioned place, built as a coaching inn
for several big houses in the vicinity. You
would not be surprised if you were to hear
the sound of horses' hooves and carriage
wheels clattering into the enormous stable
yard, or trunks being carried into the
beamed front hall, which still has the tiled
floor laid in 1720. Nothing clashes, nothing
jars, to spoil the old world charm that
brings people from far and wide. Present
owner Maureen Gelletlie (a great great
granddaughter of the original Mr Hunter)
is renowned for her individual style of
looking after guests. In a trice she manages
to get complete strangers talking in the
small bar, with bare, wide wooden floorboards, beams, and a print of the 1900
Grand National winner, Ambush 11, on the
wall, where she serves drinks. There is
good, plain cooking; a lovely garden by the
river; courtesy; glowing fires; charming bedrooms (ask for garden view); tea on the
lawn; billowing wistaria.

Recess, Co Galway

Inagh Valley, Recess, Co Galway

Tel (095) 34706
Fax (095) 34708
e-mail inagh@iol.ie **website**
www.loughinaghlodgehotel.ie

Nearby Recess; Oughterard;
Clifden; Galway.
Location in open country on shores
of Lough Inagh; car parking
Food breakfast, lunch, dinner
Price €€€
Rooms 12; 8 double; 4 twin; all with
bath and shower; all rooms have
phone, TV, radio, hairdryer, trouser
press; ironing board on request
Facilities garden, lake, fishing,
bicycles
Credit cards AE, DC, MC, V
Children welcome **Disabled**
ground-floor room
Pets acccepted
Closed mid-Dec to mid-Mar
Proprietor Maire O'Connor

Lough Inagh Lodge Hotel **Country hotel**

This solid, well-proportioned Victorian shooting lodge, romantically placed on one of the most beautiful lakes in Connemara, was boarded up when Maire O'Connor and her late husband, John, came across it looking for somewhere suitable to run as a small hotel. Remarkably, some of the old sporting record books survive and may be read by guests. Little has been overlooked in the way of comfort. Each bedroom, named after an Irish writer, has a dressing room with trouser press (not that we rate these very highly as creature comforts, but they're useful for damp Connemara days). Views are of water and The Twelve Bens mountains. Maire has kept to rich dark Victorian colours and polished wood; her careful attention to detail and service is reflected throughout the comfortable, cosy house. She arranges the fresh flowers, which are sent from Clifden. Rooms downstairs have inviting log fires and warm lighting. The green dining room with yellow curtains and gleaming, dark wood floor is delightful. Seafood and traditional wild game dishes are specialities of the kitchen. Loughs Inagh and Derryclare are on the doorstep; for walkers, there are miles of tracks through the wild and rugged landscape. The hotel also has a stable of bicycles.

Riverstown, Co Sligo

Riverstown, Co Sligo

Tel (071) 9165466
Fax (071) 9165108
e-mail ohara@coopershill.com
website www.coopershill.com

Nearby Sligo, 12 miles (20 km);
Lough Arrow; Lough Gara.
Location 1 mile (1.5 km) W of
Riverstown, off N4 Dublin-Sligo
road; in large garden on 500-acre
estate, with ample car parking
Food full breakfast, light or packed
lunch, dinner; restaurant licence
Price €€
Rooms 8; 7 double, 1 twin; , 7 with
bath and shower, 1 with shower; all
rooms have telephone, tea/coffee kit
Facilities sitting room, dining room,
snooker room; fishing, tennis
Credit cards AE, DC, MC, V
Children welcome if well behaved
Disabled no access
Pets welcome if well behaved, but
not allowed in public rooms or bed-
rooms **Closed** Nov to end Mar
Proprietor Simon O'Hara

Coopershill
Country house hotel

Brian O'Hara ran this delightful country
house with his wife, Lindy, for some fifteen years, and subtly improved the style
of the place without interfering with its
essential appeal. Since our last edition,
Brian and Lindy have handed over the running of Coopershill to their son Simon.

It is a fine house – though some may not
think it elegant by Georgian standards –
with splendidly large rooms (including the
bedrooms, most of which have four-poster
or canopy beds). It is furnished throughout
with antiques; but remains emphatically a
home, with no hotel-like formality.

The grounds are extensive enough not
only to afford complete seclusion, but also
to accommodate a river on which there is
boating and fishing for pike and trout. Five-
course dinners are available from a daily
changing, seasonal menu. Much of the food
is produced in the grounds, and the restaurant can make the unusual boast that the
distance travelled from farm to plate for
many of its ingredients is just 200 metres.
The food is described as quality Irish
country house cooking.

Reports welcome.

Shanagarry, Co Cork

Shanagarry, Midleton, Co Cork

Tel (021) 4652531
Fax (021) 4652021
e-mail res@ballymaloe.ie
website www.ballymaloe.ie.

Nearby beaches, cliff walks, fishing, golf.
Location 20 miles (32 km) E of Cork, 2 miles (3 km) E of Cloyne on the Ballycotton road, L35, ample private car parking
Food breakfast, lunch, dinner
Price €€–€€€
Rooms 33 double and twin, 31 with bath, 2 with shower; all rooms have phone **Facilities** 3 sitting rooms, conference/TV room, conservatory, library; tennis, golf, swimming pool
Credit cards AE, DC, MC, V
Children welcome
Disabled access easy; some specially adapted rooms
Pets not accepted **Closed** Christmas
Proprietors the Allen family

Ballymaloe House
Converted farmhouse

Thirty bedrooms normally rules out a hotel for this guide, but we cannot resist this amiable, rambling, creeper-clad house – largely Georgian in appearance but incorporating the remains of a 14thC castle keep – set in rolling green countryside. Readers have reported that they were 'immensely impressed' and found the staff 'as well-drilled as an army, but jolly, with abundant charm'.

The Allens, who have been farming here for over 40 years, opened as a restaurant in 1964 and started offering rooms three years later. Since then they have added more facilities and more rooms – those in the main house now outnumbered by those in extensions and converted out-buildings.

Despite quite elegant and sophisticated furnishings, the Allens have always managed to preserve intact the warmth and naturalness of a much-loved family home. But not all visitors agree: one reporter judged that Ballymaloe was becoming rather commercialized. Even that reporter, however, was impressed by the standard of food. Mrs Allen no longer takes an active role in the cooking. It is now Jason Fahey who prepares the Classic French and Irish dishes alongside original dishes, all based on home produce and fish fresh from the local quays. (Sunday dinner is always a buffet.) Just as much care is lavished on breakfast, and the famous children's high tea.

Index – Hotel names

Index – Hotel names

Index – Hotel locations

Index – Hotel locations

Austria
France
Germany
Greece
Italy
Mallorca, Menorca & Ibiza
New England
Paris
Southern France
Spain
Switzerland
Tuscany & Umbria
Venice and North-East Italy

Special offers

Buy your *Charming Small Hotel Guide* by post directly from the publisher and you'll get a worthwhile discount. *

Titles available:	Retail price	Discount price
Austria	£10.99	£9.50
Britain & Ireland	£14.99	£13.50
France	£14.99	£13.50
Germany	£14.99	£13.50
Greece	£10.99	£9.50
Italy	£14.99	£13.50
Mallorca, Menorca & Ibiza	£9.99	£8.50
New England	£10.99	£9.50
Paris	£10.99	£9.50
Southern France	£10.99	£9.50
Spain	£11.99	£10.50
Switzerland	£9.99	£8.50
Tuscany & Umbria	£10.99	£9.50
Venice and North-East Italy	£10.99	£9.50

Please send your order to:
Book Sales, Duncan Petersen Publishing Ltd, C7, Old Imperial Laundry, Warriner Gardens, London SW11 4XW enclosing:
1) the title you require and number of copies
2) your name and address
3) your cheque made out to:
Duncan Petersen Publishing Ltd
*Offer applies to this edition and to UK only.

On Foot Guides

The perfect accompaniment to the *Charming Small Hotel Guides* is the *On Foot City Guides* series.

These books feature unique aerial-view maps, which show not only the city's street layout but the look of your surroundings too.

Following these walks is like being shown around by an exceptionally knowledgeable friend.

They're fun and they'll help you fit it all together. And you'll discover plenty of interesting things you never knew about the city.

Friendly accompanying text, full of personal insights and advice, including food, drink, and shopping along the way. Introduces you to all the must-see areas.

Most of the routes take an hour; or, with stops for sightseeing, two or three hours. Or interlink the routes for longer expeditions.

Titles in the series:

London Walks

Paris Walks

New York Walks

Prague Walks

Venice Walks

Visit charmingsmallhotels.co.uk

Our website has recently been completely rebuilt. Please take a look - it includes fantastic entries from all over Europe with up to four colour photographs for each entry as well as our independent reports.

It's the best research tool on the web for finding our kind of hotel.

Exchange rates

As we went to press, $1 bought 0.74 euros and £1 bought 1.47 euros